CENSORED

"[*Censored*] should be affixed to the bulletin boards
in every newsroom in America. And, perhaps read aloud to
a few publishers and television executives."—Ralph Nader

"[*Censored*] offers devastating evidence of the dumbing-down of
mainstream news in America....Required reading for broadcasters,
journalists and well-informed citizens."—*Los Angeles Times*

"A distant early warning system for society's problems."
—*American Journalism Review*

"One of the most significant media research projects in the country."
—I.F. Stone

"A terrific resource, especially for its directory of alternative media and
organizations....Recommended for media collections."—*Library Journal*

"Project Censored shines a spotlight on news that an informed public
must have...a vital contribution to our democratic process."
—Rhoda H. Karpatkin, President, Consumer's Union

"Buy it, read it, act on it. Our future depends on the knowledge this
collection of suppressed stories allows us."—*San Diego Review*

"This volume chronicles 25 news stories about events that could
affect all of us, but which we most likely did not hear or read about
in the popular news media."—*Bloomsbury Review*

"*Censored* serves as a reminder that there is certainly more to the news
than is easily available or willingly disclosed. To those of us
who work in the newsrooms, it's an inspiration, an indictment,
and an admonition to look deeper, ask more questions, then search
for the truth in the answers we get."—*Creative Loafings*

"This invaluable resource deserves to be more widely known."
—*Wilson Library Bulletin*

"Once again Project Censored has produced an invaluable guide
to the sociopolitical landscape of the United States and the world....
A vital yearly addition to your library."—*Outposts*

CENSORED 1998

The News that Didn't Make the News — The Year's Top 25 Censored Stories

PETER PHILLIPS & PROJECT CENSORED

INTRODUCTION BY DANNY SCHECHTER
CARTOONS BY TOM TOMORROW

SEVEN STORIES PRESS
New York

Censored 1998: The News that Didn't Make the News—
The Year's Top 25 Censored Stories
ISSN 1074-5998

10 9 8 7 6 5 4 3 2 1

Seven Stories Press
632 Broadway, 7th Floor
New York, NY 10012

In U.K.:
Turnaround Publisher Services Ltd.
Unit 3, Olympia Trading Estate
Coburg Road, Wood Green
London N22 6TZ U.K.

In Canada:
Hushion House
36 Northline Road
Toronto, Ontario M4B 3E2
Canada

Designed by Cindy LaBreacht

Dedication

E. SUSAN PHILLIPS
1948–1979

Loving memories of:
desert drives
Latin beaches
coffee talks

and

Jeffrey

Table of Contents

Preface

CENSORED 1998: The News That Didn't Make the News is Project Censored's 22nd annual listing of the most important news stories that the national media failed to report or develop during the past year. We would like to say that the media are improving in their coverage and that Project Censored will no longer be needed in the near future, but in reality, it is heading in the exact opposite direction. Media are filling their time and space with trivia, entertainment, and synergistic infomercials all in the name of high returns and ideologically-oriented content. This makes freeing the media through a democratic process of realigning the Federal Communications Commission licensing requirements, and establishing/expanding an independent public-owned media in the United States an absolute necessity. At the very least, continuing in the direction we are currently going will condemn the U.S. public to a lifetime of socio-political ignorance.

This year's "most censored" news stories are a broad collection of articles about powerful individuals and organizations that have made undemocratic, and sometimes secret, decisions that affect many people's lives. These are the news stories that the mainstream media organizations tend to ignore and repress and that an independent press is willing to cover when they have adequate resources and access to these issues. In this context, supporting the alternative/independent press becomes an action in which concerned citizens can partake. It is only through a free and independent media that news stories that offend the powerful will be objectively covered. Media organizations dependent on advertising dollars from the powerful tend not to bite the hands that feed them. *Censored 1998* has an expanded listing of alternative/independent publications and resources this year. Try subscribing to several. Become part of the solution. We think that you will find it the most complete listing currently available.

The most commonly asked question to Project Censored is: Why doesn't the mainstream press cover these stories? Each year, we invite several guest writers—scholars and media critics—to write original essays that address this question, as well as other important issues in media today.

Robert W. McChesney is an Associate Professor of Communications at the University of Wisconsin. He is the author, with Edward S. Herman, of *The Global Media: The New Missionaries of Corporate Capitalism* (Cassell, 1997) and *Corporate Media and the Threat to Democracy* (Seven Stories Press, 1997). Chapter 2, comprised of his essay "This Communication Revolution Is Brought To You By U.S. Media At The Dawn Of The 21st Century," addresses concerns related to worldwide media consolidation, the decline of public broadcasting, and the impacts of the Telecommunications Act on public debate. McChesney's strengths are his ability to give a historical perspective to contemporary issues, and a reflection on the power of citizen resistance.

Norman Solomon, author of Chapter 6, "Myth of Big Media," writes a nationally syndicated column, "Media Beat," distributed to daily newspapers nationwide. He is co-author with Jeff Cohen of *Adventures in Medialand: Behind the News, Beyond the Pundits, Through the Media Looking*

THIS MODERN WORLD
by TOM TOMORROW

BOY, THE MIR SPACE STATION IS SURE FALLING APART!

IT SURE IS!

THE IRS SURE ABUSES TAXPAYERS!

THEY SURE DO!

AL GORE SURE DID A LOT OF FUNDRAISING!

HE SURE DID!

Glass: Decoding Bias and Blather in the News, and *Wizards of Media Oz: Behind the Curtain of Mainstream News.* His self-authored books include *False Hope: The Politics of Illusion in the Clinton Era,* and *The Power of Babble.* In "Myths of Big Media," Solomon challenges us to look at the erroneous assumptions prevalent in society today regarding the workings of mainstream media.

Beth Sanders and Randy Baker are the creators and producers of the new nationally-acclaimed film *Fear and Favor in the Newsroom.* Narrated by Studs Terkel, *Fear and Favor in the Newsroom* dramatically shows how bias and censorship work in the media. In Chapter 7, Sanders and Baker offer a detailed exposé of institutionalized censorship of their film by national media outlets, and the successes of a broad citizens' movement to get the film out to the public.

Also included in this year's book is original sociological research conducted and completed by Project Censored staff. In Chapter 5, we identify the corporate connections of the top media corporations in the United States and discuss how a tight network of media elites creates a similarity of interests that tend to support a pro-business orientation to the news.

Project Censored is a university-based research project that involves hundreds of concerned individuals, students, faculty, and community volunteers. We appreciate your support and encourage your participation.

Peter Phillips
Director, Project Censored

THE PROJECT CENSORED CREW (SSU FACULTY, STUDENTS, AND PC STAFF), FALL 1997.

Acknowledgments

Sonoma State University in Rohnert Park, California is the host institution for Project Censored. The Project is managed through the Department of Sociology in the School of Social Sciences. We are an applied sociological research project dedicated to freedom of information throughout the United States.

Over 125 people were directly involved in the production of this year's *Censored 1998: The News That Didn't Make the News.* University and Program Staff, students, faculty and community evaluators, research interns, funders, and our distinguished national judges, all contributed time, energy, and money to make this year's book an important resource for the promotion of freedom of information in the United States.

I want to personally thank those close friends and intimates who have counseled and supported me through another year of Project Censored. The men in the Green Oaks breakfast group, Noel Byrne, Bob Butler, Rick Williams, and Bill Simon have all been advisors and confidants through the sociopolitical trials of this past year. A special thanks goes to my Anishinabe companion and partner, Kathleen Kesterke, for her tolerance of my ups and downs during the year and our 9,000-mile cross country book tour, and her continuing active support for the important message of Project Censored. Thanks goes also to Carl Jensen, founder of Project Censored, and director for 20 years. His continued advice and support are very important to me and our work. It was his vision and dedication that made Project Censored the internationally known research project it is today.

A tremendous thanks needs to go to the people at Seven Stories Press, who, every year, create a book out of a manuscript in a record two weeks (the time between manuscript delivery and submission to the printer): publisher Dan Simon, editors Jon Gilbert, Greg Ruggiero, and Mikola De Roo, book designer Cindy LaBreacht, proofreaders Avner Gidron and Paul Abruzzo, and to the great sales staff at Publishers Group West, who see to it that every independent bookstore, chain store, and wholesaler in the U.S. are aware of *Censored* each year. Thanks also to Hushion House, our distributor in Canada, for their support up north.

Thanks also to the authors of the most *Censored* stories for 1997, for without their often unsupported efforts as investigative news reporters and writers the stories presented in *Censored 1998* would not be possible.

We are also extremely pleased to have Danny Schechter write our introduction. His past and current experiences as a television producer allow him a unique insider's perspective on censorship in the U.S. media. Thanks also to Robert W. McChesney, Norman Solomon, Beth Sanders, and Randy Baker, who each wrote an original article on an important media issue.

This year's book again features the cartoons of Tom Tomorrow. "This Modern World" appears in over 90 newspapers across the country. We are extremely pleased to use Tom Tomorrow's wit and humor throughout the book.

Our national judges, some of whom have been involved with the Project for 22 years, are among the top people in the country concerned with First Amendment freedoms and major social issues. We are honored to have them as the final voice in ranking the top 25 *Censored* Stories.

An important thanks goes to our major donors and funders, including: Anita Roddick and The Body Shop International, Office of the President at Sonoma State University, Office of the Vice-President for Academic Affairs at Sonoma State University, School of Social Sciences at Sonoma State University, Sonoma State University Associated Students, The Playboy Foundation, and hundreds of donors from throughout the United States. Without their core financial support, Project Censored simply could not continue.

The Organization of News Ombudsmen deserves a thank you for their continuing assistance with identifying the most superfluous stories published during the past year in Chapter 4, "The Junk Food News Stories of 1997."

We are also indebted to the American Library Association Associate Director, Anne Heanue, for her assistance with coordinating the inclusion of the document "Less Access To Less Information By and About The U.S. Government" in Appendix A.

This year we had 65 faculty/community evaluators assisting with our story assessment process. These expert volunteers read and rated the nominated stories for national importance, accuracy, and credibility. In November, they participated with the students in selecting this year's final top 25 stories.

Most of all we need to recognize the Sonoma State University students in the Media Censorship, Sociology 435, class who worked long hours in the library conducting coverage reports on over 160 under-published stories. Each has become an expert in library research and information retrieval. Student education is one of the most important aspects of the Project, and we could not do this work without their dedication and effort.

Jeffrey Fillmore served as our technical support this year, assisting with our World Wide Web site development and electronic outreach. Nicola Mazumdar compiled Appendix B, "The Project Censored Media Activists and Alternative/Independent Writers Resource Guide," and assisted with the timely finishing of this year's book. Cathleen Coleman wrote and researched Chapter 4, "The Junk Food News Stories of 1997." Associate Director Bob Klose wrote several portions of this book, and conducted over 60 radio interviews for the Project in 1997. Jeanette Glynn, editor/researcher of *Who Knows Who 1997* allowed us the use of her directory for research on Chapter 5.

Lastly, I want to thank our readers and supporters from all over the United States and the world. Hundreds of you nominated stories for consideration as the most *Censored* news story of the year. Thank you very much!

PROJECT CENSORED STAFF AND RESEARCH INTERNS 1997

Peter Phillips, Ph.D.	Director
Carl Jensen	Director Emeritus and Project Advisor
Bob Klose	Associate Director
Jeffrey Fillmore	Computer Systems
Kimberly Lyman	Fiscal Planning
Linda McCabe, MT(ASCP)	Promotions and Radio Announcements
Martha Wright	Grants and Development
Suzanne Z. Murphy, R.N.	Administrative Assistant
Catherine Hickinbotham	Administrative Assistant
Brian Foust	Administrative Assistant
Todd Hillstrom	Administrative Assistant
Griselda Covarrubias	Spanish Language Translations
Brian Wilson	Web Consultant
Li Li	Web Site Development and Chinese Language Translations

COMMUNITY VOLUNTEERS: Cathleen Coleman, Deb Udall, Ben Brewer, Greg Downing

WRITING AND EDITORIAL GROUP: Nicola Mazumdar, Suzanne Z. Murphy, R.N., June Wohlgethan, Kimberly Starbuck, Matt Monpas, Erik Hansen, Cathleen Coleman

ILLUSTRATIONS AND ART GROUP: Tricia Borela, Zac Wollons, Alix Jestron, Suzanne Z. Murphy, R.N.

TEACHING ASSISTANTS: Ben Brewer, Deb Udall, Jeff Fillmore

FALL 1997 PROMOTIONS GROUP: Diane Ferré, Jeff Schach, Spencer Clark, Erika Nell

SPRING 1997 PROMOTIONS GROUP: Deb Udall, Diane Ferré, Loretta Goldstein, Nancy Frankenberger, Dierdre Morrissey, Linda McCabe, MT(ASCP)

NEWS STORY MANAGEMENT TEAM: Corey Hale, Stuart Breier, Tricia Borela

NEWS STORY RESEARCHERS: Yvonne Jolley-Crawford, Brian Foust, Catherine Hickinbotham

1997 STUDENT RESEARCHERS IN MEDIA CENSORSHIP CLASS

Susan K. Allen	Sociology
Katherine A. Garey	Sociology
Kecia L. Kaiser	Sociology
Jacqueline D. Lichtstein	Sociology
Katherine R. Sims	Sociology
Bradley L. Smith	Sociology
Robin L. Stovall	Sociology
Judith A. Westphall	Sociology
Carolyn S. Williams	Sociology
Angie M. Yee	Sociology
Gavin T. Grundmann	Communication Studies
Renee L. Hamilton	Communication Studies
Lei Wang	Communication Studies
Bryan Way	Communication Studies

PROJECT CENSORED 1997 NATIONAL JUDGES

DR. DONNA ALLEN, president of the Women's Institute for Freedom of the Press; founding editor of *Media Report to Women;* co-editor: *Women Transforming Communications: Global Perspectives* (1996)

BEN BAGDIKIAN,* professor emeritus and former dean, Graduate School of Journalism, University of California, Berkeley; former editor at the *Washington Post;* author of *Media Monopoly,* and five other books and numerous articles

RICHARD BARNET, author of 15 books, and numerous articles for *The New York Times Magazine, The Nation,* and *Progressive*

SUSAN FALUDI, Pulitzer Prize-winning journalist; author of *Backlash: The Undeclared War Against American Women*

DR. GEORGE GERBNER, dean emeritus, Annenberg School of Communications, University of Pennsylvania; founder of the Cultural Environment Movement; author of *Invisible Crises: What Conglomerate Media Control Means for America and the World,* and *Triumph and the Image: The Media's War in the Persian Gulf*

JUAN GONZALEZ, award-winning journalist and columnist for the New York *Daily News*

AILEEN C. HERNANDEZ, president of Urban Consulting in San Francisco; former commissioner on the U.S. Equal Employment Opportunity Commission

DR. CARL JENSEN, founder and former director of Project Censored; author, *Censored: The News That Didn't Make the News and Why, 1990 to 1996,* and *20 Years of Censored News* (Seven Stories Press, 1997)

SUT JHALLY, professor of communications; and executive director of The Media Education Foundation, University of Massachusetts

NICHOLAS JOHNSON,* professor, College of Law, University of Iowa; former FCC Commissioner (1966-1973); author of *How To Talk Back To Your Television Set*

RHODA H. KARPATKIN, president, Consumers Union, non-profit publisher of *Consumer Reports*

CHARLES L. KLOTZER, editor and publisher emeritus, *St. Louis Journalism Review*

JUDITH KRUG, director, Office for Intellectual Freedom, American Library Association; editor, *Newsletter on Intellectual Freedom; Freedom to Read Foundation News;* and the *Intellectual Freedom Action News*

FRANCES MOORE LAPPÉ, co-founder and co-director, Center for Living Democracy

WILLIAM LUTZ, professor of English, Rutgers University; former editor of *The Quarterly Review of Doublespeak;* author of *The New Doublespeak: Why No One Knows What Anyone's Saying Anymore* (1966)

JULIANNE MALVEAUX, Ph.D., economist and columnist, King Features and Pacifica radio talk show host

JACK L. NELSON,* professor, Graduate School of Education, Rutgers University; author of 16 books and over 150 articles including *Critical Issues in Education* (1996)

MICHAEL PARENTI, political analyst, lecturer, and author of several books including: *Inventing Reality; The Politics of News Media; Make Believe Media; The Politics of Entertainment;* and numerous other works

HERBERT I. SCHILLER, professor emeritus of communication, University of California, San Diego; lecturer; author of several books, including *Culture, Inc.* and *Information Inequality* (1996)

BARBARA SEAMAN, lecturer; author of *The Doctors' Case Against the Pill; Free and Female; Women and the Crisis in Sex Hormones;* and others; co-founder of the National Women's Health Network.

SHEILA RABB WEIDENFELD,* president, D.C. Productions, Ltd.; former press secretary for Betty Ford

* Indicates having been a Project Censored Judge since its founding in 1976

PROJECT CENSORED 1996 FACULTY, STAFF, AND COMMUNITY EVALUATORS

Les Adler, Ph.D.	Provost, Hutchin School, History
Ruben Armiñana, Ph.D.	President, Sonoma State University, Political Science
Bryan Baker, Ph.D.	Geography
Melinda Barnard, Ph.D.	Communication Studies
Philip Beard, Ph.D.	German Studies
Paul V. Benko, Ph.D.	Biochemistry
Marty Bennett	Santa Rosa Community College
Barbara Bloom, Ph.D.	Criminal Justice
Noel Byrnes, Ph.D.	Sociology
Barbara Butler, MLIS, MBA	Information Research
Ray Castro, Ph.D.	Social Policy
T.K. Clarke, Ph.D.	Business
Lynn Cominsky, Ph.D.	Physics, Astronomy
Bill Crowley, Ph.D.	Geography
Randy Dodgen, Ph.D.	History, Asia
Charles Fox	Librarian
Dorothy (Dolly) Friedel, Ph.D.	Geography

Susan Garfin, Ph.D.	Sociology
Victor Garlin, Ph.D./J.D.	Economics
Robert Girling, Ph.D.	Business, Economics
Mary Gomes, Ph.D.	Psychology
Myrna Goodman, Ph. D. Candidate	Sociology/Gender Studies
Scott Gordon, Ph.D.	Computer Science
Paula Hammett, MLIS	Information Resources in Social Sciences
Debra Hammond, Ph.D.	History of Science
Dan Haytin, Ph.D.	Sociology
Laurel Holmstrom	Sociology
Sally Hurtado, M.S.	Education
Pat Jackson, Ph.D.	Criminal Justice Administration
Thomas Jacobson, J.D.	Environmental Studies and Planning
Brian Jersky, Ph.D.	Math/Statistics
Mary King, M.D.	Community Volunteer
Jeanette Koshar, Ph.D.	Nursing
John Kramer, Ph.D.	Political Science
Ellen Krebs	Librarian
Wingham Liddell, Ph.D.	Business/Economics
Linda Lopez, Ph.D.	Criminal Justice
Rick Luttmann, Ph.D./CFP	Economics/Budgets
Kenneth Marcus, Ph.D.	Criminal Justice
Perry Marker, Ph.D.	Education
Dan Markwyn, Ph.D.	History
Doug Martin, Ph.D.	Chemistry
Elizabeth Coonrod Martinez, Ph.D.	Foreign Languages
Jeffrey McIllwain, Ph.D.	Criminal Justice Administration
Robert McNamara, Ph.D.	Political Science
Andy Merrifield, Ph.D.	Public Administration
Catherine Nelson, Ph.D.	Political Science
Tom Ormond, Ph.D.	Kinesiology
Jorge E. Porras, Ph.D.	Sociolinguistics
Arthur Ramirez, Ph.D.	Mexican American Studies
R. Thomas Rosin, Ph.D.	Anthropology
Gardner Rust, Ph.D.	Music
Cindy Stearns, Ph.D.	Women's Studies
Elaine Sundberg, M.A.	Education
Bob Tellander, M.A.	Sociology
Laxmi G. Tewari, Ph.D.	Ethnomusicology
Carol Tremmel	Extended Education
David Van Nuys, Ph.D.	Psychology

Francisco H. Vazquez, Ph.D.	Liberal Studies
Albert Wahrhaftig, Ph.D.	Anthropology
Sandra Walton, MLIS	Archival management
D. Anthony White, Ph.D.	History
R. Richard Williams, J.D.	Community Volunteer
Homero Yearwood, Ph.D.	Criminal Justice
Richard Zimmer, Ph.D.	History

SONOMA STATE UNIVERSITY SUPPORTING STAFF AND OFFICES

Ruben Armiñana: President and Staff in the Office of the President
Don Farish: Vice-President for Academic Affairs and Staff
Robert Karlsrud: Dean of School of Social Sciences and Staff
William Babula: Dean of School of Arts and Humanities
Jim Myers: Vice-President for Development and Staff
Larry Furukawa-Schlereth: Vice-President Administration and Finance
Mark Resmer: Associate Vice-President for Information Technology and Staff
Susan Harris and the SSU Library Staff
Tony Apolloni and the staff at the California Institute on Human services
Carol Cinquini: Manager of School of Social Sciences
Nancy Ramsey: Development Officer, School of Social Sciences and Staff
Paula Hammett: Social Sciences Library Resources
Steve Wilson and the Staff at the SSU Academic Foundation
Katie Pierce and Staff in Sponsored Programs
Alan Murray and Staff at SSU Bookstore
Jonah Raskin and Faculty in Communications Studies
Susan Kashack and Staff in SSU Public Relations Office
Colleagues in the Sociology Department: Noel Byrne, Kathy Charmaz, Susan Garfin, Dan Haytin, Robert Tellander, David Walls, and Department Secretary Laurel Holmstrom

Introduction

BY DANNY SCHECHTER

When I think of the word censorship, I still visualize a small room occupied by a faceless man wearing one of those visors that screens out the light. He has a blue pencil in his hand and he is slashing his way through acres of copy: changing words, cleansing content, dropping whole paragraphs. His task is to uphold the party line or safeguard the approved editorial path. A man whose work never ends, he knows in the core of his being that his ass is on the line if the line curves the wrong way. A subversive phrase or an inconvenient fact can do him in. He has probably heard a story similar to the one I was told recently in Beijing, about a censor at a local TV station who lost his job after an image of the Dalai Lama inadvertently aired in a documentary on Tibet. His poignant defense was that he didn't know what the Dalai Lama looked like. He had never seen his picture because it never appears in the Chinese press. The excuse wasn't good enough. He was purged.

Many of us still think censorship operates this way. And in many parts of the world, it does. Legions of functionaries are still deployed to assure no unapproved idea sneaks out of the closet—often to the point of Kafkaesque absurdity. I still chuckle about the censor in South Africa who decided that the book *Black Beauty* had to be removed from the schools.

But in many other lands, especially ours, this kind of censorship is almost passé. Oh sure, there is still a school somewhere in Kentucky that has banished Mark Twain's *Huckleberry Finn* and the American Civil Liberties Union has its work cut out for it in protecting the Internet from the infidels. But the face of modern censorship has changed. It has gone underground in some respects, and become institutionalized well above ground in others. In his introduction to an earlier edition of *Censored,* Hugh Downs, my former colleague at ABC's *20/20,* points out that censorship is now built into "the editorial process" where decisions are made on what gets covered and how, what news gets in and what's routinely spiked.

Each day at thousands of newspapers and TV newsrooms, editors and producers gather to make their picks from a menu of story possibilities—assess pitches from reporters in the field and news running on the wire. It is there they decide what to lead with, and what to downplay. Increasingly, despite the plethora of news sources and the size of the "news army" there is a sameness to the choices. Like the word processors found on every desk, there is an idea processor at work narrowing down what future generations will come to know as the first draft of history. Increasingly those stories revolve around what's called a giga event—the O.J. Case, The Death of a Princess, Sex Scandal in the White House, etc. Like blackbirds in flight, the sky darkens with packs of reporters moving in swarms, at the same speed and in predictable trajectory. When one lands, they all land. When one leaves, they all leave.

American journalism owes Project Censored a debt of gratitude for patrolling these chilly waters whose many icebergs are so well hidden beneath the surface. The modern Titanics of the media may now have sonars and radars to avoid collisions, but their faith in techno-solutions leave them as vulnerable as that great ship that went down to its icy grave. Perhaps it is appropriate that as Hollywood's costly version of the real ship's first and last journey steams across the screens, Project Censored warns that journalism as we have known it is sinking ever deeper in a sludge of sleaze, slime, and sensationalism—news that does not belong in the news. The consequence: we as readers, watchers, and citizens are drowning.

As the mainstream becomes a mudstream, we have to try to scratch a bit deeper to understand why its happening. That's where these informative annual volumes brought to us by Sonoma State University's Project Censored together with Seven Stories Press, become so crucial.

Censorship in these pages is discussed in terms of specific and detailed hard-hitting stories that have been, in this report's words, "ignored, undercovered, or diminished by the mainstream media." In their place, we are treated to an unending diet of what's called "junk food news," stories and spectacles that "are grossly over-reported, sensationalized and hyped out of proportion to their significance." And why? As Peter Phillips, who now directs this impressive media-watch operation explains, "the structure of media organizations themselves are creating latent forms of censorship that can be just as damaging as intentional censorship." And be clear, the practices that lead to so much homogeneity in a medium which appears so diverse, are not the work of the official guardians of network standards and practices. They flow instead from a kind of group-think corporate consensus, steeped in market logic and deeply inbred in an un-brave news culture that leads to conscience-free conformity and self-censorship.

The examples in this volume abound. All you have to do is flip the dial and do what these media monitors do—take notes, write it down, and look at the pattern. The same headlines, the familiar anchors, the packaged formats with their look-alike graphics and stirring music. It is no longer about programs as a product but programming as a process that infiltrates our very beings with familiar ways of looking at the world. The stories revolve around the very important people at the top and the celebrities that their entertainment industries have created and marketed. The daily fluctuations of the business behemoths are reported, the lives of ordinary people for the most part are not. For months, to cite just one case, the "miracle" of the Asian tigers and their get rich-quick economies are marveled over until they crash with no anticipation or explanation. The speculative casino of the global economy barely infiltrates the daily news except in the business media. As global news becomes more important, it is less present. Of course there are business channels to measure the winners and losers but no labor channels to show the human costs. In an era when content is supposedly king, the connections that would help us make sense of what's happening are missing, by design. Information is everywhere; interpretation is absent.

And covered least of all—the media itself, which has gone though structural shifts, merging into cartel-sized monopolies which treat information as a subsidiary of entertainment-oriented mega-businesses. Substance is a casualty of the synergies that these arrangements produce...endless tabloidization and suffocating cross-promotional hype. The musician Polarity One denounces the result in his song *News Goo-(the more you watch, the less you know)*—"a relentless flow of information, disinformation, sob stories and sales propaganda that creates an intellectual white noise." So far, his musical manifesto (which was released non-commercially as the "soundtrack" to my recent book) has yet to be played on heavily monopolized commercial radio which has plenty of time for gangsta rap but not for trenchant social commentary that explicitly names the overmerged media corporations ruling the airwaves.

Professor Robert W. McChesney astutely details in these pages the link between hyper-commercialization with its celebrities *uber alles* paradigm and the concentration and conglomeration that characterize media control in our era. Not only does the media not report on its own power and excesses, he notes, but they have deliberately depoliticized and demoralized society by defanging dissent and seeming to assure its marginalization. And as for their responsibility to serve the public interest, it isn't discussed.

Censored 1998 shows us how and why certain stories that shed light on institutional practices, environmental dangers, corporate abuses and other threats to our well-being are routinely shuffled out of our newscasts and newspaper columns. They are forced to surface in excellent but not always widely seen alternative outlets, outlets that lack the resources to market themselves so as to effectively compete with "products" that often spend more on advertising than editorial. This book brilliantly dissects the industry and the interlocking octopus tentacles of special interests behind it. It also gives credit where credit is due.

Censored 1998 tells the story of the difficulties that the makers of *Fear and Favor in the Newsroom* have had in getting their film on censorship on the air. It reminded me of how our company, Globalvision, was initially rejected by PBS for our human rights TV series *Rights & Wrongs* because "human rights is an insufficient organizing principle for a TV series." Sadly, far too many reports like the ones in this book are considered unworthy of mainstream coverage. And too often, Project Censored, which exists to blow the whistle on censorship, is itself ignored, i.e. censored. The circle of suppression is then complete.

Please, don't just shrug or weep at these tales of woe. Do something about them. For starters, buy an extra copy of this book and send it on to Mssrs. Rather, Jennings, and Brokaw et al.—but don't stop there. Bombard their bosses too—put this book in the face of the Rupert Murdochs, Michael Eisners, and John Malones of the world. At least then, they can't say they didn't know, or, "We are only giving the people what they want."

Call it our "books for moguls" campaign.

DANNY SCHECHTER is the Executive Producer of the independent TV company Globalvision and the author of *The More You Watch, The Less You Know: News Wars/(sub)merged Hopes/Media Adventures.*

CHAPTER 1

The Top 25 Censored News Stories of 1997

BY PETER PHILLIPS & PROJECT CENSORED

Being named as an author of a "most censored" story is a high honor, as it distinguishes quality investigative journalism from the entertainment news so prevalent in today's media. The 25 news stories in this chapter are timely, factual accounts of important subjects ignored, under-covered, or diminished by the mainstream media in 1997. The chapter contains a brief synopsis by Sonoma State University (SSU) *Censored* researchers of each of the top *Censored* news stories of 1997. Each synopsis is followed by an update by the original author(s) of the stories. A dagger (†) after an article title indicates it is reprinted in Appendix D, "Top 5 Censored Reprints."

Final selection of the "most censored" is a subjective/judgmental process, involving over 150 national judges, academics, students, and community volunteers. Differences of opinion are settled through majority rule. This means that the top 25 *Censored* stories and the runners-up are all important news.

Based on the requests of our readers, at the end of this year's list, directly following comment by Project Censored judges, we have included brief citings of runners-up for 1997. Additionally, this year, we have asked our authors, in their respective comments sections, to address how readers can find out more, or become more involved in specific issues brought to light by each story. This was also a recommendation from our readers, and we think it adds a strong activist element to our stories. Most of these issues will only be addressed if local concerned individuals become involved collectively. We cannot wait for government or others to solve or, in most instances, to even address these often critical issues.

HOW STORIES ARE SELECTED

Selection of the "most censored" stories of the year is a complex task involving hundreds of people nationwide. This year, close to 1,000 nominated news stories were screened by Project Censored staff. The nominations came to us from supporters all over the world. In addition, we, in cooperation with the Data Center in Oakland, California, monitored over 700 alternative/independent media sources, looking for important under-covered stories.

After the initial screening (we set aside purely op-ed items and news stories not fitting our October 15th annual cycle), we referred 610 stories to 65 faculty and community evaluators, using a standardized grading sheet to weight the story for importance and credibility. The 160 highest-rated stories are researched by Sonoma State University students for levels of coverage in the mainstream press. The top fifty stories with the highest importance rating and lowest coverage levels are read by faculty and students, and, in November, the vote is tallied. Finally, the top 25 stories are ranked by our national judges for their national significance.

We hope you find this year's selection enlightening.

1 CENSORED

Clinton Administration Aggressively Promotes U.S. Arms Sales Worldwide

Sources:
THE BULLETIN OF ATOMIC SCIENTISTS

Title: "Costly Giveaways"†
Date: October 1996
Author: Lora Lumpe

IN THESE TIMES
Title: "Guns 'R' Us"†
Date: August 11, 1997
Author: Martha Honey

SSU Censored Researchers: Katie Sims, Deb Udall, and Susan Allen
SSU Faculty Evaluator:
Phil Beard, Ph.D.

The United States is now the principal arms merchant for the world. U.S.

weapons are evident in almost every conflict worldwide and reap a devastating toll on civilians, U.S. military personnel, and the socio-economic priorities of many Third World nations.

On June 7, 1997, the House of Representatives unanimously approved the Arms Transfer Code of Conduct. This code would prohibit U.S. commercial arms sales or military aid and training to foreign governments that are undemocratic, abuse human rights, or engage in aggression against neighboring states. Yet the Clinton Administration, along with the Defense, Commerce, and State Departments, has continued to aggressively promote the U.S. arms industry at every opportunity. With Washington's share of the arms business jumping from 16 percent worldwide in 1988 to 63 percent today, U.S. arms dealers currently sell $10 billion in weapons to non-democratic governments each year. During Clinton's first year in office, U.S. foreign military aid soared to $36 billion, more than double what George Bush approved in 1992.

Most U.S. weaponry is sold to strife-torn regions such as the Middle East. These weapons sales fan the flames of war instead of promoting stability, and ironically, put U.S. troops based around the world at growing risk. For example, the last five times U.S. troops were sent into conflict, they found themselves facing adversaries who had previously received U.S. weapons, military technology, or training. Meanwhile, the Pentagon uses the presence of advanced U.S. weapons in foreign arsenals to justify increased new weapons spending—ostensibly to maintain U.S. military superiority.

Given that international arms sales exacerbate conflicts and drain scarce resources from developing countries, why does the Clinton Administration push them so vigorously? Proponents of arms sales say that these sales are a boon to the economy and that they create jobs. However, the government's own studies reveal that for every 100 jobs created by weapons exports, 41 are lost in non-military U.S. firms. And as U.S. arms exports have soared, some 2.2 million defense industry workers have lost their jobs due to corporate layoffs.

Thus the more plausible motive is the drive for corporate profits. It is no small detail that U.S. global arms market dominance has been accomplished as much through subsidies as sales. In return for arms manufacturers' huge political contributions, much of the U.S. arms exports are paid with government grants, subsidized loans, tax breaks, and promotional activities. With the 1996 welfare reform law cutting federal support for poor families by about $7 billion annually—an amount almost equal to the yearly subsidies given to U.S. weapons manufacturers—it is the poor who will pay the price for escalating arms exports.

Lawrence Kolb, a Brookings Institute fellow and former assistant secretary of defense under Ronald Reagan, sums up the problem: "It has become a money game: an absurd spiral in which we export arms only to have to develop more sophisticated ones to counter those spread out all over the world.... [And] it is very hard for us to tell other [countries]... not to sell arms when we are out there peddling and fighting to control the market."

UPDATE BY AUTHOR LORA LUMPE: "'Costly Giveaways' was based on a longer report ('Recycled Weapons: American Exports of Surplus Arms') that my former associate Paul F. Pineo and I published in mid-1996. That study demonstrated that the Pentagon and White House had quietly implemented a major new form of military assistance in the wake of the Cold War (and the 1990-1991 Gulf War). We documented approximately $7 billion in shipments of free, 'excess,' American weapons to countries around the world during 1990-95.

"The full report and 'Costly Giveaways' garnered some mainstream media coverage. Jack Anderson and Colman McCarthy, columnists with the *Washington Post*, both wrote about it. *Harper's* ran a box on it in the May 1997 'Readings' section, and William Greider referenced the report in an excellent article on the U.S. arms industry in *Rolling Stone* (July 10-24, 1997). However, in all of the press coverage, the narrow taxpayer angle received the greatest attention, while what I consider to be the most significant aspect of the story—the impact of these weapons shipments on people working for peace, democracy, economic justice, or human rights—received little mention.

"The report and article had some policy impact. Senator Paul Sarbanes read the study and enacted several of its recommendations into law (Public Law 104-164). Most significantly, this law requires an annual State Department report listing all transfers of 'excess defense articles' (EDA) and emergency 'drawdowns' of Pentagon weapons stocks during the preceding year. The listing, by country and specifying the type of equipment, greatly enhances congressional and public oversight of these programs. According to the first iteration of this report, released in September 1997, the Executive Branch authorized over $830 million of grant surplus weapons transfers in fiscal year 1996. Among the recipients were Mexico, Columbia, Peru, Egypt, Israel, Jordan, Bahrain, and Turkey—all countries where serious political repression and/or human rights violations were reported in 1996. Senator Sarbanes' law caps future EDA shipments at $350 million a year, beginning in fiscal year 1997 (the year that ended on September 30, 1997). His law also maintains for four years a requirement that the Pentagon provide surplus arms to Greece and Turkey in a 7 to 10 ratio, allegedly balancing the arms race between these antagonistic U.S. allies.

"In a related article that ran six months after our study, *U.S. News and World Report* (December 9, 1996) exposed the ease with which civilians and foreign agents are able to purchase surplus military spare parts from the Pentagon. In thousands of instances, the Department of Defense failed to 'demilitarize' equipment before sale, allowing civilians to, for instance, convert regular helicopters into assault helicopters. This story (and an accompanying piece on *60 Minutes*) led to congressional hearings, an internal Pentagon audit of the surplus inventory, and the introduction of legislation mandating accurate classification and demilitarization of surplus parts (HR 2602, introduced in October 1997 by Representative Pete Stark).

"For more information on the issues raised in 'Costly Giveaways' and in this update, visit the Federation of American Scientists' Arms Sales Monitoring Project on the World Wide Web at http://www.fas.org/asmp."

UPDATE BY AUTHOR MARTHA HONEY: "As the sole remaining superpower, the U.S. has the opportunity to map out a new foreign policy direction towards arms reductions in this post-Cold War era. Sadly, however, the U.S. is now the world's leading arms exporter; and NATO expansion, the centerpiece of Clinton's second term, offers a bonanza to U.S. arms exporters. Arms merchants are the second greatest recipients of corporate welfare—surpassed only by farmers who receive agricultural subsidies.

"Since the article was published, the Clinton Administration's positions have, unfortunately, hardened. Washington stands nearly alone in the world in its refusal to sign the land mines treaty. In August, Clinton agreed to lift the two-decade-old moratorium on transfers of high-tech weapons to Latin America, thereby threatening to trigger an arms race in South America.

"Regarding coverage of the article, I did a number of radio interviews after it appeared, but I am not aware of any significant coverage in the mainstream print or television media."

For more information on U.S. military sales and exports, contact:

MARTHA HONEY
Foreign Policy in Focus Project
Institute for Policy Studies (IPS)
733 15th Street, NW, Suite 1020
Washington, DC 20005
Tel: 202/234-9382
E-mail: ipsps@igc.apc. org.

The Foreign Policy in Focus Project at IPS publishes a number of briefs on arms sales and subsidies, NATO expansion, defense conversion, and other related topics.

LORA LUMPE
Federation of American Scientists
307 Massachusetts Avenue, NE
Washington, DC 20002
Tel: 202/ 675-1018
E-mail: llumpe@fas.org.

Lora Lumpe has a major project on conventional arms and arms sales.

WILLIAM HARTUNG
Arms Trade Resource Center
World Policy Institute
New School for Social Research
65 Fifth Avenue, Suite 413
New York, NY 10003
Tel: 212/229-5808
E-mail: hartung@newschool.edu.

This center compiles invaluable information on defense contractors and lobbying/political contributions.

TOM CARDOMONE
Council for a Livable World
Education Fund
110 Maryland Avenue, NE, Suite 409
Washington, DC 20002
Tel: 202/543-4100
E-mail: livableworld@igc.apc.org.

Tom Cardomone runs the Conventional Arms Transfer Project.

2 CENSORED

Personal Care and Cosmetic Products May Be Carcinogenic

Sources:
IN THESE TIMES
Title: "To Die For"†; "Take a Powder"†
Date: February 17, 1997;
March 3, 1997
Author: Joel Bleifuss

Mainstream media coverage: *Chicago Tribune,* July 29, 1997, page 3, zone C

SSU Censored Researchers:
Robin Stovall, Gavin Grundmann,
and Erika Well
SSU Faculty Evaluator:
Debora Hammond, Ph.D.

Do you use toothpaste, shampoo, sunscreen, body lotion, body talc, makeup, or hair dye? These are among the personal care products the American consumer has been led to believe are safe but that are often contaminated with carcinogenic byproducts, or that contain substances that regularly react to form potent carcinogens during storage and use.

Consumers regularly assume that these products are not harmful because they believe that they are approved for safety by the Food and Drug Administration (FDA). But although the FDA classifies cosmetics, dividing them into 13 categories, it does not regulate them. An FDA document posted on the agency's World Wide Web home page explains that "a cosmetic manufacturer may use any ingredient or raw material and market the final product without government approval." (This is with the exception of seven known toxins, such as hexachlorophene, mercury compounds, and chloroform.) Should the FDA deem a product a danger to public health, it has the power to pull a cosmetic product from the shelves. However, in many of these cases, the FDA has failed to do so, despite mounting evidence that some of the most common cosmetic ingredients may double as deadly carcinogens.

Examples of products with potential carcinogens are: Clairol "Nice and Easy" hair color, which releases carcinogenic formaldehyde as well as Cocamide DEA (a substance that can be contaminated with carcinogenic nitrosamines or react to produce a nitrosamine during storage or use); Vidal Sassoon shampoo, which, like the hair dye, contains Cocamide DEA; Cover Girl makeup contains TEA, which is also associated with carcinogenic nitrosamines; and Crest toothpaste which contains titanium dioxide, saccharin, and FD&C Blue # 1 (known carcinogens).

One of the cosmetic toxins that consumer advocates are most concerned about are nitrosamines, which contaminate a wide variety of cosmetic products. In the 1970s, nitrosamine contamination of cooked bacon and other nitrite-treated meats became a public health issue, and the food industry, which is more strictly regulated than the cosmetic industry, has since drastically lowered the amount of nitrosamines found in these processed meats. But today nitrosamines contaminate cosmetics at significantly higher levels than were once contained in bacon.

The FDA has long known that nitrosamines in cosmetics pose a risk to public health. On April 10, 1979, FDA commissioner Donald Kennedy called on the cosmetic industry to "take immediate measures to eliminate, to the extent possible, NDELA [a potent nitrosamine] and any other N-nitrosamine from cosmetic products." Since that warning, however, cosmetic manufacturers have done little to remove N-nitrosamines from their products, and the FDA has done even less to monitor them.

Individual FDA scientists are speaking out. The FDA's Donald Havery and Hardy Chou, for example, proclaimed that the continued use of these ingredients contradicts what should be a social goal: keeping "human exposure to N-nitrosamines to the lowest level technologically feasible, by reducing levels in all personal care products."

UPDATE BY AUTHOR JOEL BLEIFUSS: "Cosmetics are among the most unregulated, and therefore most potentially harmful, consumer products on the market. Consumers fail to realize that what you put on your skin is absorbed into the body. Few publications put effort into investigating the cosmetics industry, which is not surprising since the industry is a major magazine and newspaper advertiser. This is especially true of the women's magazines. Consequently, there is almost no good coverage of the industry.

"The Chicago-based Cancer Prevention Coalition is a reliable source of information, though the group has a definite point of view. The government scientists who do the research on cosmetic ingredients proved indispensable in helping me understand the science and the scope of the problem. The FDA's public relations apparatus was only helpful to a point. Once I had hard questions for them, they strung me along until after my deadline had passed. For example, I wanted to know why the FDA and the Cosmetic Toiletry and Fragrance Association both cite a talc workshop which they co-sponsor as refuting the link between ovarian cancer and talc, when the review that they commissioned on the epidemiological evidence—a review presented at the workshop—concluded just the opposite. And I wanted to know why the FDA, despite ample evidence of a link between ovarian cancer and talc, had refused to take regulatory action. I never got a response."

3 CENSORED

Big Business Seeks to Control and Influence U.S. Universities

Sources:
COVERTACTION QUARTERLY
(CAQ)
Title: "Phi Beta Capitalism"†
Date: Spring 1997
Author: Lawrence Soley

DOLLARS AND SENSE
Title: "Big Money on Campus"
Date: March/April 1997
Author: Lawrence Soley

SSU Censored Researchers:
Angie Yee and Katie Sims
SSU Faculty Evaluator:
Sally Hurtado, Ph.D.

Academia is being auctioned off to the highest bidder. Increasingly, industry is creating endowed professorships, funding think tanks and research centers, sponsoring grants, and contracting for research. Under this arrangement, students, faculty, and universities serve the interests of corporations instead of the public, and in the process, academic freedom and intellectual independence are sometimes sacrificed.

At the Massachusetts Institute of Technology (MIT), a number of programs serve corporate interests. One is the MIT's Industrial Liaison Program, which charges 300 corporations from $10,000 to $50,000 per year in membership fees. The fees buy the expertise and resources of MIT's departments and laboratories. Professors participating in the program can earn points towards professional travel, office equipment, and other prizes.

Although universities often claim that corporate moneys come without strings attached, this usually is not the case. For example, a British pharmaceutical corporation, Boots, gave $250,000 to the University of California, San Francisco, (UCSF) for research comparing its hypothyroid drug, Syn-

THIS MODERN WORLD by TOM TOMORROW

EVERYWHERE YOU LOOK, IT'S *PRIVATIZATION MANIA!* HOSPITALS ARE GIVING WAY TO *HMO'S*... PRISONS ARE BEING RUN BY *PRIVATE CORPORATIONS*... AND THANKS TO WELFARE REFORM, SOME STATES ARE EVEN CONTRACTING THEIR *WELFARE SYSTEMS* OUT TO FIRMS SUCH AS *LOCKHEED*...

--AND SO ACCORDING TO *MY* CALCULATIONS, THE ONLY WAY THIS COMPANY CAN POSSIBLY TURN A *PROFIT*--

--IS TO STOP GIVING ALL THESE DAMN *BENEFITS* TO THE *POOR!*

NOW, SOME OF YOU BLEEDING HEARTS MAY FIND THIS TREND *OBJECTIONABLE*--BUT AS FAR AS WE'RE CONCERNED, IT'S *ABOUT TIME!* THERE ARE *WAY* TOO MANY HANDOUTS IN THIS SOCIETY! FOR INSTANCE, IN EVERY CITY YOU'VE GOT *LIBRARIES*, JUST LOANING OUT BOOKS FOR *FREE!* WHAT'S UP WITH *THAT?* HAVEN'T THESE PEOPLE HEARD OF *BOOKSTORES?*

YOUR FREELOADING DAYS ARE OVER NOW, OLD TIMER! NO BUCKS, NO BOOKS--*CAPICHE?*

BUT-- BUT--

throid, with lower cost alternatives. Instead of demonstrating Synthroid's superiority as Boots had hoped, the study found that the other drugs were bioequivalents. This information could have saved consumers $356 million if they had switched to a cheaper alternative, but Boots took action to protect Synthroid's domination of the $600 million market. The corporation prevented publication of the results in the *Journal of the American Medical Association*, and then announced that the research was badly flawed. The researcher was unable to counter the claim because she was legally precluded from releasing the study.

Similarly, university presidents often sit on the boards of directors of major corporations, inviting conflicts of interest and developing biases that undermine academic freedom and interfere with the ability of the university to be critical or objective. For example, City University of New York Chancellor Ann Reynolds sits on the boards of Abbott Laboratories, Owens-Corning, American Electric Power, Humana, Inc., and the Maytag Corporation. Her $150,000 salary as chancellor is approximately doubled by what she gets as a board member. University of Texas Chancellor William Cunningham, after coming under public fire for conflict of interest, resigned his seat on the board of directors of Freeport-McMoRan Corporation, and cashed in his stock options netting $650,422.

While university presidents and chancellors gain from their corporate activities, industry and business are returned favors in kind. University boards of trustees are dominated by captains of industry, who hire chancellors and presidents with pro-industry biases. New York University's board, for example, includes former CBS owner Laurence Tisch, Hartz Mountain chief Leonard Stern, Salomon Brothers brokerage firm founder William B. Salomon, and real estate magnate-turned publisher Mortimer Zuckerman.

Federal tax dollars fund about $7 billion worth of research, to which corporations can buy access for a fraction of the actual cost. This is largely the result of two 1980s federal laws that allow uni-

versities to sell patent rights derived from taxpayer-funded research to corporations—encouraging "rent-a-researcher" programs. The result has been a covert transfer of resources from the public to the private sector and the changing of universities from centers of instruction to centers for corporate R & D (research and development).

UPDATE BY AUTHOR LAWRENCE SOLEY: "Although the alternative press has increasingly examined the links between corporate and foundation-funded endowments, research grants, research centers, professorial consulting and endowing professorships, most daily newspaper stories approach each topic as though they are entirely separate issues. For example, *The Los Angeles Times,* on November 30, 1997, printed an editorial titled, 'Foreign Gifts With Strings have U.S. Colleges Fretting.' The editorial suggested that it was just foreign moneys that have the potential to pollute the impartiality of academic research and discourse. The editorial closed with the statement that the 'universities receiving the highest level of foreign and domestic donations—Caltech, UCSF Medical School, Yale and Harvard—are among the nation's best.'

"What the editorial writers fail to realize is that 'elite' institutions such as Harvard influence what is happening at other universities, just as *The New York Times* influences news coverage at other U.S. newspapers. Many universities, including Cal State Northridge, Mission College, and Cal State Fresno, which have traditionally considered themselves teaching institutions, have been trying to emulate Harvard and Yale by striking up relationships with the private sector. Since 'Phi Beta Capitalism' was written, relationships between universities and corporations have grown even cozier."

4 CENSORED

Exposing the Global Surveillance System

Source:
COVERTACTION QUARTERLY (CAQ)
Title: "Secret Power: Exposing the Global Surveillance System"†
Date: Winter 1996/1997
Author: Nicky Hager

SSU Censored Researchers:
Bryan Way and Brad Smith
SSU Faculty Evaluator:
David Van Nuys, Ph.D.

For over 40 years, New Zealand's largest intelligence agency, the Government Communications Security Bureau (GCSB), has been helping its Western allies to spy on countries throughout the Pacific region. Neither the public nor the majority of New Zealand's top elected officials had knowledge of these activities. These procedures have operated since 1948 under a secret, Cold War-era intelligence alliance between the United States, Great Britain, Canada, Australia, and New Zealand—the UKUSA agreement. But in the late 1980s, the U.S. prompted New Zealand to join a new and highly secret global intelligence system. Author Nicky Hager's investigation into this system and his discovery of the ECHELON Dictionary has revealed one of the world's biggest, most closely held intelligence projects—one which allows spy agencies to monitor most of the telephone, e-mail, and telex communications carried over the world's telecommunication networks. It potentially affects every person communicating between (and sometimes within) countries anywhere in the world.

The ECHELON system, designed and coordinated by the U.S. National Security Agency (NSA) is one of the world's biggest, most closely held intelligence projects. Unlike many of the Cold War electronic spy systems, ECHELON is designed primarily to gather electronic transmissions from nonmilitary targets: governments, organizations, businesses, and individuals in virtually every country.

The system works by indiscriminately intercepting very large quantities of communications and using computers to identify and extract messages of interest from the mass of unwanted ones. Computers at each secret station in the ECHELON network automatically search millions of messages for pre-programmed key words. For each message containing one of those key words, the computer automatically notes time and place of ori-

gin and interception, and gives the message a four-digit code for future reference. Computers that can automatically search through traffic for key words have existed since at least the 1970s, but the ECHELON system was designed by NSA to interconnect all these computers and allow the stations to function as components of an integrated whole. Using the ECHELON system, an agency in one country may automatically pick up information gathered elsewhere in the system. Thus, the stations of the junior UKUSA allies function for the NSA no differently than if they were overtly NSA-run bases located on their soil.

The exposure of ECHELON occurred after more than 50 people who work or have worked in intelligence and related fields—concerned that the UKUSA activities had been secret too long and were going too far—agreed to be interviewed by Hager, a long-time researcher of spying and intelligence. Materials leaked to Hager included precise information on where the spying is conducted, how the system works, the system's capabilities and shortcomings, and other details such as code names.

The potential abuses of and few restraints around the use of ECHELON have motivated other intelligence workers to come forward. In one example, a group of "highly placed intelligence operatives" from the British Government Communications Headquarters (GCHQ) came forward protesting what they regarded as "gross malpractice and negligence" within the establishments in which they operate, citing cases of

GCHQ interception of charitable organizations such as Amnesty International and Christian Aid.

Nicky Hager states: "The main thing that protects these agencies from change is their secrecy. On the day my book [*Secret Power*] arrived in the bookstores, without prior publicity, there was an all-day meeting of the intelligence bureaucrats in the prime minister's department trying to decide if they could prevent it from being distributed. They eventually concluded, sensibly, that the political costs were too high. It is understandable that they were so agitated."

UPDATE BY AUTHOR NICKY HAGER: "As a long-time researcher into issues of spying and intelligence, I have become all too aware of how little reliable information on these subjects ever reaches the public. Many of the 'leaks' that hit the news have been planned by the spy agencies. Fragments of correct information that do leak out of the highly secretive agencies usually remain scattered or are denied, and incorrect information is frequently repeated year after year in news stories for lack of anything more substantial.

"As far as I know, the information contained in my CAQ article comes from the most substantial leak of top secret information this decade about the electronic spying activities of the Western powers. Many intelligence staff who work in the New Zealand outposts of the U.S. spy-network risked their careers to give me hundreds of pages of interview notes about the high-tech spy systems they operate.

"Since the article was published, the main electronic spy station operating in New Zealand has expanded its operations—from intercepting e-mail, fax, and telex to telephone calls as well—confirming that the ominous capability for large-scale automated telephone monitoring has been achieved by the spy agencies.

"When governments refuse to comment on and calculatedly ignore new stories, those stories usually quickly die. That is largely what happened with my revelations. However, anyone interested in reading more about the secret inner workings of the electronic spy agencies can read my book upon which the article was based: *Secret Power* (Nelson, New Zealand: Craig Potton, 1996). The book is available from *CovertAction Quarterly* (CAQ), 1500 Massachusetts Avenue, NW, #732, Washington, DC 20005; Tel: 202/331-9763; E-mail: caq@igc.org."

5 CENSORED

United States Companies are World Leaders in the Manufacture of Torture Devices for Internal Use and Export

Source:
THE PROGRESSIVE
Title: "Shock Value: U.S. Stun Devices Pose Human-Rights Risk"†
Date: September 1997
Author: Anne-Marie Cusac

Mainstream media coverage: *Chicago Tribune*, March 4, 1997, page 5, zone N; and *Washington Times*, March 4, 1997, page 16A

SSU Censored Researchers:
Carolyn Williams and Susan Allen
SSU Faculty Evaluator:
Dan Haytin, Ph.D.

In its March 1997 report entitled "Recent Cases of the Use of Electroshock Weapons for Torture or Ill-Treatment," Amnesty International lists 100 companies worldwide that produce and sell instruments of torture. Forty-two of these firms are in the United States. This places the U.S. as the leader in the manufacture of stun guns, stun belts, cattle probe-like devices, and

other equipment which can cause devastating pain in the hands of torturers.

According to the report, the following are some of the American companies currently engaged in the production and sale of such weapons: Arianne International of Palm Beach Gardens, Florida; B-west Imports Inc. of Tucson, Arizona; and Taserton of Corona, California. Arianne International makes the "Myotron," a compact version of the stun gun. B-West joined with Paralyzer Protection, a South African company, to produce shock batons that deliver a charge of between 80,000 and 120,000 volts. Taserton was the first company to manufacture the taser, a product which shoots two wires attached to darts with metal hooks. When these hooks catch a victim's skin or clothing, the device delivers a debilitating shock. Los Angeles police officers used the device against Rodney King in 1991.

These weapons are currently in use in the U.S. and are being exported to countries all over the world. The U.S. government is a large purchaser of stun devices—especially stun guns, electroshock batons, and electric shields. The American Civil Liberties Union (ACLU) and Amnesty both claim the devices are unsafe and may encourage sadistic acts by police officers and prison guards both here and abroad. "Stun belts offer enormous possibilities for abuse and the infliction of gratuitous pain," says Jenni Gainsbourough of the ACLU's National Prison Project. She adds that because use of the stun belt leaves little physical evidence, this increases the likelihood of sadistic, but hard-to-prove, misuse of these weapons. In June 1996, Amnesty International asked the Bureau of Prisons to suspend the use of electroshock belt, citing the possibility of physical danger to inmates and the potential for misuse.

In 1991, Terence Allen, a specialist in forensic pathology who served as deputy medical examiner for both Los Angeles and San Francisco's coroner's offices, linked the taser to fatalities. With electrical current, Allen says, the chance of death increases with each use. Allen warns, "I think what you are going to see is more deaths from stun weapons."

Manufacturers of electroshock weapons continue to denounce allegations that use of their devices is dangerous and may constitute a gross violation of human rights. Instead, they are making more advanced innovations. A new stun weapon may soon be added to police arsenals: the electroshock razor wire, specially designed for surrounding demonstrators who get out of hand.

UPDATE BY AUTHOR ANNE-MARIE CUSAC: "Many citizens do not realize that the abuse of prisoners is epidemic in the United States. Since I wrote the piece, evidence that guards in the Maricopa County, Arizona, jail system mistreated inmates with stun guns (including one incident where a guard shocked a sleeping inmate) has led to a new jail policy restricting the use of 'non-lethal' weapons such as stun guns. There has also been some disturbing news; the stun belt recently appeared in South Africa.

This is the first documented export of the device.

"Meanwhile, the manufacturers have been busy. One company recently announced a device it calls 'The Sticky Shocker,' which fires an electrified high-pressure saline solution. The 'Net Gun,' another new product, uses a grenade launcher to shoot a sticky web that can deliver a 60,000-volt shock.

"The mainstream media have had no response to 'Shock Value,' and have given scant coverage to the issue as a whole. A copy of Amnesty International's report on stun devices may be obtained by phoning 212/807-8400. The American Civil Liberties Union Prison Rights Project (Tel: 202/234-4830) also has information on the devices."

6 CENSORED

Russian Plutonium Lost Over Chile and Bolivia

Source:
COVERTACTION QUARTERLY (CAQ)
Title: "Space Probe Explodes, Plutonium Missing"
Date: Spring 1997
Author: Karl Grossman

SSU Censored Researchers:
Robin Stovall and Kecia Kaiser

SSU Faculty Evaluator:
Catherine Nelson, Ph.D.

On November 16, 1996, Russia's Mars 96 space probe broke up and burned while descending over Chile and Bolivia, scattering its remains across a 10,000-square-mile area. The probe carried about a half pound of deadly plutonium divided into four battery canisters. However, no one seems to know where the canisters went. Gordon Bendick, Director of Legislative Affairs for the National Security Council, states there are two possibilities. Either the "...canisters were destroyed coming through the atmosphere [and the plutonium dispersed], or the canisters survived re-entry, impacted the earth, and...penetrated the surface...or could have hit a rock and bounced off like an agate marble."

This amount of plutonium has the potential to cause devastating damage. According to Dr. Helen Caldicott, president emeritus of Physicians for Social Responsibility, "Plutonium is so toxic that less that one millionth of a gram is a carcinogenic dose. One pound, if uniformly distributed, could hypothetically induce lung cancer in every person on earth." Dr. John Gofman, professor emeritus of radiological physics at the University of California, Berkeley, confirms the increased hazard of lung cancer that would occur if the probe burned up and formed plutonium oxide particles.

On November 17, when the U.S. Space Command announced the probe would re-enter the earth's atmosphere with a predicted impact point in East Central Australia, President Clinton telephoned the Australian Prime Minister John Howard and offered "the assets the U.S. has in the Department of Energy," to deal with any radioactive contamination. Howard placed the Australian military and government on full alert and warned the public to use "extreme caution" if they came in contact with the remnants of the Russian space probe.

In the first of a series of blunders, the day after the space probe had fallen on South America, the Space Command remained focused on Australia. Later they reported the probe had fallen in the Pacific, just west of South America. A Russian news source put the site in a different patch of the Pacific altogether. Major media in the United States reported the probe as having crashed "harmlessly" into the ocean. On November 18, 1996, the *Washington Post* ran the headline: "Errant Russian Spacecraft Crashes Harmlessly After Scaring Australia."

On November 29, U.S. Space Command completely revised its account. It changed not only *where*, but also *when* the probe fell. The final report placed the crash site not west of South America, but directly on Chile and Bolivia. The date of the crash was also revised from November 17 to November 16, the night before. Apparently, U.S. Space Command had initially tracked the booster stage of the Russian craft, and not the actual probe itself.

Yet once the U.S. had determined the plutonium might have landed on South America it did nothing to help locate and recover the radioactive canisters. "You can clearly see the double standard," charged Houston aerospace engineer James Oberg. "Australia got a phone call from the President, and Chile got a two week-old fax from somebody." Many attribute this double standard to racism.

The New York Times mentioned the incident on page 7 under "World Briefs" on December 14, 1996. The Russian government has been uncooperative, still refusing to give Chile a description of the canisters to aid in retrieval efforts.

UPDATE BY AUTHOR KARL GROSSMAN: "The fall on Chile and Bolivia of the Russian Mars 96 space probe carrying a half-pound of plutonium is important because it again reflects how accidents involving nuclear-fueled space devices can and do happen. Indeed, this was the sixth of the 41 known Soviet/Russian nuclear space shots that has met with an accident. (The U.S. also has a 12 percent failure rate—with three out of its 27 nuclear space shots meeting with accidents. The worst of these was the 1964 disintegration upon reentry into the Earth's atmosphere of the SNAP-9A plutonium system, which dispersed 2.1 pounds of plutonium widely over the planet.) In the case of the Russian Mars 96 space probe, eyewitnesses saw the probe in a fiery descent, apparently breaking up in the sky. Did the plutonium aboard the Russian Mars 96 space probe disperse? If so, what was the extent of the contamination and what are the impacts on health? We don't know the answer to those questions. More than a year later, there is still very little information about the incident.

"The mainstream press, from the time it was announced that the probe fell on South America—and not, as originally predicted by the U.S. Space Command, on Australia—has given scant attention to the accident. As Manuel Baquedano, director of the Institute for Ecological Policy in Chile, asked, 'Are the lives of Australians worth more than the lives of Chileans?' The U.S. has done virtually nothing for Chile and Bolivia in dealing with the accident despite repeated requests. Getting information on the story remains a struggle. I made numerous telephone calls to officials in the U.S. and in Latin America and have gotten precious little information."

7 CENSORED

Norplant and Human Lab Experiments in Third World Lead To Forced Use in the United States

Sources:
MS.
Title: "The Misuses of Norplant: Who Gets Stuck?"
Date: November/December 1996
Author: Jennifer Washburn

WASHINGTON FREE PRESS
Title: "Norplant and the Dark Side
of the Law"
Date: March/April 1997
Author: Rebecca Kavoussi

HUMAN EVENTS
Title: "BBC Documentary Claims
That U.S. Foreign Aid Funded
Norplant Testing On Uninformed
Third World Women"
Date: May 16, 1997
Author: Joseph D'Agostino

SSU Censored Researchers:
Carolyn Williams and Katie Sims
SSU Faculty Evaluator: Jeanette
Koshar, Ph.D.

Low-income women in the United States
and in the Third World have been the
unwitting targets of a U.S. policy to control birth rates. Despite continuous
reports of debilitating effects of the drug
Norplant, women here and in the Third
World, who have received the
implantable contraceptive, have had difficulty making their complaints heard,
and in some instances have been
deceived, according to our resources.
Norplant is a set of six plastic cylinders
containing a synthetic version of a female
hormone. It is intended to prevent pregnancy for five years. Surgery is required
for removal—at a cost far beyond the
reach of low-income women, regardless
of their nationality, if the removal is not
subsidized.

Jennifer Washburn's *Ms.* article
focuses on Medicaid rejection of Norplant
removals for low-income women prior to
the standard five-year period, even when
side effects are chronic. In the U.S. State
Medicaid agencies, for example, often
generously cover the cost of Norplant
insertion but don't cover removal before
the full five years. Although Medicaid
policy may cover early removal "when
determined 'medically necessary,'" medical necessity is determined by the
provider and the Medicaid agency, not
the patient.

Journalist Rebecca Kavoussi reports
in her *Washington Free Press* article that
the reproductive rights of women
addicted to drugs or alcohol have once
again become the focus of U.S. legislation. Senate Bill 5278, now under consideration in the state of Washington,
would require "involuntary use of long-
term pharmaceutical birth control" (Norplant) for women who give birth to
drug-addicted babies. Under this proposal, a woman who gives birth to a drug-
addicted baby would get two
chances—the first voluntary, the second
mandatory—to undergo drug treatment
and counseling. Upon the birth of a third
drug-addicted child, the state would
force the mother to undergo surgery to
insert the Norplant contraceptive.

Similarly, Norplant is figuring in
reproductive rights issues and legislative policies worldwide as well. In his
May 1997 *Human Events* article, Joseph
D'Agostino reports on the British
Broadcasting Corporation (BBC) documentary *The Human Laboratory*, which
accused the U.S. Agency for International Development (U.S.AID) of acting
in conjunction with the Population

Council of New York City, to use uninformed women in Bangladesh, Haiti, and the Philippines for Norplant tests. Many of these women were subjects in pre-injection drug trials that began in 1985 in Bangladesh, one of the world's poorest countries.

The BBC documentary contained interviews with women who complained of debilitating side effects from Norplant, but who were rebuffed when they asked to have the implants removed. These women stated that they had been told that the drug was safe and not experimental. Implantation was free.

One woman interviewed in the documentary said that after implantation, suddenly her body became weak, and that she couldn't get up, look after her children, or cook. Other women reported similar problems, stating that when they asked to have Norplant removed, they were told it would ruin the study. "I went to the clinic as often as twice a week," one woman said, "but they said, 'This thing we put in your arm costs 5,000 *takas*. We'll not remove it unless you pay this money.'" The narrator of the documentary, Farida Akhter, recounted that when another woman begged to have the implant removed—saying, "I'm dying, please help me get it out"—she was told, "Okay, when you die, inform us, we'll get it out of your body."

The documentary asserts that the women should have been told that the pre-introductory trials were to assess the drug's safety, efficiency, and acceptability. Now, says the BBC, many women who were used in the trials are suffering from

eyesight disorders, strokes, persistent bleeding, and other side effects.

However, the Norplant saga appears to have global political implications that interfere with reasonable resolution. According to the documentary, the U.S. government considers global population control a "national security issue" and has increased U.S. population control efforts around the world.

Norplant side effects have resulted in over 400 lawsuits being filed against Wyeth-Ayerst, the maker of Norplant. These lawsuits include class actions representing over 50,000 women which are only just now making their way to the courts.

UPDATE BY AUTHOR JENNIFER WASHBURN: "When Norplant hit the market in 1990, a flurry of state legislation was proposed offering AFDC recipients monetary incentives (anywhere from $200 to $700) to use Norplant. At the same time, state Medicaid agencies were crafting policies that deny coverage for early Norplant removal (before five years) even if a woman was experiencing chronic side effects, policies that still exist in many states. The mainstream media, to my knowledge, never picked up on this story, and rarely, if ever, covers issues affecting the health and reproductive rights of low-income women. Norplant usage has, however, declined dramatically in all populations largely due to the negative publicity generated from the lawsuits involving some 50,000 women which are only just now making their way to the courts.

"Since my story came out, 'child exclusion laws' that deny additional benefits to children born to mothers on welfare have spread to at least 21 states. The new federal welfare 'reform' law permits states to punitively exclude benefits to these children, despite the fact that two recent studies in New Jersey and Arkansas—the first two states to implement 'family caps' as they are euphemistically called—found no difference in birth rates between women denied benefits and those eligible for them. At the same time that welfare recipients are being asked to achieve self-sufficiency in five years or less, 34 states continue to allow Medicaid coverage of abortion services only in cases of rape, incest, or life endangerment. Meanwhile, the new law encourages competition among states for 'illegitimacy bonuses,' and dedicates an extraordinary $50 million for 'abstinence-only' education—which may not be combined with traditional sex education programs that teach about both abstinence and contraception. Many fear that this will wipe out more encompassing sex education programs from schools, hardly a viable solution for sexually active women of any class who want control over their reproduction as well as their lives."

UPDATE BY AUTHOR REBECCA KAVOUSSI:
"Although Washington state Senate Bill 5278 will take effect July 1, 1998 (if passed), there has been no mainstream media coverage of its year-long journey through the Washington state legislature.
"Technology is commonly equated with progress, and progress is believed to be positive. Accordingly, our culture seems to view advances in reproductive technology as indicators of more broad and extensive advances in freedom and autonomy for women as a group. In the case of legislation like this, however, we glimpse the stunning negative potential of technology when it is called upon to bring order to emotionally and politically loaded situations.

"In the most updated version of the bill, women targeted for mandatory contraception also face the termination of parental rights. While the writers of the bill suggest no funding for improving the resources available to pregnant addicts, they are considering extending Senate Bill 5278 to include mothers of children born with fetal alcohol syndrome.

"Both Lexis-Nexis and the Web offer the full text of legislation at state and national levels. In her book, *At Women's Expense: State Power and the Politics of Fetal Rights* (Harvard University Press, 1993), Cynthia Daniels details the relationship between reproductive technology and the state."

UPDATE BY AUTHOR JOSEPH D'AGOSTINO:
"Two crucial concerns intersect in the story of Western organizations promoting population control in the Third World at all costs: the unspoken belief that the lives of Third World people are less valuable than those of Westerners, and the perversion of women's sacred reproductive rights. Despite the well-respected BBC's report, almost nothing has appeared in the American mainstream

media on the experimental use of Norplant on unsuspecting Third World women. All that I could find was a two-sentence mention in passing by a guest on NPR's *Talk of the Nation* on February 5, 1997, and an article by Mount Holyoke College Professor of Women's Studies Asoka Bandarage in the July 14, 1997 *Christian Science Monitor*.

"The Population Council continues to insist Norplant is safe, as does the World Health Organization and U.S. AID. But the FDA has kept open the petition of the Population Research Institute (PRI) to decertify the device. Class action suits against the device are pending."

8 CENSORED

Little Known Federal Law Paves The Way for National Identification Card

Source:
WITWIGO
Title: "National ID Card is Now Federal Law and Georgia Wants to Help Lead the Way"
Date: May/June 1997
Author: Cyndee Parker

Mainstream media coverage:
The New York Times, September 8,
1996, section 6; page 58, column 1; related article in *The San Francisco Chronicle*, September 19, 1996, page A1

SSU Censored Researchers: Bryan Way, Erika Nell, and Matt Monpas
SSU Faculty Evaluator:
Peter Phillips, Ph.D.

In September 1996, President Clinton signed the Illegal Immigration Reform and Responsibility Act of 1996. Buried on approximately page 650 was a section that creates a framework for establishing a national ID card for the American public. This legislation was slipped through without fanfare or publicity.

This law has various aspects: It establishes a "Machine Readable Document Pilot Program" requiring employers to swipe a prospective employee's driver's license through a special reader linked to the federal government's Social Security Administration. The federal government would have the discretion to approve or disapprove the applicant for employment. In this case, the driver's license becomes a "national ID card."

According to author Cyndee Parker, "For the first time in American history, and reminiscent of Communist countries, our government would have the ability to grant approval before a private company enters into private employment contracts with private citizens. Because of the nature of the employment system alone, personal information would be accessible to local agencies and anyone who even claims to be an employer. The government would have comprehensive files on all American citizens' names, dates and places of birth, mothers' maiden names, Social Security numbers, gender, race, driving records, child support payments, divorce status, hair and eye color, height, weight, and anything else they may dream up in the future."

Another part of the law provides $5 million-per-year grants to any state that wants to participate in any one of three pilot ID programs. One of these programs is the "Criminal Alien Identification Program," which is to be used by federal, state, and local law enforcement agencies to record fingerprints of aliens previously arrested. A third part of this law provides that federal agencies may only accept driver's licenses that conform to new requirements—meaning only licenses which contain digital fingerprints.

The author of the national ID law, Dianne Feinstein (D-CA), stated in a Capitol Hill magazine that it was her intention to see Congress immediately implement a national ID system whereby every American would be required to carry a card with a "magnetic strip on it on which the bearer's unique voice, retina pattern, or fingerprint is digitally encoded." Congressman Dick Armey (R-TX), among others, has strongly denounced the new law, calling it "an abomination, and wholly at odds with the American tradition of individual freedom."

Shortly before the bill was signed into law, Georgia passed its own legislation, creating something similar to the federal ID program. The Georgia law requires residents to give digital fingerprints before obtaining a driver's license or state ID. This law was approved by the state legislature in April 1996 and received virtually no public or media attention at that time. Since passage, many Georgia lawmakers have tried repealing the law. Eight repeal bills were drafted in the Georgia Assembly and one in the Senate. However, all of the bills were blocked in the Senate and never voted on.

UPDATE BY AUTHOR CINDEE PARKER: "A handful of Georgians began to fight for the abolition of the fingerprints law in Georgia. Those few Georgians have now turned into a vast array of people from all 50 states, known as the Coalition to Repeal the Fingerprints Law. Our research has culminated with the knowledge that not only are Georgians required to give fingerprints in order to obtain a driver's license, but also that this is, in fact, a back door approach to not only a national ID card, but a universal ID card, all being pushed by the American Association of Motor Vehicle Administrators (AAMVA). The AAMVA, in a recent industry article entitled 'MOVE,' states that they must 'sell the public' on the idea that 'Biometric Authentication and Identification Technology' (BAIT) will help prevent 'identity fraud.' The National Highway Traffic Safety Administration, in their publication *The Highway Safety Desk Book*, similarly describes the idea: 'With a central image database of every driver in a state, the public safety community has a ready-made storehouse of photos to be used in criminal investigations. The uses for these images are limited only by the wants and needs of the public safety community.'

"We know that our new national ID card is being brought into existence through the use of driver's licensing mandates being advanced in all 50 states. Throughout the last two years, we have found that Australia, Thailand, Mexico, Canada, and many other countries all introduced similar measures for biometric identification of its citizens, including digitized fingerprints. Communist China is also one of those countries that has initiated the same form of identifying its citizens. The company that provided the Chinese equipment also was under contract to provide the new equipment for the state of Alabama.

"Thanks to much hard work by everyone in the Coalition to Repeal the Fingerprints Law, we attended a press conference in Alabama in the summer of 1997 and helped the governor of that state come to the decision to remove the equipment. That was one of our biggest successes of 1997. Stopping legislation in Washington State and Utah were other successes. In Georgia, we had a major victory last session when we saw the Senate twice vote to remove the fingerprints law—in votes of 45-7 and 49-5. At the present time, this is the most significant campaign issue for the 1998 Governor and Lt. Governor's races in Georgia.

"Though the press in the Atlanta area has given very good coverage on the driver's license/fingerprint issue, most press in Georgia and other states refuse to reveal the national mandates brought about by Congress or the internationally

documented race for a 'Universal Biometrics Card.' Information has been shared with the press, but has been almost totally ignored in the mainstream media.

"Unless 'We the People' quit acting like 'We the Sheep,' Americans will lose every bit of freedom our founding fathers fought and died for."

9 CENSORED

Mattel Cuts U.S. Jobs to Open Sweatshops in Other Countries

Sources:
THE NATION
Title: "Barbie's Betrayal:
The Toy Industry's Broken Workers"
Date: December 30, 1996
Author: Eyal Press

THE HUMANIST
Title: "Sweatshop Barbie:
Exploitation of Third World Labor"
Date: January/February 1997
Author: Anton Foek

SSU Censored Researcher:
Erika Nell
SSU Staff Evaluator: Carol Tremmel

Thanks to the North American Free Trade Agreement (NAFTA) and the General Agreement on Tariffs and Trade (GATT), U.S. toy factories have cut a one-time American work force of 56,000 in half and sent many of those jobs to countries where workers lack basic rights.

For 23 years, Dennis Mears worked as an electrician at the Fisher-Price factory in Medina, New York. In 1993, Mattel, Inc. took over the plant, welcoming the people of Fisher-Price to the Mattel family. Two years later, after Mattel had lobbied for NAFTA, touting the agreement as a boon for U.S. workers, Mears and 700 other employees, including his wife, an employee of 18 years, lost their jobs. Some of the jobs moved to the South, but 520 disappeared because of "increased company imports from Mexico," according to the U.S. Labor Department. Today, Mears works in an applesauce factory, earning half of what he made at Fisher-Price.

In the past decade, Mattel, the makers of "Barbie," bought out six major competitors, making it the largest toy manufacturer in the world. Employing 25,000 people worldwide, Mattel now only employs 6,000 workers in the United States. NAFTA has freed Mattel to further reduce its American work force and take advantage of repressive labor laws in other countries.

Delfina Rodriguez is a middle-aged woman with seven children. Until September 9, 1996, she assembled Mattel toys on the night shift at the Mabamex factory, a Mattel affiliate in Tijuana, Mexico. On that night, she reports, she came to work carrying pamphlets from a workers' rights meeting held the previous day.

Upon entering the plant she says her purse was searched and she was taken into a room by a security guard. She and two other workers say they were interrogated, accused of passing out subversive materials, detained against their will until the next morning, and prevented from going to the bathroom or making phone calls to their families. In the end, they were told they would have to quit their jobs or go to prison. They were released only after agreeing to resign. Although they have reached a settlement with the company awarding them severance pay, the women have filed a penal complaint in Tijuana, claiming their rights were violated.

In the Dynamic factory just outside of Bangkok, 4,500 women and children stuff, cut, dress, and assemble Barbie dolls and Disney properties. Many of the workers have respiratory infections, their lungs filled with dust from fabrics in the factory. They complain of hair and memory loss, constant pain in their hands, neck, and shoulders, episodes of vomiting, and irregular menstrual periods. Metha is a militant woman in her twenties who tried to start a union at the Dynamics plant. She claims the company not only fired her but threatened to shut her up "forever." She developed respiratory problems and was hospitalized. She expresses her fear to talk to a reporter by saying, "Barbie is powerful. Three friends have already died. If they kill me, who will ever know I lived?"

Though separated by distance, these Mattel workers are intimately connected by experience, as are those of countless other abused workers in toy factories in Thailand and China, where Mattel now produces the bulk of their toys.

Under pressure, the industry adopted a code of conduct, which conveniently calls upon companies to monitor themselves. There's little evidence, however, according to authors Anton Foek and Eyal Press, of any changes in these abusive practices.

UPDATE BY AUTHOR EYAL PRESS:

"A few years ago, questions about conditions in the toy industry began to be raised in the media after a fire killed more than 100 workers, mostly young women, at a factory in Thailand. Since that time, little has been done to address the unsafe and inhumane working conditions that predominate in the industry; and the media's attention has, predictably, focused on the craze for 'Elmo' dolls, the latest version of Barbie, and to the intense jostling among companies for profit and market share. The fact that so many toys are made in sweatshops is simply not a pleasant topic to dwell upon, so while it's mentioned in occasional news stories, most consumers remain uninformed and oblivious.

"My article gave a detailed, first-hand account of a previously unreported case of worker harassment and intimidation at a Mattel toy factory in Mexico. I connected this story to related events in a town in upstate New York, where, earlier in the same year, Mattel had laid off hundreds of workers, shifting production to Mexico. The strength of the story, I think, rested in the first-hand interviews I conducted with workers in both places. The article also provided a detailed look at how Mattel and other toy companies have lobbied Congress to ensure that U.S. tariff and trade agreements be separated from the question of labor rights. In the fine print of trade agreements with China and Indonesia, the industry has won special privileges eliminating all tariffs on toy imports, and it has blocked attempts to tie these privileges to improvements in labor rights.

"The short-term response to my story was positive: I was invited to speak on numerous radio shows across the country, both commercial and public. There

THIS MODERN WORLD
by TOM TOMORROW

THE MATTEL TOY COMPANY--IN A MOVE APPLAUDED BY ANIMAL RIGHTS ACTIVISTS--HAS BEGUN TO CRACK DOWN ON *FURRIERS* WHO SELL REAL, DOLL-SIZED *MINK COATS* TO *BARBIE* COLLECTORS...EXPLAINING THAT "WE WOULD NOT HAVE BARBIE WEAR REAL FUR--SHE'S A *FRIEND* TO ANIMALS..."

THAT'S PRETTY *GREAT NEWS*, ISN'T IT, BARBIE?

"YEAH! LET'S GET TOGETHER AND *CELEBRATE* WITH OUR GROUP AFTER SCHOOL!"

NOTE: IN ORDER TO GET ALL SIDES OF THE ISSUE, WE'VE INVITED *SUPER TALK BARBIE* TO SHARE *HER* SPECIAL PERSPECTIVE-- IN HER *OWN* WORDS!

WELL, MAYBE WE SHOULDN'T START CELEBRATING JUST *YET*, BARBIE...YOU SEE, THERE'S STILL THE SMALL MATTER OF *HUMAN* RIGHTS ABUSES, WHICH ARE *RAMPANT* IN THE COUNTRIES WHERE MOST MATTEL TOYS ARE MADE--SUCH AS *INDONESIA*, WHERE THOUSANDS OF MATTEL WORKERS EARN $2.25 A DAY AND HAVE *NO RIGHT TO ORGANIZE*...

"WOW! IT WOULD BE FUN TO DRIVE TO THE BEACH WITH OUR *NEW FRIENDS!*"

have also been several good stories done on conditions in the toy industry in the past year—including a program that aired on *NBC Dateline*. Nevertheless, the issues addressed in my article have not received sustained attention. In addition, I know for a fact that an award-winning reporter at a mainstream newspaper had a lengthy feature story on abuses in the toy industry killed by his editors just around the time that my story appeared. He was enraged, suspecting that his editors (and no doubt the paper's advertisers) simply did not want such a story to appear during the holiday shopping season. Given that the United States is by far the world's largest market for toys and that the industry's abuses could easily be curtailed without threatening its financial well-being, it's impossible to believe that consumers would prefer that such stories be relegated to the back pages."

UPDATE BY AUTHOR ANTON FOEK:
"In the year since my story was published, at least one of the women I wrote about died. And unsafe sweatshop conditions continue in Bangkok, Thailand, as elsewhere. A positive change, however, is that the sort of conditions I reported in 'Sweatshop Barbie,' have since garnered widespread concern, receiving publicity in *U.S. News and World Report*, on *NBC Dateline*, and in other media. As a result, companies like Mattel have publicly responded. The July/August 1997 *Humanist* featured a letter written by Sean M. Fitzgerald, Vice-President of Corporate Communications for Mattel, Inc., followed by my reply. In his letter, Fitzgerald denied or minimized what I had personally observed, photographed, and tape-recorded. But, after standing by my story, I expressed the idea that we should look beyond the toys of Mattel to the forest of the corporate world as a whole, seeing how the goal of amassing private fortunes can work at cross-purposes with the goal of extending participatory democracy.

"Though I haven't heard that my reply changed Fitzgerald's mind, I consider the corporate response sufficient. It shows that journalistic efforts can have impact. But we must do more. Consumers should write letters and send e-mail to major cor-

porations whose products carry labels indicating manufacture in developing nations, and ask about working conditions there. Further, consumer groups should be encouraged to rate products according to working conditions as well as safety. To know how best to vote with your dollars, contact The Council on Economic Priorities at 30 Irving Place, New York, NY 10001; Tel: 800/729-4237."

10 CENSORED

Army's Plan to Burn Nerve Gas and Toxins in Oregon Threatens Columbia River Basin

Source:
EARTH FIRST!
Title: "Army Plans to Burn Surplus Nerve Gas Stockpile"
Date: March 1997
Authors: Mark Brown and Kayrn Jones

SSU Censored Researcher:
Brad Smith
SSU Faculty Evaluator: Ellen Krebs

Despite evidence that incineration is the worst option for destroying the nation's obsolete chemical weapons stockpile stored at the Umatilla Army Depot, the Oregon Environmental Quality Commis-sion (EQC) gave the green light to the Army and Raytheon Corporation to spend $1.3 billion of taxpayer money to construct five chemical weapons incinerators. Despite strong protests, on February 7, 1997, the EQC made its final decision to accept the United States Army's application to build a chemical weapons incineration facility near Hermiston, Oregon.

Some examples of the chemicals to be incinerated include nerve gas and mustard agents; bioaccumulative organochlorines such as dioxins, furans, chloromethane, vinyl chloride, and PCBs; metals such as lead, mercury, copper, and nickel; and toxins such as arsenic. These represent only a fraction of the thousands of chemicals and metals that will potentially be emitted throughout the Columbia River watershed and from the toxic ash and effluents which pose a significant health threat via entrance to the aquifer.

Citizen groups, environmental organizations, health organizations, and local Native Americans have protested incineration of the chemical agents stored at the Umatilla Army depot. Extensive technical literature supports the Native American opposition to chemical agent incineration. Cancer, birth defects, reproductive dysfunction, immune system disorder, and neurological damage can occur at even very low exposure to these toxic incinerator emissions.

Their position is reinforced by the problems that continue to arise in other incinerator facilities. The Umatilla incinerator will be modeled after the Toole,

Utah Chemical Weapons Disposal Facility. Yet Toole Army manager Tim Thomas admitted there has been agent detection in heating, ventilation, and air conditioning vestibules since Toole began incinerating in 1996. Additionally, there have been agent stack alarms once or twice a week, and the Army doesn't know why. Decontamination fluid continues to leak though cracks in the Toole concrete floor into the electrical control room.

These serious revelations about chemical agent incinerator defects are a mirror of those reported at the Army's prototype facility, Johnston Atoll Chemical Agent Destruction System (JACADS), located 800 miles southwest of Hawaii. According to the Army's own reports, a fire, an explosion, 32 internal releases of a nerve agent, and two nerve gas releases into the atmosphere have resulted in EPA fines of $100,000. The JACADS facility is 450 percent over budget and had over 30 Resource Conservation and Recovery Act non-compliances in 1995.

Contrary to what incineration advocates claim, there is no urgent need to incinerate, since the stockpile at Umatilla has small potential for explosion or chain reaction as a result of decay. A 1994 General Accounting Office report estimates that the actual number of years for safe weapons storage is 120 years rather than the 17.7 years originally estimated by the National Research Council. Thus, the timeline for action could conceivably be lengthened until all the alternatives—such as chemical neu-

tralization, molten metals, electro-chemical oxidation, and solvated electron technology (SET)—are considered. A delay is supported by a National Academy of Sciences report, entitled "Review and Evaluation of Alternative Chemical Disposal Technologies," which states that there has been sufficient development to warrant re-evaluation of alternative technologies for chemical agent destruction.

UPDATE BY AUTHOR MARK BROWN: "Even a cursory glance at the facts of the Army's nerve gas incineration program shows an alarming and unacceptable risk to human health and to ecosystem integrity. Hundreds of thousands of people within the vicinity of nerve gas storage sites will be adversely affected by the incineration program. The safety violations, human health threats, and environmental degradation are too great to ignore. Incineration is an antiquated technology that is unsafe and should not be considered an option for the safe disposals of the 60 million pounds of chemical weapons stored at the eight stockpile locations across the country.

"In May 1997, Oregon activists successfully stopped the Federal Munitions Rule from taking precedence over Oregon State permits. If granted, it would have allowed nerve gas to be imported to Oregon from other sites with the approval of the Oregon Department of Environmental Quality.

"In November 1997, several alternative technologies passed preliminary testing by the federal government, yet they are not being considered for Oregon.

There is a citizen lawsuit against the Oregon Department of Environmental Quality and the Army pending in Oregon State Court to stop incinerator construction from continuing. This is our last chance in Oregon.

"More than 100 activists representing citizen groups in 40 states are backing a formal 'environmental justice' legal complaint filed December 18, 1997, against the Alabama Department of Environmental Management for approving the construction of the U.S. Army chemical weapons incinerator in Anniston, Alabama—a community highly populated by African-American and low-income people.

"The Oregon Department of Environmental Quality is scheduled to approve Raytheon as the contractor for Oregon's stockpile incineration facility at Umatilla Army Depot. Raytheon is responsible for the prototype facility in the South Pacific discussed earlier that has operated in a reckless fashion for seven years.

"The mainstream press response to my story was abysmal at best. I flew in Greenpeace Senior Scientist Pat Costner, recognized as an expert on incineration, to educate the Oregon media. We spent two hours with the board of editors of *The Oregonian* (the largest paper in Oregon) discussing the issue. They never ran any story on the alternatives, and made almost no mention of the alternatives or Pat Costner's visit. They had done a pro-incineration editorial a few months earlier, and ran two short opinion pieces (I wrote one of them). The majority of the coverage was blatantly biased in favor of incineration. One of the bidders for the Umatilla contract was Westinghouse (CBS).

"For more information, the best source is the Chemical Weapons Working Group, Craig Williams (Tel: 606/986-7565)."

11 CENSORED

Death Behind Bars

Sources:
SAN FRANCISCO BAY GUARDIAN
Title: "Death Behind Bars"; "Infected—and Ignored"
Date: February 5, 1997; February 19, 1997
Author: Nina Siegal

SSU Censored Researchers: Renee Hamilton, Carolyn Williams, and Kecia Kaiser
SSU Faculty Evaluator: Barbara Bloom, Ph.D.

A nine-month investigation by the *San Francisco Bay Guardian* found that California's prison system routinely denies women access to even minimal medical care. The investigation revealed that in many cases this failure to provide care resulted in death. Examples included breast cancer diagnoses delayed for years; ignored cardiac cases; and cases of painful post-operative treatment of surgical patients, including poor wound care, where incisions ripped and were left open to infection.

Shumate v. Wilson, the 1995 class action suit brought on behalf of hundreds of women inmates in California, is indicative of the widespread health-care crisis in women's prisons throughout the state. The suit accuses the California Department of Corrections of violating prisoners' rights under the First, Fourth, Fifth, Eighth, Ninth, and Fourteenth Amendments.

This suit charges that women's prisons are responsible for many instances of poor and grossly negligent treatment, claiming that the prison system consistently fails to provide emergency medical treatment to women in life-threatening situations. It states that inmates with chronic and terminal conditions—such as AIDS, lupus, or multiple sclerosis—are denied continuous care. The suit lists cases in which women inmates have died, suffered permanent disabilities, lost infants at full term, and been left with severe problems due to poor follow-up care. It states that inmates have difficulty getting medication prescriptions refilled, that emergency call buttons at one prison were malfunctioning, and that medical wards are often private cells with no nearby medical assistance. The suit was sponsored by a coalition of nationally renowned legal teams, including the National Prison Project in Washington, DC, the ACLU, and the Legal Services for Prisoners with Children in San Francisco. The plaintiffs are seeking prison system reform, not money.

The current lawsuit adds to prior complaints concerning medical treatment for prisoners. In the past decade, class action lawsuits filed against the California Department of Corrections have argued that the state fails to provide adequate medical health care, mental health treatment, and disability access. In most cases, courts have found those allegations to be true.

Indicative of the system-wide problems is the lack of care for AIDS and HIV positive patients. There are approximately 10,000 women inmates in California, 1,000 of whom are HIV positive. Although the prison system hired an infectious-disease specialist to check on prisoners with AIDS, women inmates at the Central California Women's Facility (CCWF) at Chowchilla—which houses two-thirds of the state's women inmates—say he only visits the Chowchilla facility once a month.

Dr. Armond Start, associate professor with the Department of Family Medicine at the University of Wisconsin Medical School said, "women in prison have an increased incidence of chronic health-care problems, and convulsive seizure disorders, because of their exposure to violence. Without proper medical treatment, even basic medical problems can become fatal."

UPDATE BY AUTHOR NINA SIEGAL: "Both [*Bay Guardian*] stories focused on inadequate health care in state prisons—particularly in the Central California Women's Facility (CCWF) and in the Valley State Prison for Women, both in

Chowchilla, California—that exacerbated inmates' problems with chronic and terminal illnesses, and led, in several cases, to unnecessary deaths.

"The problems with the health facilities at these prisons were the subject of a class action lawsuit, *Shumate v. Wilson*, filed on behalf of hundreds of women prisoners at CCWF and that California Institute for Women in Frontera, California. As a result of this lawsuit, on August 11, 1997, the State and the inmates' attorneys filed a settlement agreement on the suit which required the California Department of Corrections to give their female inmates adequate medical care. According to the draft agreement, the prisons will be required to provide appropriate screening for contagious diseases, keep medical records private, and expedite the referral process for prisoners in need of physician review. They will also be required to maintain effective emergency equipment.

"Despite the terms of the settlement, however, the problems at the prisons persist. Women are still dying behind bars in California due to lack of adequate attention to chronic, terminal, and emergency medical problems. And just as unfortunately, the mainstream press has failed to pick up on this important story.

"Anyone who wants to get involved should call the California Coalition for Women Prisoners and Legal Services for Prisoners with Children at 415/255-7036, ext. 313, or the HIV/AIDS in Prison Project of Catholic Charities at 510/834-5656."

12 CENSORED

Twenty-one States Offer Corporations Immunity from Violating Environmental Laws

Source:
RACHEL'S ENVIRONMENT & HEALTH WEEKLY, # 552

THIS MODERN WORLD   by TOM TOMORROW

CIA TIES TO OPIUM AND HEROIN SMUGGLERS DURING VIETNAM ARE A MATTER OF HISTORICAL *RECORD*... LONGSTANDING ALLEGATIONS OF AGENCY COMPLICITY IN CONTRA-COCAINE TRAFFICKING ARE SUPPORTED BY A *MOUNTAIN* OF EVIDENCE...

...MAYBE YOU SHOULD HAVE FOCUSED ON HELPING THE *CIA* "JUST SAY NO," NANCE...

AH, RONNIE, DEAR... DID YOU LEAVE THE *DOOR* OPEN AGAIN?

THE LATTER HAVE RECENTLY RESURFACED, DUE TO A SERIES IN THE SAN JOSE MERCURY NEWS--

--WHICH THE NEW YORK TIMES FINALLY DEIGNED TO ACKNOWLEDGE-- IN AN APPALLINGLY PATRONIZING ARTICLE ABOUT AFRICAN AMERICAN *OUTRAGE* THAT THE GOVERNMENT MAY HAVE HELPED BRING DRUGS INTO THEIR COMMUNITIES...

SO-- JUST BECAUSE THE U.S. GOVERNMENT HAS A LONG HISTORY OF LIES AND DECEIT-- AND CIA CONNECTIONS TO DRUG RUNNERS OVER SEVERAL DECADES ARE THOROUGHLY DOCUMENTED--

--THEY ACTUALLY THINK THIS MIGHT BE *TRUE*?

THOSE NEGROES WILL BELIEVE *ANYTHING*!

The New York Times

Title: "Right to Know Nothing"
Date: June 26, 1997
Author: Peter Montague, Ph.D.

Mainstream media coverage: related article in *The New York Times,* January 30, 1997, page B-7; National Public Radio, *Talk of the Nation*, October 17, 1997; National Public Radio, *All Things Considered*, May 8, 1997

SSU Censored Researchers:
Robin Stovall and Brian Foust
SSU Staff Evaluator: Ellen Krebs

American corporations are successfully pursuing a new strategy to evade environmental laws and regulations. One state after another has been lobbied into adopting legislation to protect companies from disclosure or punishment when they discover environmental offenses at their own plants. Called the "Right to Know Nothing Laws," they have been promoted nationwide by coalitions of big industries, including AT&T, Caterpillar, Coors Brewing, Du Pont, Eli Lilly, 3M, Pfizer, Procter & Gamble, Weyerhauser, and Waste Management.

State laws are giving corporations immunity from punishment if they self-report violations of environmental laws. Any documents related to the self-reporting become officially secret, cannot be divulged to the public, and cannot be used as evidence in any legal proceedings. "Audit privilege" laws, as they are called, have been passed in at least 21 states and are pending in 13 or 14 others. Such laws typically contain the following provisions:

➤ Corporations that report violations discovered during a self-audit are immune from prosecution for their violations. They cannot be fined or otherwise punished if they disclose violations promptly to government authorities and take "reasonable" steps to achieve compliance.

➤ Individuals who participate in conducting an environmental audit cannot be called to testify in any judicial proceeding or administrative hearing.

➤ If a corporation conducts an environmental self-audit of its operations, the information in the "self-audit" cannot be disclosed to the public or used as evidence in any legal proceedings, includ-

ing lawsuits and regulatory actions. Any information related to a self-audit becomes "privileged." The corporation decides what is related to its self-audit and what is not.

The state of Texas has even made it a crime for employees or government officials to divulge anything related to environmental self-audits. Thus citizens of a municipality in Texas can lose their "right to know" about pollution from their own local landfill if the local contractor chooses to conduct a self-audit.

The Clinton Administration has accepted self-auditing by saying companies know how to audit their own facilities better than the government does, and can do a better job of it. Last March, the U.S. Environmental Protection Agency accepted Texas's "Right to Know Nothing Law" with only minor changes, paving the way for state laws to be enacted nationwide.

UPDATE BY AUTHOR PETER MONTAGUE:
"This story represents a disturbing trend: Corporations are becoming less accountable to governments and to the public. New laws are being passed in dozens of states, exempting corporate polluters from enforcement penalties if they self-report violations of environmental laws. It is as if murderers were being declared 'innocent' simply because they confess their murders to the police. Furthermore, under most of these new laws, when polluters self-report...incriminating documents [can be kept] from the public, and from judges and juries.

"The effect of these laws is to weigh the scales of justice heavily in favor of corporate polluters. This, it seems to me, will further erode the public's confidence in government. In addition, it will encourage corporations to pollute more because they will know that penalties will be waived if they simply report their pollution to the proper authorities. As a result of increased pollution, public health will most likely be endangered. As a result of diminished public confidence in government, our democracy will most likely be weakened.

"As for developments since my story, the proposed 'federal audit privilege' legislation is still making its way through Congress, and the trend in the states has not been reversed. The mainstream press has mostly ignored this legislation. *The New York Times* published one story about it (before I did my story). Most state papers have ignored the story, even when 'audit privilege' bills were being debated in their state legislatures.

"Only one organization that I know of has been tracking this legislation across the country: The Network Against Corporate Secrecy, led by Sanford Lewis in Boston; Tel: 617/354-1030; E-mail: sanlewis@igc.apc.org."

13 CENSORED

American Drug Industry Uses the Poor as Human Guinea Pigs

Source:
COUNTERPUNCH
Title: "A Reserve Army
of Guinea Pigs"
Date: September 1997
Author: Scott Handelman

SSU Censored Researcher:
Katie Garey
SSU Faculty Evaluator:
Susan Garfin, Ph.D.

Over 40,000 human guinea pigs participate in drug testing experiments run by huge pharmaceutical companies in the United States annually. Most of these people are poor and "down-and-outers," who need the money drug testing provides.

Ever since the mid-1970s, when the Federal Drug Administration (FDA) issued stricter rules on informed consent, high compensation has been necessary to attract research subjects for pharmaceutical tests. This generally means that the lowest income people in the U.S. are the ones who participate, since few people with comfortable financial circumstances volunteer to be guinea pigs for the drug companies.

The nation's drug testing processes seem to be based on the exploitation of America's lowest classes. Last fall, *The Wall Street Journal* published an article that reported Eli Lilly, maker of Prozac, uses homeless people to test drugs for FDA approval. The Eli Lilly program, which pays $85 per day, is reportedly famous "through soup kitchens, prisons, and shelters from coast-to-coast." A nurse at the Lilly clinic in Indianapolis told the *Journal* that the majority of participants in the Phase I testing programs are alcoholics, although heavy drinkers and drug users are supposed to be excluded from experimental programs because the presence of alcohol or other drugs in the body compromises test results.

Participation in drug and medical studies is a serious gamble. No one knows the long-term side effects of the drugs volunteers take. Animal drug testing, however, the mechanism that is supposed to minimize the danger to volunteers of drugs that have never been tested on humans, is unreliable. For example, in the early 1990s, the FDA approved fialuridine for healthy human volunteers after it proved non-toxic to dogs. Dogs, however, have an enzyme that neutralizes the drug, which humans apparently do not. Five Phase II patients died after taking fialuridine.

Even Princeton University's highly rated program raises questions about the ethics of drug testing. The Princeton site makes participation especially alluring to the poor. The unit runs a courtesy van for easy access to the facility. There is a bank within walking distance, and the unit gives volunteers a letter to guarantee they won't have problems cashing their checks. Screening participants enjoy a free, all-you-can-eat lunch. Once admitted to the study, they get free meals, shelter, cable TV, and a video library.

The nation's big drug companies have never been known for high-minded ethical standards. Before 1900, orphans and street urchins were used as control groups in drug experiments. Testing remained informal in the early part of the twentieth century, as companies issued experimental drugs to doctors to try out on sick patients. But after the thalidomide scare of 1962, Congress passed laws to standardize drug testing procedures. Animal tests were then required for all new drugs, followed by experiments on healthy human subjects, who were most often prisoners.

UPDATE BY AUTHOR SCOTT HANDLEMAN: "On November 13, 1997, the FDA heard final comments on a Clinton Administration proposal that would require experiments on children and infants for the approval of new drugs that might be used in pediatric care. Following the 'voluntary' guidelines in current use, 75 companies are testing 146 new drugs on minors. The drug lords are fighting the proposed mandates—which will eventually require hundreds of new experiments—probably because they fear that minors harmed by the experiments will grow up and sue them. The drug companies allege that children who participate in the tests will be exposed to drugs that have not been deemed safe for adults, and that unnecessary tests will be performed.

"Meanwhile, in a study being conducted at the Warren Magnuson Clinic Center, at least one medically unnecessary drug study on children is already underway. The National Institutes of Health is administering Humatrope, a synthetic growth hormone developed by Eli Lilly, to mildly short children who are not growth-hormone deficient, in order to see the hormone's effects on their adult height.

"Like their adult counterparts, some of the pediatric drug studies offer generous stipends. The Children's Hospital in Columbus, Ohio is presently recruiting children between the ages of two and ten for an FDA study of Proposetimol, a fever medicine manufactured by Upsa. After their children complete the ten-hour study, parents receive a $200 savings bond or $100 dollars cash.

"For information on human drug testing, contact Guinea Pig Zero, P.O. Box 42531, Philadelphia, PA 19101; E-mail: bhlms@iww.org."

14 CENSORED

The U.S. Blood Supply is Increasingly Threatened by Parasites

Source:
LABORATORY MEDICINE
Title: "The Threat Of Chagas'
Disease in Transfusion Medicine:
The Presence of Antibodies to
Trypanosoma cruzi in the U.S.
Blood Supply"
Date: April 1997
Authors: Alfred A. Pan, Ph.D.,
and Martin Winkler, Ph.D.

SSU Censored Researchers:
Kecia Kaiser and Catherine
Hickinbotham
Community Evaluator:
Linda C. McCabe, MT(ASCP)

With increasing global migration comes the spread of infectious diseases that were once confined to specific areas of the world. A growing concern is the threat of transmission of Chagas' disease through blood transfusions. Chagas' disease affects several million individuals worldwide, and, in Latin America, causes more deaths than infection with HIV or hepatitis. The World Health Organization (WHO) considers the control of Chagas' disease to be ranked in third place after malaria and schistosomiasis control. At present, the U.S. Food and Drug Administration (FDA) has not approved any serologic test screening blood donors for antibodies to *Trypanosoma cruzi*, the parasite that causes the disease, although three U.S. manufacturers have received FDA approval of an antibody test. The *Laboratory Medicine* article focuses on the biology, transmission, prevalence in the United States, diagnostic tests, the potential for transmission, and challenges this disease presents to the U.S. blood banking and public health communities.

The disease is usually spread by the Reduviid bug (kissing bug), whose habitat ranges from northern California to northern Maryland, and south through the southern regions of Argentina. When taking a bloodmeal from a human, the insect defecates, leaving behind an infective form of the parasite known as the metacyclic trypomastigote. These trypomastigotes enter the bloodstream, either by being scratched into the bite wound or by direct contact with the host's mucosa. The parasite commonly invades cells of the liver, spleen, and lymphatic system, as well as cardiac, smooth, and skeletal muscles. The nervous system, intestinal mucosa, skin, gonads, bone marrow, and placenta may also become infected. The initial symptoms may include anemia, chills, nervous disorders, muscle and bone pain, and loss of strength. Death may occur three to four weeks after infection, although many people may live a long life even with this debilitating disease.

It is highly probable that infected donors are giving blood in North America. A study in Sacramento, California, indicated a rate of 1 in 2000 in the blood supply, and reactive specimens have been identified from blood banks in New Orleans and Miami.

Between 30,000-45,000 people with chronic Chagas' disease are estimated to be living in the United States. Until recently, diagnosis has been difficult because no simple blood test has been available. Instead, clinicians have had to rely on tissue biopsy, or the cumbersome method of xenodiagnosis, which takes several weeks to perform. Therefore, many people in the U.S. with heart disease caused by Chagas' are misdiagnosed regarding the root of their problem.

The American Red Cross has performed several studies to determine the rates of seropositive donors. They found that the median prevalence rate for all 18 centers showed 1 out of 340 donors to be at risk for *T. cruzi* infection. At present however, the FDA has not yet approved any test screening of blood donors for antibodies to Chagas' Disease. Currently, all units of blood are screened for eight separate disease markers, but Chagas' is not among them. How much more data is needed before donor screening is mandated to prevent Chagas' disease from being in our blood supply? So far, three people have been identified as getting Chagas' disease through blood transfusions in the U.S., and one person died after getting infected bone marrow. Will it take a wrongful death lawsuit before our blood supply is screened for this potentially fatal pathogen?

UPDATE BY AUTHOR ALFRED PAN, PH.D.:
"Is Chagas' disease an emerging disease in the U.S.? Perhaps we should call it an unrecognized disease. It is estimated that 16-18 million people are infected. Although these numbers appear large, few physicians know of its existence. There have been reported cases in North America and Europe. In Italy, estimates of 20,000 to 40,000 potential infectants of Chagas' disease exist (Crovato and Rebora, 1997).

"There have been four studies (i.e. more than 10,000 specimens) conducted in the U.S. using a Chagas Ab EIA (enzyme immunoassay). The first study identified 14 of 13,209 donor samples (0.105 percent) as being reactive for antibody to *T. cruzi*. When sub-classified into Hispanic donors, an incidence rate of 1.5 percent (9 in 603) was revealed (Brashear, et al., *Transfusion*, 1995). In a second study by the Red Cross (Los Angeles and Miami), 23,978 at-risk and 25,587 control donations were tested. The EIA identified 34 donors (33 and 1, respectively) (Leiby, et al., 1997a). Seroprevalence rates indicated 0.14 percent and 0.07 percent, respectively. A third study at the Stanford Blood Center tested 39,776 donations. There were three confirmed specimens (Galel, et al., 1997). The last report tested 100,089 blood donors in an Oklahoma and Texas low-risk population. There were three confirmed samples. One positive donor was born in Mexico, and the other two reported no risk for *T. cruzi*; both were born in the U.S. (Leiby, et al., 1997b). In all studies, confirmation involved a

Radioimmuoprecipitation assay (RIPA) (Kirchhoff, et al., 1987; Winkler, et al., 1995). Note that in some of the above investigations questionnaires failed to identify high-risk Chagasic antibody reactive candidates.

"Additional studies in 1997 indicated similar seroprevalence rates. In Los Angeles, 1311 of 3320 donors were at risk to *T. cruzi* infection. Seven donors were reactive by a Chagas IgG ELISA, and six were reactive with RIPA (Shulman, et al., 1997). However, a study conducted in the Southeastern U.S. (Louisiana, Alabama, Mississippi, and Georgia) indicated that zero out of 6,013 were confirmed reactive (Barrett, et al., 1997). This is in contrast to a study where two specimens were identified as being reactive by the Chagas Ab EIA and confirmed at a New Orleans, Louisiana, blood bank (Pan, unpublished results).

"Individuals seropositive for antibodies to *T. cruzi* are donating in several areas of the U.S. A summary of studies indicate seroprevalence from 0.07 percent to 4.9 percent. Compare these numbers to an HIV p 24 Ag test recently instituted. After one year of testing an identification rate of 1 out of 5.25 million units (0.000019 percent) was found (Stramer, et al., 1997). The numbers of *T. cruzi*-infected blood donors still have an uncertain effect on the safety of the blood supply and the public health system."

15 CENSORED

Mainstream Newspapers Ignore Inner City Low-Income Communities and Rural "Fringe Areas"

Source:
COLUMBIA JOURNALISM REVIEW
Title: "Trimming the Fringe:
How Newspapers Shun Low-Income Readers"
Date: March/April 1997
Author: Gilbert Cranberg

SSU Censored Researchers:
Judith Westfall and
Catherine Hickinbotham
SSU Faculty Evaluator:
Melinda Barnard, Ph.D.

Mainstream newspapers around the United States are changing how they measure success. "Market effectiveness," instead of high circulation levels, is the new criteria. Upper-class, high-income readers attract high-paying advertisers, leaving low-income subscribers with a diminished voice.

Supporting what amounts to a drive for higher-class readers, a 1995 report by the Newspaper Association of America (NAA) recommended these strategies to mainstream papers:

➤ Focus on the "good" customer who pays on time, and who, in contrast to the "marginal subscriber" doesn't need to be lured with discounts;

➤ Concentrate on aggressive consumer pricing;

➤ Eliminate "fringe circulation" which is "of little value to advertisers."

The "fringe circulation" issue has received some public attention, as papers such as *The Rocky Mountain News* and *The Des Moines Register* have cut service to readers who were deemed "too distant." But fringe circulation has another, less-discussed meaning, one that raises troubling questions. According to Miles Groves, the NAA's chief economist, "fringe circulation" has a socio-economic dimension. "We're basically delivering eyeballs to advertisers," said Groves, who added that "newspapers have to serve the whole community which is their franchise." Nevertheless, "low-income areas are not where you concentrate efforts," he said. When asked about inner-city readers' disadvantage by aggressive pricing and fewer discounts, Grove's response was, "Isn't that the American way, for the poor to pay more?"

Is this a sort of, "If you can afford it, we report it" mandate? If so, then low-income inner-city families—large numbers of whom are people of color—are being ignored by major newspapers throughout the United States. Newspapers, instead, are zeroing in on would-be subscribers with attractive demographics: homeowners with good jobs, educations, and incomes. Papers are now using "precision marketing systems" and database technologies to more effectively reach these specific populations.

In an August 1996 column, *Washington Post* ombudsman Geneva Overholser noted that unlike the *Post*, "many newspapers have essentially adopted redlining: they simply cease to serve areas of little interest to advertisers." Thus, according to author Gilbert Cranberg, with few exceptions, the profitability of newspapers in monopoly markets has come to rely on an ethically bankrupt formula that should be embarrassing for a business that has always claimed to rest on a public trust.

UPDATE BY AUTHOR GILBERT CRANBERG: "The gist of my article, 'Trimming the Fringe,' is that the demographically-challenged are of minimal interest to mainstream newspaper circulation departments; consequently, scant efforts are made to market to them. The implications are, to say the least, unhealthy, both for a press with an increasingly elite, rather than mass readership, and for a society in which the news and information needs of the inner city—and the less affluent—receive short shrift.

"I am unaware of any challenge to the facts and conclusions in the piece. Nonetheless, if discussion of this issue has appeared in the mainstream press, it has escaped my notice.

"Interestingly, it was a non-journalist, Randall Bezanson, former dean of the School of Law at Washington and Lee, a First Amendment authority who teaches communications law at the University of

Iowa, who called attention to the article and the issue. He did so in a paper at a symposium of leading communications law scholars, *The Hutchins Commission Fifty Years Later*, October 10-11, 1997, at the University of Illinois. Bezanson's paper, 'The Atomization of the Newspaper,' to be published in a forthcoming issue of *The Journal of Communication Law and Policy*, relied significantly on 'Trimming the Fringe' as compelling evidence of market-driven decision-making in journalism.

"Newspaper Association of America publications are rich sources of information about newspaper circulation strategies. Especially revealing for me was *1995 Circulation Facts, Figures and Logic*. This publication is updated periodically. The most recent issue, obtainable from the association, would be useful to anyone interested in pursuing the subject."

16 CENSORED

U.S. Paper Companies Conspire to Squash Zapatistas

Source:
EARTH FIRST!
Title: "U.S. Paper Companies Conspire to Squash Zapatistas"
Date: Summer 1997

Author: Viviana, National Commission for Democracy in Mexico

SSU Censored Researchers:
Katie Sims and Angie Yee
SSU Faculty Evaluator:
Ray Castro, Ph.D.

The passage of the North American Free Trade Agreement (NAFTA) has ushered in an era of unprecedented military and corporate domination over the already beleaguered indigenous citizens of Mexico. On the day NAFTA went into effect, the Zapatistas of Chiapas in Southern Mexico rose up in rebellion against the exploitation that they feared NAFTA portended. Though the initial violence did not last long, the Zapatistas have continued to resist intrusions into their communally held lands, known as *eijdos*. Inhabited by the indigenous people of Mexico, the *eijdos* have been farmed collectively for centuries.

With the passage of NAFTA, the Mexican government is pushing for the elimination of these communally held lands. By privatizing the land, the government hopes to make lucrative deals with multinational corporations from the U.S. and elsewhere.

Under the guise of the perpetual "War on Drugs," the U.S. has funded a massive build-up of the Mexican military over the last three years. Over 50 Huey helicopters and various other offense-capable weapons have been provided to Mexico by the U.S. government. Most of this hardware can be used to control the poor and indigenous peoples there. The

U.S. State Department admits that it is unable to account for how military aid to Mexico is used.

In recent years, the Mexican military has constructed roads deep into the Zapatista-inhabited areas of Chiapas in order to expedite movement of troops into the region. Previously a pristine and relatively remote area with few roads, the military presence in Chiapas has intimidated and isolated the various Zapatista communities, interfering with planting and harvesting their crops. This, in turn, has led to widespread malnourishment in the communities.

The absence or lack of enforcement of environmental and health and safety regulations in Mexico makes it particularly attractive to corporations from more regulated industrialized nations. Major deals have already been brokered between the Mexican government and multinational corporations for the development of forest and petroleum resources in the country.

One company, Pulsar, has presented a project to plant (non-indigenous) eucalyptus trees over 300,000 hectares throughout Chiapas and surrounding territories, and has contracted to sell the wood to International Paper (IP). In 1995, the vice president of IP sent a letter to the president of Mexico warning: "at this time, the projections of that project are not positive [since] the political environment [in Chiapas] represents a high risk." He went on to advise that "the development of a Mexican forest industry—strong and globally competitive, supported by commercial plantations—

is a national priority." The implication—that the Mexican military ought to be making a greater effort to eliminate the "Zapatista problem"—cannot be disregarded.

To make matters worse, Chiapas sits on major petroleum reserves that are second only to Venezuela in the Western Hemisphere. Many of these are under Zapatista-controlled lands. In 1996, the Mexican government made a deal with a major Canadian corporation, Hydro-Quebec International, to develop natural gas resources throughout Chiapas.

To the indigenous communities of Mexico, many of whom have inhabited their lands for hundreds of years, the loss of their homes would have ramifications which reach beyond simply the loss of their crops and livelihoods. As has happened so often in the Americas, it would mean the loss of their autonomy, their identity, and the tragic death of yet another innocent culture.

UPDATE BY AUTHOR VIVIANA: "Much of the information regarding corporate interests and plans for development of the natural resources of Chiapas remains widely unreported. However, these factors are central to understanding the depth of U.S. involvement in the politics of the region and the fate of its natural resources.

"Historically, indigenous people have repeatedly found themselves backed into the same corner, with their culture and ability to exist threatened by the race for control over their resources. The solution to the Mexican crisis depends on our awareness that we are a significant part of the problem. With this knowledge, we are challenged to participate in real solutions that support the struggle for human rights and cultural identity of the indigenous people in Zapatista communities and throughout Mexico.

"This story went unnoticed by the mainstream press, just as the Zapatista struggle has had little coverage. Because of this lack of response, the information was primarily disseminated through independent publications of non-profit organizations such as the National Commission for Democracy in Mexico, the Native Forest Network, and the *Earth First!* journal. The Internet has also played an important role (as it has throughout the work in support of the Zapatista movement) in accessing the relevant reports and articles from Mexico and in communicating the information to the United States.

"The Zapatista struggle continues as does the Mexican military's low-intensity war against the indigenous communities of Chiapas. The U.S. government has not acknowledged its role in the military presence in Chiapas, and continues to contribute to the military buildup."

17 CENSORED

Toxins and Environmental Pollution Contribute to Human Aggression in Society

Sources:
RACHEL'S ENVIRONMENT & HEALTH WEEKLY
Titles: "Toxins Affect Behavior"; "Toxins and Violent Crime"
Dates: January 16, 1997, #529; June 19, 1997, #551
Author: Peter Montague, Ph.D.

SSU Censored Researcher:
Deb Udall
SSU Faculty Evaluator:
Noel Byrne, Ph.D.

It may come as no surprise that exposure to toxic pollutants—chemical substances and heavy metals—is hazardous to your health. But according to two recent studies that examined the relationship between exposure to toxins and aggressive behavior, such exposure—which is usually preventable—has been linked to violence in society.

A 1996 study conducted by Herbert Needleman, published in the *Journal of the American Medical Association*, took into account nine variables including poverty level and minority status, as well as lead exposure, in trying to explain aggressive behavior in young boys. Needleman's study found that boys with high amounts of lead in their bones had more reports of aggressive and delinquent behavior than boys with low levels, and that their behavior got worse over a period of time, regardless of social factors.

New research by Roger D. Masters and colleagues at Dartmouth College suggests exposure to toxic pollutants—specifically lead and manganese—may contribute to people committing violent crimes. Masters developed the "neurotoxicity hypothesis of violent crime," which he hoped would help to explain why violent crime rates differ so widely between geographic areas. Masters also found that environmental pollution and high alcohol use have a strong effect on violent crime. U.S. counties with measures of neurotoxicity—lead, manganese, and alcohol—have violent crime three times the national average. "The presence of pollution is as big a factor as poverty," said Masters in a May interview in *New Scientist*. "It's the breakdown of the inhibition mechanism that's the key to violent behavior."

Despite government attempts to regulate the potential dangers of environmental exposure to toxins, such as outlawing lead in gasoline and tin cans and requiring lead paint disclosures, in 1994, an estimated 1.7 million American children ages one through five had blood lead levels of 10 micrograms per deciliter of blood (ug/dl) or more. Among African-American children in large cities, 36.7 percent have blood lead levels of above 10 ug/dl. Reduced IQ power can be measured when lead is as low as 7 ug/dl, but any amount of lead exposure seems to diminish mental power in children. Brain damage from lead exposure persists for many years, and IQ reduction is essentially *permanent*. An estimated 20 percent of American children now exhibit mental or behavioral problems.

The main source of toxic lead in children today is in dust and soil, with much of it coming from the lead-based paint of older buildings. The Centers for Disease Control (CDC) calculated that American

THIS MODERN WORLD by TOM TOMORROW

taxpayers could realize a net profit of $28 billion in social savings and increased productivity by removing all lead-based paint from old buildings.

UPDATE BY AUTHOR PETER MONTAGUE, PH.D.: "This story reveals the failure of government to require adequate testing of new chemicals while it expands the list of serious problems thought to be caused by toxic pollutants. To my knowledge, there is little new [on this subject], except an increased appreciation for the effects of chemicals on human behavior. I believe that this new view of pollution will become more widespread in the next few years. In the past, if pollution didn't kill us or make us sick, it was considered 'safe'—or at least benign. Now we are coming to learn that certain pollutants can affect our behavior—in this instance, making some of us more violent than we might otherwise be. There is also a growing body of evidence suggesting that pollutants can affect our sexual behavior (enhancing or diminishing libido, for example). I believe we are seeing the tip of the iceberg here.

"To my knowledge, this story has been completely ignored by the mainstream press."

18 CENSORED

Pharmaceutical Companies Mass Market Drugs

Source:
THE WASHINGTON MONTHLY
Title: "Pill Pushers"
Date: April 1997
Author: Greg Critser

SSU Censored Researchers: Jacqueline Lichstein and Judith Westfall
SSU Faculty Evaluator:
Paul Benko, Ph.D.

Profit-hungry pill companies are ignoring responsible medical practices and taking advantage of a growth economy to booster and advertise prescription medications directly to the public. The rush to high

sales has companies promoting some medications that have not been fully tested or approved by the FDA. As doctors can prescribe any medication they choose (even unapproved ones), drug companies are using this loophole in the law to convince patients and doctors that they should be using specific drugs even before FDA approval.

In 1990, as the success of anti-depressant Prozac proved that psychiatric drugs could create new mass markets, Abbott Pharmaceutical decided to re-register Depakote (originally a medication for epilepsy) as a treatment for bipolar disease, the diagnostic term for manic depression. Abbott filed the requisite forms with the FDA and began clinical trials, but did not wait for the FDA to render decisions about Depakote's efficacy—as required by law. Instead, they began hyping away. Using a medical education program on bipolar disease for doctors, they began to promote Depakote illegally. They were eventually caught and cited by the FDA for promoting Depakote and for collecting information about how doctors prescribed certain medications.

Over the past few years, the FDA has issued dozens of warning letters to pharmaceutical giants for promoting so-called "off-line uses." In 1996, the drug giant Pfizer received a warning letter from the FDA for promoting its antidepressant Zoloft as a treatment for "Premenstrual Dysphoric Disorder," a form of depression that accompanies premenstrual syndrome (PMS) for a small percentage of women. The FDA considered the practice of "off-line" promotions so severe at Pfizer that it sent an eight-page warning letter to William Steere, the company's chairman.

FDA Commissioner Mary Pendergast stated in 1994, "Promotion of unapproved use by company sales representatives is a major problem." The FDA has a unit specifically empowered to police drug company hype, but that arm, the Division of Drug Marketing, Advertising, and Communications (DDMAC) is increasingly understaffed and overworked, with only 29 employees nationwide.

Doctors were once the traditional gatekeepers of the public's health. However, physician-prescribing habits are increasingly circumscribed by HMOs, who prod them to prescribe more drugs, and by pharmaceutical benefits managers, who tell doctors which drugs insurance companies will cover. Doctors are losing control of their prescription-writing franchise, and are under increasing pressure from an ad-stimulated public and "off-line" drug company sales promotions. In 1996, there were over $4 billion in medical costs for treating adverse drug reactions in patients in the U.S.

UPDATE BY AUTHOR GREG CRITSER: "This story grew out of an on-going journalistic question: How do drug companies get their pills into your belly, and how do they get paid for it? One way is to market drugs to physicians for non-approved, or 'off-line' uses. This is accomplished by aggressively exploiting

FDA loopholes and staffing weaknesses. At the time I wrote this article, all such efforts violated the Food and Drug Act.

"But this is no longer the case. In 1997, President Clinton signed new legislation which, among other things, gives pharmaceutical companies permission to market drugs to doctors for uses that they have not been approved for by the FDA. This legislation was passed under the ongoing effort to 'reform' the FDA. But the reform cuts only one way—in favor of drug companies and against independent government oversight. The new law permits drug companies to use private firms to evaluate new drugs instead of being evaluated by FDA staff. This means that the agency Americans believe is the last word in product safety and efficiency is increasingly unable to do that job independently. Witness the recent recall of the diet drug Redux.

"There was no mainstream response to the *Washington Monthly* article. To find out more, you may want to explore the Web site of the FDA, which posts all enforcement actions. All of the major pharmaceutical companies have extensive Web sites. The trade publication *Medical Advertising News* provides a varnished, but nevertheless revealing, look at marketing practices. Of the big three national newspapers, only *The Wall Street Journal* is worth reading on this subject."

19 CENSORED

Evidence of Fluoridation Danger Mounts— With Little Benefit to Your Teeth

Sources:
AUSTRALIAN AND NEW ZEALAND JOURNAL OF PUBLIC HEALTH
Title: "New Evidence on Fluoridation"
Date: 1997, Vol. 21, No. 2
Authors: Mark Diesendorf, John Colquhoun, Bruce J. Spittle, Douglas N. Everingham, and Frederick W. Clutterbuck

TELEGRAM & GAZETTE (Worcester, MA)
Title: "Panelists Critical of Fluoride: Chemical Linked to Health Problems"
Date: October 25, 1996
Author: John J. Monahan

THE GUARDIAN (London)
Title: "Clear and Present Danger"
Date: June 7, 1997
Author: Bob Woffinden

SSU Censored Researchers:
Brian Foust and Deb Udall
SSU Faculty Evaluator:
Peter Phillips, Ph.D.

Over two-thirds of U.S. public drinking water is fluoridated. "Experts" have told us that fluoride helps re-mineral enamel and that it prevents tooth decay. They have asserted its beneficial effects and claimed that its negative impacts were non-existent. New studies show this to be false, however, and there is mounting evidence of serious side effects of fluoride ingestion that can result in bone decay, infant mortality, and brain damage.

Large-scale blind studies show there are no differences in tooth decay rates between fluoridated communities and unfluoridated communities, and therefore conclude that people are receiving too much fluoride. One study that compared levels of tooth decay in Los Angeles and San Francisco found no difference between the two cities, even though fluoride is added to the San Francisco water supply and not to the water supply of Los Angeles. During the '90s there has been a steady trickle of scientific reports on the health-related problems of fluoride. One report found a statistically significant association between water fluoridation and increased risk of hip fracture. Research at the National Toxicology Program (NTP) in 1990 and 1991 showed a possible increase in osteosarcomas, a form of cancer, in males exposed to fluoride.

Evidence shows that for reducing dental decay, fluoride acts topically (at the surface of the teeth) and that there is negligible benefit in ingesting it. In an as yet unpublished paper, Ian Packington, a toxicologist on the advisory panel for the National Pure Water Association,

records that in the years 1990 to 1992, perinatal deaths in the fluoridated parts of the West Midlands were 15 percent higher than in neighboring unexposed areas. His analysis of Department of Health statistics also concludes that in the period 1983 to 1986, cases of Down's Syndrome were 30 percent higher in fluoridated than non-fluoridated areas. In the 1970s, Dr. Albert Schatz reported that the artificial fluoridation of drinking water in Latin American countries was associated with an increased rate of infant mortality and death due to congenital malformation. As long ago as the 1950s, Dr. Lionel Rapaport published studies showing links between Down's Syndrome and natural fluoridation.

Why has there been such an unrelenting administrative pressure to fluoridate? One theory is that aluminum manufacturers, and petro-chemical and fertilizer industries—for whom fluoride was a waste product and a dangerous pollutant—welcomed the opportunity to both launder the image of fluoride and to sell to water companies something they would otherwise have to pay to get rid of.

The final irony is that fluoridation, packaged and marketed in part as a way to bridge the socio-economic gap by providing better dental protection for those with poor nutrition, may be most adversely affecting the poor. It is those suffering poor nutrition and vitamin and mineral deficiencies who are most vulnerable to fluoride's toxic effects.

UPDATE BY AUTHOR MARK DIESENDORF: "The publication of our paper in the *Aus-*

tralian & New Zealand Journal of Public Health, the subsequent media stories, and the Project Censored story reveal to the public that there is informed opposition to the fluoridation of drinking water on scientific and public-health grounds. This is a challenge to the medical and dental power structure which strongly supports fluoridation in English-speaking countries.

"Subsequent to publication of this article, attacks were made on the paper in the letters section of the journal and elsewhere by medical and dental proponents of fluoridation, but shortly after the paper was published, I was lucky to be invited as a scientific panelist at a major symposium for medical and health journalists on *Medicine in the Media.* I drew attention to the paper and challenged journalists to report it. As a result, the main thrust of the paper was covered in two major Australian newspapers and on national radio. Such publicity is rare for questioning fluoridation, since medical journalists normally defer to 'expert' spokespeople from medical and dental associations."

For further information, see:
➤ Diesendorf, Mark, "Fluoridation: Breaking the Silence Barrier," in B. Martin, ed., *Confronting the Experts.* Albany, NY: State University of New York Press, 1996.
➤ Diesendorf, Mark, "How Science Can Illuminate Ethical Debates: A Case Study on Water Fluoridation," *Journal of the International Society for Fluoride Research,* volume 28 (1995): 87-104.

➤ Martin, B., *Scientific Knowledge in Controversy: The Social Dynamics of the Fluoridation Debate.* Albany, NY: State University of New York Press, 1991.

UPDATE BY AUTHOR JOHN J. MONAHAN: "The [*Telegram & Gazette*] story that detailed concerns about possible health risks associated with fluoridation of drinking water appeared in advance of a citywide referendum on whether to fluoridate the city water supply in Worcester, Massachusetts, at a time a new water treatment plant was being completed.

"The referendum posed a dual controversy, first whether the possible health benefits of fluoridation outweighed possible health risks, and secondly whether fluoride should be essentially forced upon those who rely on the water supply but did not want to have fluoride in their water.

"City Health officials ordered fluoridation, and that decision was endorsed by a majority vote of the City Council, but challenged by a group of concerned citizens who sought to give residents a choice by direct referendum. No doubt many readers were unaware of the relative toxicity of fluoride and possible risks associated with it, and the story gave them a chance to learn just what critics were saying about possible health effects despite the dismissal of those concerns by many public-health officials and elected officials in the city.

"In the end the binding referendum on the November city election ballot prohibited city officials from implementing their plan to begin fluoridating the water supply. Voters rejected fluoridation by nearly a 2 to 1 margin, with 28,972 opposed to fluoridation and 17,826 in favor. As a result, the city did not ever use the new equipment installed for fluoridation at the new water treatment plant, and public-health officials have said they do not expect to try to impose fluoridation on residents in the future. While the city's public-health director later described the referendum results as a victory of 'quackery over science,' the grass-roots organizers of the campaign against fluoridation claimed the outcome was a victory for people's rights to not have toxic agents imposed on them through their public water supply."

For additional information, contact John J. Monahan, Environment Writer, Worcester *Telegram & Gazette*, Worcester, Massachusetts; E-Mail: MonahanJ @aol.com; Tel: 508/793-9172.

20 CENSORED

Environmental Regulations Create Jobs and Make American Corporations More Competitive

Source:
DOLLARS AND SENSE
Title: "Does Preserving Earth Threaten Jobs?"

Date: May 1997
Author: Eban Goodstein

SSU Censored Researchers:
Robin Stovall and Katie Sims
SSU Faculty Evaluator:
Charles Fox

Corporate lobbyists often claim that most of the jobs lost in the U.S. over the past decade were due to overblown environmental regulations. In 1990, the U.S. Business Roundtable published a study predicting that the Clean Air Act amendments would lead to the loss of between 200,000 and 2 million jobs. Six years later the job loss figure had not reached even six thousand.

Almost all economists agree that there is no trade-off between jobs and the environment. Actual layoffs from regulation have been quite small, and regulations have not damaged the international competitiveness of U.S. manufacturing. In 1995, in spite of spending $160 billion per year on environmental protection, the Federal Reserve decided the U.S. economy was growing too fast. Too many people employed might raise inflation rates, so the Federal Reserve hiked interest rates several times in an effort to "cool" the economy and to raise unemployment to the 6 percent level.

Environmental regulation can be expensive. But it is a mistake to confuse costs of environmental protection with job losses from environmental protection. Indeed, environmental costs translate into environmental spending, which also creates and provides jobs. Most studies find that jobs created in environmental and related sectors outweigh jobs lost due to higher regulatory costs. This leads to an actual, overall 'net' employment gain. Environmental spending pumps demand into the economy during recessions. Also, environmental protection is often more labor intensive than the alternative, actually leading to more jobs. Environmentally preferable means of meeting our energy needs would actually yield more jobs than our current reliance on fossil fuels and uranium.

In recent years, corporate downsizing has become a much greater threat to U.S. workers than environmental regulations ever were. A U.S. Department of Labor survey concluded that layoffs due to environmental regulation were less than one-tenth of 1 percent of all major layoffs in manufacturing. The major source of job loss has been "corporate restructuring."

Still, aren't we losing manufacturing jobs to countries overseas that have lax environmental standards? For decades, economists have been looking for exactly these effects; but recently most have concluded that environmental regulations have had no observable effect. This is because, for most industries, environmental costs are little more than 1 percent of total business costs. Also, most trade flow occurs between developed countries, all of which already have comparable regulations. Finally, one Harvard professor argues that regulations, while imposing short-term costs on firms, actually enhance their competitiveness over the long term.

UPDATE BY AUTHOR EBAN GOODSTEIN:
"The fact that there is no significant job loss when protecting the environment is one of those surprising 'good news' stories. It was surprising to me when I first started to investigate the subject five years ago. The conventional wisdom (that there was significant job loss)—manufactured largely by corporate PR offices, but also endorsed by significant parts of the environmental and labor movements—seemed so plausible. It is a 'good news' story because it means that we don't have to worry (much) about factories shutting down or fleeing overseas as we tighten regulations to clean up our environment.

"Is the conventional wisdom changing? Possibly. Along with Hart Hodges, I wrote an article in the November/December 1997 *American Prospect* ('Polluted Numbers') which examined initial cost estimates for past environmental regulations, and found them to be uniformly excessive. We were pleased when President Clinton echoed those sentiments a month later in his global warming speech at the National Geographic Society. Of course, allegations of massive job loss are still being leveled against the recently-signed Kyoto agreement. But we have come a long way from 1992, when President Bush threatened to boycott the Rio Conference in order to 'protect American jobs from environmental extremists.'

"If you would like more information about these issues, I can be contacted at e-mail: eban@clark.edu."

21 CENSORED

Blood Tests Suggest Reason Behind Gulf War Syndrome

Source:
INSIGHT
Title: "Sickness and Secrecy"
Date: August 25, 1997
Author: Paul M. Rodriguez

SSU Censored Researchers:
Robin Stovall and Kecia Kaiser
SSU Faculty Evaluator: Andy Merrifield, Ph.D.

Gulf War-related illnesses are rampant among American war veterans. One suggestion as to the cause of the illnesses has surfaced with new blood tests on the most seriously ill victims. A synthetic substance, squalene, banned for use in humans, has been found in blood tests of hundreds of sick Gulf War veterans, some of whom never left U.S. soil. Complicating the issue is the U.S. Department of Defense's "loss" of over 700,000 service-related immunization records, which might provide a clue as to why squalene is showing up in Gulf War veterans' blood samples.

Analysis of the blood samples has shown antibody levels of the experimental adjuvant compound known as squalene. This compound, not approved for internal human use other than in highly controlled experiments, has been studied on animals and humans as a promising tool that might help boost the body immune systems against influenza, herpes simplex, and HIV. Only government agencies are involved in human experimental tests using adjuvants (including squalene) yet the government has denied that experimental HIV immunization tests were ever expanded to the general population of sick people or military personnel.

The military has rejected any claim that immunizations administered to Gulf War military personnel prior to leaving for the war contained any adjuvants, but actual immunization records for the period have either been lost or destroyed. This has led to speculation in several circles that the government used military personnel to test experimental immunizations.

Military samples of blood drawn from the vets showed positive reactions for squalene antibodies. Samples of test subjects involved in federal experimental HIV studies also show positive reactions for squalene. It should be noted the medication administered to those involved in this HIV study contained the adjuvant squalene. These test subjects have never served in the military.

A military lab researcher interviewed by *Insight* was quoted as saying, "We have found soldiers who are not sick that do not have the antibodies, and we found soldiers who never left the United States, but who got shots (administered by the military) who are sick—and they have squalene in their systems. We found people who served overseas in various parts of the desert that are sick who have squalene. And we found people who served in the desert but were civilians who never got the shots, who are not sick and do not have squalene."

Many people believe that there is probably no single cause for Gulf War Syndrome. Due to the disappearance of the inoculation records, even the most elementary checks cannot occur.

UPDATE BY AUTHOR PAUL M. RODRIGUEZ: "Since publication, none of the so-called mainstream press has followed up on the original story (or subsequent reports) by *Insight*. This may be due to the controversial nature of the issue and/or obstruction by military and politicos who alternatively have denied, rejected, or brushed aside the story.

"The *Insight* stories were (and are) based on preliminary and ongoing medical tests by one of the country's most prestigious laboratories. This laboratory, which plans soon to seek 'peer' reviews, has initially confirmed the highly unusual discovery of antibodies to a polymer compound called squalene in the blood of sick Gulf War soldiers who served overseas as well as in the blood of those who never left the United States. In both camps, the sick soldiers received multiple inoculations and immunizations.

"At first, Defense Department and military/veterans' officials denied they had such a substance, even experimentally. Then slowly over many months it was learned—and officials conceded— that squalene has been, in fact, tested extensively as a promising new 'adjuvant' compound in experimental drugs to protect troops against malaria, herpes, and potentially even HIV. However, to this day, the government denies it ever used squalene during the Gulf War period.

"This poses several intriguing questions, not the least of which is: Why does something that's not supposed to be there show up in sick vets? Bipartisan members of Congress and the General Accounting Office are now looking into the issue. *Insight* will continue to report what is found, and, of course, what is not found."

22 CENSORED

FBI: Sloppy, Out of Touch, and Very Powerful

Source:
THE NATION
Title: "The FBI"
Date: August 1, 1997
Author: David Burnham

SSU Censored Researchers:
Katie Sims and Ben Brewer
SSU Faculty Evaluator:
Patrick Jackson, Ph.D.

The Federal Bureau of Investigation (FBI) for years was perceived as the nation's preeminent crime-fighting agency. That image took a blow from events at Waco and Ruby Ridge, where the FBI had major confrontations with citizens, as well as from a reported mess at the FBI crime lab. Now, after examining the bureau's own records, a law enforcement reporter concludes that the FBI today is a sloppy, unresponsive, badly managed, uncooperative, and out-of-touch agency that is aggressively trying to ex-and its control over the American people.

The bureau concentrates on drug dealers, credit-card scams, and bank robbers, all tasks that could easily be left to state and local agencies. Meanwhile, insufficient attention is given to the financial loss and the physical pain and deaths that result from the work of the nation's army of white-collar criminals.

Records also show that the success rate of FBI cases is dismal. Justice Department prosecutors find much of the FBI's investigative work inadequate. From 1992 to 1996, only one-fourth of all FBI cases referred to prosecutors resulted in convictions. The much-touted FBI lags behind the Drug Enforcement Agency, Internal Revenue Service, Immigration and Naturalization Service, and Bureau of Alcohol, Tobacco and Firearms in prosecution success rates.

Given the current system in which the FBI runs with a free hand, there's little reason to expect the bureau to improve or change. Because the FBI operates within the Justice Department, most people assume that it is accountable to the Attorney General. This is incorrect. From his appointment in 1924 to his death in 1972, FBI Director J. Edgar Hoover was his own boss. This was largely due to the fact that Hoover under-stood the importance of information and how it could be used to garner power and influence. Hoover was untouchable. After his death, Congress attempted to put some controls on the FBI. Now the director serves a 10-year term and can be removed from office only for "just cause." Subsequently, new FBI directors have a 10-year period to be their own masters with little accountability or oversight.

The FBI is continually pushing for greater control over and access to the private domains of American citizens. Evidence of this is given in a program quietly signed into law by President Clinton in October 1994. This program required the nation's telephone companies to install a new generation of FBI-approved equipment that will make it much easier for the bureau to tap telephones throughout the country. The implications of this mandate are made even more far-reaching by the subsequent development of computer technologies that are able to monitor these wiretaps with little or no help from human operatives—making wiretapping considerably cheaper.

Testifying before the House Judiciary Subcommittee on Crime in June, Louis Freeh, the current FBI Director, said, plainly: "We are potentially the most dangerous agency in the country."

UPDATE BY AUTHOR DAVID BURNHAM:
"The Federal Bureau of Investigation is the most powerful and secretive agency in the United States. Decade after decade, with no consideration of alternatives, it has continuously sought to expand its reach over the American people. Despite

this steadily growing authority, the 'B,' as special agents refer to it, has rarely been subject to informed scrutiny.

"Most news organizations are satisfied with press releases and leaks that are always carefully crafted to serve the FBI's purposes. While FBI Director Louis Freeh frequently testifies before Congress, the information he provides is almost always anecdotal. Public interest groups, lawyers, and scholars frame their questions about the FBI around individual horror stories that are easily dismissed as exceptions to the rule.

"The FBI article in *The Nation* was important because for the first time ever, it used the comprehensive internal records of the Justice Department to document what the bureau does and does not do, and how well or poorly it does it. FBI investigations result in thousands of convictions for drug crimes, bank robberies, and small-time fraud against the banks, but only a handful of convictions of big time white-collar criminals, fraudulent medical providers, or brutal cops. Even by its own standards, other agencies like the DEA appear to do a better job than the FBI in the enforcement of the nation's drug laws.

"The data that served as the foundation of this article were obtained under the Freedom of Information Act by the Transactional Records Access Clearinghouse (TRAC), a research organization associated with Syracuse University. I am a founder and co-director of TRAC. At the time *The Nation* published the FBI article, we mounted an FBI Web site with more than 20,000 pages of maps, charts, graphs, textual material, and other information about the bureau's operations. This information is available to every citizen, every reporter, every public interest group, and every congressperson who is concerned about the FBI, at http://trac.syr.edu/tracfbi. TRAC has created similar sites about the IRS, DEA, and BATF.

"Post Script: On August 5, 1997, just as *The Nation* was coming off the presses and TRAC's Web site was going up, ABC's *Nightline* ran a favorable program on TRAC and its FBI findings. For a transcript of the program, call me at 202/544. 8722 or e-mail me at trac@syr.edu. The Web site of TRAC is: http://www.trac.syr.edu."

23 CENSORED

The Scheme to Privatize the Hanford Nuke Plant

Source:
COUNTERPUNCH
Title: "Clinton Crowd Said Yea! Plot to 'Cure AIDS,' Make H-Bombs and $5 Billion"
Date: April 1997
Authors: Jeffrey St. Clair and Alexander Cockburn

SSU Censored Researchers
Susan Allen
SSU Staff Evaluator: Charles Fox

A consortium of energy contractors plotted to gain control of the Fast Flux Facility at Hanford Nuclear Reservation, convert it to tritium production for H-bombs, and profit to the tune of billions. The Hanford Fast Flux, sitting at the heart of a radioactive wasteland in eastern Washington State, was scheduled for decommissioning. But the government's emphasis on privatizing public facilities—promoted under Vice President Gore's program for "reinventing government"—made it a tempting target for profit.

Contemplating the shutdown and the potential for profit, the consortium of about a dozen large corporate contractors at Hanford (including Westinghouse, Lockheed, Batelle, Bechtel, TRW Environmental, Fluor, and Informatics) actively lobbied to have the Fast Flux transferred to the consortium and retooled for tritium production at taxpayer expense. Tritium—the substance needed to put the "oomph" into an H-bomb—could earn profits of $4 to $5 billion a year for the consortium.

Sales to the U.S. government were to be the major source of profit, since tritium has a half-life of only 12.3 years and must be regularly replaced. But the consortium recognized that approval would be hard to obtain as the Department of Energy (DOE) had already selected two other facilities as the primary future providers of tritium. Approval of a "tritium-only" plan at the Hanford site was sure to fail unless a new strategy was developed.

At a November 20, 1995 meeting in Washington, DC, representatives of the consortium met with Washington congressional delegation staffers, Terry R. Lash, director of the DOE's Office of Nuclear Energy, and Richard Thompson, a Democratic wheeler dealer/entrepreneur who was impresario of the conclave. Thompson suggested that they should be "riding the AIDS cure bandwagon," and outlined a plan to promote Hanford as the last American producer of medical isotopes to be used in AIDS and cancer research.

The Hanford consortium then faced the delicate task of convincing the DOE they needed to be paid for making tritium in order to finance the future production of medical isotopes. Negotiations in Washington began by labeling Hanford an "interim" tritium project. To sell this idea to the White House, the consortium launched lobbying and PR campaigns, hiring Hugh Rodham, Hillary Clinton's brother, to lobby on their behalf, and making campaign donations to insure access to the President, who gave "thumbs up" to the proposal during the Democratic National Convention in Chicago. One of Secretary of Energy Hazel O'Leary's last acts before leaving the DOE for a position on the board of directors of a major energy company was to approve Hanford's role as a potential site for tritium production.

Fatefully, when the consortium moved to the next step—arranging for financing and plutonium fuel rods supplies—they turned to Randall Bonebrake, then an employee at Advanced Nuclear Medicine Systems. Bonebrake states that when placed in contact with European sources of supply, he suddenly found himself "...in the center of an international market in nuclear waste. It was bizarre and frightening." He stated he woke up to the fact that he was involved in what appeared to be a conspiracy to breach the International Atomic Energy Treaty, which forbids trade in commercial nuclear fuel for the production of nuclear weapons.

Carrying internal documents from Thompson and the DOE, Bonebrake first approached the IRS in Seattle. He was told there was nothing they could do and they recommended he approach *The Seattle Times*. Instead, Bonebrake turned to Greenpeace, who counseled leaking the affair to the media and seeking some protection of his status as whistleblower by unburdening himself to the Government Accountability Project. When Bonebrake learned that Thompson was about to sign a contract with the DOE commencing privatization of the Fast Flux, he leaked the news report to the German weekly, *Der Spiegel*, thus raising alarm in Europe and blocking the shipments of fuel rods from Europe.

At the time of the article, the Fast Flux remained on "hot standby" and had not been decommissioned.

UPDATE BY AUTHOR JEFF ST. CLAIR:

"Our story shows how easy it is for a group of venture capitalists to get their hands on government nuclear reactors capable of making fuel for hydrogen bombs. Taking advantage of the widespread privatization of DOE sites and some slick public-relations work, a small company from Ellensberg, Washington was nearly awarded title to the Fast Flux Breeder Reactor at the Hanford Nuclear Site in Washington State. Though the deal ultimately collapsed (after it was exposed in *CounterPunch*), the firm, Advanced Nuclear Medicine Systems (ANMS), successfully persuaded the DOE to keep the Fast Flux in 'hot stand by' as a possible source of tritium production rather than being shut down as advised by DOE staffers. The DOE is currently searching for another company to take over operations of the Fast Flux.

"One of the key sources for our story was a former employee of ANMS by the name of Randall Bonebrake. Bonebrake left ANMS when he discovered that the company's professed intention to operate the Fast Flux in order to produce radioactive isotopes to treat AIDS and cancer patients was a ruse to hide the company's real objective: production of tritium for hydrogen bombs. Bonebrake turned over ANMS papers to Greenpeace, the Government Accountability Project, and *CounterPunch*. He was later arrested for theft. After our story ran, Bonebrake's trial ended in a hung jury and the prosecutors decided not to retry the case.

"The story was largely ignored by the mainstream press, although it received quite a bit of attention from public radio. We did interviews for stations in Los Angeles; Portland, Oregon; Spokane, Washington; and Moscow, Idaho. The combination of our story and the radio coverage was cited as a major factor in ANMS's decision to withdraw its proposal, according to Bill Sykes, the company's president, who complained that his company had been 'tarred by bad publicity.' The privatization of DOE sites, many of them highly toxic, remains one of the great uncovered stories in America."

24 CENSORED

Profits-Before-People Delays Release of New AIDS Drug

Sources:
SAN FRANCISCO BAY TIMES
Title: "The Fight For 1592: AIDS Activists Battle Glaxo Over Access To Anxiously Awaited New Drug"
Date: May 15, 1997
Author: Bruce Mirken

SAN FRANCISCO BAY GUARDIAN
Title: "OTC Drugs to be Boycotted: AIDS Activists Announce Boycott of Drug Company"
Date: July 2, 1997
Author: Nina Siegal

Major media coverage: *The Wall Street Journal,* November 12, 1996, section B, page 1, column 3

SSU Censored Researchers: Kecia Kaiser, Deborah Udal, and Bryan Way
Community Evaluator: Mary King, M.D.

A decade after the high price of AZT caused AIDS activists to declare a war on Burroughs Wellcome pharmaceutical company, the AIDS community is again gearing up for battle with drug giant Glaxo-Wellcome over access to what San Francisco AIDS Foundation Director of Treatment Education and Advocacy Ron Baker calls "the most important AIDS drug in the research pipeline."

That drug, known as 1592U89, or 1592, belongs to the class of drugs called nucleoside analogs, (a.k.a. "nukes") the same category as AZT, 3TC, ddC, ddI, and d4T. For full effectiveness, nukes must be, "cocktailed," or combined with other protease and non-protease inhibitor drugs. Many AIDS patients have already used the older nukes and have HIV strains that have become resistant to these drugs. For them, 1592, which in earlier tests demonstrated far more anti-HIV punch and appears to be less toxic, represents the only hope for building a drug cocktail that can keep them alive.

Realizing the need for 1592, advocates began meeting with Glaxo-Wellcome last summer to persuade the company to offer the drug immediately on a "compassionate use" basis. Glaxo said they would consider it, but unveiled a plan with only three minuscule programs—one for children, one for those suffering from severe dementia, and a third for adults without dementia—which would enroll a total of 2,500 patients. Equally alarming is the fact that access will be restricted to only 30 to 50 sites worldwide. Adults will have to enroll at unspecified "geographically dispersed centers"—which is also unusual.

The company doesn't expect to file for FDA approval until mid-1998 because of concerns that there is a serious lack of general information on its effects, and because studies have included so few people. Glaxo claims that it is a lack of knowledge around the specifics of how viral resistance works that is holding up their filing for FDA approval.

AIDS activists aren't buying Glaxo's assertions. The 1592 Access Coalition says Glaxo-Wellcome has been stalling development of the drug for nine years because it already manufactures most of the current AIDS medications available. Since these provide a large share of Glaxo's profits, 1592 may make the older drugs become very unpopular, even extinct. Many believe Glaxo is stalling to maximize profits from current AIDS drugs. In other words, profits stand in the way of millions of desperate and dying people.

UPDATE BY AUTHOR BRUCE MIRKEN:
"This article was written after nearly a year of glowing media stories that all but declared AIDS over as a result of new anti-HIV drugs that became widely available in 1996. Doctors, researchers, and AIDS activists knew that the drugs weren't working for everyone and that access to promising new compounds was becoming a critical issue for thousands who were running out of options, but little of this was being reported. This story is significant because it represented the tip of a much larger iceberg: That the much-heralded protease inhibitors, though important, were not a miracle cure and that the pharmaceutical industry's responsibilities to people with AIDS had not ended.

"I must add that Project Censored's decision to recognize this piece is significant in another, equally important way. Project Censored has had a long and unhappy history of paying little attention to the gay and lesbian press, for which it has been taken to task repeatedly. I fervently hope this means we're finally on the radar screen for good.

"The campaign for access to 1592 continued through the summer, with a series of protests staged by ACT UP/New York, ACT UP/Golden Gate (based in San Francisco), and others. Over a dozen organizations united to call for an international boycott on Zantac, Glaxo's top-selling product. For months there was little progress, but in October 1997, the company agreed to make the drug available on a larger scale in early 1998, in a program with fewer restrictions, and some activists considered the company's offer good enough to allow them to call off the boycott.

"I am not aware of any mainstream press response to my story, but the protests organized by ACT UP did attract some mainstream media attention beginning in June and July. In San Francisco both daily papers and some radio and TV stations did stories on 1592 and the boycott of Glaxo."

For more information on this and related AIDS-treatment access and research issues, some good places to start are:

ACT UP/Golden Gate, Tel: 415/252-2900; Web site: http://www.actupgg.org; ACT UP/East Bay, Tel: 510/568-1680; ACT UP/New York, Tel: 212/966-4813; Web site: http://www.actupny.org; Project Inform, Tel: 415/558-8669; *AIDS Treatment News,* Tel: 800/ TREAT-12 (for subscription information).

UPDATE BY AUTHOR NINA SIEGAL:
"In addition to the boycott of Glaxo-Wellcome by the San Francisco chapter of AIDS activist group ACT UP/Golden Gate, Mothers' Voices, a group of mothers of people with AIDS or otherwise related to people who had died from AIDS, then urged the heads of two New York State public employee retirement systems to divest from Glaxo-Wellcome. The two investment funds sent letters to Glaxo threatening to pull out a million shares, worth more than $50 million, if the company did not expand its compassionate use program.

"As a result of the pressure exerted by a four-month boycott, on October 13, the company met with ACT UP to discuss the group's demands, and on October 31, the company agreed to implement an expanded drug access program with no limits. The only criteria would be that the patient be unable to put together a triple combination therapy program.

"The announcement of the boycott was covered in San Francisco by the local gay newspapers and was later picked up by the Associated Press. But according to John Iversen, co-founder of ACT UP/East Bay, the AP story only ran in the *San Francisco Examiner.* The threat of divestment was covered by *The New York Post* on August 8, but that story received no other press attention, according to Iverson. To publicize the boycott, ACT UP brought advertisements in *The Nation* and *In These Times,* but neither of those publications ran a story on the boycott."

25 CENSORED

Black Elected Officials Targeted by Law

Source:
EMERGE
Title: "Targets For Scrutiny"
Date: October 1996
Author: Joe Davidson

SSU Censored Researchers:
Amber Knight, Yvonne Jolley-Crawford, and Brian Foust
Community Evaluator:
Rick Williams, J.D.

Statistical evidence indicates that black elected officials have tended to be investigated by law enforcement agencies at higher rates than white elected officials. According to the Washington-based Joint Center of Political and Economic Studies, in the past 25 years, 70 members of Congress have faced criminal charges. Fifteen percent of those investigated have been minorities—four times their percentage in the legislative body.

The *Washington Post* reported that black elected officials were the target of investigations for corruption in 14 percent of the 465 political corruption cases launched between 1983 and 1988—a period in which blacks were just 3 percent of all office holders. *Gentleman's Quarterly* (GQ) magazine noted that about half of the Congressional Black Caucus members were the subject of investigations or indictments between 1981 and 1993. States GQ, "For the numbers to be equal for white representatives, 204 of the 409 whites...would have been subjected to the same scrutiny during that time...Yet, according to Justice Department figures, only 15 actually were."

In an interview with author Joe Davidson, Robert Moussallem, an FBI informant charged with getting incriminating information on black officials in Atlanta, sets forth his experience with the policy of harassing of black officials. He states, "Shortly after I began working with the FBI in 1979, I was made aware of an unofficial policy of the FBI which was generally referred to by Special Agent John McAvoy as *Fruhmenschen* [German for early or primitive man]. The purpose of the policy was the routine investigation without probable cause of prominent elected and appointed black officials in major metropolitan areas throughout the United States. I learned from my conversations with special agents of the FBI that the basis for this policy was the assumption by the FBI that black officials

were intellectually and socially incapable of governing major government organizations and institutions." (Moussallem's assignment, according to a 1989 affidavit, was to entice Birmingham Mayor Richard Arrington and other black officials to take bribes on a phony land deal.)

Mary Sawyer, a professor at Iowa State University who has studied the treatment of black officials, says, "The magnitude of the harassment cannot be measured solely in terms of numbers of cases...the higher the level of office, or the more outspoken the official, or the greater the influence and power, the higher the incidence of harassment."

While law enforcement agencies deny specifically targeting black elected officials, there are considerable differences in the levels of investigations and the degree of punishment between black and white elected officials in the United States.

UPDATE BY AUTHOR JOE DAVIDSON:
"In 'Targets for Scrutiny,' I explored the accusation that black elected officials are unfairly scrutinized by comparing the treatment of Mel Reynolds with other current and former members of Congress who had been accused of sex-related crimes or misconduct. The importance of the piece is that it provided real examples of disparate treatment.

"The article certainly did not say that the now-imprisoned Reynolds, former Congressman from Chicago and certain southern suburbs, was innocent, nor the white men mentioned, guilty. But the story did demonstrate, with specific detail, how somewhat similar behavior was treated so differently. It showed that the likelihood that black people will fall victim to the double standard of justice does not diminish with status.

"While complaints about the double standard by black officials have been carried by the mainstream press, the *Emerge* article went beyond that to show how white officials generally were treated much more leniently than Reynolds.

"Resources for this topic are less abundant than for other issues in the fields of criminal and social justice. Places to begin include the Leadership Forum, Tel: 202/789-3500; the Black Caucus, Tel: 202/222-7790; and the National Black Caucus of State Legislators, Tel: 202/624-5457."

Project Censored Honorable Mentions for 1997

TOWARD FREEDOM
Title: "Criminalizing Charity"
Date: June/July 1997
Author: Jenna E. Ziman

Food Not Bombs activists, in trying to feed homeless people in San Francisco and 130 other locations around the United States, are increasingly being harassed and arrested by police demanding food-serving permits.

THE WEEKLY STANDARD
Title: "Eugenics, American Style"
Date: December 2, 1996
Author: Tucker Carlson

Amniocentesis testing leads to pressures on women to abort Down's Syndrome fetuses.

SAN FRANCISCO BAY GUARDIAN
Title: "The Sack of San Bruno"
Date: December 11, 1996
Author: Savannah Blackwell

San Bruno Mountain was a national model for decimating the Endangered Species Act. Developers use habitat conservation plans (HCPs) to bypass the Endangered Species Act.

E MAGAZINE
Title: "The Ties that Blind: Big Oil Goes Hunting for Electric Cars in California"
Date: March/April 1997
Author: Jim Motavalli

Big oil goes hunting for electric cars in California. Deep-pocket lobbyists encouraged the California Legislature to dilute the zero-emission mandates for automobiles.

WORLD WATCH

Title: "Asia is Losing Ground"
Date: November/December 1996
Author: Gary Gardner

The development boom is eating away at Asia's cropland. Unless the trend is reversed, the continent's leaders may find themselves facing a new national security problem: food.

THE NATION

Title: "Inherit the Wind"
Date: June 16, 1997
Author: Harvey Wasserman

Despite predictions that wind power will be the next century's cheapest sources of power, the United States is ignoring advances in wind power technologies in favor of a policy dependent on fossil fuels.

Z MAGAZINE

Title: "All MOXed Out"
Date: May 1997
Author: Tom Johnson

Energy Secretary Hazel O'Leary approved the processing of plutonium from nuclear warheads and its "burning" in civilian nuclear reactors. Six months after a January 1997 letter from 171 medical, environmental, and activist organizations in the U.S. and 18 other countries to President Clinton asking him to overrule this decision, their call was still being ignored.

IN THESE TIMES

Title: "Fishy Business"
Date: May 26, 1997
Author: Jeffrey St. Clair

Giant factory trawlers are wiping out independent boat operators and wreaking havoc with the marine ecosystem.

BUSINESS WEEK

Title: "The Black Market v. The Ozone: Despite Global Limits on CFC Production, the Traffic is Brisk"
Date: July 7, 1997
Authors: Catherine Arnst and Gary McWilliams

$500 million worth of chlorofluorocarbons (CFS) are smuggled into the U.S. annually. CFCs still threaten the ozone layer.

INTELLIGENCE REPORT

Title: "Crossing the Threshold: The Increasing Threat of Biochemical Terrorism has Security Experts on High Alert"
Date: Winter 1997
Author: Klanwatch Staff

Right-wing extremist groups in the United States believe that the government is preparing biological agents to kill them. Some have initiated strategies to strike first.

MULTINATIONAL MONITOR

Title: "Fueling Strife in Chad and Cameroon: The Exxon-Shell-ELF-World Bank Plans for Central Africa"
Date: May 1997
Author: Korinna Horta

The planned oil and pipeline project organized by Exxon, Shell, ELF, and the World Bank—Africa's largest oil development project ever—fuels civil strife and threatens watersheds, forests, and biodiversity.

EARTH ISLAND JOURNAL

Title: "Microwaving Our Planet"
Date: Summer 1997
Author: Arthur Firstenberg

Proponents of microwave telecommunications systems continue to claim that electromagnetic bombardment is harmless to life despite new research to the contrary.

RACHEL'S ENVIRONMENT & HEALTH WEEKLY

Title: "Dioxin In Chickens and Eggs"
Date: July 17, 1997, #555
Author: Peter Montague, Ph.D.

The federal government has found evidence of dioxin contamination in chickens, eggs, and farm-raised catfish. Dioxin has been classified as a Class 1 carcinogen and is much more toxic than previously believed.

EARTH ISLAND INSTITUTE

Title: "Oil Spills in the Sky"
Date: Summer 1997
Author: Gar Smith

NASA scientists have reported that both the vapor trails and voluminous soot produced by heavy jet plane traffic have negative impacts on the hydrospherical cycle and contribute to global warming.

RACHEL'S ENVIRONMENT & HEALTH WEEKLY

Title: "Infectious Disease and Pollution"
Date: January 9, 1997, #528
Author: Peter Montague, Ph.D.

Our immune systems—the vital protectors of human health—degenerate in the continual presence of pesticides and pollution. There is increased evidence of immune system failures in the general population.

EARTH ISLAND INSTITUTE

Title: "Food Pets Die For"
Date: Fall 1997
Author: Ann N. Martin

Misnomers describing pet food ingredients as "real meat" and "bone meal" mislead consumers about the actual constituents which may include all parts of rendered, hormone-laced, and infected livestock—and even "roadkill" and euthanised pets.

COMMENTS BY PROJECT CENSORED NATIONAL JUDGES

SUSAN FALUDI, Pulitzer Prize-winning journalist: "The selections this year were rife with ironic connections: Some people forced to take drugs they don't want, while others are denied medical aid and medicine they desperately need. One low-profile government agency conducts massive global surveillance while a high-profile one (the FBI) mishandles one investigation after another...and no government, in spite of their bottomless appetites for monitoring, can find those canisters of spacecraft plutonium. One entry—that the press ignores lower-income communities—is all too well proved by another entry, the censored tale of Mattel's sweatshops. The media *have* issued endless reports about Barbie's new waistline...while oblivious to the gaunt profiles of the women who are sick from making Barbie under Dickensian conditions. As the press becomes increasingly preoccupied with marketing itself to the 'quality' consumer, more and more such stories will be censored. Only they won't be censored for the traditional reasons—to serve the interests of the rich and powerful, etc. They will be eliminated merely to clear the columns/aisles for more salable stories/wares for the new reader/shopper."

BEN H. BAGDIKIAN, professor emeritus and former dean of the Graduate School of Journalism, University of California, Berkeley: "Project Censored has become more important than ever at a time when national legislation deals mainly with secondary social issues. Washington's major lobbies have made corporate goals the primary priorities in national politics, and these always become the centerpiece of mainstream daily news. Project Censored, as always, reminds the public—and mainstream editors—of the urgent social issues and events mistakenly left in the shadows."

MICHAEL PARENTI, author, lecturer, political analyst: "For all their range and variety, most of the *Censored* stories of 1997 offer the same fundamental theme. They reveal something about the immoral, profit-driven, anti-human abuses of the giant corporations. It is the very reason why the mainstream corporate-owned media find these stories so untouchable.

"The mainstream media do not usually deal with the underlying problems of unaccountable economic power confronted in these stories because they themselves are part of that problem. They are monopoly media not just in their pattern of concentrated ownership but also in their ideological uniformity, their readiness to close ranks in defense of the capitalist, global 'free market,' and in defense of the national security state whose task is to make the world safe for the favored few filthy-rich investors at the very top of the social pyramid.

"What is at stake is not just this or that particular issue but the ability of an informed citizenry to develop the collective consciousness and take collective action that enables it to protect itself against the abuses of wealth and power. Such protection is the essence of democracy itself. So let us keep lighting our candles in the darkness. Every effort helps."

CARL JENSEN, professor emeritus of Communications Studies at Sonoma State University, founder of Project Censored, and author of *20 Years of Censored News* (Seven Stories Press, 1997): "In 1997, America's mainstream journalism was characterized by its extended coverage of Princess Diana's death, its exposé of Marv Albert's sexual proclivities, its investigation of the Frank Gifford affair, amongst other junk food news coverage.

"America's alternative journalism, on the other hand, was distinguished by its coverage of President Clinton's efforts to promote U.S. arms sales to Third World countries, its exposé of drug scientists who use poor people as human guinea pigs, its investigation of a federal law that could force you to carry a national identification card, and a host of other important issues.

"If the major print and electronic news media were to spend more time on the latter issues, and leave the junk food news to the tabloids, you just might see more Americans interested in subscribing to newspapers and watching television news programs.

"As it is now, the news media honchos are trying to figure out why they're losing millions of readers and viewers. In response, some publications, such as *The Los Angeles Times*, are merging their marketing, advertising, and news departments in an effort to give the public what it says it wants rather than giving the public what it needs—reliable information on issues that affect the public.

"It's time for journalism to get back to basics—reporting on issues that 'comfort the afflicted and afflict the comfortable,' as Finley Peter Dunne's Mr. Dooley said."

JULIANNE MALVEAUX, economist and syndicated columnist, King Features and Pacifica radio talk show host, president and CEO, Last Word Productions: "Because the macroeconomic indicators of economic well-being have been positive, I do not think enough Americans pay attention to issues of concentration of economic power and how it affects our daily lives. We are especially ignorant of ways that a set of rights we assume are basic do not exist for those who have little economic power. Several of this year's under-covered stories reflect this theme. From the cutting of jobs at toy manufacturers, to the way that human beings are used in medical experiments at home and abroad, it is clear that some people's rights and options are literally 'for sale.' Similarly, the extent to which corporations will withhold drugs that can cure AIDS, or interfere in the politics of another country for economic reasons ('U.S. Paper Companies Conspire to Squash Zapatistas') suggest that profits are consistently valued over people at home and abroad. The spin on this can be partly controlled by the synergy that exists between big business and universities that have long been assumed to be 'impartial' filters of data. Now, however, we learn that the collusive relationship between business and some universities may skew results of some findings.

"I am most concerned about the extent to which we take the valuation of profits over people for granted, the extent to which some eyes glaze over as they read these under-covered stories, wondering what's new about human experiments, environmental abuse, inhumane prison conditions, and other abuses. There may be bias in the media that results in these stories being under-reported, but there is also an apathy and inertia that suggests that even the best coverage of human experimentation might result in shrugs from some readers."

GEORGE GERBNER, Bell Atlantic Professor of Telecommunication, Temple University, Philadelphia: "All news is necessarily selective. The test of validity of news is not how factual but how *relevant* (as well as factual) it is—relevant to the public interest. The *Censored* list reveals a selective process relevant to the interests of corporate sponsors and to repressive policies undermining the foundations of a democratic press."

HERBERT I. SCHILLER, professor emeritus of Communication, University of California, San Diego: "This year marks another step in the push for *total corporate control* in the country's informational/cultural structure. This process occurs not with Orwellian measures of coercion, but develops in the institutional changes that have been underway for decades. It is observable, most crucially, in the drives to privatize the entire culture, eliminate the social sector, and wipe out all social accountability ('deregulation'). Though not a complicated process, it has already moved the U.S. to the brink of democratic dysfunctionality."

JUDITH F. KRUG, Director, Office for Intellectual Freedom, American Library Association: "Each year, as I review the selections for the top *Censored* stories, I am reminded anew of the importance of information to our society. How can we govern ourselves effectively if we don't have the information we need to make wise decisions? The answer is that we can't. Hopefully, the information in these stories will lead to better decisions in a few areas of our society."

AILEEN C. HERNANDEZ, urban consultant, community activist, and former Commissioner on the U.S. Equal Employment Opportunity Commission: "The stories that made this year's list involve situations that can impact the lives of millions of people—and that, for the most part, target the poor and the disenfranchised. All too often, they involve the potential for massive profits to a small segment of the society and significant physical danger for many people.

"The public's right to know is seriously impeded by the 'blackout' of these news stories by the mainstream press. And what you don't know *can* hurt you. If these stories, slighted by the media, have validity, we are all in danger from media co-opted all too frequently by the greed of a few corporate interests or the dishonesty of a few politicians."

WILLIAM LUTZ, professor of English, Rutgers University, New Brunswick, NJ: "If anything, 1997 will be remembered as the year in which news became more dominated by 'entertainment' and 'commercialism.' News is no longer news, it's a product to be used as a vehicle to make money, either through high ratings or by promoting products. All of which underlines the need for the *Censored* awards, so we will remember what news is supposed to be and what it should do."

RHODA H. KARPATKIN, president, Consumers Union, non-profit publisher of *Consumer Reports*: "For democracy to work, news organizations have to work hard to find and report the tough stories, even when doing that raises the hackles of government, corporations, and advertisers. Investigative journalism is a prerequisite for ensuring public accountability.

"Once again, however, this year's selections show how important facts that Americans need to know about the environment, foreign policy, consumer health and safety, and human rights are often obscured, covered up, or just not reported at all. Each example shows that the mass media is not meeting its responsibility to report on public and private abuses of power.

These include violations of civil liberties and human rights, corporate misconduct, and efforts to roll back and undercut environmental protections."

JUAN D. GONZALEZ, columnist, New York *Daily News,* and co-host of Pacifica Radio's *Democracy Now*: "During a year when such inordinate news space was consumed by Princess Diana's death and the campaign finance scandals, the mainstream media's failure to tackle the critical stories that formed the top *Censored* news stories was, at best, gross negligence."

JACK L. NELSON, professor, Graduate School of Education, Rutgers University, New Brunswick, NJ: "There are many stories which are of great human significance, but which are terribly under-reported in the mass media. The stories under consideration this year included such stories—ones which would have been in the top ten of my selections, but did not make my top ten received some, although inadequate, coverage in mainstream media. This makes selection difficult, because it may suggest that such stories are of lesser importance. However, that would be a misreading. My selections leaned more toward stories that were virtually ignored in mass media, but which had major implications for life in a democracy. This year, my selections seemed to focus on health and secrecy/conspiracy issues that the public deserved to have better and more thoroughly reported."

DONNA ALLEN, founding editor in 1972 of *Media Report to Women*: "The disgraceful lack of coverage of these stories, so vital to the public's democratic participation in the decision making affecting our lives, suggests that we need to build our own means of communication. I'm pleased that Project Censored now has e-mail and World Wide Web access, because one of the most censored stories of all is the story of the media's failure to cover important stories, even while claiming their function in society is to tell the public 'what it needs to know.' Project Censored plays a valuable role in inspiring us to raise the media issue until we have forced the mass media to acknowledge a wider range of information than that which only affects their special economic interests. Remember that all mass media owners, from owners of networks reaching 98 percent of American households to owners of mass media in small towns, do not total more than two million people—that's less than one percent of the population telling *us* what they think we need to know. But times are changing fast and there are now new technologies through which we can speak for ourselves and begin participating in the making of the new, more democratic decisions of society."

RICHARD BARNET, Fellow of the Institute for Policy Studies: "The stories on the arms race and corporate power were especially strong."

SHEILA ROBB WEIDENFELD, president, D.C. Productions, former press secretary for Betty Ford: "It seems to be getting harder to find truly 'censored stories.' Thanks to the Internet, there is greater ease in accessing information. There is a lawsuit, however, which threatens this open access to ideas. It holds the Internet service providers liable as 'publishers' of the information delivered through their facilities. This lawsuit against *The Drudge Report* seeks to hold America OnLine responsible for contents on the Internet. *The Drudge Report* is one of many kinds of 'cyber' publications available on the 'information superhighway.' Publications like these sometimes circulate stories that Project Censored highlights. (They also circulate a certain amount of misinformation.) But, if Internet service providers become liable for the contents of the Internet, a new class of censor will be created and access to ideas will be curtailed.

"The authors of libel must be responsible for the damage they cause. Irresponsible journalism will not do. But unlike traditional publishing, electronic re-publishers are not, and should not be, in control of content. Internet censorship is a concern for those who care about freedom of speech. It is time for organizations like Project Censored to address this issue."

BARBARA SEAMAN, co-founder of the Women's Health Network: "In addition to the important issues of lack of coverage already raised by Project Censored, the Norplant story in particular has endless ramifications:

"Norplant is a clear case of 'welfare for the rich.' At last report, Norplant cost Wyeth-Ayerst about $23 per set, which is its sale price in developing countries. Wyeth-Ayerst sells these kits in the U.S. for $350 wholesale, and the ultimate user is charged around $600 per kit in the end. The high resale cost cannot be justified by claiming there are development costs to recoup, since Norplant was developed by the Population Council. Wyeth-Ayerst spokesman Mark Deitch, M.D., has testified that the high price was intended to protect a marketing image and to prevent middle-class women from shunning Norplant as a drug for the poor. However, since 50 to 60 percent of Norplant bills are paid by Medicaid, U.S. taxpayers are, in fact, lavishly underwriting Wyeth-Ayerst.

"Another deeply disturbing issue is the absence of knowledge of long-term effects on nursing infants. It is well established that levonorgestrel, the powerful synthetic hormone in Norplant, gets into breast milk.

"A third issue is that Norplant creates 'menstrual chaos' in most users. A regular menstrual cycle is disturbed, and there are unpredictable weeks or even months of continuous bleeding, and then no bleeding at all. Such irregularity sometimes masks serious conditions such as ectopic pregnancies or uterine cancers."

THIS MODERN WORLD

by TOM TOMORROW

THIS WEEK--A LOOK AT SOME OF AMERICA'S BIG-GEST *WELFARE BUMS*--SUCH AS *ED RENSI*, PRESIDENT AND CEO OF *McDONALDS*, WHICH RECEIVED $466,000 FROM THE U.S. GOVERNMENT IN 1992 TO PROMOTE *CHICKEN McNUGGETS* OVERSEAS...

THINK OF IT AS A CULTURAL EXPORT!

McDonald's
HAMBURGER
GAZILLIONS SOLD

OR *JOHN F. SMITH, JR.*, PRESIDENT AND CEO OF *GENERAL MOTORS*, A COMPANY WHICH RE-CEIVED MORE THAN $110.6 MILLION IN FEDERAL TECHNOLOGY SUBSIDIES AS PART OF A PROGRAM TO CREATE JOBS FROM 1990-1994--DURING WHICH TIME THEY *SLASHED* 104,000 JOBS...

HEY--WHAT'S GOOD FOR *GENERAL MOTORS* IS GOOD FOR--

--WELL, FOR *MY STOCK OP-TIONS*, ACTUALLY...

AND THEN THERE'S *MICHAEL EISNER*, CEO OF THE *DISNEY CO.*, WHOSE RESEARCH INTO *BRIGHTER FIREWORKS* IS BEING SUBSIDIZED BY TAXPAYERS TO THE TUNE OF $300,000 THRU THE DEPARTMENT OF ENERGY "COOPERATIVE RESEARCH AND DEVELOPMENT" PROGRAM...

WHAT'S THE *MATTER?* YOU DON'T LIKE *FIRE-WORKS?* OR *MICKEY MOUSE?*

WHAT ARE YOU, SOME KINDA COMMUNIST?

FINALLY, WE CAN'T OVERLOOK WELL-KNOWN WELFARE RECIPIENT *SAM DONALDSON*, WHO COLLECTS $97,000 ANNUALLY FROM THE U.S. GOVERNMENT IN THE FORM OF SUBSIDIES FOR HIS *SHEEP RANCH* IN NEW MEXICO...

ER--WOULDN'T YOU REALLY RATHER HEAR ABOUT ALL THOSE WEL-FARE MOTH-ERS RECEIV-ING $67 A MONTH...?

HEH, HEH...

BAAA

A COMPLETE SET OF CORPORATE WELFARE POSTER BOYS IS AVAILABLE FROM WOMEN'S INT'L LEAGUE FOR PEACE & FREEDOM, 215-563-7110

CHAPTER 2

This Communication Revolution Is Brought To You By U.S. Media at the Dawn of the 21st Century

By Robert W. McChesney

Over 40 years have passed since the publication of C. Wright Mills's *The Power Elite*, arguably one of the most insightful and prescient critiques of U.S. political culture written this century. In that book Mills discusses the paradox of the postwar United States. On the one hand, it is a nation abuzz with technology, celebrity, and commercialism, a radical society in which tradition is torn asunder and all that is solid melts into air. On the other hand, it is a highly depoliticized society—only formally democratic in key respects— where most important political decisions are made by the few for the few, with public relations to massage the rabble should they question their status. The commercial media system plays a major role in maintaining the social order. The final third or so of the book reveals the United States as a fundamentally conservative society and a deeply troubled one at that. In my mind, when one looks at the core argument, it could well have been written in 1998.

Mills also provides us with a useful schemata to make sense of what seem like revolutionary changes in our media system on the verge of the 21st century. The Internet and the broader developments in digital and satellite communication present us with a picture of staggering, almost incomprehensible, change in media and communication—indeed, in our entire social fabric—in the coming decade. Writers from Nicholas Negroponte and Douglas Rushkoff to George Gilder and even Newt Gingrich inform us that we are entering a period of fundamental social change the likes of which may occur once in a millennium, with the very essence of human social life and cognition undergoing qualitative change. It will be a future where individuals will have vastly greater power over their own lives. Yet, when one cuts through the rhetoric, the promises, and the projections, the digital revolution seems less a process about empowering the less powerful than it is a process that will further the corporate and commercial domination of life in the United States. Following Mills's analysis, the logical trajectory of the current patterns is to assist in the continued depoliticization, polarization, and demoralization of social life, unless the citizenry arises to demand that these technologies be employed in a different manner.

THE CORPORATE MEDIA CARTEL

There are three striking features of the U.S. media system in the 1990s: concentration, conglomeration, and hyper-commercialism. Each of these is, in fact, a long-term phenomenon that has accelerated in the 1990s and each looks to continue for the visible future, well into the digital age. To some extent the astonishing degree of concentrated corporate control over the media is a response to the rapid increase in channels wrought by cable and satellite television. In this sense, the corporate media giants are having a trial run for how they might dominate the Internet when it converges with digital television.

The U.S. mass-media industries have been operated along non-competitive oligopolistic lines for much of the 20th century. In the 1940s, for example, broadcasting, film production, motion picture theaters, book publishing, newspaper publishing, magazine publishing, and recorded music were all distinct national oligopolistic markets, with each of them dominated by anywhere from a few to a dozen or more firms. In general, these were different firms dominating each of these industries, with a few exceptions. Throughout the 20th century there have been pressing concerns that these concentrated markets would inhibit the flow and range of ideas necessary for a meaningful democracy. Rarely, however, did these concerns spill over into public debate, for any number of reasons. In particular, the rise of the notion of professional journalism in the early 20th century attempted to disconnect the editorial process from the explicit supervision of the owners and advertisers of the mass media, hence making the editorial product more credible as a public service. To the extent this process was seen as successful, the corporate commercial domination of the media was a less pressing, perhaps even insignificant, matter.

In the final decades of the 20th century, the conglomeration of media ownership began. This was the process whereby media firms began to have major holdings in two or more distinct media sectors, such as book publishing, recorded music, and broadcasting. To some extent this was fueled by a desire to build the extremely lucrative vertical integration, meaning that media firms would not only produce content but also own distribution channels to guarantee having places to display their wares. In the current era, the classic form of vertical integration is the combining of film and television show production with the ownership of cable channels, broadcast networks and stations, and motion picture theaters. But it was also stimulated by something more profound in the 1980s, and especially in the 1990s: the desire to increase market power by cross-promoting and cross-selling media properties or "brands" across numerous different media sectors that were not linked in the manner suggested by vertical integration. Hence, if a media conglomerate had a successful motion picture, it could promote the film on its broadcast properties and then use the film to spin off television programs, music CDs, books, merchandise, and much else. In the new world order of conglomerated media, the profit whole can be vastly greater than the sum of the profit parts. This process is often called synergy. And, ironically, the conversion of all media to digital format has the effect of not putting an "iceberg" before the corporate media giants but, rather, making it easier and more profitable for them to work in several media sectors at once.

A look at Disney's recent operations shows how a media conglomerate attempts to employ synergy. Its *Home Improvement* show is a big hit on its ABC television network. So Disney then has *Home Improvement* star Tim Allen take roles in Disney movies and write books for Disney's book publishing firms. The other giant media conglomerates are increasingly emulating this pattern. In an another example, Disney takes it lucrative ESPN cable channel and uses the name to generate other properties. In 1998, Disney launched ESPN *Magazine* to compete directly with Time Warner's *Sports Illustrated*. Likewise, Disney is launching a chain of ESPN Grill restaurants to appeal to those who wish to combine sports with a meal.

The degree and pace of market concentration and conglomeration over the past 20 years is little short of breathtaking. In 1983, the first edition of Ben Bagdikian's seminal *The Media Monopoly* was published. In that book, Bagdikian chronicled how some 50 firms dominated the entirety of U.S. mass media, ranging from newspapers, books, and magazines to film, radio, television, cable, and recorded music. In each of the subsequent four editions, mergers and acquisitions reduced the number of dominant firms, until the most recent edition in 1997 put the figure at around 10, with another dozen or so firms rounding out the system. Though few thought it possible, the 1990s has seen an acceleration of this process.

The largest U.S. (and global, for that matter) media firms like Time Warner, Disney, Viacom, and Rupert Murdoch's News Corporation have all doubled or tripled in size, due to major acquisitions of other media firms as well as internal growth of existing assets. This is due to relaxed regulatory standards in this era of "free market" capitalism, new technologies that make consolidation more feasible, and, especially, the immense profit potential that comes with size. Indeed, there is no longer the option of being a small- or middle-sized media firm anymore: a firm either gets larger through mergers and acquisitions or it gets swallowed by a more aggressive competitor.

If the early and middle 1990s were marked by huge media mergers, like Time Warner's purchase of Turner Broadcasting or Disney's purchase of ABC, the late 1990s has seen a more surgical addition of assets, and occasional prunings, all to improve market power. The overall trajectory, nonetheless, remains that of increasing concentration both within distinct media sectors, and in the number and size of the largest media conglomerates. In the newspaper industry, for example, the emerging trend is that of "clustering," whereby metropolitan monopoly daily newspapers purchase or otherwise link up with all the smaller dailies in the suburbs and surrounding region.

In cable television, six firms, divvying up the nation, have effective monopolistic control over more than 80 percent of the nation, and seven firms control nearly three-quarters of cable channels and programming. As Time Warner's Ted Turner puts it, "We do have just a few people controlling all the cable companies in this country." *Variety* notes that "mergers and consolidations have transformed the cable-network marketplace into a walled-off community controlled by a handful of media monoliths." At the retail end, concentration proceeds apace. In motion picture theaters, for example, the era of the independent or even small-chain theater company has gone the way of the Dodo Bird. Several colossal deals in 1997 left the industry dominated by a few huge multiplex chains, many of which connected to larger media conglomerates.

But concentrating upon specific media sectors fails to convey the extent of concentrated corporate control. This only comes when one addresses the holdings of the largest media corporations. For nearly all of the dominant firms in each of the major media sectors are owned outright or in part by the 20 largest U.S. media firms, and, among those firms the largest half-dozen rule the roost. Hence Time Warner, the world's largest media firm with 1997 sales of around $25 billion, has holdings that rank it among the top few firms in: film production, TV show production, cable systems, cable TV stations, broadcast TV networks, magazine publishing, book publishing, recorded music, amusement parks, and movie theaters. The other corporate media giants like Disney, Viacom, News Corporation, General Electric's NBC, TCI, Seagram's Universal Studios, CBS, and Sony all have or are in the process of building similar arsenals. NBC, for example, is known to be eager to acquire a film studio while even giant Time Warner is rumored to be in the market for a major television network. As one media analyst puts it, "consolidation among distribution and content players rages on" (Mermigas, Diane, "TCI Headed in the Right Direction," *Electronic Media*, September 1, 1997: 20).

Moreover, the smart money is betting on a further thinning in the ranks of the giant media corporations. Gordon Crawford, who manages the Capital Research mutual fund that has significant stakes in nearly all of the media giants forecasts that the eventual outcome will be a global media oligopoly dominated by six firms: Time Warner, Disney, Viacom, News Corporation, Sony, and Seagram. Crawford is more than a silent investor; he works quietly but persistently to coordinate deals among the media giants to increase all of their profitability.

But this barely begins to indicate how noncompetitive the media market is becoming. In addition to an oligopolistic market structure and overlapping ownership, the media giants each employ equity joint ventures with their "competitors" to an extraordinary extent. These are media projects where two or more media giants share the ownership between them. They are ideal because they spread the risk of a venture and eliminate the threat of competition by teaming up with potential adversaries. Each of the eight largest U.S. media firms averages having joint ventures (often more than one) with five of the other seven media giants. Rupert Murdoch's News Corp. has at least one joint venture with every single one of them. Viewed this way, the U.S. media market has cartel-like tendencies. While competition can be and is ferocious in specific markets, the overall thrust is to reduce competition and carve up the media pie to the benefit of the handful of giants. By any known theory of market performance, this degree of collaboration can only have negative effects for consumers.

If synergy is the principle that makes becoming a media conglomerate more profitable and, indeed, mandatory, the other side of the coin is branding. All media firms are racing to give their media properties distinct brand identities. Although the media system has fewer and fewer owners, it nonetheless has a plethora of channels competing for attention and branding is the primary means of attracting and keeping audiences while also offering new commercial possibilities. Cable channels and even broadcast networks each strive to be regarded as brands especially desirable to specific demographic groups desired by advertisers. Hence Viacom's Nickelodeon cable network battles its new competition from News Corp.'s Fox Kids Network and the Disney Channel by hammering home the Nickelodeon brand name incessantly on Nickelodeon, and in its other film, television, and publishing holdings. Branding also opens up for the media giants the entire world of selling retail products based on their branded properties to the media giants, and it is a course they have been pursuing with a vengeance. Disney now has 590 retail stores to sell its branded products while Time Warner has 160 stores. Viacom has entered the market too and some of the other media giants are moving in this direction as well.

FAREWELL TO PUBLIC SERVICE

The other side of the coin of commercialization is the decline and effective elimination of any public service values from the media, placing the status of nonmarket public service in jeopardy across society. It is often assumed that the United States has always been a business society where commercial values have reigned supreme, and there is a strong element of truth to this. But this assertion must be qualified: there is an enormous, difference between the degree and nature of commercialism in the United States in, say, 1830 or 1880 or 1950 and what is emerging today. Those were commercial societies, but nonprofit and noncommercial institutions and values also played notable roles. Today's hyper-commercialized society is such a sharp, quantitative change that it is also producing a qualitative change. In this environment, the commercial values of profit maximization and sales have overwhelmed the main vestiges of public service in media. The areas in marked retreat to the point of extinction are public service broadcasting, the regulations that require commercial broadcasting to serve some public service values, and journalism. I will concentrate here upon journalism, because that is clearly the most important vestige of public service in U.S. media.

Indeed, journalism has been regarded as a public service by all of the commercial media throughout this century. It is something that newspapers, magazines, broadcasters, and journalism schools regarded as an activity directed to noncommercial aims fundamental to a democracy that could not be bought and sold by powerful interests. Professional journalism was predicated on the notion that its content should not be shaped by the dictates of owners and advertisers, or by the biases of the editors and reporters, but rather by core public service values. For much of the 20th century the media corporations have brandished their commitment to journalism as their main explanation for why they deserve First Amendment protection and a special place in the political economy. Professional journalism has never enjoyed the independence from corporate or commercial pressure suggested by its rhetoric, and indeed in some respects has been a mixed blessing if not detrimental to democracy, but whatever autonomy journalism has enjoyed is presently under sustained attack by the corporate media giants and commercial values. Whatever the limitations of professional journalism, it shines in comparison to much of what is called "news" today.

The decline, even collapse, of journalism as a public service is apparent all across the media. For network and national cable television, news has gone from being a loss-leader to enhance prestige to being a major producer of profit. NBC at present enjoys what is regarded as "the most profitable broadcast news division in the history of television," with annual advertising revenues topping $100 million. NBC is renowned not for the quality of its news as much as for the extraordinary manner it squeezes profit from it. NBC uses QNBC, a high-tech statistical service, to analyze its news reports to see exactly how its desired target audience is reacting to the different news stories and to the ads. Its goal is to have a "boundaryless" flow across the program so as to satisfy those paying the bills. In 1996, the news story that NBC gave the most time to was the Summer Olympics in Atlanta. That story did not even rank on the top 10 list of most covered stories for CBS, ABC, or CNN. What explains NBC's devotion to this story? NBC had the television rights to the Olympics and it used its nightly news to pump up the ratings for its primetime coverage.

Beside using the news to promote corporate fare, the main way to make journalism profitable is to have fewer reporters, therefore concentrating upon inexpensive and easy stories to cover, like celebrity lifestyle pieces, court cases, and visually compelling stories like crashes and shoot-outs. It is also good business. This caliber of journalism rarely offends people in power—since serious investigative work is far too expensive to be conducted—and therefore does not get the parent corporation enmeshed in controversy.

Examples of these trends abound. The annual number of crime stories on network TV news programs tripled from 1990–92 to 1993–1996. In the summer of 1997, CNN addressed a decline in ratings by broadcasting a much publicized interview with O.J. Simpson. One almost had to feel sympathy for the CNN correspondent who was reprimanded after he did a television commercial as a spokesperson for Visa USA; his role in the commercial had been originally cleared by CNN and it certainly seemed in keeping with the commercial thrust of television journalism. His crime, it would appear, was being caught. As bad as this seems, local television news is considerably worse. One recent detailed content analysis of local TV news in 55 markets in 35 states concludes that the news tended to feature crime and violence, triviality, and celebrity, and that some programs aired more commercials than news (Kite, Paul, Robert A. Bardwell, and Jason Salzman, *Baaad News: Local TV News in America*, February 26, 1997 [Denver: Rocky Mountain Media Watch, 1997]; see also Bannon, Lisa, "In TV Chopper War, News Is Sometimes A Trivial Pursuit," *The Wall Street Journal*, June 4, 1997: A1, A10).

The attack on journalism is every bit as pronounced in the nation's newspapers. The concentration of ownership into local monopolies that are part of large national chains gives the media corporations considerable power to reduce the resource commitment to journalism so as to fatten the bottom line. Gannett showed the genius of this approach as it built its empire over the past 35 years. Since purchasing the once highly acclaimed *Des Moines Register* in the 1980s, for example, it has slashed that paper's once extraordinary coverage of state affairs down to the bone. These corporate giants are

also increasingly using temporary labor to fill reporters' and photographers' jobs. In addition, there is implicit pressure on editors and reporters to accept marketing principles and be "more reader friendly." This means an emphasis upon lifestyle and consumption issues that strongly appeal to desired readers and advertisers alike. "Marketing," one reporter stated in 1997, "these days means spending more time focusing on the things that concern the people who have all the money and who live in the suburbs." In a bold new measure, the *Los Angeles Times* in 1997 appointed a business manager to be "general manager for news," and directly oversee the editorial product to see that it conform to the best commercial interests of the newspaper.

What is happening at the prestigious *Los Angeles Times* in fact only makes explicit what had been increasingly implicit in journalism over recent years: to serve commercial needs first and foremost. Magazine journalism has had less concern on balance with keeping a formal separation between advertising and editorial content for years; in 1997 *The Wall Street Journal* reported that some major national advertisers demanded to know the contents of specific issues of magazines before they would agree to place ads in them. This caused a public outcry, with magazine editors and publishers formally denouncing the practice. But even if advertisers are not officially vetoing magazine contents, the message has been underlined and boldfaced, again, for publishers and editors, that what they do will affect their commercial fortunes directly.

There are some who argue that this shift to trivia and fluff masquerading as news is going to ultimately harm the media corporation's profitability, as people realize they no longer have any particular need to read or watch news, and news is competing with the entire world of entertainment for attention. Whether that is true or false is impossible to say, but the media corporations

by their actions have made it clear that they prefer to take their profits now rather than spend and make a lot less money now for the chance at pie-in-the-sky profits far down the road. "Our big corporate owners, infected with the greed that marks the end of the 20th century, stretch constantly for ever-increasing profit, condemning quality to take the hindmost," Walter Cronkite observes. They are "compromising journalistic integrity in the mad scramble for ratings and circulation."

Few defend the new journalism, except to say half-heartedly that the media are now "giving the people what they want," as if the people have had any particular choice or as if what generates the best market for advertisers was ever a satisfactory determinant for journalism. This defense stinks of apologia. And there are still many dedicated journalists working under existing conditions to produce as high quality fare as possible; but the trajectory is unmistakable. A recent examination of TV news concludes that consumption of this "distorted diet of information has profound side effects, contributing to public cynicism, desensitization, alienation, ignorance, and the American culture of violence" (Klite, Paul, Robert A. Bardwell, and Jason Salzman, "Local TV News: Getting Away with Murder," *Harvard Journal of Press/Politics* 2(2): 102-112). What is clear is that this is a journalism that makes perfect sense for media corporation shareholders and for advertisers— and it makes perfect sense for those who prefer a depoliticized and quiescent public—but it is absurd and indefensible for citizens in a democracy.

The decline of journalism as a public service independent of commercial values also has clear implications for preserving and extending social inequality. As the notion of journalistic autonomy from owners and advertisers weakens, the journalistic product will increasingly reflect the interests of the wealthy few that own and advertise in the news media. This is the main reason why U.S. conservatives are so obsessed with taming the "liberal" news media; what they desire is for journalism to more closely reflect the political agenda of the business class. As Newt Gingrich informed a meeting of the Georgia Chamber of Commerce in 1997, business and advertisers need to take more direct command of the newsroom. Some of the corporate media owners maintain their journalism holdings not merely to make profit, but to promote their pro-business, anti-labor view of the world. Rupert Murdoch, for example, is an outspoken proponent of the view that the main problems with the world are the prevalence of taxation on business and the wealthy; regulation of business; government bureaucrats; and labor unions. As TCI CEO John Malone stated, Murdoch would be willing to keep his Fox News Channel on the air even if it was not profitable because Murdoch wants "the political leverage he can get out of being a major network." "It is curious," the famous graphic designer Milton Glaser wrote in 1997, "that after the triumph of capitalism, American business is embracing the politburo practice of censoring ideas it deems unacceptable."

THE SQUASHING OF PUBLIC DEBATE

Even among those who acknowledge corporate concentration, conglomeration, and hyper-commercialism as main trends in U.S. media today, and who regard the social and political implications of these trends as extremely negative, there is a fatalistic sense that this is the way it must be, because the United States is a business-run society. In fact, the nature of the U.S. media system is the result of a series of political decisions, not natural law or holy mandate. Even when media are regulated preponderantly by markets, it is in the end a political decision to turn them over to a relative handful of individuals and corporations to maximize profit. The U.S. media system of the late 20th century looks substantially different from the media system of the late 19th century and is diametrically opposed to the press system of the Republic's first two generations. All modern U.S. media as well as advertising are affected directly and indirectly by government policies, regulation, and subsidies. Specifically, the development of radio and television broadcasting has been and is the direct province of the political system. If at any time the U.S. people had elected to establish a fully nonprofit and noncommercial radio and television system, for example, it has been within their constitutional rights to do so. The seminal law for U.S. broadcasting was the Communications Act of 1934; it was only superseded recently with the passage of the Telecommunications Act of 1996.

What is most notable about media policy making in the United States is not that it is important and that it exists, but, rather, that virtually the entire American population has no idea that it exists and that they have a right to participate in it. The Telecommunications Act of 1996 had virtually no public participation or general news media coverage, despite the fact that it will probably set the terms for the development of the media for the coming generations. It is a stunning testament to how undemocratic U.S. society is on basic issues of resource allocation.

The effects of the Telecommunications Act on media were evident in the discussion of the contemporary media market earlier in the chapter. The one media sector most thoroughly overturned by the Telecommunications Act has been radio broadcasting. The Telecommunications Act relaxed ownership restrictions so that a single firm can own up to eight stations in a single market. In the 20 months following the law's passage there has been the equivalent of an Oklahoma land rush as small chains have been acquired by middle-sized chains, and middle-sized chains have been gobbled up by the few massive giants who have come to dominate the national industry. In that time 4,000 of the nation's 11,000 radio stations changed hands and there were over 1,000 radio firm mergers. The deregulation now made it possible for giant radio firms to control enough of a market to compete with television and newspapers for advertisers. This sort of consolidation also permits the giant chains to reduce labor costs as redundant editorial and sales staffs can be "downsized," and programming can be coordinated from national headquarters. According to *Advertising Age,* by September 1997 in each of the 50 largest markets, three firms controlled over 50 percent of the radio ad revenues. And in 23 of the top 50, three companies controlled more than 80 percent of the ad revenues. CBS, formerly Westinghouse, ranks as the national leader with 175 stations, predominately in the 15 largest markets, where it has "maxed out" to the new legal limit. As *The Wall Street Journal* puts it, these deals "have given a handful of companies a lock on the airwaves in the nation's big cities."

When one ponders these developments in radio, the implications of the Telecommunications Act of 1996 for media become more stark. Relative to television and other media technologies, radio is inexpensive for both broadcasters and consumers. It is ideally suited for local community service and control. Yet it has been transformed into a profit engine for a handful of firms, so that they can convert radio broadcasting into the most efficient conduit possible for advertising. Across the nation these giant chains use their market power to slash costs, providing the same handful of formats with only a token nod to the actual localities in which the stations broadcast. On Wall Street, the corporate consolidation of radio is praised as a smash success, but by any other standard this "brave new world" is an abject failure.

The ultimate importance of the Telecommunications Act of 1996, however, was to establish that the private sector would determine the future of U.S. electronic media and digital communication. Since the market is presumed infallible and competitive, there are minimal or nonexistent public service requirements. What the law established, therefore, was that Congress, and, by extension, the public, had formally passed the matter along to the corporate community, and to the FCC, which is in charge of coordinating the "deregulation." And so it is that from the World Wide Web to digital television, the corporate sector has taken the lead in the United States, with little discussion or opposition.

MEDIA REFORM

Following the vision of Mills, the U.S. media at the dawn of the 21st century present an apparent paradox. On the one hand, there is a mind-boggling technological explosion, seemingly scripted in the pages of science fiction novels, that promises unprecedented consumer choice. On the other hand, the clear tendencies of our media and communication world are those of corporate concentration, media conglomeration, and hyper-commercialism. Notions of public service—that there should be some motives for media other than profit—are in rapid retreat if not total collapse. The implications for democracy are entirely negative. Moreover, public debate over the future of media and communication has been effectively eliminated by the corporate media sector, which metaphorically flosses its teeth with politicians' underpants in both major parties. But as Mills understood, this is no paradox at all: the illusion of consumer choice and individual freedom provide the ideological oxygen necessary to cement a media (and broader social) system that serves the few, making it appear accountable and democratic.

But that could change. Indeed, the missing character throughout this chapter has been the public, relegated to its proverbial couch and commanded to shut up and shop. Yet public enthusiasm for commercial media, arguably never as great as the PR industry proclaimed, may be beginning to fray under the hyper-commercialism and semi-monopolistic corporate rule that typifies the 1990s. Some municipalities are beginning to provide city-owned cable services, reminiscent of the great public ownership movement of the Progressive Era. Other activists have taken new developments in radio technology to begin providing unlicensed microradio channels on the parts of the dial unused by the commercial broadcasters. Moreover, local media watch organizations have sprouted across the nation in the 1990s, determined to improve the quality of news and entertainment in their communities, and to oppose the commercialization of public broadcasting, schools, and neighborhoods. At the national level, too, media reform organizations like Fairness and Accuracy in Reporting and the Cultural Environment Movement have blossomed, with clear mandates not merely to get the best of what is currently possible, but to extend the range of what can be possible in the way of media reform. In all of these activities, reformers find significant public support in addition to apathy and disinterest, but very little public hostility on the grounds that the current media system is a success. There is seemingly the climate for the building of a viable public media reform movement for the first time in generations.

Although in certain respects the media system and the handful of firms that sit atop it appear politically and ideologically all-powerful, the system is simultaneously producing considerable disenchantment across society. Should citizens become active in media reform—a prospect the corporate media are doing everything in their power to prevent—all bets would be off concerning the future of U.S. media and society writ large. In the end, the nature of our media system will be determined by people and social activity, not technology.

ROBERT W. McCHESNEY is an Associate Professor of Journalism at the University of Wisconsin-Madison. He is the author, with Edward S. Herman, of *The Global Media: The New Missionaries Of Corporate Capitalism* (Cassell, 1997) and *Corporate Media And The Threat To Democracy* (Seven Stories Press, 1997).

CHAPTER 3

Censored Déjà Vu: What Happened to Last Year's Most Censored Stories

By Peter Phillips, Bob Klose, Matt Manpas, Erik Hansen, and Project Censored

Chapter 3 is designed to give readers an update on the top *Censored* stories from previous years that have been covered in the news in 1997. This year's reviews focus on coverage of stories from 1996. For follow-ups on previously under-covered news stories in the United States, an excellent reference is *20 Years of Censored News* by Carl Jensen & Project Censored (Seven Stories Press, 1997). *20 Years* gives updates on the most *Censored* stories for the years 1976 to 1995 and is available direct from the publisher (Tel: 800/596-7437) and in bookstores nationwide.

1996 # 1 CENSORED STORY

RISKING THE WORLD: NUCLEAR PROLIFERATION IN SPACE

In October 1997, NASA launched the Cassini space probe. Its destination: Saturn. The probe carried 72.3 pounds of plutonium to run electrical equipment. Never before has so much plutonium been used in any space mission.

There are a number of risks involved in using plutonium in space missions. First, the probe was to be propelled by a Titan IV rocket, a rocket with a history of launch accidents. For example, in 1993 a Titan rocket exploded shortly after launch, destroying a $1 billion spy satellite system.

Also, Cassini will not have enough momentum to reach Saturn directly, and will have to circle Venus twice and then fly back toward Earth using Earth's gravity to reach its final destination. During the flyby, which will occur in August 1999, the probe will reach a speed of 42,300 mph at an altitude of just 500 miles above Earth. If the probe comes in too close and enters the Earth's atmosphere during the flyby, it will burn up and discharge plutonium into the atmosphere.

In an environmental impact statement, NASA estimated that if plutonium from the probe were to be released into the Earth's atmosphere, 5 billion of the earth's estimated population at the time would receive 99 percent or more of the radiation exposure. NASA projects that over 50 years, an estimated 2,300 people would die and many others would

fall victim to latent cancer fatalities and nuclear fallout. Other scientists claimed that hundreds of thousands of people could die.

The energy generated by the plutonium is not substantial (745 watts) and could be produced by solar panels, but NASA, the Department of Energy's national nuclear laboratories, and the corporations that manufacture the nuclear hardware for NASA insisted on using plutonium.

SOURCES: "Risking the World: Nuclear Proliferation in Space," *CovertAction Quarterly*, Summer 1996: 56-62, and "Don't Send Plutonium Into Space," *Progressive Media Project*, May 1996, both by Karl Grossman.

COVERAGE 1997: Karl Grossman's original reports on Cassini and the plutonium dangers were reported in May and the summer of 1996. Yet very little mainstream coverage of the issue appeared before the March 25 publication of *Censored 1997: The News that Didn't Make the News*. The *San Francisco Examiner* on March 26, 1997, reported that the Marin County (California) Board of Supervisors had voted to send a letter to President Clinton to order an investigation into the hazards of Cassini. But beyond that there was little coverage before June 1997. Ironically, one of the first articles (*Rocky Mountain News*, June 1, 1997) examined the Cassini issue in terms of criticism of Project Censored for selecting it as the top *Censored* story of the year.

Initially, coverage began to show up

with some regularity in Florida newspapers whose readers were closest to the scheduled launch of the probe. On June 9, 1997, the *Orlando Sentinel* published a story inside its main news section, "Plutonium Worries Cassini Opponents." The next day, The *Sun-Sentinel of Fort Lauderdale* carried a 486-word story, "Nuclear Launch Raises Concerns," in which the pros and cons of the mission and the rise of a protest movement were fairly reported. The *Seattle Times* ran The *Sun-Sentinel* story on the same day, and the New York *Daily News* ran its own 982-word story citing NASA officials saying it is perfectly safe to have a "sky full of radioactivity." On June 15, 1997, *The Palm Beach Post* ran a 1,578-word story on critics' fears and NASA's confidence in the Cassini project, and *The Dallas Morning News* reported on a growing protest movement, both worldwide and in cyberspace.

NASA won a brief reprieve from critics when world attention was turned in July to the landing of the Mars Pathfinder and transmission of pictures of Mars' surface to Earth. Cassini received some upbeat press attention when the Associated Press published a story in late August reporting that Cassini would carry 600,000 signatures, paw prints, and baby scrawls from 81 countries along for the ride to Saturn, a story that even made the Sunday edition of *The New York Times* on August 24, 1997.

But that was a brief holiday for the Cassini probe. Reports on concerns over the mission continued to pour out of Florida and creep across the country.

During August, stories relating the risks of the Cassini launch were carried in *The Detroit News*, the Minneapolis *Star Tribune*, and *The Fresno Bee*.

The rate of national exposure began to accelerate on September 3, 1997, when the headlines reported problems aboard Cassini. Cox News Service reported a cooling glitch with the Cassini spacecraft could delay the October 6 scheduled launch. That story was picked up on September 4 by, among others, the *Chicago Tribune, New Orleans Times-Picayune,* and *Bloomington* (IL) *Pantagraph. The New York Times* carried its own story by correspondent John Noble Wilford, "Delay Expected for Spacecraft Going to Saturn."

Attention increased with a *Los Angeles Times* story on problems and protests exasperating NASA scientists and then exploded with another *New York Times* story, 1,461 words published on September 8, on a former Kennedy Space Center emergency preparedness officer's concerns about Cassini. *The Times* story was picked up around the country, and the worried officer's comments found their way into other newspapers' own reports including another one by Cox News Service, "Protesters Ask Clinton to Block Plutonium Powered Spacecraft." The most mainstream of American mainstream papers, *USA Today*, ran its own story on September 9, "Clinton Urged to Block N-Powered Space Mission." *USA Today* later published pro and con arguments on its editorial page. Other reports were carried in St. Louis, Seattle, Pittsburgh, Fort Worth, Des Moines, Dayton,

San Francisco, Buffalo, Boston, Atlanta, Santa Fe, and Denver.

Arguments for and against Cassini were carried via the Internet. On September 5, 1997, *Wired News* reported that two San Francisco Bay Area members of Congress, Democrats Ron Dellums and Lynn Woolsey, asked NASA to delay the launch until alternatives to plutonium could be researched.

Talk radio and network television carried the Cassini story, as did CBS's *60 Minutes*. *60 Minutes* interviewed Karl Grossman, who credited Project Censored for exposure of his stories which led to his national broadcast programs.

Despite much concern and criticism, the space probe was launched successfully without radioactive disaster on October 15, 1997. However, Project Censored's goal—a national dialogue in the media on the merits and demerits of the Cassini program—was reached. Any American who regularly watches television news and reads a daily paper would have been hard pressed not to have seen something about Cassini and the controversy surrounding it. The next test of this mission and the media's role in covering it will be in August 1999, when the spacecraft will make that close (and the critics say dangerous) pass by Earth on its final shot to Saturn.

SOURCES: *San Francisco Examiner,* March 26, 1997; *Rocky Mountain News,* June 1, 1997; *The Palm Beach Post,* June 15, 1997; *The Detroit News,* August 25, 1997; the Minneapolis *Star Tribune,* August 30, 1997; Associated Press, September 1, 1997; *Los Angeles Times,* September 4, 1997; *The New York Times,* September 8, 1997; Cox News Service, September 8, 1997; and *USA Today,* September 9, 1997.

1996 # 2 CENSORED STORY
SHELL'S OIL, AFRICA'S BLOOD

In October 1990, Nigerian military forces fired on protesting villagers when they attempted to gain compensation for damaged farm lands by occupying a Shell facility. Nearly 80 people were killed and 495 homes were devastated. A Nigerian jury later found that the protests were peaceful. As a result, the

THIS MODERN WORLD by TOM TOMORROW

SINCE JOURNALISTS ON SHOWS LIKE *THE McLAUGHLIN GROUP* ARE PRIMARILY INTERESTED IN BECOMING *MARKETABLE COMMODITIES*--

EXIT QUESTION! HOW LOW WILL YOUR LECTURE FEES *PLUMMET* IF I KICK YOU OFF THIS SHOW?

ER--

PLEASE DON'T.

--PERHAPS THEY SHOULD START MERCHANDISING THEMSELVES IN *EARNEST*...WITH A LINE OF *ACTION FIGURES*, FOR INSTANCE...

LOOK OUT! HERE COMES *ELEANOR CLIFT* WITH SPRING-LOADED *CONVENTIONAL WISDOM*!

HAH! JOHN McLAUGHLIN'S *INVECTIVE BOLTS* WILL *CLOBBER* HER!

movement for the Survival of Ogoni People (MOSOP) was founded by writer/activist Ken Saro-Wiwa. However, in 1995, the Nigerian government, using trumped-up charges of murder and despite worldwide protests, executed Ken Saro-Wiwa along with eight other environmental activists.

Ninety percent of Nigerian foreign exports comes from oil, of which 50 percent is imported to America by Shell Oil. Shell has claimed that it is not involved in Nigeria's political affairs. However, journalists and human-rights groups have revealed that Ken Saro-Wiwa's brother, Dr. Owens Wiwa, has given testimony regarding meetings between Brian Anderson, the managing director of Shell Petroleum Development Co., and The Ogoni's People's Movement, in which Shell offered to prevent the executions of Wiwa and the other activists if they would call off their protests. The Ogoni People's Movement refused and the executions proceeded.

There also was supporting evidence that Shell paid Nigerian military officials for action against protesters, and bribed prosecution witnesses to unjustly incriminate Saro-Wiwa in his trial.

SOURCES: Bielski, Vince, "Shell Game," *San Francisco Bay Guardian,* February 7, 1996: 21; Nixon, Ron, and Michael King, "Shell's Oil, Africa's Blood," *Texas Observer,* January 12, 1996; Stein, M.L., "Rejected Ad Flap," *Editor & Publisher,* March 23, 1996; Sachs, Aaron, "Dying for Oil," *World Watch,* May/June 1996: 10-21; Bright, Chris, "Eco-Justice in Nigeria," July/August 1996: 9; and Durbin, Andrea, "IFC Pulls Out of Shell Deal," *Bank Check,* February 1996.

COVERAGE 1997: Given the minuscule amount of coverage the story received in 1997, the U.S. press does not appear to have kept pace with the continuing tribulation over the politics of oil as 19 more Nigerian environmentalists have been arrested and remain jailed on the same murder charges that took Saro-Wiwa and his supporters to the gallows. Yet, in the British press, the *Financial Times, The Times, The Guardian,* and *The Daily Telegraph* dominate a list of 72 stories located in a computer search using

key words "Shell Oil" and "Nigeria."

Shell Oil felt the pressure, however, from the attention that began to pile up shortly before the New Year. *The Wall Street Journal* reported on November 11, 1996 on a federal lawsuit filed in New York by the survivors of Saro-Wiwa and one other executed activist. The suit accused Shell of conspiracy in the hangings. On December 17, 1996, *The Village Voice* reported that Shell had admitted its representatives paid the Nigerian military to police the Ogoni's People's Movement and that environmental problems did exist as a result of their oil operations. In its December 20 edition, *The Texas Observer* described the unsuccessful efforts to impose an embargo on Nigerian oil exports.

The New Year brought condemnations from the World Council of Churches which, meeting in Geneva in January, accused Nigeria of oppression and Shell of causing environmental devastation to the country. The story was carried by the *Washington Post, Chicago Tribune*, and *Journal of Commerce* in the U.S., and the *Financial Times* and *The Guardian* in Britain.

In These Times, in its February 3, 1997 issue, published "Hired Guns," an extensive report warning that the Nigerian military was preparing for "another campaign on behalf of its patron, Shell Oil."

The *Washington Post* ran two stories in March on a clash between Shell Oil workers and protesters. *The Wall Street Journal* on March 28 reported the protests but only in one paragraph and in

terms of its impact on oil exports. *The Journal* did, however, publish a 560-word story on April 7 that explored the apprehension oil officials were feeling in the wake of the successful occupation of Shell's facilities by demonstrators. The tone of the story reflected *The Journal's* primary interest in financial implications. On May 9, *The Journal* reported on crude oil and unleaded gasoline futures based on concerns over refinery closures and strikes in Nigeria.

On May 10, *The New York Times* published a 787-word story covering the Nigerian military dictator's plan to legitimize his reign by running for president. The story made only a brief mention of the Shell Oil issue. *The Atlanta Constitution* on May 17 reported on a delegation of Nigerians making a tour of five U.S. cities to dispel, they said, the belief that Saro-Wiwa was a hero. The group contended Saro-Wiwa was indeed guilty of murder for inciting rioters to kill.

Writer Nadine Gordimer, winner of the Nobel Prize for Literature in 1991, wrote a major piece on Nigeria for *The New York Times* on May 25 entitled "In Nigeria, the Price for Oil is Blood." Gordimer's report outlined the risks Nigerians face if they run afoul of the government's oil policies. The report said that Nigeria's ruling General Sani Abacha "has responded to strikes by oil workers and demands for increased revenue-sharing by local communities by declaring the death penalty on anyone who interferes with the government's efforts to revitalize the oil industry." Similarly, the government has tried to silence the media on the oil issue: "Many journalists have been detained; some have disappeared—dead or alive."

May also saw reports by *The San Francisco Chronicle* and *The Boston Globe* on protests in those two cities against Shell's Nigerian operations. *The Christian Science Monitor* in early July reported on reports of sabotage of oil pipelines by poor Nigerians as a job-creating measure. Also in July, *The Wall Street Journal, San Francisco Chronicle*, and *Journal of Commerce* reported on the growing number of municipalities in the U.S. boycotting Shell products, as well as President Clinton's decision to review American foreign policy regarding Nigeria. The *Journal of Commerce* reported on July 21 that the U.S. Conference of Mayors had passed resolutions calling for Nigeria's government to release political prisoners, including environmental protesters.

Express, a San Francisco Bay Area weekly, ran an extensive story in July 11 on "Heart of Darkness: Adventures of an Eco-warrior." The story features Steve Kretzmann, a leader in the campaign against Shell's policies, who went to Nigeria in the spring to meet with environmental dissidents.

Project Censored's researchers could find little additional coverage of this issue covered by mainstream media. Shell Oil, in mid-year, made overtures to reconcile with Nigerian environmentalists. But reports of those efforts by a wide-ranging group of new sources, including the Inter Press Service, *Journal of Commerce*, *American Political Network's Greenwire*, the *Financial Times*, and the African News Service, were apparently overlooked or ignored by the U.S. media.

Meanwhile, there was little coverage of Shell's program for oil exploration in the Amazon forests of Peru, and no word on the 19 Nigerian environmentalists who remain in custody and under a threat of death for crimes for which the government hanged Ken Saro-Wiwa and his supporters in November 1995.

SOURCES: *The Wall Street Journal*, November 11, 1996, March 28, April 7, and May 9, 1997; *The Village Voice*, December 17, 1996; *The Texas Observer*, December 20, 1996; *In These Times*, February 3, 1997; *Washington Post*, March 28, 1997; *The New York Times*, May 15 and May 25, 1997; *The Christian Science Monitor* July 10, 1997; and *Journal of Commerce* July 21, 1997.

1996 # 3 CENSORED STORY
BIG PERKS FOR THE WEALTHY HIDDEN IN MINIMUM WAGE BILL

The minimum wage bill was supposed to help lower income families deal with the increased cost of living. Congress, however, inserted big breaks in the bill for some of the most powerful lobbies in Washington. For example, American multinational corporations no longer have to pay taxes on foreign income and no longer have to invest foreign profits in factories overseas.

Insurance companies also benefit from the bill. It allows them to invest pension funds in high-stake ventures and then claim higher fees for themselves by effectively reversing the Employee Retirement Income Security Act (ERISA) of 1974. Insurance companies can now use and abuse worker retirement funds for their own interests.

The minimum wage bill also changed the law that forbade multi-tiered health benefit plans, so now companies can offer lower quality health packages to new employees or lower-paid workers and give deluxe health-care packages to executives.

Also, managers that engage in risky leveraged buyouts can do so exclusively for themselves and their investment advisors. In the past, the only employee buyouts that were rewarded were of companies that otherwise would have closed. Now managers receive half interest payments on loans for all employee buyouts. This essentially encourages managers to act in their own interests and not the interests of their employees.

SOURCES: Judis, John, "Bare Minimum: Goodies for the Rich Hidden in Wage Bill," *The New Republic*, October 28, 1996, (reprinted in *The Press Democrat*, Santa Rosa, CA, and *The Commercial Appeal*, Memphis, TN, October 13, 1996).

COVERAGE 1997: Although the minimum wage bill was supposed to have widespread positive effects on the economy, the mainstream press has given the issue scant attention. Only *The Buffalo News* made reference to the issue, quoting Representative Jack F. Quinn: "The preliminary effects (of the bill) are all very positive." This comment, however, goes unsubstantiated, as no figures, stud-

ies, or other documentation were cited to support the assertion. *The Buffalo News* also quoted Senator Edward Kennedy as saying that the bill provided "plums for the rich and crumbs for everyone else."

Nationally, the press completely ignored the shady, underhanded aspects of the bill, including the provision that gives tax incentives for leveraged buyouts (LBOs). The provision gushes tax incentives to multinational corporations, and is the same piece that weakens pension protections and health care benefits for workers. Despite this glaring deficiency of coverage, two lesser-known aspects of the bill did receive attention. One is the provision that created tax breaks on college savings plans. Currently, about 12 states offer some kind of investment program to help parents meet college tuition expenses. Often called "prepaid-tuition" programs, or savings plans that are similar to individual retirement accounts, the plans generally allow parents (depending on the program) to either pay tuition early for lower rates, or accumulate enough savings to cover tuition by the time the child enters college. One drawback to the latter program, however, is that funds earned in the program are subject to taxation. Under the new law, however, college savings plans will not be taxed until the funds are withdrawn to pay tuition. This translates into a smaller burden on parents trying to save for college expenses.

Another aspect of the bill covered in the mainstream press had to do with the Savings Incentive Match Plan for

Employees, a retirement-savings method for small businesses.

SOURCES: *The Buffalo News*, July 23, 1997; *The Wall Street Journal*, October 28, 1996; and *The Wall Street Journal*, November 11, 1996.

1996 # 4 CENSORED STORY
DEFORMING CONSENT: THE PR INDUSTRY'S SECRET WAR ON ACTIVISTS

The public relations industry, using the enormous financial resources of their corporate clients, creates false non-profit agencies as fronts which target activists and lobby against legislation threatening big business. Most of these organizations are aimed at environmental, consumer, and labor issues. "Astroturf lobbying" as Lloyd Bentsen named it, utilizes private detectives, lawyers, and undercover spies, influences editorial and news decisions, launches phony "grass-roots" campaigns, and uses high-tech information systems to influence and manipulate public opinion and policy.

In one instance, the Health Insurance Association of America created the Coalition for Health Insurance Choices in an attempt to create opposition to Clinton's attempt at health care reform.

Astroturf lobbying allows big businesses to create a false impression of activism while actually promoting the interests of the companies. With multimillion dollar budgets, the power of large corporations sadly outweighs that of many citizen reformers.

SOURCES: "The Public Relations Industry's Secret War on Activists," *Covert Action Quarterly*, Winter 1995/1996: 18, and "Public Relations, Private Interests," *Earth Island Journal*, Winter 1995-96: 27-29, both by John Stauber and Sheldon Rampton.

COVERAGE 1997: While the mainstream media has virtually ignored the issue, the alternative/independent publication *Extra* reported on one of the most high-profile deceptive PR campaigns in recent history. The case involves Contributions West, a phony watchdog group established by Philip Morris's PR firm. The cigarette maker's objective was to plant "manufactured" stories in newspapers, hoping not only to shape public opinion, but also to advance an important objective: the reform of product-liability laws. This is especially important for Philip Morris since cigarettes have been proven to be unhealthy, and current product-liability laws make it easy to sue for damages caused by unsafe products.

Operating under the guise of Contributions Watch, Philip Morris's strategy was fairly simple: spoon-feed stories to newspapers deemed friendly to their interests and deflect questions from reporters who ask real questions. It proved to be an effective strategy. *Extra* reported Philip Morris managed to get several articles published in major newspapers around the country.

Philip Morris is not alone in its manipulation of the media. *Extra* reports that a good percentage of what appears in newspapers is actually placed by public relations firms: "A 1991 survey by Jericho Promotions, a New York-based PR firm, claimed that 38 percent of 2,432 journalists surveyed said they got half of their stories from public relations flacks, and an additional 17 percent said they used PR people for every story."

Meanwhile, *E Magazine* reports that some industries, especially big polluters, continue to use "greenwashed" advertisements. Examples of "greenwashed" advertisements include "sea lions applaud(ing) a passing oil tanker with their flippers," "a young girl talk(ing) about her dad's tree planting for a timber company," and "an animated dove (flitting) from smokestack to smokestack as a voice-over speaks about chemical companies cleaning up their acts." These ads were part of a $1 billion campaign to create the perception that industry is genuinely concerned with the environment. Similar types of campaigns have been used for years, especially as the American public has become more environmentally conscious.

SOURCES: Helvarg, David, "Perception is Reality," *E Magazine*, November/December 1996; Silverstein, Ken, "Manufactured News," *Extra*, November 25, 1996; and Stauber, John, and Sheldon Rampton, "A Wolf in Sheep's Clothing," *Extra*, January/February 1997.

1996 # 5 CENSORED STORY

WHITE-COLLAR CRIME: WHITEWASH AT THE JUSTICE DEPARTMENT

Centralized records from the Department of Justice (DOJ) show that white-collar crime is hardly ever brought to court. Out of 51,000 federal criminal indictments in 1994, only 250 involved criminal violations of the nation's environmental, occupational health and safety, and consumer product safety laws. Nonetheless, business organizations such as the U.S. Chamber of Commerce and the National Association of Manufacturers fight to lift regulations concerning environmental, health, and safety issues, maintaining that the federal government restricts businesses

THIS MODERN WORLD   by TOM. TOMORROW

with unnecessary regulations. Despite the fact that white-collar crime costs America 10 to 50 times more money than street crime, the Justice Department continues to show little interest in taking the problem seriously.

The impact of the Occupational Safety and Health Act (OSHA) in 1970 was greatly reduced by a number of insertions that underfunded the program and made it hard to enforce regulations. In 1987, 50,000 to 70,000 workers died on the job from exposure to toxins—nearly three times the 21,500 people that were murdered in the same year. Even in cases where corporate executives have knowingly exposed workers to hazardous conditions that resulted in death, the cases seldom get to court.

SOURCE: Burnham, David, "White-Collar Crime: Whitewash at the Justice Department," *CovertAction Quarterly*, Summer 1996: 24-26.

COVERAGE 1997: Although corporate crime is a common problem in the U.S., news about it remained scarce in 1997. *The Wall Street Journal* was one of the few mainstream newspapers to run stories about corporate crime during this period. *The Nation* pulled several stories from *The Journal* to create an article titled "A Year in Corporate Crime." Among the stories reported by *The Nation*:

➤ Archer Daniels Midland Company (ADM): This company, the world's largest grain producer, was caught by a Justice Department sting operation in 1996. The company pleaded guilty to fixing prices on two products: Lysine, a feed supplement for livestock, and citric acid, which is used in soft drinks and detergents. Although the Justice Department fined the company $100 million, it proved to be a bargain. After all, the company cheated its lysine customers alone out of more than $170 million and had revenues of $13.6 billion for its last fiscal year. The fine was a pittance—not an uncommon punishment for corporate crime.

➤ Insurance Company Fraud: Prudential was fined $35 million and is currently paying more than $1 billion in restitution to policy holders. The company was caught by insurance regulators for using

a deceptive sales practice called "churning," which diverted as many as 10 million people into policies they couldn't afford, thus giving them no coverage.

➤ Allegations of Money Laundering: The Justice Department conducted an investigation to determine if Citibank had helped Raul Salinas, brother of Mexico's former president, Carlos Salinas, launder more than $100 million by transferring it to bank accounts abroad. In addition, some question how Salinas cycled $100 million through the bank, but never earned more than $190,000 per year.

➤ Cheating Defense Contractors: Companies that supply the government with defense weapons, tools, and machinery have been caught for selling defective products. One of the most recent cases involves United Telecontrol Electronics, which knowingly sold the government defective bolts used to hold missile launchers in place on military planes. In another case, Lucas Industries pleaded guilty to falsifying quality control records of its gearboxes, which are used in Navy F-18 fighters; the gearboxes were later found to be defective. The Navy blames the defective gearboxes for 71 emergency landings, several in-flight fires, and an F-18 crash during the Gulf War.

➤ Workplace Crime: According to *The Wall Street Journal*, failure to pay for overtime work is a common problem: "Violations are so common that the Employer Policy Foundation, an employer-supported think tank in Washington, estimates that workers would get an additional $19 billion a year if the rules were observed."

➤ Discrimination (age, race, sex): Texaco, Astra USA, WMX Technologies, Monsanto, and Mitsubishi Motors were among some companies recently charged with discrimination cases.

➤ Unenforced Antitrust Laws: "When is a crime not officially a crime? Simple: When the laws against that activity are not enforced," according to *The Nation*. Increasingly, mega-mergers in the telecommunications business and aerospace industry are proving this to be the case. Moreover, according to *The Wall Street Journal*, the outlook for mergers is "as good as it gets" because "looser regulation is changing the competitive landscapes in telecommunications, utilities, and broadcast, among other industries."

SOURCE: Sherrill, Robert, "1997: A Year in Corporate Crime," *The Nation*, April 7, 1997.

1996 # 6 CENSORED STORY
NEW MEGA-MERGED BANKING BEHEMOTHS = BIG RISK

The massive mergers of banks has resulted in 71.5 percent of the U.S. banking assets belonging to less than one percent of the total banks in the nation. The Federal Reserve, under the Bank Merger and Bank Holdings Company Act, is supposed to consider whether the needs of the public are being met when considering the application of a merger. Critics charge that the Federal Reserve is not sufficiently observing this regulation, and is doing a disservice to the American public.

Analysts are concerned that the growth and monopolization of the banking industry will result in a number of "consumer inconveniences."

Banks in controlled markets tend to charge higher interest rates for loans while paying lower interest rates on deposits. In 1995, fees on checking and savings accounts increased at twice the rate of inflation from 1993 to 1995 as the bank merger trend appeared.

Also, having the majority of the nation's bank assets in just a few companies increases the amount of money that taxpayers would have to pay in case of a bank failure. The Federal Reserve caps the amount that financial institutions have to cover with insurance at only $25 billion. As a results only 1.25 percent of all deposits in the United States are actually insured against loss.

SOURCE: Lewis, Jake, "The Making of the Banking Behemoths," *Multinational Monitor*, June 1996.

COVERAGE 1997: Although banks continued to merge in 1997, the mainstream media failed to explain the larger significance of this topic. Instead, most of the articles explored the mergers at a shallow angle: explaining the issue with numbers, quotes from bank analysts, quotes from bank representatives, and from state bank officials.

For example, in explaining the Wells Fargo-First Interstate merger, the Minneapolis *Star Tribune*, on July 16, 1997, reported: "Between June 30, 1996 and June 30, 1997, Wells lost about $9.2 billion in deposits, and the bank has nearly $1.2 billion in deposits slated for divestiture."

The *Star Tribune* also reported that earnings per share would be about 30 percent lower than in the first quarter. "This is the nail in the coffin for calling First Interstate a bad integration," said Thomas K. Brown, analyst with Donaldson, Lufkin & Jenrette. "As opposed to costs of doing the integration, this reflects the cost of doing it poorly."

Absent from the reporting, however, were personal horror stories—like long lines, poor service, processing errors, lost deposits, computer breakdowns, and other problems associated with bank mergers. Some references were made to such problems, but no in-depth coverage was printed.

One recent merger getting attention is that of Minneapolis-based First Bank System with Portland, Oregon-based U.S. Bankcorp. The Federal Reserve Board of Governors happily approved the deal in just one day, adding another merger to a list of 1,500 since 1993. One customer, upset by the merger wrote, in a letter to bank regulators, "My concern is that these takeovers appear to be mainly for the benefit of the bank hierarchies and the stockholders, and the customers be damned."

Indeed, the problems associated with bank mergers can mean a disruption of service for customers. Despite this, First Bank says it intends to minimize these disruptions. The *Star Tribune* reported, "First Bank is expected to act decidedly unlike Wells Fargo, which sold 200 branches and pushed customers toward

ATM machines after acquiring First Interstate..." Time will tell whether this holds true.

While individual bank mergers received coverage, what's missing from press coverage are larger, more in-depth articles about what the mergers mean. What isn't being discussed, for example, is how the mergers are resulting in higher service fees, fewer branches, an enormous concentration of political and economic power, and banks that are so huge they become almost impossible to regulate. Also absent from the mainstream news is how these mega-banks will eliminate jobs, make it harder for small borrowers to get loans, and how, if one of these behemoths were to fail, taxpayers would be forced to pay for a bailout, similar what happened in the savings and loan mess of the 1980s.

SOURCE: Minneapolis *Star Tribune*, July 16, 1997.

1996 # 7 CENSORED STORY
CASHING IN ON POVERTY

In the United States, 60 million people without bank accounts or access to competitive-rate loans rely on second-rate financial institutions such as pawn shops and high-interest mortgage lenders. Because of these businesses, people living in poverty end up paying more interest on loans and credit cards than middle-class citizens. While more affluent credit-card holders pay as little as six to eight percent annual interest, lower income holders pay as much as 240 percent from a pawn broker, or even an astronomical 2,000 percent for fast "payday" loans from check-cashing outlets.

Interestingly, many of these second-rate financial service chains are owned or subsidized by large companies such as American Express, Bank America, Citibank, Ford, Nations Bank, and Western Union. Such business chains can generate yearly revenues of $200 to $300 billion. Ford, for instance, gets three-fifths of its earnings from car-loans, mortgages, and consumer loans, and subsidizes Associate Corporations of North America (ACNA). ACNA targets low-income, blue-collar, and minority consumers, charging as much as 300 percent for used-car loans in some states.

Many low-income consumers are also victimized by hidden fees, forged loan documents, and harassing collection tactics.

SOURCES: "Cashing in on Poverty," *The Nation*, May 20, 1996: 11-14; and "Bordering on Scandal: What Some Pay for Credit," *The Houston Chronicle*, July 15, 1996: 17, both by Michael Hudson.*

*Both sources are excerpts from *Merchants of Misery: How Corporate America Profits From Poverty*, Hudson, Michael, ed., Common Courage Press, 1995.

COVERAGE 1997: *Censored* story # 7 for 1996 was closely related to another *Censored* story in 1993 entitled, "There's a Lot of Money to be made in Poverty," from *Censored 1994*. Bill Brenner with the Atlanta Legal Aid Society told Project Censored that ABC's *Primetime*

Live got their idea for a 1997 special on Ford Motor Company's exploitation of low-income borrowers from our 1994 story. An April 23 *Primetime Live* special exposed Ford on national television for its practices of soaking low-income people with high-pressure sales tactics and exorbitant interest rates. However, few other major media outlets have followed up on this issue.

The Knight-Ridder News Service released a story on August 22 by Toyna Jameson that specifically addressed the issue of check-cashing services charging high rates for their services. Citing The Consumer Federation of America, the article was similar in content to Hudson's work and represented some media coverage on this important story. *The Denver Post* was one major paper to pick up the Knight-Ridder article.

Several factors contribute to the growth of financial services that cater to low-income Americans such as check-cashing services, credit services and other banking alternatives. Corporate downsizing and increased cost of living create a large market of low-income Americans who have restricted access to banking services. Because of the recent trend in bank mergers, the market is controlled by an elite few. Banking services have risen in cost in recent years and local branches have closed, driving more poor people away from regular banks and forcing them into "fringe banking."

SOURCE: Knight-Ridder News Service, August 22, 1997.

1996 # 8 CENSORED STORY
BIG BROTHER GOES HIGH-TECH

Governments and corporations are now discovering new surveillance, identification, and networking technologies. These new technologies allow regular surveillance of large segments of the population without the need of warrants and court orders. In Great Britain, nearly all public areas are monitored by over 150,000 closed circuit television cameras. Resistance to "Big Brother" type surveillance has been strong in the United States as rights to privacy and freedom from unreasonable search are part of our national culture. Privacy rights, however, have been rapidly changing with new technologies.

The city of Baltimore is planning to install 200 cameras in the city center. The cameras are on a closed circuit and can be controlled remotely to zoom, pan, tilt, and focus. These cameras are easily installed anywhere.

A new type of camera known as the passive millimeter wave imager can see through walls and clothing to detect concealed weapons, plastic explosives, or drugs. Controversy as to whether the right to be secure against unreasonable search and seizure, guaranteed by the Fourth Amendment, would be violated by the use of such equipment has resulted.

Another emerging technology, Intelligent Transportation Systems (ITS), tracks the movement of all people using private or public transportation. These systems create records of drivers including the name, address locations, and times where tolls were charged, and are linked to an ordinary bank account. Nine states in the U.S. already use such systems and 12 more states plan to implement such systems.

SOURCES: Banisar, David, "Big Brother Goes High-Tech," *CovertAction Quarterly,* Spring 1996: 6; Rust, Michael, and Susan Crabtree, "Access, Privacy and Power," *Insight,* August 1, 1996; and Price, Joyce, "New Surveillance Camera Cheers Police, Worries ACLU,"* *Insight,* September 9, 1996.

*Reprint from *Washington Times.*

COVERAGE 1997: The mainstream press in 1997 has tended to applaud the use and expansion of high-tech surveillance equipment for citizen monitoring. In April, the *Press Democrat* (Santa Rosa, CA) reprinted a *New York Times* story entitled "New Gun Detectors Excite Law Agencies." The story describes electromagnetic devices capable detecting weapons 60 feet away, and x-ray imaging devices that show everything the person is carrying.

Last February, the city of Baltimore installed 200 cameras on downtown streets. The cameras operate 24 hours a day and are monitored from a central kiosk. Sixty-five other cities including New Orleans, Cincinnati, Honolulu, and Portland, are now interested in setting up their own camera systems.

Another system of surveillance that has been developed is the Urban Gunfire Location System, already utilized by Redwood City, California. The system consists of 20 high-tech microphones mounted on street lights. The system is capable of instantly pinpointing gunfire to within 20 feet. A more advanced system is being developed that automatically provides a mug-shot of the person discharging the firearm.

In Pasadena, California, police use infrared tracking systems originally developed for use by military helicopters. The device, called CAATS (Compact Airborne Tracking System) is a helicopter mounted, heat-reading camera capable of detecting fresh footprints, tire treads of fleeing vehicles, and can also see through walls to observe body movement or detect the hot lamps of indoor marijuana gardens. Over the last year, nearly a dozen other police departments have started using infrared technology. Phoenix, Boston, and New York use a similar technology—infrared goggles that are used by officers on the ground.

Independent/alternative news sources are the primary media questioning the trend toward surveillance in U.S. society. ACLU representative John Crew told *The Bay Guardian* in San Francisco that, "generally speaking, the more invasions of our privacy society accepts the more will follow...it is creeping Big Brotherism."

So far, there have been few legal cases that question the constitutionality of the new high-tech surveillance systems. A case last October in the 10th Circuit Court of Appeals in Denver ruled that the use of infrared technology to search homes for indoor marijuana cultivation without first obtaining a warrant was a violation of police procedure. Other courts, however, have ruled that similar cases are completely constitutional. It is expected that such cases will eventually be taken to the Supreme Court.

Critics fear that the use of high-tech equipment by police forces will encourage military style behavior that will harden police culture. "This new technology serves to entrench a hierarchical, crisis-response, impersonal, military model of policing which is very dangerous and not effective in reducing crime," charges criminologist Tony Platt. "The hardware fetish flies right in the face of the traditional model of police as public servants," Platt goes on. "It's been shown time and again that the sort of policing that does work is labor intensive, involves a lot of communication and mutual respect among cops and community." The question remains as to whether the use of high-tech equipment is the type of policing that is appropriate for a democratic society.

SOURCES: *San Francisco Bay Guardian*, April 9, 1997; *Press Democrat* (Santa Rosa, CA), April 7, 1997; *The Nation*, February 3, 1997; and *Reason*, May 1997.

1996 # 9 CENSORED STORY
U.S. TROOPS EXPOSED TO DEPLETED URANIUM DURING GULF WAR

The Persian Gulf War in 1991 was the first time that the United States used depleted uranium (DU) in a war situation. Weapons that use DU, though highly effective, are extremely toxic and require special protective gear to handle.

Even though training manuals were made in the 1980s to inform soldiers of the dangers of DU weapons, it wasn't until eight days *after* the war had ended that soldiers were warned of these dangers by the United States government. Without the use of protective clothing, the 144th Army National Guard Service and Supply Company performed DU battlefield cleanup for three weeks in Kuwait and southern Iraq, where at least 14,000 rounds (40 tons) of DU ammunition had been used.

DU has been linked to many illnesses, including the "Gulf War Syndrome." Despite protests from public activists, the United States government and defense contractors are selling DU weapons to allies worldwide.

Through the use of DU weapons, the U.S. government has the option of using toxic waste material in weapons instead of disposing of it properly. The department of energy has collected 500,000 tons of DU since the Manhattan Project and has spent billions of dollars trying to come up with a suitable site for its disposal. Such disposal projects come into fierce opposition from local communities.

SOURCES: Solnit, Rebecca, ed., "Radioactive Battlefields of the 1990s: A Response to the Army's Unreleased Report on Depleted Uranium Weaponry," *Military Toxics Project's Depleted Uranium Citizens' Network*, January 16, 1996; Cohen, Gary, "Radioactive Ammo Lays Them to Waste," *Multinational*

Monitor, January/February 1996: 10-14; Triplett, Bill, "Depleted Uranium: One Man's Weapon, Another Man's Poison," *The VVA Veteran*, March 1996: 13-16; and Casa, Kathryn, "Depleted Uranium, First Used in Iraq, Deployed in Bosnia," *National Catholic Reporter*, January 19, 1996: 3.

COVERAGE 1997: Hard work by the Depleted Uranium Education Project in New York and numerous other organizations along with Project Censored's coverage of the DU story in 1997, assisted in prompting some mainstream coverage on this issue. The *San Francisco Examiner* published a front page story on August 17, 1997 with the headline, "New Link to Gulf War Ills: Bullets of Uranium." *The Hartford Courant*, published a similar news story entitled, "Uranium Shells in Gulf Sickened Many Soldiers, Experts Say." *The Nation* published a full report on DU on October 21, 1996 (missing the Project Censored deadline for awards in 1996 by one week), reporting that hundreds and perhaps thousands of GIs were exposed to these tank shells. Noticeably absent from coverage in 1997 are DU stories from most of the mainstream media.

Until recently, news about DU ammunition was kept secret. Although some soldiers suspected the tank shells of being radioactive, most dismissed the idea as unfounded rumor. Combat engineer Dwayne Mowrer, who began suffering fatigue, memory loss, bloody noses, diarrhea, bloody stools, bleeding gums, rashes, and problems with motor coordination after exposure to DU shells, summarized the general opinion at the time: "We really thought we were in the new 'enlightened Army.' We thought all that Agent Orange stuff and human radiation experiments were a thing of the past." Like most soldiers, Mowrer was unaware that radioactive shells were even being used. Because of this, Mowrer and others "didn't worry when a forty-ton HEMTT transport vehicle packed with DU rounds exploded near their camp." Soldiers also didn't realize the dangers, for example, of climbing on newly destroyed Iraqi vehicles and tanks, such as those found on the fairly infamous "highway of death." Many of these vehicles, hit by DU shells, were contaminated with radiation.

SOURCES: *The Nation*, October 21, 1996; *San Francisco Examiner*, August 17, 1997; and *The Hartford Courant*, August 14, 1997.

ALSO AVAILABLE: *Metal of Dishonor Depleted Uranium: How The Pentagon Radiates soldiers and Civilians with DU Weapons*, International Action Center, Tel: 212/663-6646.

1996 # 10 CENSORED STORY
FACING FOOD SCARCITY

Because of the increasing growth of the world population and the loss of agricultural land to suburbs and housing, the world food supply is becoming insufficient to feed the world population. Studies by the Japanese Ministry of Agriculture project that world grain prices will double by the year 2010 and the world prices for wheat and rice will exceed twice that of the base year of 1992. Conversely, the economists that project supply and demand of grain for the World Bank predict that grain prices will continue to fall throughout the next few decades. The Japanese studies are based on past experience in finite environments, whereas the reports by the World Bank are not.

As the demand for grain increases, poor countries, which have the highest population growth rates, will become increasingly responsible for feeding their own population without the aid of wealthier nations.

Because of the World Bank reports, the problem of food scarcity is not being addressed. The reports generate a false impression of security, making it difficult to gain support for agricultural and population control movements.

SOURCES: "Facing Food Scarcity," *World Watch,* May/June 1996, and "Japanese Government Breaks With World Bank Food Forecast," *World Watch,* May/June 1996, both by Lester R. Brown.

COVERAGE 1997: In 1997 the mainstream U.S. media ignored the report from the Japanese Ministry of Agriculture that predicted a doubling of world prices for grains by the year 2010. However, several serious articles on projected world food shortages were well in evidence in alternative publications.

Alison Maitland of the *Financial Times* wrote a lengthy article in October 1996 entitled "Will There Be Food Enough?" that was reprinted in several ` newspapers including the *San Francisco*

Chronicle. Maitland cited U.N. figures reporting that over 11 million children under five years of age die each year of hunger and malnutrition, and that this will probably only get worse in the future.

Wendy Koch of the *Hearst Papers* (March 1997) cited meat consumption as the main reason for continued hunger in the world. She quoted the Washington-based Population Reference Bureau and the World Watch Institute stating, "...if everyone adopted a vegetarian diet and no food were wasted, current (food) production would theoretically feed 10 billion people, more than the projected population for the year 2050." Current world population is approximately 5.8 billion.

A Johns Hopkins University study released in December 1997 predicted that there will not be enough land to grow food for world population by the year 2025. The study stated that 100 million women wanted better access to contraceptives, but that birth control was often unavailable or too expensive for Third World women.

Generally speaking, the U.S. mainstream media has discussed the issue of world food shortages often in connection with the "population problem" or cultural practices that blame the malnourished for their own circumstances. However, there seems to be a reluctance by the press to critically address U.S. policies and practices that are contributing factors.

SOURCES: *San Francisco Examiner*, October 27, 1996; and *The Press Democrat* (Santa Rosa, CA), March 18, and December 11, 1997.

Other Project Censored Stories In the News In 1997

1996 # 12 CENSORED STORY
MILKING THE PUBLIC

New research suggests that our milk supply may be increasingly unsafe. With the increased use of bovine growth hormones such as rGBH and antibiotics in milk-producing cows comes an increase in the levels of the naturally occurring growth hormone regulator known as "insulin-like growth factor-I" (IGF-I). IGF-I has been linked to major health problems. Drinking milk with high levels of IGF-I may lead to an increase in breast or colon cancer.

The growth hormone regulator IGF-I is present in both cows and humans. IGF-I controls milk production and growth, but the Consumer Policy Institute's Jean Halloran asserts that it is also known to be a "tumor growth promoter." This means that while IGF-I helps us to grow, it also accelerates the multiplication of cancer cells. Studies done on rGBH-injected cows show that IGF-I levels are increased anywhere from 25 to 700 percent.

Dr. Samuel S. Epstein, professor of occupational and environmental medicine at the University of Illinois School of Public Health and chairman of the Cancer Prevention Coalition states that "IGF-I is a growth factor for human breast cancer cells, maintaining their malignancy, progression, and invasiveness. IGF-I has been similarly associated with colon cancer."

In short, Dr. Epstein charges that the FDA has, "allowed for uncontrolled, unlabeled sales of treated milk to unwitting customers," and believes that the FDA should revoke its restrictions on the labeling of milk and consider banning the use of the hormones.

SOURCE: Varner, Hilary, "Milking the Public," *Chicago Life Magazine,* October 1995.

COVERAGE 1997: Because of its questionable safety, the recombinant bovine growth hormone, or rBGH, controversy has received a lot of media attention in 1997.

Among the biggest rBGH stories making news was a lawsuit filed by Monsanto, the maker of rBGH, against Pure Dairy of Waco, Texas. The suit was filed after Pure Dairy labeled its milk as coming from non-injected cows, a move that Monsanto believed would jeopardize its business and imply that milk from treated cows was unsafe. In the end, most of the case was thrown out and Pure Dairy was allowed to continue its labeling practices.

Another case of litigation concerning rBGH is Ben & Jerry's. The company, opposed to the use of rBGH, wanted to label its products "rBGH-free," but Illinois, Nevada, Hawaii, and Oklahoma have laws forbidding this practice. After spending $250,000 in legal fees, the company reached a settlement with Illinois, resulting in a compromise label: "We Oppose Recombinant Bovine Growth Hormone." Because of the settlement, which was reached in August 1997, it's expected that the company will be allowed to use the label nationwide. Among those carrying this story were *USA Today*, *Washington Post*, *The Houston Chronicle*, and the *Chicago Tribune*.

Despite their coverage, the mainstream media remained silent on the issue of the safety of this hormone. Only *In These Times* and *Natural Health* ran stories on this topic. *In These Times* reminded readers that rBGH "is known to cause udder infections in cows, and evidence exists showing a possible link between rBGH and cancer in humans." Meanwhile, *Natural Health* reminded people that milk drinkers should be concerned about the hormone.

On a more encouraging note, the mainstream media ran a story concerning the public's opposition to allowing rBGH-milk to be served to school children. Appearing in the New York *Daily News*, the story reported that rBGH-milk would not be banned from schools. School officials argued that there is no way to test for the presence of rBGH in milk, thus making a ban on the milk unenforceable.

Whatever the story, the coverage by the mainstream press seemed to have a common characteristic: the rBGH issue got air time only if it had a local tie-in. Meanwhile, the larger and more important issue of public health was ignored, replaced by local rBGH stories that didn't

begin to explain the more complex reasons of why it exists, or the potentially deadly consequences rBGH-produced milk may present.

SOURCES: "The Devastation Caused By Corporate Lawyers," *Washington Afro-American*, January 4, 1997; "Sour Milk," *In These Times*, May 26, 1997; "Which Peach Should You Pick," *Natural Health*, May 15, 1997; *The Houston Chronicle*, August 15, 1997; *Washington Post*, August 15, 1997; *USA Today*, August 14, 1997; *Chicago Tribune*, August 14, 1997; and New York *Daily News*, April 17, 1997.

1996 # 19 CENSORED STORY
CORPORATE AMERICA SPENDS BIG $$ ON PRO-CHINA PR

In its annual battle to preserve "most favored nation" (MFN) trade status, the Chinese government received a big boost from a powerful dose of U.S. corporate money—funneled through the public relations firm of Hill & Knowlton. The PR firm's lobbying effort, dubbed the "China Normalization Initiative," was paid for by such Fortune 500 companies as Boeing, AT&T, General Motors, Allied Signal, General Electric, and the Ford Motor Company.

American companies involved in the pro-China PR blitz spent over $1 million on the campaign, which was supposed to convince the public that the Chinese leadership is deserving of greater sympathy. Critics argue that 11,000 Chinese were executed last year by their government—some for minor crimes—and that an even greater number of abuses go unreported. The wretched conditions of Shanghai's orphanages are also an ongoing human rights violation that is largely absent from the annual debate over the renewal of China's MFN status.

Among their many activities, Hill & Knowlton was instrumental in networking corporate representatives with members of Congress. Hill & Knowlton also hired scholars to draft op-ed articles for major newspapers and to speak at media events. These "third party" advocates, as they are dubbed by industry, are well paid for their labors but seldom reveal their affiliations to the public.

Hill & Knowlton's PR blitz clearly demonstrates how corporate America, aided by the U.S. government, distorts the image of a foreign government whose value as a trading partner conflicts with its disregard for international standards of conduct.

SOURCES: "The New China Lobby," *CounterPunch*, April 1-14, 1996, and "China's Hired Guns," *Multinational Monitor*, April 1996, both by Ken Silverstein.

COVERAGE 1997: Exposing the China-Democratic Central Committee financial connection has been a substantial event in 1997 that overlapped with the # 19 *Censored* story for 1996.

Coverage of U.S corporate interests in China and the privately funded corporate lobby effort to maintain the most favored nation trade status designation was widely covered in 1997. The *News Tri-bune* headline, "Boeing Co. a Big Player in Corporate China Lobby," was a typical lead. Other media covering this issue included the Minneapolis *Star Tribune*, *The Chattanooga Times*, *The American Prospect*, *Los Angeles Times*, *San Francisco Chronicle*, and *St. Louis Post–Dispatch*.

Ken Silverstein completed an expanded update on his story that was published in *The Nation* on February 17, 1997. He cites the U.S. China Business Council as advocating the position that elimination of the most favored nation trade status for China would result in a decline in human rights. The Council claims that human rights will come naturally as a result of increased trade. Silverstein argues that it is not the human rights issue that is motivating U.S. corporate interests, but rather access to a cheap labor pool of 1.2 billion workers who will work in factories for $50 a month. Boeing recently shut down a plant in Kansas and transferred operations to a factory in Xian, China. Motorola expects to have 12,000 workers in China by the year 2000.

SOURCES: *The Nation*, February 17, 1997; *Sacramento Bee*, February 23, 1997; *The News Tribune*, May 12, 1997; *San Francisco Chronicle*, April 10, 1997; and *Los Angeles Times*, May 11, 1997.

1996 # 23 CENSORED STORY
TROUBLE IN MIND:
CHEMICALS AND THE BRAIN

Scientists are discovering that chemicals in our environment are impacting our hormones and permanently changing how we live and who we are. Everyone is exposed throughout their lives to large numbers of man-made chemicals.

In a statement issued by a group of international scientists and physicians who attended a workshop in Erice, Italy, great concern was expressed regarding the effects of hormone-disrupting chemicals on the brain and the central nervous system.

Industrial hormone-disrupting chemicals are found in native populations from the Arctic to the tropics and, because of their persistence in the body, can be passed from generation to generation. These synthetic chemicals are found in pesticides, plastics, shampoos, detergents, cosmetics, and other products we use in our everyday lives.

According to Dr. Theo Colborn, one of the participants at the workshop and author of a book on the subject, most research funds used for testing new chemicals concentrate on cancer and ignore other risks, like hormone disruption.

"This preoccupation with cancer," she points out, "has blinded us to evidence signaling other dangers. It has thwarted investigation of other risks that may prove equally important, not only to the health of individuals, but also to the well-being of society."

SOURCE: Montague, Peter, "Chemicals and the Brain," *Rachel's Environment & Health Weekly*, June 20, 1996.

COVERAGE 1997: On July 14, 1997 the *Chicago Tribune* front paged a story enti-tled, "Impostor Hormones Raising Fears." The story covered a meeting of scientists and policy makers sponsored by the U.S. Environmental Protection Agency in Chicago to specifically address how to test for hormone disrupters in the environment.

While little is known about how to measure the often subtle effects of hormone disrupting chemicals, the federal government is taking it seriously enough to fund over 400 studies to work on this problem.

One study cited was that of Joseph and Sandra Jacobson's work on children born to women who had eaten PCB-laden fish from Lake Michigan during the early 1980s. Tests now show that the children have lowered IQ levels, decreased memory, and limited attention spans. The study suggested that because PCBs are widely evident in industrialized countries that we may be gradually affecting all children raised in these environments.

There was no mention of the work in Europe on this issue in *The Tribune* article leaving readers to think that it is only the U.S. government that is working on this problem.

SOURCE: *Chicago Tribune*, July 14, 1997.

1996 # 24 CENSORED STORY

DARK ALLIANCE: TUNA, FREE TRADE AND COCAINE

If recent history is any guide at all, one can only conclude that President Clinton's free trade policies have been immensely valuable to drug-smuggling cartels based in Italy, Colombia, Venezuela, and Mexico. The ongoing dolphin-safe tuna debate sharply illustrates U.S. indifference to the problem of international drug trafficking. According to the administration's own Drug Enforcement Agency (DEA), approximately 90 percent of the world-wide flow of cocaine and heroin is transported and maintained by fishing fleets—with Mexico as one of the most successful traffickers.

By the late 1980s, the Mexican fleet, with 70 big boats, dominated smuggling operations. The country's boats and canneries were privatized—with tuna industry shares divided up between prominent Mexicans in the ruling PRI party.

In the early 1990s, legislation for dolphin-safe standards on tuna fishing closed the lucrative U.S. and western European tuna markets to Mexican, Venezuelan, and Colombian fleets that continued to use the outlawed "purse-seine net" technique. As a result, the Mexican fleet began to shrink, thus limiting their overall smuggling capacity.

On May 8, 1996, the Clinton Administration's legislative reversal of the ban cleared the House Resource Committee. With this passing, the Mexican tuna fleet, owned by narcotraffickers and high-ranking Mexican officials, is expected, once again, to expand.

SOURCE: St. Clair, Jeffrey, and Alexander Cockburn, "Tuna, Free Trade and Cocaine," *Earth Island Journal,* Summer 1996.

COVERAGE 1997: In September 1996 then White House Chief of Staff Leon Panetta met privately with members of Congress and officials from the drug and intelligence community. The topic of discussion was drug trafficking by the tuna industry in Latin America. The discussion lead to the White House's last minute pull-out for supporting changes in the laws that would have allowed resumption of importation into the U.S. of tuna caught using the "purse-seine net" practice.

To her credit, California Senator Barbara Boxer had threatened a filibuster on the "Dolphin Death Act." However, new "Dolphin Death" bills were reintroduced into Congress this year (HR 2823 and SB 1420). A compromise bill passed in August 1997 and was signed into law by President Clinton.

The Cali drug cartel and its Mexican affiliates are estimated to be the wealthiest criminal organization in the world with a net worth over $200 billion. U.S. officials have stated that the Cali Cartel spends $500 million a year on bribes in Mexico. At the same time the *El Financiero* estimates that the drug cartels annually spend $500 million bribing U.S. officials as well.

SOURCES: *Earth Island Journal,* Spring 1997; and *San Francisco Chronicle,* August 1, 1997.

CHAPTER 4

The Junk Food News Stories of 1997: Why We Need a More Balanced Diet

By Cathy Coleman, Project Censored, and News Ombudsmen from around the world

> Instead of endeavoring to genuinely increase our understanding of the events and forces that shape our society, much of the media presents stories ensured to be as superficial as possible. They have mastered rather than obliterated obfuscation. An artificial appetite for titillation and sensationalism has replaced our demand for the truth.—Marianne Williamson, *The Healing of America*

In what has become a sad-but-repetitiously-true scenario, 1997 was another banner year for Junk Food News (JFN). This topic was so-named to designate those stories that bear a startling resemblance to junk food: they fill us up, but don't satiate. Like their sugarcoated counterparts in the culinary world, these stories give us a rush, but soon let us down with the nagging realization that we're hungry for more. They are the stories of people and events that are so grossly over-reported, sensationalized, and hyped out of proportion to their significance, it becomes difficult to differentiate between tabloid and the so-called mainstream forms of media. It is important to stress that the term "junk food news" is not necessarily an indictment against or a judgment about the subject, but rather about the content and coverage, particularly when weighed against the top *Censored* news stories of the same period.

Selected by ombudsmen who serve as independent reviewers and public complaint reporters for major newspapers around the world, the Top Ten Junk Food News stories of 1997 are:

1. Marv Albert
2. Princess Diana/the British Royals*
3. Frank and Kathie Lee Gifford
4. Michael Jackson's baby
5. JonBenet Ramsey
6. Tyson-Holyfield match
7. O.J. Simpson (Part IV)
8. TIE BETWEEN Andrew Cunanan and the anniversary of Elvis's death
9. Howard Stern
10. Paula Jones

*For some of the voters, this is qualified to coverage prior to Diana's death

Rounding out the top 25 JFN news stories were: the Kennedy dynasty, Tiger Woods, Lt. Kelly Flinn and military sex scandals, Autumn Jackson, Chelsea Clinton entering Stanford, Heaven's Gate, movie release hype, celebrity breakups, Ellen's "coming out," Bill Gates, Clinton's knee injury, cigars, the 63-year-old woman who gave birth, and Rosie O'Donnell.

Stories centered on sex and perversion are becoming a mainstay of news, and, as in the past, several of the features chosen as the top Junk Food News stories fall into these categories. To cover the fields of both sex and perversion, Marv Albert made a slam dunk to become the number one Junk Food News story of the year. And as if Howard Stern himself weren't perverse enough, we were pummeled by coverage of the Tyson-Holyfield match/munch.

In a category all his own, O.J. Simpson holds the dubious distinction of appearing in the Top Ten for the fourth straight year, admittedly in a lower rank (seventh place, rather than his previous positions at first and fifth). The civil case filed against him by the Goldman family ended with a unanimous verdict in favor of the plaintiffs, and an $8.5 million award they will most likely never see. Simpson's house went into foreclosure and many of his trophies and other valuables claimed by the court "mysteriously" disappeared. But through it all, we remained informed of his activities (golfing) and the hardship of his fall from grace (having to play at a public golf course instead of the more exclusive and luxurious private clubs).

Celebrities were too busy breaking up this year to repeat last year's number one JFN story: celebrity pregnancies. The notable exception was the much-heralded birth of Michael Jackson's son, the aptly named Prince Michael. Jackson, another perennial JFN favorite, and his blushing bride, Debbie, have (as of this writing) managed to fool all those wags who predicted a custody battle even before the baby arrived. The couple is currently providing further titillation with unconfirmed rumors of another pregnancy, thereby almost ensuring their inclusion in next year's JFN listing.

The topic chosen as the eighth highest-ranking JFN story of 1997 was Andrew Cunanan, whose killing spree spread half-way across the continent and claimed six lives, including his own. There is an old maxim in media circles that "if it bleeds, it leads." Yet, we are so inundated with heinous acts of violence in the daily news, we're becoming numb to them, and competition among the media for our attention intensifies. Did the Cunanan story grow out of all proportion because of the grizzly aspects of his rampage? Or was it the lackluster performance of several law enforcement agencies, including the FBI, that invited the media scrutiny? Did the celebrity status of his fifth victim, fashion designer Gianni Versace, fuel the frenzy? Joe Sheibley of the *News Sentinel* in Fort Wayne, Indiana, asserts that "the news is driven by media capitals. There are Andrew Cunanan and JonBenet Ramsey-type stories occurring almost every weekday across the country, but unless they occur in or near one of the major media capitals of the world, you don't hear much about them." Sheibley described a news story wherein a serial killer was kidnapping, raping, and murdering women throughout the southern part of Indiana. State news accounts reported the killings that occurred along Interstate 70 from St. Louis, Missouri to Columbus, Ohio, but this story never made national news. Whatever the reasons for the excessive coverage, Cunanan's ignominious acts and ignoble death brought him infamy, rather than the fame and glory he vainly sought.

The fifth-ranked story this year is the horrendous murder of a six-year-old beauty queen, although several of the voting ombudsmen did not feel this was a story that could be over-reported. Harry Themal believes, "The murder of a small child is something that people want to hear about. Plus you have the added factor of police ineptitude. This case remains unsolved, so it can't be overdone." Carl Jensen agrees: "I don't think, on par, that JonBenet got that much coverage. It came in spurts, partly because the Denver authorities kept a lid on it, unlike the O.J. Simpson case where everybody was constantly talking to the media." Although Felix Winternitz did not include this story in his JFN vote, he observed that JonBenet's story was a natural for national coverage: "There was just too much film footage of a beauty queen—so many videos existed of her," videos that could be shown on major news outlets and tabloid shows alike, with professional photos available for newspapers and magazines. He agrees that class may be a factor in all the publicity given "the celebrity of her parents being millionaires," as well as the power and social status inherent in their financial wealth. On the other hand, because of the type of coverage given to the Ramsey murder case, Elissa Papirno listed it among her Top Ten choices.

The British Royals round out our list of Top Ten JFN annual favorites, but it was a strange and tragic twist of fate that kept the media spotlight so sharply and relentlessly focused on them this year. As previously noted, some of our respondents specified that their vote for this topic was for the "absurd amount of coverage" given to the Royal family and especially Princess Diana prior to her death. We knew Diana's whereabouts, who her companions were, and what she was wearing several days out of any given week. When she found a new romantic interest, the reports and speculation by the press increased so dramatically, it appeared there was little else of consequence going on in the world (an assumption that is dramatically disproved by our top *Censored* stories). Focusing solely on Diana's death, several ombudsmen disagreed that this nomination qualified as junk food news. Their comments include:

"There was a wide general interest in both Princess Diana and JonBenet Ramsey. The deaths of young people are more than gossip. These are real events— the other stories are just gossip."—Jean Otto, *Rocky Mountain News*

"The outpouring of grief made it a big story. The media couldn't have done less; it was simply reflecting public feeling. Some stories just automatically generate a public outcry."—Harry Themal (retired), *The News Journal*

"[Princess Diana and Jon Benet] were major news stories that enormous amounts of people were interested in. They were legitimate news stories that captivated people. It's undeniable that the world was captivated by [Diana], it's what folks wanted.—Arthur Nauman, *Sacramento Bee*

But on a dissenting note, Project Censored founder Carl Jensen stated, "The nation was deluged with Princess Diana. The media went totally overboard, worse than the O.J. Simpson case. The public didn't start out wanting that much coverage of Diana. Mother Theresa was a more important figure, and she didn't get that much coverage."

THE CHICKEN OR THE EGG

While most media ombudsmen would agree that junk food news is an easy escape for news sources, they don't agree on the root cause. Some blame the producers of the news for resorting to the quick, simple and inexpensive route, while others place the responsibility on the audience. It has been commented that, much like drug use, while people crave junk food news, it still takes a junk pusher to stimulate and build that craving.

As Project Censored founder Carl Jensen puts it, "The audience has been trained to want junk food news. While the media say they give the public what it wants, in reality, they give the public what is most fashionable and least expensive to produce."

Felix Winternitz of the *Cincinnati City Beat* summed it up nicely: "It's easier to serve up junk food than a thoughtful five-course meal. Perhaps the old definition of news of 'when man bites dog' should be updated to 'When man wears women's underwear.'"

Excluding Princess Diana and JonBenet Ramsey, Jean Otto of the *Rocky Mountain News* described this year's nominees for JFN as "'who cares?' stories, of no value to the public beyond titillation and voyeurism. The media play to the public's worst impulses and, by spending their own space and time on stories of little or no value, take themselves off the hook for delivering news of genuine import."

Echoing some of his colleagues' remarks, Kenneth Starck (*Cedar Rapids Gazette*) explains that there's no simple answer to the question of why the media tend to sensationalize selected stories: "It has to do with perceived public interest, not necessarily real interest. It has to do with a general malaise in society in which many people are eager to spice up their own dreary existence vicariously. It has to do with appealing to the largest and often lowest common denominator of public taste. It has to do with appealing visuals (such as JonBenet and Princess Di) that are shown over and over again, becoming instant iconography. And all of it has to do with economics, namely: the first obligation of a free press in a society driven by market forces is to make money."

According to Elissa Papirno of *The Hartford Courant*, "[These stories] are tantalizing, voyeuristic, freakish in some cases, [using] a cheap hook to grab an audience's or reader's attention."

The end result of this ongoing trend toward sensationalism, according to Mirio Vitor Santos of *Folha de Sao Paulo*, is that "we are losing track of public interest. We are losing the ethics of our activity."

The other predominate view holds that the audience is responsible by continuing to support the type of journalism that promotes junk food news. Phil Record of the *Fort Worth Star-Telegram* describes this view most succinctly: stories are sensationalized "because the readers eat them up."

Joe Sheibley of *The News-Sentinel* in Fort Wayne, Indiana, says, "Tabloid-style journalism has become part of the one-upmanship battle between competing media in the major markets. National media passes it down, and the rest of the media drag their readers and viewers into it, but not kicking and screaming, as tabloid newspaper circulations and tabloid TV ratings attest. Tabloid journalism won't stop until readers and viewers say they've had enough and then prove it by putting their money where their mouths are."

"Many news stories go beyond the control of journalists and editors, so they become a sort of Frankenstein's monster with no father, but with a life of its own," says Roger Jimenez of *La Vanguardia* in Barcelona, Spain.

Takeshi Maezawa, a lecturer at Tokyo Keizai University, seems to feel that the answer lies somewhere in the middle: "People's curiosity to know (about) prominent persons outweighs their right of privacy, and media use such tendencies for their business."

Many thanks to the members of the Organization of News Ombudsmen who participated in this year's survey of Junk Food News:

Lynn Feigenbaum	*The Virginian-Pilot*, VA
Jerald Finch	*The Richmond Times-Dispatch*, VA
Roger Jimenez	*La Vanguardia*, Barcelona, Spain
Arthur Nauman	*The Sacramento Bee*, CA
Osami Okuya	*The Yomiuri Shimbun*, Tokyo, Japan
Jean Otto	*Rocky Mountain News*, CO
Elissa Papirno	*The Hartford Courant*, CT
Phil Record	*Fort Worth Star-Telegram*, TX
Mario Vitor Santos	*Folha de Sao Paulo*
Joseph Sheibley	*The News-Sentinel*, Fort Wayne, IN
Kenneth Starck	*The Gazette*, Cedar Rapids, IA
Felix Winternitz	*Cincinnati City Beat*, OH
Carl Jensen	Cotati, CA
Harry Themal	Wilmington, DE

Typically, ombudsmen are directed by their editors or publishers to critique published articles, and to investigate and report on public concerns and complaints regarding the newspaper. In the United States, less than 1 percent of 1,800 daily newspapers employs an ombudsman. More papers might employ these guardians of the press if the public came to expect and demand such an outlet for public concern.

The Junk Food News survey represents the ultimate irony and stark contrast to our Top 25 *Censored* News Stories of the year. The features chosen as the top JFN stories underscore the imbalance of news presentations, and the periodic absurdity that prevails when stories about men biting each other, biting women, and "when man wears women's underwear" take precedence over stories such as the number one *Censored* story this year on the aggressive promotion of U.S. arms sales.

Several questions remain: What's news, and what's not? What is an "appropriate" amount of coverage, and what constitutes "excessive" media coverage? Art Nauman of *The Sacramento Bee* questions the efficacy of making subjective judgments about journalistic stories: "The stories selected are of interest to somebody, and some of them, to a lot of people. It makes me somewhat queasy to make these kind of pronouncements," regarding which stories qualify as junk food news.

While certainly it's important to remember that one man's poison is another man's meat (or in this case, cheeseburger and shake), it's equally essential to remember that too much sugar and fat in our media diet can be toxic. The analogy of these stories to junk food is quite apropos: They are toxic in their excess and in their frequent lack of substance. And like chocolate, French fries, burgers, and Twinkies, they are addictive. We become caught up in the media frenzy, and lose sight of the fact that we're missing out on the stories of greater import that have been bumped, overlooked, under-investigated, or deemed threatening by major news outlets. It won't help to point the finger of blame: We are all responsible, media and audience alike. Now we must learn to take care of ourselves by demanding proper nutrition in the form of more appropriate and truthful news reporting.

CHAPTER 5

Self-censorship and the Homogeneity of the Media Elite

By Peter Phillips with research assistance from Bob Klose, Nicola Mazumdar, and Alix Jestron

Images of the zealous censor or "public relations official" imply that censorship is an intentional act. However, contemporary analysis tends to stress that the structure of media organizations themselves are creating latent forms of censorship that can be just as damaging as intentional censorship.

The operation of latent censorship is analyzed in *Manufacturing Consent* (1988; and updated in Herman, 1996). The authors Ed Herman and Noam Chomsky claim that because media is firmly imbedded in the market system, it reflects the class values and concerns of its owners and advertisers. They hold that the media maintains a corporate class bias though five systemic filters: concentrated private ownership; a strict bottom-line profit orientation; over-reliance on governmental and corporate sources for news; a primary tendency to avoid offending the powerful; and an almost religious worship of the market economy, devaluing alternative beliefs. These filters limit what will become news in society and set parameters on acceptable coverage of daily events.

The danger of these filters is that they produce subtle and indirect forms of censorship which are all the more difficult to combat. Owners and managers share class identity with the powerful and are motivated economically to please advertisers and viewers. Their conceptions of what is "newsworthy" are influenced by their social background, and their values seem, to themselves, only "common sense." Journalists and editors are not immune to the influence of owners and managers. Journalists want to see their stories approved for print or broadcast, and editors come to know the limits of their freedom to diverge from the "common sense" world view of owners and managers. The self-discipline which this structure induces in journalists and editors filters down as "common sense" to these employees as well. Self-discipline becomes self-censorship. Independence is restricted. And the filtering process is hidden and often denied, or rationalized away.

Media news organizations like ABC, NBC, CBS, and Time Warner are massive bureaucratic organizations that function like all other bureaucracies. Survival into perpetuity and ever-increasing profits are logical and necessary measures of their success. Corporations have evolved to work in exactly this way. Policies towards these ends are set through privately-owned hierarchical command structures whose number-one consideration is the bottom-line success of the corporation.

Management theorists use the term "corporate culture" to distinguish the internalization of "common sense" understandings that operate within the corporate environment. Employees who continually clash with the corporate culture are gradually weeded out.

In large media organizations, journalists and writers trained in critical thinking, analysis, research, and freedom of information values must become acculturated to the "common sense" understandings of the organizational

THIS MODERN WORLD by TOM TOMORROW

HARD AT WORK, I SEE... I BET I CAN GUESS WHAT *THIS* WEEK'S CARTOON IS ABOUT...

YEAH, THE MEDIA HAVE REALLY BEEN TRUMPETING THIS NOTION OF A *BOOMING ECONOMY*... SOMETHING'S JUST NOT *RIGHT* THERE...

I MEAN-- THEY'RE REPORTING THE *GREAT NEWS* THAT 30% OF CORPORATIONS ARE HIRING -- BUT DOESN'T THAT MEAN THAT 70% *AREN'T*?

AND IF THERE ARE MORE JOBS FOR GRADS BECAUSE TOO MANY *OLDER* WORKERS HAVE BEEN DOWNSIZED-- DOES THAT *REALLY* CONSTITUTE GOOD ECONOMIC NEWS?

OF COURSE, THE RAGING *STOCK MARKET* IS ULTIMATELY WHAT'S FUELING THESE STORIES... AND IF YOU'RE AMONG THAT SMALL PERCENTAGE OF AMERICANS WHO HAVE A DIRECT STAKE IN WALL STREET, THINGS PROBABLY *DO* LOOK ROSY...

structure in order to remain employed. Understandings regarding objective reporting, standards of critical inquiry, socio-political perspectives, conflict of interests, and other abstract values are organizationally created and interpreted to new employees as "the way we do things." These organizational values are understood by veteran news workers, and communicated to new employees through both word and action. At times a special mentor arrangement develops between a senior worker and new employee that will accelerate the assimilation of the organizational culture and the positive chances for the new employee's advancement and promotion.

The responsibility for development of a corporate culture lies with the Chief Executive Officer (CEO). CEOs are selected by and receive direction from the corporation's board of directors. These directors are elected to the board by stockholders and hold the ultimate responsibility for the success or failure of the corporation. Consequently, CEOs are generally like-minded individuals similar to the corporate board of directors. CEOs, in turn, hire executives, who in turn hire staff who reflect the values and profit orientation of the CEO and board. That this happens is neither surprising nor unusual in the corporate world of international capitalism.

What has been surprising and unusual is how rapidly so many large media corporations have embarked on a massive merging and buy-out process that is realigning our information systems into global corporate structures (Bagdikian, 1997; Herman & McChesney, 1997). Again, there is nothing illogical about this process. Monetary capital seeks the most profitable return on investment, and media/information technology properties are seen as the future growth market of the world.

What changes within media organizations with conglomeration is that traditional core values having to do with freedom of information and a belief

in the responsibility of keeping the public informed on critical issues give way to the "common sense" values of bottom-line oriented CEOs and boards of directors. Freedom of information is a value as long as it sells advertising and attracts viewers, readers, and listeners. But information or news that discourages advertising, offends or challenges the audience, or is contrary to the interests and values of the CEO/Executive Board is not deemed valuable information within the logical fiscal orientation of the organization.

Corporate fiscal concerns are changing our media systems. For example, in 1997, the new CEO of the *Los Angeles Times* found it necessary to assign a business manager to each section of the newspaper in order to insure that a proper profit-oriented product was developed and to help maintain a corporate climate that reflected the management desires of the board of directors.

Even the *Columbia Journalism Review*, a leading publication monitoring journalism, has, under the leadership of former *Fortune* editor Marshall Loeb, been steering itself towards "gossip and celebrity" in order to increase sales (Cohen, 1997). Similarly, book reviews that appear in *The New York Times* are now linked to a Barnes and Noble Web site so that if a book is sold, *The Times* gets a percentage of the sale (Stone, 1997).

With the changing structure of media organizations, an important focus for study of global media systems will be the values and biases of the boards of directors, and their corporate interests, connections, and understandings. Simply allowing the logic of private profit-taking to determine the outcome of access to information in our society puts democracy and freedom dangerously at risk. If the corporate media elite are to be the ultimate decision makers, policy formers, and corporate-culture determiners, then we must focus our research attention on them to determine the implications of their burgeoning power for democracy and freedom of information in the world.

PROJECT CENSORED RESEARCH SUMMER 1997

Roya Akhavan-Majid and Gary Wolf (*Critical Studies in Mass Communications*, June 1991) describe how mass media studies have focused on both the libertarian model and the authoritarian model. The former is a pluralist model of independent news sources watching the government and the powerful, and the latter a consolidated governmental authority model in which elites tell the population what to think. Akhavan-Majid and Wolf argue that a modified model of elite power groups working in cooperation with government fits contemporary society more accurately.

It is with this elite model in mind that we began our analysis of the interconnectedness of the American media elite (see Figure 1). After selecting the top six broadcast corporations and the largest five newsprint organizations, we identified the individual members of each corporate board of directors. Our research interests were to gain an understanding of the relationships between the media elites in the United States and to examine their direct affiliations with other multinational corporations.

The six largest or most influential broadcast corporations in the United States are General Electric Company (NBC), Viacom Inc. (cable), The Walt Disney Company (ABC), Time Warner Inc. (CNN), Westinghouse Electric Corporation (CBS), and The News Corporation Ltd. (Fox). Collectively, these six multinational corporations had 81 directors in 1996. Of these 81 directors, only nine were women, including Rupert Murdoch's wife, Anna Maria Murdock (News Corp.), making the group 89 percent male. These 81 directors, a group small enough to fit in a medium-size university classroom, also hold 104 directorships on the boards of *Fortune* 1,000 corporations in the United States including: Chase Manhattan Corp., J. P. Morgan & Co., PepsiCo. Inc., Columbia HCA Healthcare Corp., Bank of America, Chevron Corp., Mobil Corp., Philip Morris Inc., and some 95 others.

These directors are the media elite of the world. While they may not agree on abortion and other domestic issues, they do represent the collective vested interests of a significant portion of corporate America and share a common commitment to free market capitalism, economic growth, internationally protected copyrights, and a powerful government dedicated to protecting their interests.

The following overviews offer a sampling of the backgrounds of a few of these media elites:

FRANK C. CARLUCCI III (Westinghouse), former deputy director of the CIA 1978-81, and Secretary of Defense 1987-89, Harvard graduate 1956, board of directors for Ashlind Inc., BDM International Inc., Bell Atlantic Corp., Kaman Corp., Pharmacia & Upjohn Inc., Quaker Oats Co.;

DAVID T. MCLAUGHLIN (Westinghouse), President of the Aspen Institute, board of directors for ARCO, Atlas Air Inc., Standard Fusse, graduate of Dartmouth 1954, member of the San Francisco Bohemian Club;

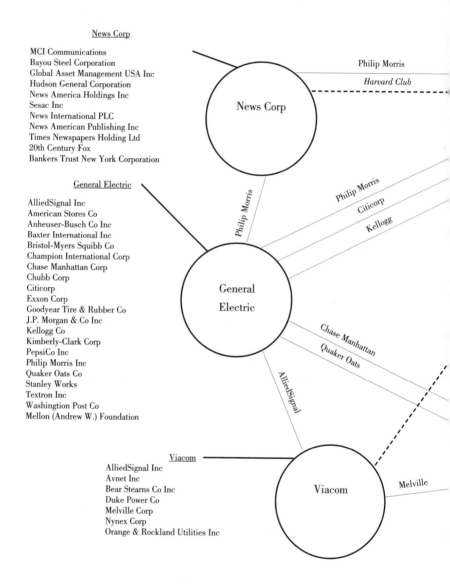

News Corp

MCI Communications
Bayou Steel Corporation
Global Asset Management USA Inc
Hudson General Corporation
News America Holdings Inc
Sesac Inc
News International PLC
News American Publishing Inc
Times Newspapers Holding Ltd
20th Century Fox
Bankers Trust New York Corporation

Philip Morris

Harvard Club

News Corp

General Electric

AlliedSignal Inc
American Stores Co
Anheuser-Busch Co Inc
Baxter International Inc
Bristol-Myers Squibb Co
Champion International Corp
Chase Manhattan Corp
Chubb Corp
Citicorp
Exxon Corp
Goodyear Tire & Rubber Co
J.P. Morgan & Co Inc
Kellogg Co
Kimberly-Clark Corp
PepsiCo Inc
Philip Morris Inc
Quaker Oats Co
Stanley Works
Textron Inc
Washingtion Post Co
Mellon (Andrew W.) Foundation

Philip Morris

Philip Morris
Citicorp
Kellogg

General Electric

Chase Manhattan
Quaker Oats

AlliedSignal

Viacom

AlliedSignal Inc
Avnet Inc
Bear Stearns Co Inc
Duke Power Co
Melville Corp
Nynex Corp
Orange & Rockland Utilities Inc

Viacom

Melville

Figure 1
Major Media Corporate Relationships, 1996

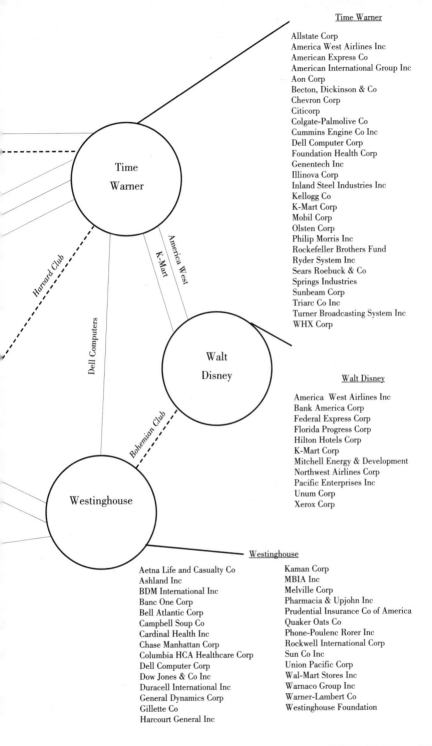

Time Warner

Allstate Corp
America West Airlines Inc
American Express Co
American International Group Inc
Aon Corp
Becton, Dickinson & Co
Chevron Corp
Citicorp
Colgate-Palmolive Co
Cummins Engine Co Inc
Dell Computer Corp
Foundation Health Corp
Genentech Inc
Illinova Corp
Inland Steel Industries Inc
Kellogg Co
K-Mart Corp
Mobil Corp
Olsten Corp
Philip Morris Inc
Rockefeller Brothers Fund
Ryder System Inc
Sears Roebuck & Co
Springs Industries
Sunbeam Corp
Triarc Co Inc
Turner Broadcasting System Inc
WHX Corp

Walt Disney

America West Airlines Inc
Bank America Corp
Federal Express Corp
Florida Progress Corp
Hilton Hotels Corp
K-Mart Corp
Mitchell Energy & Development
Northwest Airlines Corp
Pacific Enterprises Inc
Unum Corp
Xerox Corp

Westinghouse

Aetna Life and Casualty Co
Ashland Inc
BDM International Inc
Banc One Corp
Bell Atlantic Corp
Campbell Soup Co
Cardinal Health Inc
Chase Manhattan Corp
Columbia HCA Healthcare Corp
Dell Computer Corp
Dow Jones & Co Inc
Duracell International Inc
General Dynamics Corp
Gillette Co
Harcourt General Inc

Kaman Corp
MBIA Inc
Melville Corp
Pharmacia & Upjohn Inc
Prudential Insurance Co of America
Quaker Oats Co
Phone-Poulenc Rorer Inc
Rockwell International Corp
Sun Co Inc
Union Pacific Corp
Wal-Mart Stores Inc
Warnaco Group Inc
Warner-Lambert Co
Westinghouse Foundation

Circle labels: Time Warner, Walt Disney, Westinghouse

Connection labels: Harvard Club, Dell Computers, K-Mart, America West, Bohemian Club

HAMISH MAXWELL (News Corp.), board of directors for Philip Morris Inc., Bankers Trust New York Corp., graduate of Cambridge University, England 1949 former CEO of Philip Morris Inc.;

ANDREW CLARK SIGLER (General Electric), board of directors for Bristol-Myers Squibb Co., Chemical Bank, AlliedSignal, Champion International, Chase Manhattan Corp., graduate of Dartmouth 1953;

DOUGLAS A WARNER III (General Electric), board of directors for Bechtel Group Inc., Anheuser–Busch Co., CEO of J.P. Morgan & Co., member of the private New York River Club, and Meadowbrook Club on Long Island, graduate of Yale 1968;

EDWARD S. FINKELSTEIN (Time Warner), board of directors for American Eagle Outfitters Inc., Finkelstein Associates, former CEO of Macy's, Harvard graduate 1946, member of the Harvard Club.

These six individuals are typical of the media elite. Their shared characteristics include: professional corporate careers, private educations, multiple corporate interests, metropolitan lifestyles, and often private club memberships or affiliations.[1] The media elite share a commonality of interests and socio-economic characteristics that reflect the homogenous lifestyle and class background that they tend to bring with them to their positions as decision makers on the boards of directors of their respective media corporations.

The media elite also tend to have direct connections to one another through membership on several boards and private affiliations. News Corporation, General Electric and Time Warner all have board members who also sit on the Philip Morris board of directors. Overall, there are 15 direct corporate or club membership links between the six major broadcasting corporations, making them an interlocking network of shared affiliations and economic interests.

The directors of the five largest or most influential newspaper corporations (publishing over 160 dailies) in the United States share a similar pattern of corporate affiliations with their broadcast counterparts. Gannett Co. Inc., Knight-Ridder Inc., New York Times Co., Washington Post Co., and the Times Mirror Co. have 76 directors who are interconnected with 66 other *Fortune* 1,000 corporations.

---

[1] The media elite list membership in 21 private clubs clubs including: Beefsteak, Bohemian Club (San Francisco), Brooks (N.Y.), California Yacht Club, Cosmopolitian Club (N.Y.), Harvard Club, Hasty Pudding Club (Harvard), Los Angeles Yacht Club, Meadowbrook Club (Long Island), Republican Club 100, River Club (N.Y.) San Diego Yacht Club, St. Francis Yacht Club (San Francisco) Transpacific Yacht Club, and the Yale Club.

GANNETT CO. INC. SHARED DIRECTORSHIPS: Airborne Freight Corp., American Express Co., Bancorp Hawaii Inc., Bank America Corp., Continental Airlines Inc., E.I. du Pont De Nemours and Co., FPL Group Inc., Ford Motor Co., Frontier Corp., Kellogg Co., Navistar International Corp., PHH Corp., Union Pacific Corp. (2 directors);

KNIGHT-RIDDER INC. SHARED DIRECTORSHIPS: ALCO Standard Corp., Champion International Corp., Chubb Corp., Delta Air Lines Inc., Digital Equipment Corp., Eli Lilly and Co., Great Atlantic & Pacific Tea Co., J.P. Morgan & Co. Inc., Kimberly-Clark Corp., Phillips Petroleum Co., Raytheon Co. (2 directors), State Street Boston Corp., Tandy Corp., Texas Instruments Inc.;

THE NEW YORK TIMES CO. SHARED DIRECTORSHIPS: Bristol-Myers Squibb Co., Campbell Soup Co., International Business Machines Co., Lehman Brothers Holding Inc., PepsiCo Inc., Springs Industries Inc., Texaco Inc., U.S. Industries Inc.;

TIMES MIRROR CO. SHARED DIRECTORSHIPS: Amoco Corp., Black & Decker Corp., Boeing Co., Cox Communications Inc., Edison International (2 directors), Marsh & McLennan Cos. Inc., Nordstrom Inc., Procter & Gamble Co., Rockwell International Corp., Ryder Systems Inc., Sun America Inc., Talborts Inc., Travelers Group Inc.;

WASHINGTON POST CO. SHARED DIRECTORSHIPS: American Express Co., American Stores Co., Ashland Inc., Bank of New York Co. Inc., Berkshire Hathaway Inc., Coca-Cola Co., Conrail Inc., Darden Restaurants Inc., Geico Corp., General Electric Co., Gillette Co., H. J. Heinz Co., Home Depot Inc., J. P. Morgan & Co. Inc., Lexmark International Group Inc., McDonald's Corp., Morgan Stanley Group Inc., National Services Industry Inc., Polaroid Corp., Rohm and Haas Co., Salomon Inc., Textron Inc., Union Pacific Corp., Wells Fargo & Co.

Collectively these 11 major broadcast and print media corporations represent a major portion of the news information systems, providing multiple links to most every household in the United States. For many people, this means that their entire source of news and information comes through the filters of these 11 corporations.

An analysis of the interconnectedness of the top 11 media organizations in the United States shows that they have 36 direct links (see Figure 2) creating a solid network of overlapping interests and affiliations. The 11 media corporations collectively have directorships interlocking with 144 of the *For-*

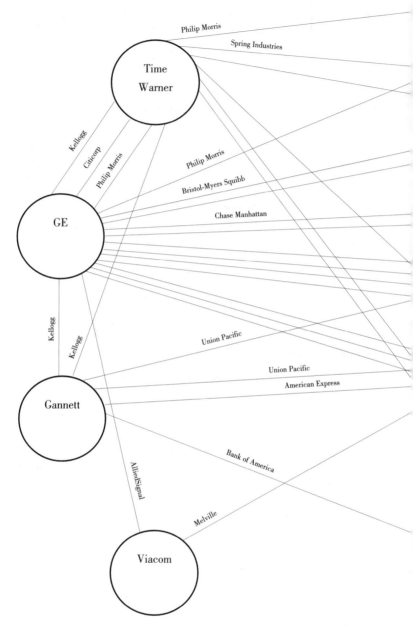

Figure 2
Major Media Corporate Interlocks, 1996

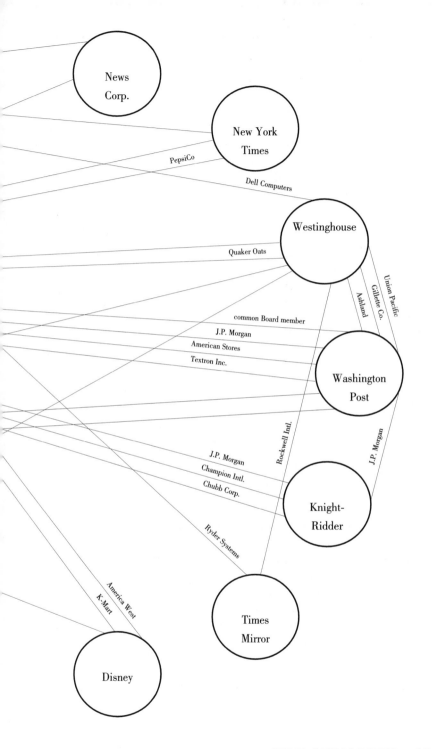

tune 1,000 corporations. All 11 media corporations have direct links with at least two of the other top media organizations. General Electric, owner of NBC, has the highest rate of shared affiliations with 17 direct links to 9 of the 11 corporations. Time Warner Inc. came in second with ten links to seven of the other media corporations.

What becomes clear from the charts presented in this chapter is the top media corporations in America are directly linked to 14 percent of the *Fortune* 1,000 corporations. Additionally, they receive advertising money from a significant portion of the other *Fortune* 1,000. Given this networking system, it is safe to say that the media in the United States effectively represents the interests of corporate America, and that the media elite are the watchdogs of what constitutes acceptable ideological messages, the parameters of news and information content, and the general use of media resources.

Do the media elite directly censor the news? Without being privy to insider conversations, it is difficult to prove direct censorship by management of particular stories in the news. But clearly there is a widespread tendency among media corporations to comply with the general corporate culture, and this culture is shored up by career-minded employees with "common sense" understandings. This combination tends to achieve what direct censorship cannot, that is a general compliance with the attitudes, wishes, and expectations of the media elite and, in turn, corporate America.

BIBLIOGRAPHY

Akhavan-Majid, Roya and Gary Wolf, "American Mass Media and the Myth of Libertarianism: Toward an 'Elite Power Group' Theory," *Critical Studies in Mass Communications*, June 1991: 139-151.

Bagdikian, Ben, *The Media Monopoly*, Fifth Edition. Beacon Press, 1997.

Chomsky, Noam & Edward Herman, *Manufacturing Consent: The Political Economy of the Mass Media*. New York: Pantheon, 1988.

Chomsky, Noam, *Necessary Illusions: Thought Control In Democratic Society*. Boston: South End Press, 1989.

Cohen, Richard, "CJR—Cheating Journalism," *The Nation*, June 9, 1997.

Glynn, Jeannette, *Who Knows Who*. Berkeley, CA: Who Knows Who Publishers, 1997.

Herman, Edward, "The Propaganda Model Revisited," *Monthly Review*, vol. 48, no. 3, (New York: Monthly Review Press), 1996.

Herman Edward, and Robert W. McChesney. *The Global Media—The New Missionaries of Global Capitalism*. Cassell, 1997.

Stone, Martha, "All the Ads That Are Fit to Print," *ZDNN*, September 11, 1997.

CHAPTER 6

Big Media Myths

By Norman Solomon

Over time, repetition can make certain false assumptions begin to seem natural. Every day, the media scenery provides us with views so familiar that we're apt to see them as common sense. In the process, the mass media have propagated many enduring illusions. And perhaps none of them are more important than prevalent myths about the media industry itself.

MYTH: "THE LIBERAL MEDIA"

In recent years, the myth of "the liberal media" has gotten a boost from surveys showing that journalists are much more likely to vote for Democrats than Republicans. But these surveys tell us nothing about the content of news media.

We don't often hear about key realities: The higher you look up the ladder of media institutions, the more conservative it gets. In general, editors are more conservative than reporters, and managers are even farther to the right; the CEOs, boards of directors, and owners are the most conservative of all. In the media business, as in other industries, people at the top of the hierarchy have much more power to determine policies and constraints than rank-and-file employees do. Ultimately, what affects the public is the finished media product—which reflects the priorities and choices of top management.

Television's most eminent political programs feature styles that range from genteel exchanges on *Washington Week in Review,* to high-decibel simplicities of *The McLaughlin Group,* to forehead-crinkling discussions on the nightly *NewsHour With Jim Lehrer.* But in every case, the corporate logos of sponsors and underwriters, dancing on the screen, hint at the choreography and orchestration. Those who pay the piper call the tune—not every note, but the main themes.

When yet another TV pundit show premiered in 1988—*The Capital Gang* with Patrick Buchanan and Robert Novak squaring off against Mark Shields and *Wall Street Journal* Washington bureau chief Al Hunt—no one pointed out the double meaning of its name. *The Capital Gang* stayed well within bounds acceptable to institutions of big capital, some of which were sponsors of the show and investors in the network. A CNN promotional spot for *The Capital Gang* was right on the money as it described the program: "A select few make judgments that affect us all."

In 1997, the media watch group FAIR noted that "forceful right-wing advocates enjoy prominent positions in national mainstream media—as television commentators, radio hosts, and syndicated columnists.... They are often heard denouncing `liberal media bias' even as their collective voices overwhelm those of unabashed left-wing commentators."

On major TV networks, the "liberal media" include such outspoken conservatives as Buchanan, Novak, George Will, John Sununu, Mona Charen, Pat Robertson, William Kristol, Fred Barnes, Morton Kondracke, Paul Gigot, Ben Wattenberg, Lynn Cheney, William F. Buckley, John McLaughlin, James Glassman, and Laura Ingraham. Their routine opponents—if any—are mushy centrists and tepid liberals along the lines of Shields, Hunt, Jack Germond, Geraldine Ferraro, Eleanor Clift, and George Stephanopoulos.

Populism, historically and in the present day, has taken two general paths. Only one of them is well represented on television and radio. The road of virulent intolerance—blaming the poor, racial minorities, feminists, gays, and immigrants—is well traveled by the Buchanans and the Novaks, the Rush Limbaughs, and the G. Gordon Liddys. But those who have taken the other fork in a populist journey—strong progressives—are rarely found in the mass media.

Overall, in the United States, the news media offer the public either conventional pundits who differ on exactly how to shore up the status quo, or populists of the right-wing variety. Largely excluded are progressive populists who challenge the power of large corporations and explicitly reject scapegoating.

MYTH: FREE PRESS = PRIVATELY-OWNED PRESS

Equating freedom of the media with private ownership of the media is a convenient myth for the likes of Time Warner, Disney, and General Electric. In the real world, however, the freedom of expression that flourishes in mass media is confined to messages that are acceptable to such corporations.

Although dissenting voices are heard once in a while, the essence of propaganda is repetition—and what's repeated does not rock the big corporate boats. The favorite perspectives of economic elites are commonly mistaken for journalism. The narrative is usually narrow; for example, we hear much more about the concerns of investors and shareholders than workers or consumers. Mass-media employees seem to rise to the level of their utility to corporate America.

Bankrolled by major corporations, mainstream media have done a lot to render "big government" one of the leading pejoratives of American political rhetoric. In contrast, the private sector largely eludes media scrutiny; we rarely hear warnings about "big business." Not coincidentally, the Pentagon's huge sacrosanct budget is a cash cow for some companies that own large media outlets, such as General Electric (NBC) and Westinghouse (CBS). Many more firms are hefty advertisers—as well as contributors to the campaigns of politicians selectively lambasting "big government."

As corporations increase their power, they meld with the journalistic air and blend into the media atmosphere—so that a *de facto* corporate state appears to supply us with the oxygen we breathe. Under such circumstances, accepting corporate power seems natural and neutral; opposing it seems "ideological."

The corporatization of media is part of broader developments in public and private life. We're invited to choose from choices made for us by wealthy and powerful elites. Democracy has very little to do with the process.

MYTH: AT LEAST WE HAVE PUBLIC BROADCASTING

Mythology aside, "public broadcasting" is second to none for corralling minds that might otherwise wander. For propaganda in the guise of quality journalism, the Public Broadcasting Service and National Public Radio can't be beat—a reality that became more flagrant in 1991, during the Gulf War, when the PBS *MacNeil-Lehrer NewsHour* (now *The NewsHour with Jim Lehrer*) cheer-led U.S. missile attacks on Iraqi cities and NPR seemed to stand for National Pentagon Radio. Such pseudo-alternative media outlets receive plenty of acclaim. Providing more in-depth coverage than commercial networks, they perform high jumps over low standards.

Taken as a whole, NPR's news coverage swamps its islands of laudable journalism with oceans of avid stenography for the powerful. Sociologist Charlotte Ryan examined the transcripts of every weekday broadcast of *All Things Considered*, and *Morning Edition*—totaling 2,296 stories—during the last four months of 1991. Her study, commissioned by FAIR, concluded that NPR is in sync with "the tendency to allow Washington officials and establishment pundits to set the news agenda." When selecting and quoting sources, NPR relied most heavily on government officials (26 percent of all sources). Journalists, academics, lawyers, and other professionals accounted for another 37 percent.

Twenty-eight percent of NPR's domestic stories originated in Washington, a city with think tanks of every sort. But for analysis, NPR repeatedly turned to corporate-funded outfits of the establishment center (such as the Brookings Institution, 11 quotes) and the right (such as American Enterprise Institute, eight quotes). Think tanks to the left of center, or allied with labor, were generally ignored; for example, the Institute for Policy Studies was never quoted.

Other FAIR studies have documented that television programs like ABC's *Nightline* and the PBS *NewsHour* allow little air time for representatives of public interest and grass-roots action groups. Such voices were no more audible on NPR—only 7 percent of total sources. Ryan's study found that the numbers of advocates for any single movement were tiny—racial or ethnic groups (1.5 percent); organized labor (0.6 percent); feminism (0.4 percent); environmentalism (0.3 percent); gay rights (0.2 percent).

Propaganda is scarcely mitigated by occasional exceptions. It's the routine that counts: the political clichés supplied by Cokie Roberts, for instance, or the mind-constricting repartee of Shields and Gigot. Narrow territory must be traversed, endlessly, as though it were the alpha and omega of political terrain. The routine discourse runs the gamut from A to C.

The crown jewel of PBS nightly programming, *The NewsHour With Jim Lehrer*, puts out press releases hailing itself as "one of the most influential news sources in the world." Credit where due: *The NewsHour* has excelled at serving as a steady transmission belt for elite opinion. Most of the time, disagreements are well within the range to be found among powerful politicians and lobbyists in Washington. It's fitting that the show has been praised as "balanced" by right-wing groups that normally bash network TV news for being too "liberal."

The NewsHour has always depended on corporate largess. In the past, underwriters have included AT&T and PepsiCo. These days, two politically active firms—the agribusiness giant Archer Daniels Midland and the New York Life Insurance Co.—team up to provide about $10 million a year, which amounts to half of the program's total budget.

In December 1994, the private media conglomerate TCI purchased two-thirds of MacNeil/Lehrer Productions. The PBS network president, Ervin Duggan, promptly called it "a welcome infusion of capital into the *NewsHour.*" Since then, the program's top producers have continued to resist introspection. In 1995, I asked the president of MacNeil/Lehrer Productions to comment on charges that the program lacks diversity. "I think that's an outrageous criticism of our program," Al Vecchione replied. "It's in a class by itself in terms of being fair and evenhanded."

In autumn of 1997, PBS moved to augment public TV's schedule of political discussion shows, which already included a half-dozen weekly programs hosted by conservatives like William F. Buckley, John McLaughlin, Ben Wattenberg, and James Glassman. PBS added a new series, *National Desk,* with three rotating hosts: In a nod to diversity, white conservatives Fred Barnes and Morton Kondracke were joined by black conservative Larry Elder.

MYTH: NEW TECHNOLOGIES ARE CREATING MORE DEMOCRATIC MEDIA

Whether trumpeted two decades ago with the advent of cable technology, or today, with nonstop prattle about "the information superhighway," the myth of the techno-fix is a distraction from a key truth: We cannot solve political problems by technological means. No digital breakthrough or cyberspace marvel can rectify a chronic and severe shortage of democracy.

In countless media forums, we're encouraged to fixate on technology—and speculate on the market prospects of corporations like Microsoft, Oracle, Apple, and the like. As mere mortals, we are cast in the roles of spectators while the multibillion-dollar media gods clash and cooperate. The new technologies are impressive. But power is more centralized than ever.

It's pleasant to believe that the Internet will provide a free flow of information and opinion. Popular rhetoric makes plenty of egalitarian claims—but the emerging reality is something else. "The Internet is in full transition from a participatory interactive communications network to a broadcast medium dominated by electronic commerce," observes Frank Beacham, an independent journalist who monitors technology.

Viewed from corporate boardrooms, the ideal Internet users will be passive consumers. Lots of publicity—and multimedia leverage—will be crucial to steer a mass audience to particular spots on the vast Internet. The biggest players in cyberspace aren't just guiding us through the media terrain—they're altering it in fundamental ways, pointing us in some directions and away from others.

The way things are going, Beacham warns, the Internet will soon undergo a profound shift—"from being a participatory medium that serves the interest of the public to being a broadcast medium, where corporations deliver consumer-oriented information. Interactivity would be reduced to little more than sales transactions and e-mail."

It's easy to be mesmerized by dynamic new technology that seems to offer a way of cutting through knotty social problems. To substitute for figuring out how to create systems of communication that are genuinely democratic, believers in the techno-fix assume that technological change can dissolve the bottlenecks.

It never works. From radio to television to modem, each new gizmo has arrived with inspiring potential—undermined by extreme disparities in people's access to economic resources and political clout.

MYTH: NEWS REPORTS CAN BE "OBJECTIVE"

Despite all the pieties about objective journalism, the truth is that value judgments infuse everything in news media.

After decades as a reporter and editor in the newspaper business, Ben Bagdikian wrote *The Media Monopoly*. The book describes a few of the subjective choices that go into any daily paper: "Which of the infinite number of events in the environment will be assigned for coverage and which ignored? Which of the infinite observations confronting the reporter will be noted? Which of the facts noted will be included in the story? Which of the reported events will become the first paragraph? Which story will be prominently dis-

played on page 1 and which buried inside or discarded? None of these is a truly objective decision."

It's not a matter of merely reporting the news. Mass media literally *make* the news. Subjective decisions, suffused with judgments based on values, are constant and inevitable. Familiar types of coverage can come across as "objective" precisely because they're so ubiquitous, blending in with the customary media landscape.

MYTH: NEWSPAPERS CORRECT
THE MOST IMPORTANT INACCURACIES

On the second page of *The New York Times,* on the last Sunday of October 1997, the listings were typical under a headline that said "Corrections":

➤ Because of a mechanical error, a picture on page 44 of *The Times Magazine* today, with an article about notable art collectors, is printed upside down and in mirror image. In the painting by David Hammons, called "Bag Lady in Flight," the handles seen on the top left should appear at the bottom left.
➤ A listing in the "New & Noteworthy Paperbacks" column of the *Times Book Review* on Oct. 5 misidentified the distributor of Yury Dombrovsky's autobiographical novel "The Faculty of Useless Knowledge." Like other books from Harvill Press, it is now distributed in the United States by Farrar, Straus & Giroux—no longer by HarperCollins World.
➤ An article on page 16 of the "Travel" section today about the Caribbean island of Saba misstates the height of a cliff where the airport was built. It is 400 feet, not 4,000.

Such inconsequential corrections are routine. In general, the more minor an inaccuracy is, the greater the chances that a correction will appear. The major distortions and imbalances of media coverage, however—the ongoing biases

of race and gender and class, or the stenographic reliance on governmental and corporate sources—don't qualify for correction. They're much too important. And they're not mistakes.

MYTH: IN THE U.S.A., JOURNALISTS WORK FREE OF CENSORSHIP

While a few huge conglomerates now control most of the flow of news and information, the effects are more insidious than overt. Intermittent cases of blatant corporate censorship are much less significant than the unspoken limits that journalists learn to accept.

"Circus dogs jump when the trainer cracks his whip," George Orwell wrote, "but the really well-trained dog is the one that turns his somersault when there is no whip." A half-century after Orwell's caustic gibe at compliant editors, self-censorship is one of the least discussed media constraints.

When a dictatorial government decides what can reach print or get on the airwaves, the heavy hand of the censor is apt to be obvious. But in a society where the First Amendment protects freedom of speech, the most important limitations are obscured.

In contrast to dramatic storms of brazen censorship, the usual climate of U.S. journalism is as unobtrusive as morning dew. The dominant seems normal, like a ubiquitous odor. "We scent the air of the office," the great American journalist George Seldes noted in 1931. "We realize that certain things are wanted, certain things unwanted."

Today's media milieu hardly encourages intrepid journalism. At a time of merger mania in the news industry, journalists are especially aware that it's risky to challenge the corporate elephant fattening in the middle of the newsroom.

It is illustrative that *The Today Show* on NBC—a network owned by General Electric—removed mention of defective GE-made bolts from a correspondent's news report in November 1989. And it's telling that the program's producers told a guest expert on consumer boycotts not to mention a major boycott targeting GE. But it's unlikely that anyone from GE's front office specifically ordered *Today Show* producers to protect the company's image. No one had to. That's how self-censorship works.

And nobody needs to instruct the editor of a magazine dependent on cigarette advertising revenue not to launch a crusade against the tobacco industry.

Blatant instances of owner or advertiser pressure on journalists, while significant, are mere tips of icebergs that must be taken into account when navigating a journalistic career. Flagrant intrusion by media owners or sponsors is not a frequent occurrence; far more common, below the surface, are the preemptive decisions made in silence.

The biases of mass media don't amount to a conspiracy, as longtime TV producer Danny Schechter says in his book *The More You Watch, The Less You Know,* published in late 1997: "No, rarely is someone picking up the phone and telling some producer to skew the news. The boardroom rarely faxes orders to the newsroom. But then again, they don't have to if they hire professionals who share the same world view and language, rely on the same sources, and tend to shape their reporting the same way."

Self-censorship gains power as it becomes automatic. Former FCC commissioner Nicholas Johnson summarized the process when he told of "a reporter who first comes up with an investigative story idea, writes it up, and submits it to the editor and is told the story is not going to run. He wonders why, but the next time he is cautious enough to check with the editor first. He is told by the editor that it would be better not to write that story." Johnson added: "The third time he thinks of an investigative story idea but doesn't bother the editor with it because he knows it's silly. The fourth time he doesn't even think of the idea anymore."

Journalists are probably no less courageous than people in other professions. But it's daunting, especially in tough economic times, to consider biting the hand that signs the paycheck. Options have been particularly sparse during this decade, with news departments shrinking at many media outlets.

In the mid-1990s, soon after transferring from a top post at General Mills, the new chief executive at Times Mirror Co., Mark Willes, lowered the corporate boom—closing *New York Newsday* and ordering big layoffs at *The Los Angeles Times.* Willes did not seem to be embarrassed when he compared managing newspapers to marketing Cheerios.

The journalists who insist that they are hardly akin to Orwell's circus dogs—that they function without severe constraints—should try harder to prove such assertions in daily work. Few whips are in evidence as most American journalists labor with well-trained caution.

MYTH: TELEVISION PUTS US IN TOUCH WITH EACH OTHER

In the mass culture of television, what gets inculcated is intimate and global. Television powerfully normalizes duplicity; winks and nods become unnecessary. Commercials have tremendous impact on people who "understand" cerebrally that those ads are untruthful and manipulative. News reports and commentaries also have enormous effects—even on those who watch with great skepticism.

In her book *When Society Becomes an Addict*, Anne Wilson Schaef describes television as one of the habitual commodities that "make us numb to our own reality—to seeing what we see and knowing what we know." But behind the madness of TV is a lucrative method. Informing, entertaining, and dunning become interchangeable. Replete with technical virtuosity, ads on television have become ersatz art forms. Sales pitches are to entertain, and entertainment is to pitch for consumption. Television programs, layered with commercials, synthesize complementary messages that foster passivity among the population. All we're really encouraged to do is go out and buy things.

MYTH: THE NEWS MEDIA ARE PROMOTING SOCIAL CHANGE

If current types of journalism were in place generations ago, the coverage might have gone something like this:

CBS EVENING NEWS, SPRING 1913.

DAN RATHER: "Tensions are high in the nation's capital tonight, hours after a militant march down Pennsylvania Avenue by suffragettes. Police say 3,000 ladies were there. Protest leaders claim twice that number. For some perspective, we turn now to CBS news analyst Laura Ingraham."

LAURA INGRAHAM: "Dan, anyone watching the march had to be concerned about the polarization of America. Gender conflict is on the rise. What's next? Refusal to wear corsets? Brassiere burning? Female lawyers? The latest fashion statements are coming from feminists with an anti-male agenda. It's as though men can't do anything right."

RATHER: "But what about the idea that women should have the right to vote, just like men?"

INGRAHAM: "Sounds like some kind of envy to me, Dan. Those of us who are secure in our womanhood don't make these demands. We may not like the results of the male electorate, but it's the height of elitist arrogance to assume that other voters could do any better."

ABC'S THIS WEEK, MARCH 1933.

SAM DONALDSON: "A new president—in a wheelchair no less—entering the White House after a landslide. How's this going to play out? Cokie?"

COKIE ROBERTS: "Sam, it's important that our new president avoid doing anything rash. Let's remember, he wisely campaigned on a moderate platform. Now, as usual, some Democrats want to push him to the left. It would be political suicide."

GEORGE WILL: "The leveling impulse has always been a hazard to democracy, as Alexis de Tocqueville pointed out a century ago. He warned that Americans were overly enamored of equality, which can only lead to the tyranny of the mob. Right now, I fear for this republic."

DONALDSON: "George, surely you're not saying Franklin Roosevelt is dangerous. I mean—"

WILL: "Time will tell. There's talk of a federal social-security program. And unemployment insurance. The kind of welfare-state mentality that undermines family values and frays the moral fabric of the free-enterprise system."

ROBERTS: "But I'm convinced cooler heads will prevail. That's the word on Capitol Hill."

HEADLINES, JULY 1946.

People Magazine: "Bob Oppenheimer, the Sexy Brain Behind the Bomb Tests"

The Wall Street Journal: "Bikini A-Bomb Blasts Encourage Investors"

USA Today: "*We're* Happy About Atomic Weapons!"

ABC'S 20/20, SEPTEMBER 1957.

HUGH DOWNS: "It's not so easy being a governor these days. Is it, Barbara?"

BARBARA WALTERS: "Certainly not if your name is Orval Faubus. I visited him yesterday at the governor's mansion in Little Rock. He was kind and charming. But his life has been quite stressful with all the well-publicized controversy about integration at Central High School. Next: a look inside the private life of the governor of Arkansas, a gentle man in a difficult time."

THE MCLAUGHLIN GROUP, APRIL 1963.

FRED BARNES: "This kind of lawlessness can't be tolerated. It's outrageous."

MORTON KONDRACKE: "A big publicity stunt, that's what we're seeing. Some of my gullible colleagues in the press corps are falling for this smear campaign against the city of Birmingham, the state of Alabama, and the United States of America. These demonstrations give comfort to our country's enemies."

PATRICK BUCHANAN: "The protesters say they want 'civil rights.' What a laugh. They want special rights. If the media would ignore these trouble-makers, we'd have some racial tranquillity in America. The police measures have been entirely justified."

JACK GERMOND: "Gosh, I can't agree with that. Maybe the fire hoses are necessary. But using attack dogs on those young demonstrators seems too extreme."

JOHN McLAUGHLIN: "Jack, is that the bleating sound of a bleeding-heart liberal?"

KONDRACKE: "Ha ha."

BARNES: "Ha ha."

NORMAN SOLOMON is a nationally syndicated columnist on media and poli-tics. His most recent books are *Wizards of Media Oz: Behind the Curtain of Mainstream News* (co-authored with Jeff Cohen) and *The Trouble With Dil-bert: How Corporate Culture Gets the Last Laugh.* He is an associate of the media watch group FAIR.

CHAPTER 7

Fear and Favor in the Newsroom

By Beth Sanders and Randy Baker

Back in 1990 we started work on *Fear and Favor in the Newsroom*, a documentary narrated by Studs Terkel which shows that ownership of the press by a small elite constricts the free flow of ideas and information upon which our democracy depends. We wondered to what extent the corporate influence over the mass media, which we documented in the film, was going to undermine our own ability to complete and then distribute the film to the public.

Seven years later, we found those pressures have weighed heavily on *Fear and Favor in the Newsroom*. On a more optimistic note, however, we also found that there are a considerable number of people who want to challenge the corporate stranglehold on the news, and those people have helped us bring *Fear and Favor in the Newsroom* to the public.

We made *Fear and Favor in the Newsroom* to challenge the pervasive assumption that the major news outlets provide us "fair" and "objective" reporting. Organizations such as Fairness and Accuracy in Reporting (FAIR) and Project Censored have long exposed the mainstream media's partiality to what can be termed a "Fortune 500" point of view. We hoped to use the medium of video to bring this analysis to a broader audience.

Typically what the public hears about the corporate news media is the story they like to tell about themselves: that they do not favor the interests of the wealthy and the powerful. Indeed, defenders of the corporate press buttress their case by pointing to the news they report that does antagonize the powers that be.

That there are instances in which news stories critical of the wealthy and powerful in America come from the corporate media itself is true enough, but this proves too little. The partiality of the corporate press lies in the fact that when a reporter discloses unflattering facts about the powerful, he or she is "in a dangerous area," as Lowell Bergman, a producer at CBS's *60 Minutes* explains in *Fear and Favor in the Newsroom*. Pursuing those stories too often can damage a journalist's career.

As a result, to be safe, journalists usually cover such stories only if these reach a "higher threshold of drama and documentation" than other stories, to borrow Ben Bagdikian's apt expression. In other words, the major news outlets employ a double standard, one for stories that could offend the powers that be, and one for all other news. It is this double standard that gives the news its "Fortune 500" spin.

Fear and Favor in the Newsroom is a film about this double standard, its effect on journalists, and its consequences for the news. Of course, as the journalists explain in the film, this double standard is not written on a bulletin board. Owners and editors don't walk through newsrooms telling journalists to lay off their wealthy and powerful friends and business associates. The standard is generally expressed more subtly. Editors tell reporters, "no one is interested in that," which, as Ben Bagdikian, Dean emeritus of the Journalism School at the University of California, Berkeley, tells viewers, would be legitimate if it were true. Or they might ask the reporter, as former *Atlanta Journal Constitution* Assistant Managing Editor Wendall Rawls explains, "What else you got on your plate?"

To make this double standard clearer, *Fear and Favor in the Newsroom* looks at what happened to journalists, and to their work, when they didn't take the hints, and when they proceeded to cover the powers that be as professional journalists, rather than as followers of the double standard. Even though our subjects were all award-winning journalists at prestigious news organizations, they met a pattern of obstruction by superiors, suppression of stories, and in some cases, suffered severely damaged careers.

One of the stories we present is that of Sydney Schanberg, a Pulitzer Prize-winning journalist at *The New York Times*. Schanberg explains to viewers how, while he tried to report on abuses of power by the wealthy and a city government closely tied to elites, his superiors at *The Times* consistently interfered with his work—and how, ultimately, they took away his column because of such reporting. We were also able to interview Sydney Gruson, the man who canceled Schanberg's column. Sydney Gruson, the former assistant to the Publisher and Vice Chairman of the New York Times Corporation, substantially acknowledged Schanberg's contention, explaining that *The Times* canceled Schanberg's column because it disapproved of the unflattering light in which Schanberg's writing had cast *The New York Times* itself.

Fear and Favor in the Newsroom also examines the case of reporter Jon Alpert, winner of numerous Emmy Awards, who brought NBC News the first uncensored footage from Iraq during the 1991 Persian Gulf War. The footage depicted widespread damage to civilians inflicted by U.S. bombing—evidence which contradicted the official story of "surgical" strikes against Saddam Hussein. Jon Alpert explains to viewers that he was able to sneak the footage out of Iraq and beat their censors, but he was unable to beat the censors in the U.S. After the staff of the *NBC Nightly News* had scheduled it for broadcast, Michael Gartner, then President of NBC News, personally spiked the story and then fired Alpert on the spot. Any doubts that Gartner's actions were censorious are put to rest when Michael Gartner justifies his actions by citing a two-year-old infraction, which Alpert had committed before the Iraq story— shooting a reenactment of a flag raising—and after which NBC had continued to air Alpert's work.

In another case, *Fear and Favor in the Newsroom* shows footage deleted by editors at PBS's *MacNeil-Lehrer NewsHour* (now *The NewsHour with Jim Lehrer*) from a story produced by award-winning reporter Peter Graumann. The story concerned a controversy over the construction of a proposed radioactive waste storage facility in Ward Valley, near the small California town of Needles. The deleted footage depicted the "technology" to be employed at the facility—an unlined pit in the ground—and the dismal track record of serious radioactive waste leakage established by other radioactive waste facilities, including those operated by the same firm that was proposed to manage the Ward Valley facility. Graumann then explains to viewers that, after he watched the edited story on *MacNeil-Lehrer*, he realized that the edits created the impression that opponents of the facility, i.e. residents near the California site and environmentalists, were a bunch of anti-technology nuts. Essentially, the deleted footage prevented *MacNeil-Lehrer* viewers from seeing the compelling evidence on which opponents of the waste facility had based their opposition. Conversely, Graumann explains the editing reinforced the credibility of the large corporations and the government, which supported the construction of the radioactive waste facility.

Based on the critical response the show has received, *Fear and Favor in the Newsroom* is a success. *The San Francisco Bay Guardian* labeled it a "landmark documentary" and the *Village Voice* described it as "tough, gutsy and vital." Moreover, a broad range of commentators, unconnected with the alternative press, including journalist and former State Department Spokesperson Hodding Carter, Columbia Journalism School Professor James Carey, and reviewers at *The San Francisco Chronicle, Boston Globe*, and *The Quill* (the journal of the Society of Professional Journalists) found that *Fear and Favor in the Newsroom* cogently and accurately documents how journalists are discouraged from pursuing stories that challenge accounts put forth by the wealthy and the powerful. The most unfavorable review we have encountered appeared in the *San Jose Mercury News* (a paper negatively covered in the film) and even that reviewer said that the program merited a broadcast on public television.

Despite the broad and highly favorable recognition the show has received, however, public television has been, on the whole, extremely resistant to the show. In fact, we first encountered this resistance during production.

At several points we sought production assistance from public television's *Frontline* series, from *P.O.V.* (PBS's special series for independent documentaries), and from the Independent Television Service (established by Congress for the purpose of funding independent film). Each time, we were rejected. Of course, given the large corporate influence in public television, a documentary exposing unflattering facts about corporate power—including corporate influence over public broadcasting—this resistance was not entirely unexpected.

However, we were surprised by how brazenly one public television executive announced his pandering to corporate sensibilities. After viewing a sample clip of the show early in the production process, *P.O.V.* executive producer Marc Weiss told us straight out that *P.O.V.* probably would not be interested in the project because it was not likely to be favorably reviewed in venues such as *Redbook*. (Randy, handicapped by his ignorance of this publication, nonetheless intuited that *Redbook* was not the kind of journal that reviewed films exposing the dark sides of corporate power.)

With public funding closed off, support from private foundations was not forthcoming. Most foundations were not sympathetic to the film's thesis and even several foundations otherwise sympathetic to the film's ideas would not fund media as a matter of policy. (Apostles of the "Fortune 500" world view should have this problem.) This is why it took us six years to complete the documentary. Ultimately, the show was financed through grants from several small foundations, a few individuals, and in-kind contributions. When we had shot the film and required only access to "on-line" facilities for the final edit of the show, we literally had no place to go. Then Danny McGuire, the executive producer at KTEH, San José's "renegade" public television station, came to our rescue. McGuire provided us a professional editor, an edit suite, and left control of the content of the program entirely to us. McGuire recognized that *Fear and Favor in the Newsroom* was "the story the corporate media won't report," and explained that was why he and KTEH "wanted to see it completed, aired, and distributed." This, of course, is the *raison d'être* for public television. Regrettably, as Trudy Lieberman noted in her June 23, 1997 column in *The Nation*, KTEH's commitment to the goals of public broadcasting is extremely unusual.

For example, two considerably larger public television stations, KQED in San Francisco and WTTW in Chicago (which had won a regional Emmy with Beth Sanders for broadcasting her first documentary film), declined to provide any support whatsoever for *Fear and Favor in the Newsroom*. Even after the program was completed with KTEH's assistance, PBS rejected the program for national broadcast. *P.O.V. American Program Service* (APS), a smaller source of public television programming, also rejected the program. It was, according to APS, "not balanced enough."

Finally, in the summer of 1997, after a year of negotiations, KTEH's Danny McGuire secured a satellite feed of the show to all public television stations nationwide through the National Educational Television Association (NETA). NETA is apparently the smallest and least influential source of national programming for public television. Because this meant we were effectively at the bottom of the public television programming food chain, we essentially had to persuade each local public television station to download the satellite feed, and then to broadcast it.

To aid us in our efforts, we asked people to contact their local PBS program directors to urge them to broadcast *Fear and Favor in the Newsroom*. Some producers had warned that this technique could backfire by annoying program directors. In our case we felt we had nothing to lose. How many public television stations would air a documentary that exposed the undersides of corporate power, including corporate power at public television, if their viewers and members did not demand it?

The lobbying effort picked up steam when Citizen Vagrom, a group of media activists in Seattle, produced a video segment on *Fear and Favor in the News-*

room and on public television's resistance to the show. In addition to distributing the segment through their free video magazine, they put the segment on their Web site and linked it to Free Speech TV's Web site. FAIR and other grass-roots activist groups posted their own Web-site notices, as did our educational distributor, California Newsreel. Suddenly an Internet/e-mail campaign to air *Fear and Favor in the Newsroom* was born. Viewers and activists around the country, including media activist groups in Seattle, Chicago, and Los Angeles began to lobby their local PBS affiliates around the country to air the show, often e-mailing us the responses they were getting from their public television programmers.

The Internet campaign became so strong that it generated widespread interest all over the U.S. Numerous alternative newspapers began publishing stories about *Fear and Favor in the Newsroom* and its fate in public broadcasting. *Wired Magazine* published a story on it and on the Internet campaign to get it aired.

One participant in the campaign, Andrew Barbano, a Nevada journalist and activist, began using his newspaper column as a virtual battering ram in order to "raise hell" so that Nevada's public television stations would air the program. Barbano connected with local labor and environmental activists who then joined the campaign. As a result, Barbano just reported to us, public television in Reno has scheduled *Fear and Favor in the Newsroom* for a prime time broadcast. Las Vegas public television, and other stations in the region have not committed thus far, but Barbano and the activists are proceeding apace.

Several community radio stations, including those in Minneapolis; Seattle; Madison, Wisconsin; Austin, Texas; and Portland, Oregon, did programs on *Fear and Favor in the Newsroom* and its fate at public television, as did *Hightower Radio, Making Contact,* and *Democracy Now.* KPFA, the Pacifica affiliate in Berkeley, did numerous shows on the program. FAIR's national radio show *Counterspin* did a segment on the program. These radio shows also seem to have made a considerable impact. When several public television stations were called to get a sense of how many had already been contacted about *Fear and Favor in the Newsroom,* those located in markets where there had been local radio interviews seemed to have had the most calls to the program director.

In one case the impact was manifest. After Beth was on the *Peace and Social Justice* show on public radio in Chico, California, we were told the local PBS station was inundated with calls encouraging the station to air *Fear and Favor in the Newsroom.* The station agreed, but there was a catch. Although the documentary was offered to the station for free, the station required an underwriter. Thankfully, a small, feisty, (they had been bombed, apparently in response to their reporting) independently owned newspaper, the *Sacramento Valley Mirror*, came forward to underwrite the documentary.

One place where the campaign almost certainly made a difference was at KQED, San Francisco's public television station. *Fear and Favor in the Newsroom* began to attain visibility in San Francisco after a local screening jointly sponsored by Project Censored and The Northern California Chapter of the Society of Professional Journalists. Shortly thereafter, KTEH in neighboring San Jose aired the program. This resulted in reviews in the *San Francisco Examiner*, in the alternative San Jose weekly, the *Metro*, in the *Berkeley Voice*, and in *Disgruntled*, a Berkeley-based, on-line magazine. KQED radio, the principal NPR affiliate in San Francisco, also devoted a full hour to the program.

About this time, Dennis Bernstein and Julie Light, investigative reporters and producers at Berkeley's listener-supported KPFA radio, began the first three programs on *Fear and Favor in the Newsroom* and its troubles with public television. Chris Welch and Philip Muldari, who co-host a public affairs show at KPFA, also did several programs on the show. KPFA news often issued reports on our progress, or lack thereof, in getting broadcast time.

The result, we were told from several sources, was a barrage from the community for KQED in San Francisco to air the program. KQED's president made a public statement that the station would consider the program for broadcast when it was offered. And, indeed, when we subsequently submitted the show to KQED, they aired it in a favorable time slot, which earned the show a favorable review by the *San Francisco Chronicle's* television critic. We, of course, were not privy to KQED's decision–making process. However, given their utter lack of interest in helping us finish the show during the earlier production stages, it is difficult to imagine that pressure from the public to air it was not a factor.

Public pressure does not always prevail, however. One station, for example, that we know will not run *Fear and Favor in the Newsroom* despite public interest is San Diego's KPBS. Responding to persistent inquiries by activist Bill Lott, KPBS's program director complained to Lott about all the telephone calls and faxes people were sending her about *Fear and Favor in the Newsroom.* She then sent Lott a written explanation of their decision not to broadcast the show, including in it such criticisms as that the film shouldn't have shown Ralph Nader suggesting that the public was interested in nuclear power stories, because he had no expertise in television "psychographics."

At the time of this writing, *Fear and Favor in the Newsroom* has been, or is scheduled for, broadcast in Seattle, San Francisco, Chicago, Minneapolis,

St. Paul, St. Louis, and Reno, as well as more than half a dozen smaller locations across the U.S. Some of these stations, such as those in Chicago and St. Louis, have scheduled it outside prime viewing time, thereby substantially reducing the number of people who would otherwise see the show. So, while *Fear and Favor in the Newsroom* has not been entirely frozen out of public television, at least as things stand now, the vast majority of the public television audience will not be able to see it.

Another vehicle we had thought would have helped us increase the show's visibility and thereby enhance its chances for television broadcast was public screenings. Our belief and hope was that the screenings would help by generating interest from newspapers, magazine reviewers, and radio shows. We were wrong.

Fear and Favor in the Newsroom screened at the national convention of the Society of Professional Journalists (SPJ) in Washington, DC. In addition, local chapters of SPJ held screenings in Philadelphia, and several in New Jersey. To our knowledge, these screenings did not generate a single story, which seems somewhat surprising and ironic given that journalists obviously were aware of and interested in the show—having screened it themselves. Even publications that focus on journalism, such as *Columbia Journalism Review*, and *American Journalism Review* (formerly the *Washington Journalism Review*), have ignored the program.

Fear and Favor in the Newsroom was also screened at New York University's journalism school and the screening was followed by a panel discussion with several of the journalists who appeared in the film. The event attracted over 300 persons, including a number of journalists from local and national media. Yet, only Raymond Schroth in the *National Catholic Reporter* reviewed the film in an article titled "Corporate Influence Makes Sure You'll Never Get to See This Show." As Trudy Lieberman noted in her June 23, 1997 column in *The Nation*, "Almost no one, including the city's media organizations, had come to write about it—a twist consistent with the film's central thesis: The media avoid uncomfortable topics that strike too close to home."

One exception to this pattern was *The Boston Globe*, which published a story after a screening at the Boston Museum of Fine Arts. The screening was followed by a discussion that included such participants as Bill Kovach, curator of Harvard's Nieman Foundation (whose story is discussed in the documentary).

Unfortunately, with some notable exceptions, most of the major alternative press outlets ignored the show until the grass-roots campaign to air it began—one full year after the show was completed and brought to their attention by our distributor, California Newsreel. In light of the power the alternative press had to mobilize people on this issue elsewhere, this was particularly distressing.

Our challenge remains to get our documentary seen by as large and varied an audience as possible. One venue in which the show is being widely seen is colleges and universities, where California Newsreel has already sold hundreds of copies. Several professors have reported that their students consistently find the film stunning and that lively debates follow each screening. Interestingly, one journalism school decided not to purchase *Fear and Favor in the Newsroom* because students would find it "discouraging."

The broader problem at hand, however, is less about the televising of *Fear and Favor in the Newsroom* and more about insuring the public's access to news that is not distorted by a "Fortune 500" spin. That, of course, will require establishing a news media with a large revenue source which is independent of the discretion of corporate interests and of the government.

There is plenty of money available to support such a news media. Dean Baker, an economist at the Economic Policy Institute, points to calculations by several respected mainstream economists, including Lawrence Summers of Harvard University (currently Deputy Secretary of Treasury) showing that a 1/2 percent transaction tax on securities would raise about $30 billion per year. Moreover, Summers' analysis shows that such a tax would actually benefit the economy by reducing unproductive speculation, thereby rendering securities markets more stable.

Financing the press through such a tax would also be extremely equitable. Since the vast majority of the public derives very little of its income from securities transactions, even when pension funds are considered, only persons whose incomes place them in the top 3-5 percent of earners would pay any significant amount towards the tax. Essentially, the burden of the tax would fall on those best able to bear it, those with incomes over $150,000 per year.

Baker has also suggested a fascinating, simple, and highly attractive method of allocating such funds—letting individual citizens do the allocation. Thirty billion dollars in revenues works out to about $150 per adult citizen. Using the analogy of taxpayer check-offs to political parties, Baker proposes allotting to each adult citizen (regardless of tax status) the opportunity to direct the government each year to allocate $150 to the news organization of his or her choice (or relegating portions to several such organizations).

Presumably it would be desirable to require such organizations to satisfy the criteria for non-profit status; otherwise, large private firms might use their tremendous marketing power to bring most of the funds back into their own pockets. But, as it stands, an extremely wide range of social, cultural, educational, and activist organizations have satisfied these relatively easy and non-discretionary IRS rules, so it would not pose a great opportunity for government to intervene in the content of what is produced by such organizations.

The potential impact of such a policy on journalistic freedom and the breadth of public discourse could be revolutionary. Large corporations, small corporations, advertisers, governmental appointees, Congress, and foundations could be entirely removed from the process of selecting, evaluating, writing, and distributing the news. The purse strings of news organizations would lie in the hands of their audience.

Moreover, the gap between professional journalist and citizen would narrow in the sense that virtually anybody could become a journalist. If a journalist could persuade 100 fellow citizens to direct their $150 (or 200 citizens to allocate half their $150) to his or her newsletter, for example, that newsletter would have a $15,000 annual operating budget. That may not be enough to live on, but it could cover significant expenses and yield some compensation for the journalist. Given the number of community and non-profit organizational publications and Web sites already in existence, such a policy would almost certainly yield an explosion of these institutions.

And that sort of explosion of persons involved in investigating, analyzing, writing about, and discussing issues of concern to them and their communities is what we need to move from the increasingly corporate-dominated society to a more democratic one.

We outline this proposal here in order to illustrate the wide range of possibilities that are available if we successfully organize a movement to democratize the press. In the long run, the measure of *Fear and Favor in the Newsroom*'s success will be the extent to which it contributes to public understanding of the need for such a movement.

BETH SANDERS and **RANDY BAKER** are independent film makers and the producers of *Fear and Favor in the Newsroom*. They live in Seattle, Washington.

CHAPTER 8

Reviews of Current Books on Media, Censorship, and the First Amendment

By Sonoma State University Faculty

This book review chapter is designed to give readers a brief update on important recent books on media that address key issues in structural censorship, monopolization, the First Amendment, equal access to information, and the media's impacts on society. The following nine books were selected by the Project Censored staff for review by scholars from various disciplines.

TABLE OF CONTENTS—CURRENT BOOKS

THE MEDIA MONOPOLY, 5TH ED.

Ben Bagdikian
Boston: Beacon Press, 1997.
Reviewed by Charles Fox

"Media power is political power."

In erudite, often poetic terms, Ben Bagdikian delineates the size and power of the huge media conglomerates and their rapidly escalating political and economic influence in American society. Bagdikian makes a compelling argument that concentrated private ownership of mass media has become a threat to the American democratic process and suggests remedial action to create a media industry that operates in the public interest.

The Telecommunications Act of 1996 has made it possible for leading corporations to acquire vast combinations of media including television, radio, cable, newspapers, magazines, book publishing, film, and video production. Less than ten corporations now control a majority of the information and images flowing into American minds. Information will not reach the public unless a handful of corporate decision makers decides that it will. Through ownership of media outlets, military-industrial giants such as General Electric and Westinghouse have acquired extensive power to create and manipulate public perceptions. They utilize this ability to represent themselves in benevolent, even heroic terms. Not surprisingly, editorial and news content of their wholly owned subsidiaries has been "adjusted" to advance the corporate paradigm. There is increasing contempt for journalistic independence, and "zones of silence" often surround news topics that depart from the promotion of corporate values. The media conglomerates are successfully promoting their own national agenda.

With special emphasis on newspapers, Bagdikian describes the insidious process by which the pursuit of mass advertising has rearranged media priorities, steadily destroying competitive daily papers and impoverishing the marketplace of ideas. Ninety-eight percent of American cities are now "one paper towns." In some localities, advertising departments must approve stories involving local businesses before they can be printed. Seventy-five percent of daily newspaper budgets now come from advertising revenues. In broadcasting, the figure is close to 100 percent. Mass communications have become a vehicle for the promotion of a frantic level of consumption with news content designed to appeal to the "right kind" of audience.

American society currently faces a number of social and environmental crises. According to Bagdikian, these problems have remained largely invisible and untended due to the failure of commercial media to adequately report on the issues. The chronic failures of mass media to reasonably report urgent information and to present socially responsible entertainment present serious threats to social health.

In this astute analysis of media monopolization and its effects, Bagdikian suggests several steps to undo the dangerous excess of media concentration and revitalize American culture:

➤ Dilute the concentration of media ownership through reform of the Telecommunications Act of 1996;

➤ Ban paid political advertising from broadcasting;

➤ Improve financing for public broadcasting;

➤ Reform the Federal Communications Commission;

➤ Restore the Fairness Doctrine, ensuring a reasonable opportunity for opposing viewpoints to be expressed on critical issues;

➤ Create a non-partisan commission to study the performance of the country's media;

➤ Teach serious media literacy in schools.

Bagdikian asserts that social justice and economic success are not mutually exclusive goals, a myth that has been perpetuated in the mass media. He suggests that ultimately we need to make a conscious decision about the role of mass media in the construction—or destruction—of our society. Finally, he reminds us that the airwaves do not belong to the broadcasters. They are, by law, the property of the American people.

CHARLES FOX is a librarian at Sonoma State University and a Project Censored evaluator.

THE GLOBAL MEDIA: The New Missionaries Of Global Capitalism
Edward S. Herman and
Robert W. McChesney
Cassel, 1997.
Reviewed by Robert McNamara, Ph.D.

In *The Global Media*, Herman and McChesney have written a well-researched, up-to-date critique of the role of Transnational Corporations (TNCs) in the international capitalist system. Through a tracing of the emergence of the global media system with an account of those political, economic, and technological factors that have led to its ascension, the authors ask an important question: Have the central features of the global media process contributed to or inhibited "the public sphere," an important determinant of the quality of democracy? Given that the media are the primary vehicles through which the public participates in the political process, the authors' conclusions can hardly leave any advocate of the democratic process feeling optimistic. Rather than providing societies with the information they need to make informed decisions on important political matters, the primary objective of the global media process has been to deliver affluent audiences to advertisers, thus serving the interests of TNCs and the upper classes. While this thesis is hardly an original one (e.g., Ben Bagdikian's *Media Monopoly*), the authors, nevertheless, offer a convincing argument that the emergence of a truly global media system is actually a rather recent development, driven by the globalization of the market economy.

The discussion of the historical rise of neoliberalism and its relationship to global media is quite informative for any student of international politics. Specifically, the authors recount the efforts of the Non-Aligned Movement (NAM) in the 1970s and 1980s to bring the campaign for a New World Information and Communication Order (NWICO) to the attention of world audiences. Using UNESCO (United Nations Educational, Social, Cultural Organization) as their forum, the NAM (consisting of primarily Third World nations) accused the global media of cultural imperialism and 'flagrant quantitative' imbalances between the North and the South in information resources due to western monopoly of global news services. Yet, in the end, the movement was more of a rhetorical 'whining' than a true political threat. Instead, it provoked both the United States and Great Britain to withdraw from UNESCO, thus signaling the onslaught of neoliberal policies imposed by both Reaganism and Thatcherism.

The neoliberal policies of both Reagan and Thatcher, the authors argue, were aggressively applied to global media and telecommunications, thus stimulating their commercial development. Deregulation and the assault on organized labor were two significant factors in the 1980s that, along with new technologies, provided the basis for a new wave of corporate consolidations in the media industry. As the 1980s closed, the leading transnational media firms were rejecting national identities and regarding themselves as 'global concerns.'

THIS MODERN WORLD   by TOM TOMORROW

Although dominated by firms based in the United States, a critical development of the 1980s was a diffusion of ownership of the global media concerns among investors in the advanced capitalist world. An example is the Japanese purchase of U.S.-based media firms. The authors quote Herbert Schiller who aptly noted that American cultural imperialism was being replaced with "transnational corporate cultural imperialism with a heavy American accent."

The impact of neoliberalist policies of the 1980s was just the beginning of what we have more recently witnessed in the 1990s. While the commercialization and deregulation of national television systems worldwide began in the 1970s and was furthered in the 1980s under Reagan and Thatcher, this process gained full speed in the 1990s. Public broadcasting systems worldwide have seen their subsidies slashed, forcing many (e.g., PBS and BBC) to become commercial enterprises in order to succeed. Yet, it was the 1996 U.S. Telecommunications Act that "opened up a Pandora's box of consolidations." Deregulation has been the order of the day as the 1990s have witnessed an unprecedented wave of mergers and acquisitions. With the continued encouragement of the major media lobbies, a commercial spirit now permeates all national and regional (e.g., European Union) debates concerning media. This 'liberalization' drive can be most noted in the 1997 World Trade Organization's telecommunications agreement. This agreement, signed by 68 countries representing 90 percent of the telecommunications market, requires the signatories to open their markets to foreign competition and to allow foreign companies to buy stakes in domestic operators.

As for the impact of the Internet on the global media process, Herman and McChesney conclude that the future is "far from certain." Thus far, however, the authors note that the Internet has yet to become a lucrative market for the media TNCs. As long as that is the case, the Internet will hardly be in a position to effectively challenge the dominance of traditional commercial media. Still, all of the major media firms have significant stakes in the Internet since none of them wants to be 'outflanked' by their competitors if and when the Internet does become a profit-making venture.

In their final chapter, the authors note four specific neo-imperialist exports of the media TNCs, with the United States being the primary exporter: 1) commercial values; 2) displacement of the public sphere with entertainment; 3) the strengthening of conservative political forces; and 4) the erosion of local cultures. Yet, rather than ending on an entirely pessimistic note, Herman and McChesney recognize that there are forces struggling to assure that the public sphere continues to have its influence on the political process (e.g., organizations like Fairness and Accuracy in Reporting and the Campaign for Press and Broadcasting Freedom). Quoting Noam Chomsky, the authors conclude, "if you act like there is no possibility for change, you guarantee that there will be no change."

ROBERT MCNAMARA is an Assistant Professor of Political Science at Sonoma State University and a Project Censored evaluator.

THE MORE YOU WATCH, THE LESS YOU KNOW:
News Wars/[sub]Merged Hopes/Media Adventures
Danny Schechter
New York: Seven Stories Press, 1997.
Reviewed by Daniel Markwyn, Ph.D.

Thoughtful analysis and colorful anecdote characterize Danny Schechter's powerful tale of the sad decline of "truth-telling" in American broadcast journalism. But Schechter has written much more than a jeremiad against the mindlessness of TV. In the first place, he has nearly 30 years of experience in the field. A graduate of Cornell University and a veteran of the contentious politics of the Sixties, Schechter went on to the London School of Economics before signing on with WBCN in Boston in 1970. Schechter took the job writing the news and later broadcasting it, he tells us, because it provided a platform for ideas, not because it fulfilled a dream of life in broadcasting. His perception of himself as an "outsider" and his insistence on practicing public service journalism defines his career and helps to make this book as good as it is. In many respects he remained "Danny Schechter the news dissector" as he moved from WBCN to a prestigious Nieman fellowship at Harvard, to CNN, to ABC, and on to the co-founding of his independent production company, Globalvision. Secondly, Schechter seems a likable sort with wide associations in the world he dissects, despite his strong views and his willingness to challenge the media establishment. Thus, Ted Turner, Jesse Jackson, Rupert Murdoch, and other familiar figures from the media wars appear in Schechter's dramatic—and often amusing—accounts. Furthermore, he possesses an accessible and energetic style, and weaves personal anecdote and thoughtful analysis into a very good read.

Since his first visit there in 1967, South Africa has claimed Schechter's attention and he has produced important independent films, as well as a TV series on South African issues. In this book, he writes much about those experiences and draws upon his work there to sharpen his analysis of the American media and their role in American democracy. For example, at the close of an informative and moving section on post-apartheid South Africa, Schechter asks readers whether a "TV system that only serves the market [can] adequately market democratic ideas?" This question, whether asked about South Africa or the United States, lies at the heart of *The More You Watch, The Less You Know*. Again and again, Schechter concludes, the role of responsible media journalism has been compromised and diminished by an emphasis on profits. This emphasis has lowered both the standards and the content of media journalism and has encouraged the rise of immensely powerful global conglomerates.

What is to be done? Shunning such flamboyant steps as "killing your TV," Schechter urges instead that we consider his "Declaration of Media Independence," which includes specific steps toward wide-ranging reforms. He then ends his book with an admittedly visionary plan for a Media Channel devoted to waking "America from its media-conditioned stupor." The likelihood of achieving these reforms and launching the Media Channel depends on finding "a new force...to break the logjam that only celebrates the status quo." Exactly where that new force may be found remains problematic, but Schechter suggests that serious efforts should be undertaken to recruit on its behalf the "growing number of media professionals" who are presently unhappy inside the system.

In *The More You Watch, The Less You Know*, Danny Schechter writes authoritatively of a world in which communication about ideas and issues has declined dangerously in the face of market-driven decisions. It should be otherwise, and Schechter's book makes a significant contribution to the discussion of how best to make it so.

DANIEL MARKWYN, PH.D., is a Professor of History at Sonoma State University and a Project Censored evaluator.

CONGLOMERATES AND THE MEDIA

Eric Barnouw, et al.
New York: New Press, 1997.
Reviewed by Debora Hammond, Ph.D.

This collection of essays on the cultural implications of recent media mergers grew out of a lecture series at New York University. While the writing is uneven and similarly, the editing reflects some of the cost-cutting measures discussed in Mark Crispin Miller's article on the publishing industry, the cumulative effect of the perspectives offered by key figures in communications studies, journalism, media analysis, and television news production, is sobering. Dominating the cover is an octopus, spreading its tentacles across the entire surface, its suction cups reaching ominously toward the reader. Reminiscent of Frank Norris's novel, *The Octopus*, about railroads and nineteenth-century robber barons, the image suggests that the twentieth-century monopolies of information and communication technologies are even more insidious than the transportation monopolies of a previous era.

In his introduction, Todd Gitlin describes the "culture trust," including such entities as Disney, Time Warner, and News Corp., "bestriding the earth" via movies, television, cable, radio, print media, consumer goods, and a variety of other entertainment forms. Highlighting the inherent conflict of interest between news and entertainment, a central theme throughout the book, he asks what kinds of values are reinforced by increasingly concentrated decision-making power and the incessant drive for greater profits. With American culture rapidly becoming world culture, this question becomes even more critical. Most troubling along these lines is the fact that the United States, the supposed leader of the democratic world, is the only nation that charges its political candidates for access to the primary means of communication.

Eric Barnouw, author of *The History of Broadcasting in the United States,* offers a fascinating historical account of radio and television, chronicling the battles between educational and commercial interests throughout their respective evolutions. Radio was initially hailed as ushering in a "new era in adult education." By 1924, the driving force in radio had shifted from public service to advertising. The broadcasting range of educational stations, deemed "special interest," was limited, while that of commercial stations, owned by AT&T, Westinghouse, and GE, was unlimited. As then President Calvin Coolidge put it, "the chief business of America is business." Non-profits were slowly forced off the air. With the emergence of television in 1952, the government reserved channels (but no funds) for educational programming.

The saddest (and most compellingly written) story is Mark Crispin Miller's account of the implications of cost-cutting and market pressure for the publishing industry. With publishing dominated by eight media giants, distribution dominated by Baker & Taylor and Ingram, and sales by Borders Books and Barnes and Noble, smaller trade houses are increasingly vulnerable and academic presses are struggling. The drive for profits is especially brutal in an industry that has never been particularly lucrative. Editing and proofreading are being sacrificed to the bottom line. Quality work isn't profitable; footnotes and indexes are said to scare people off. Critical works don't last long if they are published at all: "The bigger the mogul, the deader any book which might offend him." Adding to market pressure is a 1979 Supreme Court ruling eliminating inventory cost write-offs for tool companies that the IRS has decided also applies to books. In this environment, what sells is sensationalism and big names: O.J. Simpson's *I Want to Tell You,* Donald Trump's *The Art of the Deal,* Newt Gingrich's *To Renew America.*

The overriding question that emerges from these essays is whether or not commercial culture and democracy can coexist. The view put forth in Thomas Frank's essay on "Liberation Marketing" is dismal. He sees business culture as completely displacing civil society: "The world of business is the world, period...The defining fact of American life in the 1990s is its reorganization around the needs of the corporations."

Patricia Aufderheide, editor of *In These Times*, and professor of communications at American University, offers a slightly more optimistic perspective, seeking a balance between visions of doomsday and cyber-utopia. She argues that communications networks are a social resource that could be used to expand public spaces and encourage a more active civil society. How this is to be done remains unanswered. The inside jacket cover suggests that *Conglomerates and the Media* is "sure to raise a storm of discussion within the media and beyond." Would that this were true.

DEBORA HAMMOND, PH.D., is an Assistant Professor of the History of Science in the Hutchins School at Sonoma State University and a Project Censored evaluator.

MASS MEDIA AND FREE TRADE, NAFTA AND THE CULTURAL INDUSTRIES

Emile G. McAnany and
Kenton Wilkinson, eds.
University of Texas Press, 1996.
Reviewed by Tony White, Ph.D.

Because of their fear of U.S. cultural dominance, France and Canada succeeded in exempting cultural industries from recent trade agreements, including GATT, FTA, and NAFTA. However, since cultural exports are only second to aerospace products among U.S. exports, the United States considers these efforts to preserve national culture as an excuse for economic protection of cultural industries. Given the new distribution technologies of film and television and the already dominant position of the U.S. media, renewed fears of cultural dominance and charges of "cultural imperialism" are in full force.

Several of the studies in *Mass Media and Free Trade*, however, provide evidence that the fears of a loss of cultural sovereignty because of U.S. dominance in film and television are exaggerated. For example, while the U.S. has an advantage of large-scale production for an English market, some formats do not translate across cultures, even with dubbing or subtitles, and when an American format is adopted, it has to be adapted to local culture, if it is to be effective.

Since locally-produced programs are more popular than imported U.S. television programs in Mexico and French-speaking Quebec, language and culture still provide effective barriers to cultural dominance. Even in border areas, with maximum exposure, cultural erosion is insignificant. Moreover, media giants like Televisa in Mexico and TV Globo in Brazil not only dominate their respective markets, but their telenovelas attract mass audiences in the rest of Latin America, Europe, and the United States.

These are just some of the issues addressed in *Mass Media and Free Trade*, a collection of scholarly studies presented at a conference on the impact of new technologies and NAFTA on Canadian and

Mexican cultures at the University of Texas, Austin, in 1994. Convened to create a dialogue between academicians, policy makers, and cultural industry representatives, the conference brought together a wide range of theoretical, technical, and empirical perspectives on the issues of cultural dominance and resistance, trade in cultural products, cultural identity in Mexico and French Canada, and intellectual property rights.

Although most of the contributors predict that the U.S. will continue to dominate in television and film production, and probably expand its cultural exports, this does not necessarily imply cultural dominance. Not only do we see examples of successful resistance and competition, but some of the evidence and analysis raises questions about the assumptions on which the cultural imperialism argument is based, including who defines national culture and which social class or ethnic group it reflects. Furthermore, national cultures are not static but are constantly evolving.

While *Mass Media and Free Trade* provides a constructive starting point for a discussion of these issues, it does not address the issue of whether the locally-produced programs foster the same values or promote the same brand-name products as imported programs. In the wake of recent mergers among mass media outlets and the current trend of trade liberalization, the valuable dialogue generated by this conference and published in *Mass Media and Free Trade* should be expanded.

TONY WHITE, PH.D., is a Professor of History at Sonoma State University specializing in Latin America and a Project Censored evaluator.

REAL MAJORITY, MEDIA MINORITY: The Cost of Sidelining Women in Reporting

Laura Flanders
Monroe, Maine: Common Courage Press, 1997.
Reviewed by Catherine Nelson, Ph.D.

In this book, Laura Flanders argues that the biggest problem with the media is that it has become "an industry that has

THIS MODERN WORLD
by TOM TOMORROW

WELL, SPARKY-- ACCORDING TO THE NEW YORK TIMES WEEK IN REVIEW, WE'VE REACHED AN "APPOMATTOX IN THE CULTURE WARS" --A NEW ERA OF *CIVILITY!*

HOLD THAT THOUGHT, BIFF-- LISTEN TO WHAT CONSERVATIVE COLUMNIST *LINDA BOWLES* WROTE AFTER THE *ELLEN* BROUHAHA...

SHE COMPLAINS THAT "CLINTON HAS BEEN CARRYING THE TORCH FOR HOMOSEXUALS FOR A VERY LONG TIME ... FOR YEARS, HE HAS ENTHUSIASTICALLY BENT OVER BACKWARD AS WELL AS FORWARD IN HIS SERVICE TO THEM."

GET IT? BENT OVER *FORWARD?*

ARE THESE CONSERVATIVES A RIOT OR WHAT?

SHE CONTINUES: "IF SAME-SEX ANAL ORIENTATION IS MANDATED BY A...FLAWED GENE, DOES IT NOT FOLLOW THAT THOSE WHO...COPULATE WITH ANIMALS, LUST AFTER CORPSES, CROSS DRESS, EXPOSE THEMSELVES... AND HOLD DYING INSECTS IN THEIR MOUTHS FOR SEXUAL THRILLS MAY LIKEWISE BE UNDER THE COMMAND OF FLAWED GENES?"

AS GOD IS MY WITNESS, I'M NOT MAKING THIS UP.

created a numbness to a whole range of ideas." The under-representation of women extends beyond reporters, sources, and commentators, into the focus of the story. In a collection of columns, essays, and interviews whose topics range from Paula Jones to women in New York's Chinatown restaurant industry, Flanders suggests that the treatment of women by the media is a choice that undermines the very search for truth in which the media claims to be engaged.

Flanders' book is a blizzard of information. Several examples from the book illustrate the power of her argument that gender bias in the media perpetrates the silencing of an essential component of the "truth" found in women's voices. The first example is an interview with Frances Fox Piven entitled "The Willie Horton of Welfare," which establishes how the media reflects politicians' use of women, the poor, and persons of color as scapegoats in the welfare debate. Piven argues that in America there is "...a kind of ferocious and unrealistic ethic of individual responsibility, and we're preoccupied with sex." And, even though most of the women on welfare are white, most of the pictures we see are of black women. "You can always talk about those women and their out-of-wedlock babies; it's a kind of Willie Horton issue." Americans "don't like women very much or...the poor." Or people of color.

Similar evidence of gender bias is apparent in Flander's critique of Catharine MacKinnon's appearance at the United Nations World Conference on Human Rights in June 1993, where MacKinnon spoke about the systematic rape of women by Serbian forces in the war in Bosnia and Herzegovina as an 'unprecedented' tactic. Flanders says MacKinnon casts all those who took a different approach from hers as 'whitewash feminists' who dilute the real crisis in Bosnia with talk of other not-so-relevant or immediate events. Flanders calls this a one-woman-equals-all, for-us-or-against-us ideology, a finite universe of right versus wrong with little space for difference: "Even raising questions can get one characterized as enemy, pimp, or rapist. That way lies feminist fundamen-

talism...." Most frightening for Flanders is that it could lead to a simplistic picture of human rights and marginalize the diversity of the women's movement.

Flanders offers hope in the form of the independent media. And, while she is quite critical of the dominance of women from the right as commentators and columnists in major media outlets, if she is true to her own emphasis on diversity, she would have to argue that these voices should be heard. They do, however, need to be effectively met by their more progressive counterparts.

There are a few improvements that could be made to the book. More comprehensive introductions to each part of the book, and a more orderly conclusion, would create a more powerful theoretical statement. Despite these flaws, this is not just another book saying that men "don't get it." All of us are indicted for our complacency, even those who think they do "get it."

CATHERINE NELSON, PH.D., is an Assistant Professor of Political Science at Sonoma State University and a Project Censored evaluator.

THE NEW CENSORS:
Movies and the Culture Wars

Charles Lyons
Philadelphia: Temple University Press, 1997.
Reviewed by Elizabeth Coonrod Martínez, Ph.D.

Do protesters in front of movie theaters stop interest in a controversial film? Do letter-writing campaigns or demonstrations that block film production force movie makers to lose money or cancel films? Most movie viewers are more likely to consider contemporary cinema art for art's sake than to ponder these questions. However, Charles Lyons' thought-provoking book shows that in some cases, pressure for movie censorship *is* effective (but usually only if the censors are members of the majority population holding political power).

The New Censors reveals the economic power and protest of those who would censor films because of oppositional beliefs, along with the voices of those who struggle to be represented as equal citizens. On one side, liberal groups tend to seek to change the stereotypical nature of their representation (that gays are murderers, that women desire to be raped and chopped into pieces, and that people of color are more lazy, weak, or devious than their white counterparts, for example). On the other side, fundamentally religious groups usually seek to bar depictions of sexual or religious interpretations with which they do not agree. The censors who are most successful are those who are well-connected financially, while the unsuccessful censors remain mere protesters.

Lyons' focus is more social than political. He presents a valuable history of cultural forces around controversial film production and presentation in the twentieth century. The introductory chapter is somewhat tedious, describing the demise of the Hays Production Code (the governing office which granted or withheld its Seal of Approval prior to the present rating system) in 1968. But this background is helpful in the subsequent five chapters. Lyons tackles specific environmental, feminist, ethnic, gay, and religious issues in film, with in-depth examples of censoring attempts. He rounds up historical data and facts that may be only vaguely remembered by movie viewers, and presents these facts in vivid sequences.

In the 1970s, movies became critical of the dominant values of society, with such films as *All the President's Men* and *The Deerhunter*. Then special interest groups began to put pressure on movie makers for abusive representations of ethnic groups, women, gays, and lesbians. Lyons shows how demonstrators first sought censorship of pornography and violence in films (especially regarding the psychotic violence of the 1976 film *Snuff*, and *Dressed to Kill*, made in 1980.) Protesters then asked for greater sensitivity to violence against women, and greater awareness of women's civil rights.

Gay and lesbian groups protested their representation as psychotic and lonely individuals out of step with the heterosexual world. Their efforts also evolved from censorship to raising sensitivity. By the time the 1991 film *Basic Instinct*—negative in its portrayal of lesbians—appeared, there was no need to attempt censorship; national protests were loud and clear.

Asian Americans demonstrated against and boycotted *Year of the Dragon* (1985) to call attention to white supremacist attitudes, as well as to anti-Chinese bigotry and misogynist themes. As with gay efforts, their protests and pressure seem to have affected the movie making business from the inside. Recent films such as *The Joy Luck Club* and *Heaven and Earth* (Asian), and *Philadelphia* and *The Crying Game*, are examples of more sensitive portrayals of these groups.

Lyons saves his most alarming example of censorship for his final chapter. In 1951, religious groups heatedly protested *The Miracle*, a film considered by Christians to be sacrilege, but attempts to censor it were foiled by the Supreme Court. Films in the early 1970s, such as *Jesus Christ Superstar*, elicited little protest, despite liberal interpretations of the Bible, but by the late 1970s, a strong religious coalition and the election of Ronald Reagan, Lyons believes, helped foment a conservative backlash on gains by the left. This "collective rage" of the religious right was unleashed—effectively, according to Lyons—in the form of censorship against the 1988 film *The Last Temptation of Christ*. The coalition achieved what none of the other groups had achieved: three major movie chains decided not to show *The Last Temptation*, and several small cities canceled the film's engagements. Lyons shows how criticism of this film also fanned anti-Semitism, and how a prominent Evangelical leader (who offered to buy the film from Universal Studios so that it could be destroyed) used the news media to gain publicity for his cause by placing a letter outlining his offer in several major newspapers. Indeed, the new media often plays a role in censorship efforts, by following "majority" thought.

The New Censors aptly documents a cultural history of the changes in movie making in this century, while illustrating how the power of economic clout joins with political or majority rule. While gains have been made and lost in recent decades, Lyons confirms the dominance of white, Eurocentric control over "independent" movie making in this country.

ELIZABETH COONROD MARTINEZ, PH.D., is an Assistant Professor of Spanish and Latin American Literature at Sonoma State University and a Project Censored evaluator. She has published books for children on Mexican history and Hispanic leaders, and articles on film, Latin American, and Latino literature.

WIZARDS OF MEDIA OZ:
Behind the Curtain
of Mainstream News

Jeff Cohen and Norman Solomon
Monroe, Maine: Common Courage Press, 1997.
Reviewed by Rick Luttmann, Ph.D.

The authors of *Wizards of Media Oz* have written and spoken widely on media matters. Jeff Cohen is the founder and executive director of the media-watch organization, Fairness and Accuracy In Reporting (FAIR). Cohen and Solomon write a syndicated weekly column called "Media Beat."

Like their previous book, *Through the Media Looking Glass: Decoding Bias and Blather in the News*, which was reviewed in *Censored* 1997, this book is essentially a compilation of the authors' weekly columns. Most were written in 1995 and 1996, and so deal with events of that period.

Like their last book, *Wizards of Media Oz* again puts forth the author's philosophy and intent that the mainstream press in the U.S. is failing to report the news Americans need to make democracy work. There are two big problems with the new book: First, it has very little new to say that the authors didn't tell us in their last book. Second, most of the events they discuss are now "old news"—one feels as if one is reading through newspapers that have been stored in the garage for a year or two. One would do better, having read one Cohen/Solomon book, to try to find a source for their weekly column itself, and read that on a regular basis.

Despite its general redundancy, the new book, like its predecessor, covers an interesting range of subjects, including the following:

➤ PBS: Hold the cheers, it's far less "public." Notice how the "non-ads" for the corporate sponsors are getting longer and longer? The corporate mindset has invaded public television.

➤ HMOs: In a few short years our health care has fallen into the hands of companies whose first interest is their profits and whose last is our health.

➤ Affirmative Action: Don't count on the press to come to its defense; in fact, count on it to hype the backlash.

➤ Labor: There's a Business Section in most daily papers, but no Labor Section.

The major dailies seem blatantly devoted to union-busting.

➤ The Ecology movement: Environmentalists are portrayed as tree-hugging nuts; news agencies regard them as much a threat as the CEOs of large corporations do.

➤ Prisons: Silencing prisoners is a crime against journalism, but few papers are willing to fight for the right of prisoners to a voice; when the public cannot hear that voice, all manner of abuses can easily be concealed behind those iron bars.

➤ Heroes and Villains: Colin Powell, Ted Koppel, Bill Gates, Robert McNamara—these are the darlings of the mainstream press; George Seldes, Robert Parry, Jim Hightower, Noam Chomsky, Daniel Ellsberg—they might as well be invisible.

➤ Sanitizing the history of the Vietnam War: The press stresses entirely the wrong point—that "the war was unwinnable"; in fact the war was stupid as well as immoral.

➤ FBI: This much-vaunted, almost sacrosanct government agency is incompetent as well as politically tainted.

➤ CIA: The press is ready to carry their water. The slightest criticism—that it is a rogue agency, out of control, answerable to no one, willing to sacrifice any means to its ends, completely outside the sphere of normal standards of ethical behavior—is sure to be trivialized and mocked by the mainstream press.

➤ East Timor: A third of its population has been extirpated by the Indonesian government, in violation of every princi-

ple of international law, not only without our protest, but using weapons we have given them.

➤ The drug war in Colombia: The real story is quite different from the one the government and its corporate and media co-conspirators would like you to believe.

➤ U.S. Military Aid to Mexico and the Chiapas Rebellion: Again, the real story is quite different.

➤ Selective reporting on both Egypt and Israel: The top two recipients of our foreign aid couldn't possibly do anything unethical, could they?

➤ Russia: Is capitalism really the best road for the Russians to take? Are its capitalist reformers really serving the best interests of the Russian people?

➤ "Reform": Forget it—the media and the entire establishment it supports are not unhappy with the status quo.

RICK LUTTMANN, PH.D., is a Professor of Mathematics at Sonoma State University and a Project Censored evaluator.

ILL EFFECTS: THE MEDIA/VIOLENCE DEBATE

Martin Barker and Julian Petley, eds.
London: Routledge, 1997.
Reviewed by Barbara Bloom, Ph.D.

There is widespread debate concerning the media's influence on individuals, and on children in particular. Martin Barker and Julian Petley question whether film, television, and video can be blamed for social aggression and violence, and provide a provocative re-examination of the "media effects" debate. *Ill Effects* questions not only whether the media are capable of directly influencing people, but also whether the idea of "effects" is the most useful way of conceptualizing the relationship between the media and audiences.

Antimedia-violence campaigns generally employ slogans about the need to protect children. Barker and Petley assert that anyone can make wild claims about the effects of the media, in that all they have to say is that they are "protecting society" or "concerned for the young." This, according to the authors, provides these pundits with the credentials one needs to "pontificate about the media."

A primary theme that runs through *Ill Effects* is how issues of media effects are used for purposes of control and censorship. "Effects research" asks how we might be influenced by the media: what is it, and what problems are caused by it; what also needs to be examined, however, are the political, financial, and bureaucratic interests that lie *behind* the media effects research.

A summary of chapters illustrates some main points. In the first chapter, Barker discusses a report by professionals in Great Britain who claim that "new kinds of film have disturbing messages" for children. The aftermath of a sensational British murder case involving two young boys gave rise to a case against television, film, and video. At the trial, the judge speculated that violent videos may have prompted the killing. In response to these events, Barker asks how we can know the message of a film. He argues that anti-media campaigns need to be the focus of research so that their motives and self-interests can be examined.

Chapter 2 places children in the center of the debate about media effects. Barker discusses how media violence is seen not only to encourage children to commit violent acts, but is, itself, literally a form of violence. He cites anti-media campaigns which imply that media violence is a form of "electronic child abuse." Barker proposes that we explore what children themselves identify as upsetting or violent. In a debate that is dominated by adults purporting to speak on children's behalf, children's voices have been almost entirely unheard. He argues that we need to find ways of supporting parents' and children's attempts to regulate their own viewing, rather than seeking the state's control over private citizens.

In Chapter 6, "Us and Them," Jason Petley claims that, from its inception, the film industry has been regarded by moral entrepreneurs as a cause of decline and deterioration of society, and as a "textbook" of bad examples to the young, the easily influenced, and the working class. Petley's main concern has been with how films, television, and videos have been seen as affecting the working class "worse" than the middle class.

Chapter 9, "Going Public with Young Offenders and the Media," explores the role of the media in the lives of young people. It examines whether there were differences in the viewing habits or preferences of young offenders and their peers. The research revealed few differences; offenders neither watched more television nor selected more violent programs or films.

The authors argue throughout the text that those who blame the media for crime and violence are on a "doomed mission in search of a simple solution to a complex problem." They effectively assert that there is an urgent need for an informed and interdisciplinary approach to the study of the media.

BARBARA BLOOM, PH.D., is a lecturer in the Department of Criminal Justice Administration at Sonoma State University and a Project Censored evaluator. She also serves as a consultant to national, state, and local criminal and juvenile justice agencies.

APPENDIX A

Less Access to Less Information by and about the U.S. Government

XXVIII, A 1997 Chronology: January-June
and XXIX, A 1997 Chronology: June-December
By the American Library Association (ALA) Washington Office

INTRODUCTION

For the past 16 years, this ongoing selective chronology has documented efforts to restrict and privatize government information. It is distributed as a supplement to the *ALA Washington Office Newsletter* and as an electronic publication at http://www.ala.org/washoff/lessaccess. While government information is more accessible through computer networks and the Freedom of Information Act, there are still barriers to public access. The latest damaging disclosures facing the Clinton Administration involve allegations of concealing information and claiming "executive privilege." Continuing revelations of Cold War secrecy show how government information has been concealed, resulting in a lack of public accountability and cost to taxpayers.

Another development with major implications for public access, is the growing tendency of federal agencies to use computer and telecommunication technologies for data collection, storage, retrieval, and dissemination. This trend has resulted in the increased emergence of contractual arrangements with commercial firms to disseminate information collected at taxpayer expense, higher user charges for government information, and the proliferation of government information available in electronic format only. This trend toward electronic dissemination is occurring in all three branches of government. While automation clearly offers promises of savings, will public access to government information be further restricted for people who cannot afford computers or pay for computer time?

On the other hand, the Government Printing Office (GPO) Access system and the Library of Congress THOMAS system have enhanced public access by providing free on-line access to government databases.

Recognizing that some federal agencies are succeeding in using technology to enhance public access to government information, this update includes selected examples of such successes.

ALA continues to reaffirm its long-standing conviction that open government is vital to a democracy. A January 1984 resolution passed by ALA's Council stated that "there should be equal and ready access to data collected, compiled, produced, and published in any format by the government of the United States."

In 1986, ALA initiated a Coalition on Government Information. The coalition's objectives are to focus national attention on all efforts that limit access to government information, and to develop support for improvements in access to government information. Since 1989, the coalition has presented the James Madison Award to champions of the public's right to know.

With access to information a major ALA priority, library advocates should be concerned about barriers to public access to government information. Previous chronologies were compiled in two ALA Washington Office indexed publications, *Less Access to Less Information By and About the U.S. Government: A 1981-1987 Chronology*, and *Less Access to Less Information By and Bout the U.S. Government: A 1988-1991 Chronology*. The following selected chronology continues the tradition of a semi-annual update.

CHRONOLOGY

JANUARY

National Security Agencies Blunder

The end of 1996 saw several public relations blunders that drew unfavorable attention to various federal agencies that are part of the national security establishment. The decision of the Central Intelligence Agency to make major cuts in personnel and in the budget for its popular Foreign Broadcast Information Service (FBIS) caused the service's fans to protest. "For them to be talking about massive cutbacks is a tragedy," said Representative W. Curtis Weldon (R-PA). "If anything, we need more information." FBIS, which provides English-language translations of more than 3,500 publications from around world, is considered essential reading among diplomats, journalists, academics, and politicians who follow foreign affairs. Additionally, FBIS provides one of the few visible products that the public receives from the annual $29 billion investment in intelligence collection.

In another incident, the Air Force leaked the news that it had determined that no Air Force person should be held responsible for the bombing of an Air Force housing complex in Saudi Arabia where 19 Americans had been killed and 500 wounded. But the Air Force withheld release of the report on which it based the blanket clearances, pending further legal reviews. The Air Force finding contradicted the conclusions of a Pentagon investigation that found that the base's military leaders had failed to react to a number of intelligence warnings about terrorist attacks planned in Saudi Arabia. (Kitfield, James, "Ready, Aim...Oops!" *National Journal*, January 4, 1997: 45)

Timing of Ethics Report Release Causes Controversy

In early January, the bi-partisan membership of the House Ethics Committee agreed on several days of public hearings into the acknowledged ethical violations of House Speaker Newt Gingrich (R-GA) prior to the House vote on the Speaker's punishment. But when Democrats complained that they would be required to vote before the report of the committee's Special Counsel, James Cole, was turned in, the agreement fell apart. The dispute concerned the Special Counsel's role in the hearings and what information (relevant to the vote) he would present. Representative Nancy Johnson (R-CT), chair of the ethics panel, said she had told Cole to complete the committee's final report by January 16 for circulation to the public and to every member of Congress. Following that, she stated, she anticipated a public hearing. (Blomquist, Brian, "Gingrich Hearings Deferred," *The Washington Times*, January 10, 1997: A1)

More Kennedy Assassination Records Made Public

Continuing a story that *Less Access* has documented for many years, the Federal Bureau of Investigation transferred to the National Archives 15,121 more pages of records related to President John Kennedy's assassination. The latest files include documents reviewed by the House Select Committee on Assassinations in 1978 and 1979, during which time the committee examined various assassination conspiracy theories. The FBI has transferred more than 666,000 pages of Kennedy assassination records to NARA under a 1992 law that provides public access to the records. (Associated Press, "FBI Turns Over More Files on Kennedy Assassination," *Washington Post*, January 14, 1997: A13)

Ethics Report Made Available on Publicly Inaccessible Web Site

When the Ethics Committee's report on House Speaker Newt Gingrich (R-GA) was released, the GPO Conference's photocopier could not meet the demand for copies. The leadership then posted the report in the Member Services section of its Web site, a part of the site the public cannot access. (Henry, Ed, "Spin Begins Even Before Counsel's Report Is Out," *Roll Call*, January 20, 1997: A-1)

White House Acknowledged Conflicting Statements

White House officials acknowledged that they had on three occasions in recent months provided incorrect or incomplete statements concerning their knowledge of key events in the campaign fundraising activities that have resulted in numerous investigations. These occasions were explained as "the innocent results of internal miscommunications" rather than a deliberate attempt to mislead the public. The three occasions were:

➤ The hiring of Webster Hubbell (the long-term Clinton friend and former associate attorney general who was convicted of bilking clients of his old law firm) by an Indonesian firm owned by Democratic financial benefactors. In December 1996, the White House said that it did not know of the hiring before it was disclosed by news media. Later it was found that Bruce Lindsey, a senior Clinton adviser, was aware of the arrangement as early as 1994.

➤ The meetings of President Bill Clinton, Indonesian firm executive James Riady, and Democratic fundraiser John Huang were first characterized as social chats. Later it was revealed that these "chats" included discussions of U.S. policy toward Indonesia and China.

➤ The assertion by Vice President Al Gore during the 1996 campaign that he did not realize a controversial event he had attended at a Buddhist temple was actually a Democratic fundraiser. He recently stated that his staff had sent him a memo informing him that those attending had paid to belong to the party committee that hosted the events. (Baker, Peter, "White House Acknowledges Another Foul-up," *Washington Post*, January 24, 1997)

Disclaimer Issued by Foreign Relations of the United States

Volume XXII of *Foreign Relations of the United States*, covering the years 1961 to 1963, has been published with an unprecedented disclaimer. According to a committee of historians, "this published compilation does not constitute a 'thorough, accurate, and reliable documentary record of major United States foreign policy decisions.'" The censored material involves U.S. actions in Japan from 1958 through 1960, and marks a victory by CIA classifiers over history. "A frightening precedent," said Steven Aftergood of the Federation of American Scientists. "The government would rather people imagine the worst rather than know the truth." (Kamen, Al, "And the Truth Shall Make You [Deleted]," *Washington Post*, January 24, 1997)

Runyon's Stock Worth More

Postmaster General Marvin Runyon had a much larger holding of Coca-Cola stock than he had previously disclosed. Runyon, under investigation for possible conflict of interest violations for his involvement in a proposal that would have given the company exclusive rights to place soft drink machines in the nation's post offices, sold his Coca-Cola stock holdings last summer for between $350,000 and $360,000 after questions were raised about his role in the deal. His 1995 disclosure statement indicated the value of his Coca-Cola stock to be between $50,000 and $100,000. The 1996 disclosure statement, subsequently released by postal officials, placed the value of the Coca-Cola stock between $250,000 and $500,000. Runyon said he never believed the vending machine deal would benefit him, and once he learned his role was being questioned, he sold his stock. (McAllister, Bill, "Runyon's Coca-Cola Stock Worth More Than Stated," *Washington Post*, January 24, 1997: A21)

Crop Freeze Blamed on Lack of Weather Data

A freeze in Florida, the worst in seven years, caused $93 million in damage to winter vegetable and fruit crops in Dade County. Losses for all crops could total $250 million statewide. Officials said one reason for the severity of the losses was that farmers did not receive warning of the weather in sufficient time to take precautions. Due to budget cuts, the National Weather Service stopped forecasting temperatures for agricultural areas in April 1996, forcing farmers to rely on local forecasts of populated areas, which tend to be warmer. "This was the first year we haven't had a weather forecast coming from the government specifically for farming areas," said Bob Crawford, Florida Agriculture Commissioner. "It really left farmers in the lurch not knowing this freeze was coming." ("Worst Freeze in Years Ruins Florida Crops," *The New York Times*, January 24, 1997: A20)

CIA Taught, then Dropped, Mental Torture Techniques

According to documents released by the CIA, the agency taught techniques of mental torture and coercion to at least five Latin American security forces in the early 1980s, although it formally dropped these methods of interrogation in 1985. A 1983 manual advised against physical torture, but discussed using intense fear, deep exhaustion, solitary confinement, unbearable anxiety, and other forms of psychological duress against a subject. The agency's role in training Latin American security forces was discussed in the press and in closed Congressional hearings in the mid-1980s. The 1983 manual on interrogation and the 1985 prohibition against coercive methods were made public through a Freedom of Information Act request filed by *The Baltimore Sun* in preparation for a series on the CIA's relationship with a Honduran military battalion. On January 28, 1997, the CIA's office of public affairs acknowledged for the first time, the agency's prior teaching and subsequent repudiation of psychological torture. (Weiner, Tim, "CIA Taught, Then Dropped, Mental Torture in Latin America," *The New York Times*, January 29, 1997: A11)

Quality of Data and Quality of Life Linked

Questions about the data being used to calculate the Consumer Price Index (CPI) has generated a great deal of news, but the problem of inadequate measurement goes much deeper than current headlines. According to journalist Susan C. Strong, shortsighted congressional attacks on funding for data collection and preservation "will significantly damage everyone's quality of life, not just those affected by changes in the CPI." She observes that in its haste to reduce the federal deficit, over the next ten years Congress plans to cut funding substantially for data collection for federal agencies, including funds for conducting the year-2000 census. "The cuts will hurt quality-of-life measurement projects at every level—federal, state, and local. Even local projects depend on federal data gathering for many important categories of information about their environments, social conditions, and economies." Strong concludes: "There is a lot of loose talk these days about what kind of debt we are passing on to our children. But a 'know nothing' information policy at the dawn of the information age is a contradiction neither we nor our children can afford." (Strong, Susan C., "The Link Between Quality of Data and Quality of Life," *The Christian Science Monitor*, January 30, 1997)

Specificity Limited of Airline Safety Data

The Federal Aviation Administration announced it will use the Internet to disseminate airline safety data previously considered confidential. The FAA was pressured by Congress to release more airline safety performance data after the May 1996 ValuJet Airlines crash in Florida. But airline safety records will not be ranked in the same way as FAA ranks on-time and luggage-handling performance. Apparently, airline officials convinced the FAA and Congress to limit the specificity of the data on airline safety, asserting that certain FAA data could be misinterpreted and should not be released. Information about maintenance violations—such as engine trouble or missed repair schedules—will not be included because of FAA concerns that airlines might be discouraged from volunteering such information if it were released. Previously, it would have required a Freedom of Information Act request to access much of the information that will be available on the FAA Web page located at: http://www.faa.gov. (Mintz, John, "FAA to Release Data on Safety of Airlines," *Washington Post*, January 30, 1997: D1)

IRS Admits it Lacks the Intellectual Capital to Modernize

Arthur Gross, an Assistant Commissioner of the Internal Revenue Service, told the National Commission on

Restructuring the IRS that it had spent $4 billion developing modern computer systems that "do not work in the real world." He said he doubted the agency was capable of developing modern computer systems because it lacked the intellectual capital to do the job. Gross also proposed contracting out the processing of paper tax returns filed by individuals, a move that would permit non-government workers to see confidential financial information on tax returns. (Johnston, David Cay, "IRS Admits Lag in Modernization; Urges Contract Plan," *The New York Times*, January 31, 1997: A1)

FEBRUARY

Federal Contractor Denies Access to Organ Transplant Data to the Public and Government

The United Network for Organ Sharing (UNOS), a non-profit organization based in Richmond, Virginia, is a public/private partnership intended to manage the acquisition and distribution of the nation's scarce supply of donated organs. Although the Division of Organ Transplantation of the U.S. Department of Health and Human Services regulates UNOS—and in 1995, paid about 18 percent of its $13.1 million revenue—in recent months UNOS has repeatedly told the government that it cannot have data on rejected organ offers in transplant centers, access to records and meetings of UNOS's Council on Organ Availability, and minutes of some of UNOS's public board and committee meetings.

While the government increasingly finds itself helpless when UNOS says "no," some people think the government has abdicated its responsibility. "You can't delegate public policy to a private contractor," said Dr. John Roberts, a liver transplant surgeon at the University of California at San Francisco. "You can't have the people who are in control—essentially competitors—make policy."

UNOS Executive Director Walter Graham disagrees. "I personally believe that the essence of democracy is self-regulation," he said. *The Plain Dealer* filed a request under the Freedom of Information Act for data listing the reasons transplant programs turn down offers of organs for centers that transplant hearts, lungs, kidneys, pancreases, and livers, because it wanted the information for a series of articles. Officials of the U.S. Department of Health and Human Services agreed to ask UNOS for the data last summer, but UNOS officials denied the request, maintaining that the data was "misleading" and that they were "meaningless" indicators of the quality of a transplant center. Following the newspaper's appeal, U.S. Department of Health and Human Services official Remy Aronoff said of UNOS, "They think if it's given out and publicized, it will jeopardize their ability to get that same data from their sources." When asked, "Because it's potentially embarrassing?," Aronoff replied, "Well, yeah, right." (Davis, Dave, and Ted Wendling, "Contractor Keeps Government in Dark on Transplant Data," *The Plain Dealer* (Cleveland, OH), February 3, 1997: 6-A)

IRS Sued for Failure to Protect its Records

The American Historical Association, the Organization of American Historians, the Society of American Archivists, and Tax Analysts of Arlington joined in a lawsuit against the Internal Revenue Service in U.S. District Court alleging that the IRS is not taking care of its records and has huge gaps in its documents for the 1890s, 1910s, and the 1940s. The suit alleges that IRS records, if maintained, would help document the history of taxation in the United States and the transformation of the income tax from a "class tax" to a "mass tax" which occurred after the Depression and World War II. According to the historians, tax records are scattered throughout IRS headquarters, with no inventory, while others are rotting in leaky basements. The lawsuit maintains that the IRS and the National Archives and Records Administration have failed to comply with the Federal Records Act, which requires all federal agencies to turn over historically significant documents to the Archives. (Locy, Toni, "IRS's Record-Keeping Found Lacking," *Washington Post*, February 11, 1997: A19)

CIA Critic Leaves State Department

Richard Nuccio, an adviser in the State Department's Latin America bureau, left his post to become an aide to Senator Robert Torricelli (D-NJ). Nuccio lost his security clearances last year because of his role in revelations about CIA activities in Guatemala. In March 1995, he took to Torricelli his concerns that the CIA had withheld information about a paid CIA informant involved in a cover-up of the killings of an American citizen and the Guatemalan husband of an American woman. Torricelli's decision to make public the information upset the CIA, which places high priority on the secrecy of its agents' identities. In his resignation letter to President Clinton, Nuccio wrote that the CIA continues to rely on disreputable agents for information although such persons are the "principal enemies of the policies of democracy and human rights." (Gedda, George, "CIA Critic Quits State Department to Push Reform," *Washington Post*, February 25, 1997: A14)

Army Warned Early of Gulf Chemical Exposure

The CIA provided the Army with information in February 1991 suggesting that an ammunition dump in Iraq—which American troops blew up a month later—might have contained chemical weapons. The Pentagon said that the information was never passed on to the American troops who demolished the ammunition dump. These soldiers learned only last year that they may have been exposed to nerve gas as a result of the blasts. The Pentagon has estimated that 20,000 troops may have been exposed, although they state there is no conclusive evidence that anyone was made sick as a result. The newly declassified CIA reports undermine the Pentagon's repeated assertions that it was only last year that they were aware of the possibility of exposure of American troops to chemicals at the depot. The documents raise new suspicions about the credibility of the Pentagon and the CIA. Senator John Rockefeller (D-WV) said the CIA had clearly hidden information about the issue. "The CIA is every bit as implicated as the Department of Defense," he said. "The CIA has known since 1991 and totally failed to come forward until late last year." (Shenon, Philip, "Pentagon Now Says It Knew of Chemical Weapons Risk," *The New York Times*, February 26, 1997: A20)

White House Tries to Control Damage from Release of Documents

The White House released more documents with new disclosures about President Clinton's role in Democratic fundraising. These follow thousands of other documents released over the past month that show how the Democratic National Committee (DNC) raised money by bringing top supporters to the White House. Presidential aides declared the White House had nothing to hide. Having disclosed the documents, the White House was forced to explain what they meant. Some documents refer to the DNC-sponsored "coffees" at the White House as fundraisers, which are illegal on federal property. White House spokesman Michael McCurry said the events were inaccurately described. (Harris, John F., "Hundreds of Pages Added to White House Experiment in Disclosure," *Washington Post*, February 26, 1997: A8)

New Documents Show Senator Involved in Controversial Fundraising

Newly released White House documents contradict the claim of Senator Chris Dodd's (D-CT) that he was not involved with the Democratic National Committee's (DNC) controversial fundraising practices while he was the party's general chairman during the last election. Until the release, Dodd had blamed his former co-chair, Don Fowler, for the DNC's fundraising mistakes, although a July 1995 memo showed that Dodd—over Fowler's objections—encouraged the White House to continue offering "premier" access to $100,000 DNC contributors. (Henry, Ed, "Democrats Tied to DNC Scandal," *Roll Call*, February 27, 1997: A1)

Pentagon Reveals it Lost Chemical Weapons Logs

The Department of Defense (DOD) revealed that all full copies of the chemical-warfare logs from the 1991 Persian Gulf War had disappeared, although paper and computer-disk copies had been stored after the war in locked safes at two U.S. locations. An exhaustive search found only 36 pages of the estimated 200 pages of the classified logs that were supposed to record any incident in which chemical or biological weapons were detected. The DOD report increased speculation by veterans groups and Members of Congress that there had been either criminal incompetence with the Defense Department or a cover-up. (Shenon, Philip, "Pentagon

Reveals It Lost Most Logs on Chemical Arms," *The New York Times*, February 28, 1997: A1)

Government Has Too Many Secrets

The Report of the Commission on Protecting and Reducing Government Secrecy, released in early March, said that the federal government's system for classifying and keeping secrets is out of control. The Commission was chaired by Senator Daniel Patrick Moynihan (D-NY). According to the report, about a half-million government officials and contractors have the power to stamp a document "secret," and they do so on more than 3 million documents a year. Government vaults contain approximately 1.5 billion pages of documents stamped secret that are more than 25 years old. About a half-million requests to make documents public under the Freedom of Information Act (FOIA) are received each year, but it can take months or years to respond. The cost of processing FOIA requests runs more than $100 million a year. In 1995, President Clinton ordered that all secrets more than 25 years old should be automatically declassified by the year 2000—with certain exceptions for national security. So far, only about ten percent of those documents have been declassified. (Thomas, Evan, "Taming Uncle Sam's Classification Compulsion," *Washington Post*, March 9, 1997: C2)

White House and FBI Clash over Briefing

The White House and the FBI gave conflicting versions of their contacts with each other regarding briefing the President on an alleged Chinese plan to influence the 1996 U.S. congressional elections. President Clinton complained that he had only recently found out about the allegation because the FBI agents who had briefed National Security Council staff at the White House asked that the information not be revealed, and White House aides complied. Within hours, the FBI issued a public statement rebutting this account, insisting that it had placed no restriction on the dissemination of information within the White House. The White House insisted the FBI statement was in error. (Baker, Peter, "Clinton, FBI Clash Publicly Over China Probe Briefing," *Washington Post*, March 11, 1997: A1)

Eisenhower Secretly Recorded White House Conversations

President Dwight Eisenhower used a secret dictabelt machine to record conversations in the Oval Office. The dictabelts—old, creased, flattened out, and stuffed into letter-sized envelopes with dates and other notations scribbled by Eisenhower or his secretary, the late Ann Whitman—went unnoticed at the Eisenhower library in Abilene, Kansas, for more than 40 years. The conversations were recorded on machines that are now obsolete. "We thought they were damaged and unplayable," library director Dan Holt said. But last summer a New

York researcher, William S. Doyle, asked to listen to them. With the help of the Dictaphone Corporation and other experts the conversations will be released to the public. When it was in operation "the Eisenhower recording system was a closely held secret," said Doyle. (Lardner, George, "Eisenhower Secretly Recorded Oval Office Sessions," *Washington Post*, March 15, 1997: A6)

FBI Director Admits Giving Inaccurate Data

Following the request of the Department of Justice Inspector General that he correct his testimony as promptly as possible, Louis Freeh, director of the FBI, acknowledged providing inaccurate information to Congress about the suspension of a crime-lab whistleblower. Senator Charles Grassley (R-IA), chair of a Senate subcommittee that oversees the FBI, released several letters describing the inaccuracies in Freeh's testimony. An FBI statement said that Freeh "totally rejects any contention that he deliberately misled the Congress or the public." According to the FBI statement, Freeh promptly corrected the record when his "inadvertent omission" was pointed out to him. (Davidson, Joe, "FBI's Director Admits Giving Inaccurate Data," *The Wall Street Journal*, March 18, 1997)

Administration Proposes Legislation to Protect Humans from Secret Experiments

Continuing an ongoing story in this chronology, the Clinton Administration said it would propose legislation to protect Americans involved in secret government experiments from abuses like those committed in Cold War-era human radiation tests. Additionally, Secretary of Energy Federico Peña announced that the administration would expand current law and compensate roughly 600 uranium miners who developed lung cancer. Lack of records of government experiments, many dating from the '40s, '50s, and '60s, have hampered efforts to compensate victims or their survivors. (Strobel, Warren, "Rules Set to Protect Human Subjects," *The Washington Times*, March 29, 1997: A2)

APRIL

EPA Admits Error in Health Benefits Data

The Environmental Protection Agency (EPA) conceded that it had overestimated by about one-fourth the health benefits of the stricter air pollution standards the agency wants to impose this summer. The admission provides ammunition to those who oppose the proposed regulations. The EPA now says the new standards, designed to reduce smog and soot in American cities, would prevent 15,000 premature deaths each year, down from the 20,000 originally projected. The recalculation came at an inopportune time for EPA because critics allege that the proposals were not supported by scientific evidence. Supporters said the error does not change the fundamental problem of unhealthy levels of industrial soot in the air which leads to needless loss of life. (Warrick, Joby, "EPA Concedes Error in Air Pollution Claim," *Washington Post*, April 3, 1997: A19)

Too Much Useless Information Hampered Troops in Bosnia

A Pentagon study has determined that too much useless information was overwhelming troops in Bosnia and that a "major weakness" existed in providing computerized human intelligence. The report, prepared by a task force of the Defense Science Board, said that while there is good news in that information flowing down to the troops is "much more robust," we must make sure we don't "saturate the warrior with data while starving him of useful information." Widespread computer viruses were identified as a second problem. The task force recommended using guards and establishing training to prepare for the possibility that enemies might exploit the vulnerability of U.S. computer-run operations. (Pincus, Walter, "Information Glut Hampered U.S. Troops in Bosnia, Pentagon Say," *Washington Post*, April 3, 1997: A22)

Weather Service Cuts Said to Cost Lives

Some employees of the National Weather Service are fighting personnel cuts being made at the agency, maintaining that the cuts will impair forecasting and endanger both lives and property. The weather service also said it would temporarily defer maintenance on vital computer and forecasting systems and freeze its program for replacement of equipment in order to meet a funding cut of $27.5 million in fiscal year 1997. The administration has proposed an increase of $10.8 million for the weather service in fiscal year 1998, but unless Congress approves this level, further deep personnel cuts will be necessary.

As an example of the risk to public safety resulting from these cuts, National Weather Service officials point out that three Coast Guard crewmen died off the coast of Washington in February when their boat capsized in rough seas during a rescue. The seas were forecast to be 12-to-15 feet high, but were actually as high as 24 feet. A weather service buoy in the area could have given a more accurate reading of sea height, but the buoy was not operating because the service had stopped maintaining it. (Rivenbark, Leigh, "Storm Brews Over RIFs," *Federal Times*, April 7, 1997: 3)

CIA Says It Failed to Share Information about Chemical Dump

The CIA released a report suggesting that intelligence errors may have led to the destruction of an Iraqi ammunition dump, possibly exposing thousands of American troops to nerve gas. In an unusual televised press conference, the CIA apologized to the veterans for the mistakes. The report revealed that the CIA had solid evidence in 1986 that thousands of weapons filled with mustard gas had been stored at the Kamisiyah ammunition depot in southern Iraq. Yet the agency failed to include the depot on a list of suspected chemical-weapons sites provided to the Pentagon before the war. (Shenon, Philip, "CIA Report Says It Failed to Share Data on Iraq Arms," *The New York Times*, April 10, 1997: A1)

Justice Department Says CIA Failed to Refer Ames Information to the FBI

A Department of Justice (DOJ) report concluded that "the CIA must bear the primary responsibility" for the failure of investigators to focus early attention on spy Aldrich Ames in the late 1980s. DOJ Inspector General Michael Bromwich reported that "potentially incriminating information concerning Ames," available at the CIA in late 1989, "was not properly referred to the FBI for investigation." Additionally, the summary of Bromwich's still-classified 400-page report complained of the FBI's slow start in investigating the loss of two FBI-recruited agents who had been working inside the Soviet Embassy in Washington. Ames, a veteran counterintelligence officer, spied for Moscow for nine years. He provided information that led to the deaths of ten Soviet and other officials who were working for the United States in clandestine agencies. (Pincus, Walter, "Report Faults CIA's Delay in Ames Case," *Washington Post*, April 22, 1997: A6)

President Expands Public Access to Environmental Information

After considerable internal debate within the administration, President Clinton marked Earth Day by issuing new federal regulations requiring thousands more industrial facilities to report the toxic chemicals they emit into air, land, and water. The rules expand the "community-right-to-know" program that provides detailed public information on toxic materials in local communities. "By expanding community right-to-know, we're giving Americans a powerful—very powerful—early warning system to keep their children safe from toxic pollution," Clinton said. "We're giving them the most powerful tool in a democracy—knowledge." Citizens can tap into the Internet or visit local libraries to find out what toxic materials are being discharged in their neighborhood.

Administration officials had considered softening the plan because of complaints from industry officials and congressional Republicans who maintain that the requirements are too burdensome. Critics say that compliance with the rules costs too much, particularly for small businesses, which pay an estimated $7,000 a year in paperwork. (Baker, Peter, "Clinton Marks Earth Day by Widening Scope of Toxic Release Reporting Rules," *Washington Post*, April 23, 1997: A15)

MAY

National Academy of Sciences Committees Must Provide Open Public Access

The U.S. Court of Appeals for the District of Columbia ruled that advisory committees of the National Academy of Sciences

(NAS), the premier independent scientific body in the United States, must provide open public access to their deliberations and documents. The private, congressionally-chartered organization plans to appeal the ruling to the Supreme Court on the grounds that such access could threaten the objectivity and quality of its research reports. (The lawsuit resulting in the ruling involved an attempt by the Animal Legal Defense Fund and other groups to prevent the U.S. Department of Health and Human Services from using the NAS committees' proposed revisions to the principal federal guide for the care and use of laboratory animals.)

The plaintiffs in the case argued that the NAS committees should be subject to the 1972 Federal Advisory Committee Act which requires bodies advising the federal government to open their proceedings and to follow strict government regulations in appointing committees and conducting meetings. For decades, NAS has exercised exclusive control over committee membership and usually has met behind closed doors on such controversial topics as nuclear energy, air quality, pesticide safety, and electrical and magnetic fields. Even when acting under congressional mandates, funded by federal agencies, and producing reports intended to influence government policy, NAS has followed its own rules. Bruce Alberts, the academy's president, said this practice ensures that the panels can provide "independent, objective scientific advice, free of political pressure of partisan influence." (Suplee, Curt,

"Court Orders Public Access at National Academy of Sciences," *Washington Post,* May 7, 1997: A19)

Social Security Administration Shuts Down On-line Access to Database

In April, the Social Security Administration (SSA) shut down on-line access to its database of Personal Earnings and Benefits Estimate Statements for 60 days after some members of Congress, privacy advocates, and the public complained that personal privacy was too easily compromised at the site. Recent congressional hearings were held to determine what kind of security would allow the SSA to safely resume posting the sensitive financial records on the Internet. It only took five items of personal information to unlock personal information on the database: a name, Social Security number, mother's maiden name, birth date, and place of birth. The purpose of the site was to make it easier for workers to see their financial records and plan for retirement. The acting Social Security Administrator James Callahan testified, "Nothing is more important to Social Security Administration than maintaining the public's confidence in our ability to keep confidential the sensitive data we maintain on American citizens." But he pointed out that the security problem is shared by other government agencies that are increasingly using the Internet to conduct business. (Saffir, Barbara, "Sharing the Secrets with the Right Party," *Washington Post,* May 8, 1997: A25)

White House Will Appeal Court Decision that it Must Turn Over Lawyers' Notes

The White House appealed to the Supreme Court the decision of an 8th U.S. Circuit Court of Appeals requiring that the White House to turn over notes subpoenaed by Whitewater independent counsel Kenneth Starr. The subpoenaed notes were ones taken by White House lawyers during the questioning of Hillary Rodham Clinton on her involvement in Whitewater real estate dealings in Arkansas. The efforts of the White House to keep the lawyers' notes away from investigators were not known before this ruling. (Biskupic, Joan, "Lawyers for White House Ask High Court to Shield Notes," *Washington Post*, May 13, 1997: A4)

Report Says Secret Army Chemical Spraying Did Not Harm Health

A National Research Council report stated that the secret spraying of zinc cadmium sulfide, a potentially toxic chemical, in tests conducted by the Army in the 1950s and 1960s apparently did not harm health. According to the NRC report, the chemical, sprayed from airplanes, rooftops and moving vehicles in 33 urban and rural areas of the United States and Canada, did not expose residents to chemical levels considered harmful. Sites for the secret spraying included Minneapolis and surrounding areas; Corpus Christi, Texas; Fort Wayne, Indiana; and St. Louis, Missouri. (Leary, Warren, "Secret Army Chemical Tests Did Not Harm Health, Report Says," *The New York Times*, May 15, 1997: A24)

President Apologizes for Government Deception

President Clinton formally apologized to the eight survivors of secret government experiments that became known as the "Tuskegee experiment." In a White House ceremony, the President said, "What was done cannot be undone, but we can end the silence." The Tuskegee experiment (entitled "The Effect of Syphilis on the African-American Male" and carried out by the U.S. Public Health Service) began in 1932 and ended in the 1970s when a newspaper article revealed the deception involved in the study. Participants were promised free medicine and meals, but were never told their venereal disease was being left untreated. (Harris, John, and Michael Fletcher, "Six Decades Later, an Apology," *Washington Post*, May 17, 1997: A1)

Fate of Many Families Cut Off Welfare Unknown

A General Accounting Office (GAO) study found that states have cut off welfare benefits to 18,000 families in recent years, in most cases because the families failed to find work or move far enough toward that goal. About three-fourths of those who lost benefits were still receiving some federal assistance, such as Medicaid, food stamps, disability payments, or housing aid. About one-third of the families were returned to welfare rolls when they agreed to comply with state requirements. But GAO said that a lack of information made it impossible to know whether the circumstances of the families who lost benefits had improved or if they had fallen deeper into poverty. Frequently, states could not say what had happened to as many as half the families that had lost benefits. "This is the first indicator that people—when they go out of the welfare system—you're not in touch with them," said Senator Daniel Patrick Moynihan (D-NY), who requested the study. (Vobejda, Barbara, "States Cut 18,000 Families from Welfare Rolls, GAO Reports," *Washington Post*, May 16, 1997, A11)

"Fugitive Documents" Decrease Public Access to Information

Representative Steny Hoyer (D-MD) inserted a report by the Government Printing Office (GPO) into the Congressional Record concerning the extent of the problem of "fugitive government publications." "Fugitive government publications" are those that should be available to the public in the nation's depository libraries but have been excluded for a variety of reasons. The GPO report documents the scope of this problem and recommends solutions. Hoyer said, "It is important that people know just how serious this problem is."

GPO said four major factors have contributed to increased losses of key general-interest publications in the Federal Depository Library Program (FDLP): 1)

electronic information dissemination via agency Web sites without notification to the FDLP; 2) decreasing compliance with statutory requirements that agencies print through the GPO or provide copies of publications not printed through GPO to the FDLP; 3) an increasing trend for agencies to establish exclusive arrangements with private sector entities that place copyright or copyright-like restrictions on the products involved in such agreements; and 4) an increasing use by agencies of the rationale that publications must be sold in order to be self-sustaining. (Hoyer, Steny, "People's Right To Access," *Congressional Record*, May 22, 1997: E1045-46)

CIA Destroyed Documents on the 1953 Coup in Iran

The CIA said that it had destroyed or lost almost all of the documents related to its secret mission to overthrow the government of Iran in 1953—records which the agency has promised for more than five years to make public. Apparently the two successive directors of the CIA who pledged the documents would be released (Robert Gates in 1992 and James Woolsey in 1993) did not know there was little left to open. These pledges were made as part of the "openness" initiatives made to counter criticisms of the agency. Almost all these documents were destroyed in the early 1960s. "If anything of substantive importance that was an only copy was destroyed at any time," Woolsey said, "this is a terrible breach of faith with the American people and their ability to understand their own history." Nick Cullather, a historian on the CIA staff in 1992 and 1993, said that the records were eliminated by "a culture of destruction born of secrecy." (Weiner, Tim, "CIA Destroyed Files on 1953 Iran Coup," *The New York Times*, May 29, 1997: A19)

JUNE

Lack of Data Hampers Agency Compliance with Law

The General Accounting Office (GAO) has determined that many federal agencies are having difficulty fulfilling the intent of the 1993 Government Performance and Results Act. GAO predicted that although agencies will meet the September deadline for filing strategic plans and annual performance goals, "those documents will not be of a consistently high quality or as useful for congressional and agency decision making as they could be." Among the challenges agencies face are a lack of information on program performance. GAO questioned the equality and accuracy of information on program performance even when the data exists. The GAO report, "The Government Performance and Results Act: 1997 Government-wide Implementation Will be Uneven" (GAO/GGD-97-109) was posted on the GAO's Internet site, www.gao.gov. (Barr, Stephen, "Agencies Are Having Difficulty Measuring Success, GAO Finds, *Washington Post*, June 3, 1997: A17)

Legislation Moves Forward to Allow Federal Employees to Provide More Secrets to Congress

The Senate Select Committee on Intelligence approved legislation that would permit federal employees, including those who work for the CIA, to give classified information to senators and representatives with the approval of their superiors if it exposes inaccurate statements made to Congress, gross mismanagement or waste, fraud, or abuse. Since the Reagan Administration, Executive Branch policy has prohibited federal employees from giving classified material to legislators or congressional committees without first clearing such action with their bosses. Senator Robert Kerrey (D-NE), vice chairman of the committee, said that current administration policy left federal workers in doubt about whether they could go to Congress with classified information as whistleblowers. "This [uncertainty] undermines Congress's ability to fulfill its constitutional responsibility and is particularly troubling when intelligence agencies are involved," he said. (Pincus, Walter, "Panel Votes to Let Agency Staff Pass More Secrets to Capitol Hill," *Washington Post*, June 6, 1997: A3)

Federal Agencies Disagree About Evidence Regarding Veterans' Illnesses

The Pentagon took the unusual step of disputing a General Accounting Office (GAO) draft report before its tentative release later the same month. The GAO report asserted there is "substantial evidence" that low-level exposure to poison gas weapons could cause delayed or long-term ailments of Gulf War veterans. The Pentagon and a presidential panel appointed by President Clinton to look into the Gulf War veterans' illnesses said the GAO had reached different and unwarranted conclusions after analyzing the same scientific research and data they had reviewed.

In a 10-page rebuttal, Joyce C. Lashof, chair of the Presidential Advisory Committee on Gulf War Illness, said overall the GAO report "misrepresents" her panel's work, is "lacking in substantiation and analytic rigor," and makes statements that are "specious and misleading." The presidential advisory committee concluded that "stress, rather than Iraqi chemical and biological weapons, were the likely cause of veterans' health problems." The GAO said the presidential panel had "overemphasized stress as a factor."

Like the Pentagon, members of the presidential advisory committee have also been accused by veterans' advocates and others as part of a government-wide cover-up of the facts about Gulf War veterans' illnesses. (Priest, Dana, "GAO Draft Report Suggests Link Between Gas, Gulf Vets' Illness," *Washington Post*, June 17, 1997: A2)

[Ed. Note: The 140-page General Accounting Office report, *Gulf War Illnesses: Improved Monitoring of Clinical Progress and Reexamination of Research Emphasis Are Needed* (GAO/NSIAD-97-163), can be found on the World Wide Web at: http://www.gao.gov.]

House Committee Criticizes U.S. Intelligence Agencies

The U.S. House of Representatives Intelligence Committee criticized U.S. intelligence agencies in a sharply written report on the fiscal 1998 intelligence authorization bill. The report said the agencies have "limited analytical capabilities" and an "uncertain commitment and capability to collect human intelligence on a worldwide basis through espionage." The committee also said the continued expenditure by the Central Intelligence Agency of "billions" on high-tech satellites is disturbing because it failed to allocate adequate funds to review, analyze, and present the data to policy makers and military commanders in a usable form. "Expending resources to collect intelligence that is not being analyzed is simply a waste of money," the report said.

The House panel pointed out that other countries are learning how to block satellite coverage that "will affect how the intelligence community collects information and...what targets remain viable." Joining earlier criticism by the Senate Intelligence Committee, the House panel cited "a largely inexperienced work force, lack of foreign language skills, and limited in-country familiarity." (Pincus, Walter, "Intelligence Community Faulted by House Panel," *Washington Post*, June 19, 1997: A19)

Research Needed Before Government Databases can be Easily Accessible to Public

According to a new report, "Toward the Digital Government of the 21st Century," private industry and government need to research how public information can be aggregated, updated, and made easily accessible through several World Wide Web sites. Herbert Schorr, executive director of the University of Southern California's Information Sciences Institute and co-author of the study, said, "The Internet has exacerbated the expectations of people. We need to provide citizens with more access to the information the government has about them as well as other data they seek."

The report states, "The federal government is still providing information services using technology that is, in large measure, several generations behind the current Internet and Web style of information." Among the actions the authors recommend to the government are: 1) the coordinating of agency research so that more government databases are compatible and simpler to connect to the Internet; 2) the creation of standards for maintaining federal and local statistics so they can be easily combined and published on-line; 3) the admission of data that can be seen using multiple interfaces; and 4) the building of "virtual agencies" so that people can access documents or services. (Macavinta, Courtney, "Report: Government Files a Mess," news.com, June 25, 1997, http://www.news.com/News/Item/0,4,11926,00.html)

Army Charged with Destroying Sex Survey Data

A researcher charged a secretive Army panel looking into sexual misconduct with destroying some highly sensitive data it had collected from a survey of 9,000 troops. Leora Rosen, who works in the department of military psychiatry at Walter Reed Army Medical Center, said, "the panel's apparent intention is to suppress this information in order to avoid making the Army look bad." Rosen, who has filed a whistleblower complaint with the Office of Special Counsel, analyzed 613 surveys that escaped destruction. The purged data included questions about the use of prostitutes and pornography in Army units.

Rosen added, "A spokesman for the Army confirmed that some survey data had been destroyed. According to Colonel John Smith, 'The raw data from those sex questions no longer exists.'" An Army statement said the questions destroyed were "inflammatory and offensive and felt by some soldiers to be an invasion of privacy to the extent that some of them refused to comply with the survey." Rosen said Army officials had spoken at a panel meeting about the possibility of destroying all the raw survey data, not just the most controversial questions, in order to control how the results were interpreted. The Army would not say whether the raw data would be available in full, although the survey results will be released in some form.

The panel, appointed by Army Secretary Togo D. West, Jr. after revelations of widespread sexual abuse at the

Aberdeen Proving Ground, has gone to extraordinary lengths to keep its work secret. Madeline Morris, a Duke University law professor who consulted with West, said the Army's actions "raises questions about why the Army would eliminate data they had already collected, rather than analyze it, when that data could be relevant to the question they are asking: What causes sexual harassment?" (Priest, Dana, "Army Panel Destroyed Data on Sex Survey," *Washington Post*, June 27, 1997: A21)

More Troops Were Exposed to Chemicals in Area of Iraqi Dump

The Pentagon has again revised the number of troops estimated to have been exposed to an Iraqi chemical dump when it was destroyed in 1991. The estimate was said to be 27,000, an increase from the estimate of 21,000 made earlier in 1997. Thousands of Persian Gulf War veterans have complained of illness, but no cause has been found for the complaints. Congress has accused the Pentagon and White House of failure to properly investigate the matter. (Reuters, "Raises Estimate of Troops Near Iraqi Chemical Arms," *Washington Post*, June 27, 1997: A26)

ALA Joins in Suit to Preserve Electronic Federal Records

Several independent researchers and non-profit organizations, including the American Library Association, filed a lawsuit in federal court against the Archivist of the United States because he issued guidances in 1995 authorizing government agencies to destroy electronic mail and other computerized records without regard for their content. The regulation permits destruction of electronic records once they have been copied on paper or some other format and are "no longer needed for updating or revision." The complaint sought to invalidate the rule and accused Archivist John Carlin of abdicating his responsibility to appraise the value of the electronic records on an agency-by-agency basis. "It's the electronic shredder," protested one of the plaintiffs, author-researcher Scott Armstrong.

Justice Department lawyers argued that the regulation was solidly grounded and that federal agencies cannot have efficient records-management programs if they cannot get rid of unneeded records. Justice Department Attorney Anne Weismann said that "the vast majority" of government agencies are not equipped to preserve computer records in an electronic format. Public Citizen attorney Michael Tankersley said, "The archivist has opened the floodgates, allowing agencies to destroy records without regard for their historical value." (Lardner, George, "Record-Destruction Order Assailed," *Washington Post*, June 28, 1997: A8)

[Ed. Note: On October 22, U.S. District Court Judge Paul Freidman ruled that the Archivist was wrong to allow federal agencies routinely to destroy the electronic versions of word processing and electronic mail records even if paper copies were made. (Miller, Page Putnam, "Court Rules Against the National Archives in Case on Regulations for Destroying Electronic Records," *NCC Washington Update*, vol. 3, #44, November 6, 1997)]

Right to Know Week Celebrated

An editorial in *The San Francisco Chronicle* announced that the American Society of Newspaper Editors had designated "Your Right to Know Week" to celebrate the First Amendment and sunshine laws that help the public keep an eye on the inner workings of government. It pointed out that with a few clearly defined exceptions, "there is relatively little official business that legally can be kept secret from the public. However, there continues to be a struggle between reporters who always want more and bureaucrats whose instincts are often to conceal, especially information that might embarrass them or their bosses." The editorial also said that the Internet has brought new opportunities for government access, and that the press and public must be alert to new technology that can expand access to government. ("Your Right to Know Week," *San Francisco Chronicle*, June 30, 1997: A22)

JULY

Freedom of Information Act Implemented Unevenly

After President Lyndon Johnson signed the Freedom of Information Act (FOIA) in 1966, it was amended in the 1970s to make it quicker and easier to use. Since then, its use has increased steadily, and currently, about 600,000 FOIA requests are filed with the federal government each year. Most experts estimate that reporters file about 5 percent of the requests. The act's users also include historians, prisoners, and individual citizens trying to discover, for example, what files the government has on them. According to John Fialka, a *Wall Street Journal* reporter and author, however, 60 percent of FOIA requests are filed by businesses trying to gather information on competing firms. He said it costs up to $100 million a year to carry out the federal law, and believes fees for commercial users should be sufficient to cover the law's overhead. "Otherwise, the law should be abolished," he said. "The backlog of FOIA requests at some agencies is so great that users often wait one to three years."

Some researchers and reporters have waited up to 10 years to have requests filled. The act's nine exemptions cover national security, confidential business information, and records that would violate an individual's privacy. Experts say the latter exemption has been used increasingly to deny access to records. "The approach that some agencies have taken is that anything that has somebody's name on it will be withholdable, either in whole or part," said Jane Kirtley, executive director of the Reporters Committee for Freedom of the Press. Tom Blanton, director of the National Security Archive, has had to battle the impulse of many agencies to deny requests even when disclosure of records would appear harmless. Blanton said, "It's a reflexive secrecy. You tap on a knee and the foot kicks out. You call an agency and the top-secret stamp hits the page."

But the author says that some agencies are forthcoming with records, like the Food and Drug Administration, the Department of Health and Human Services, and the Defense Department. Agencies notorious for responding slowly include the State Department, the Federal Bureau of Investigation, and the Central Intelligence Agency. (Armstrong, Ken, "The Trickle of Information Act Is Closer to Truth," *Chicago Tribune*, July 4, 1997: 19)

AUGUST

State Department Implements 900 Number for Passport Information

Americans seeking passport information were charged as much as $60 on their phone bills when they called a 900 number operated by AT&T Corporation. Unlike the 800 number system used by agencies such as the Social Security Administration and IRS, the 900 is not toll free. Customers are charged 35 cents to hear basic recorded information or $1.05 per minute to talk to a representative. The telephone representatives are no longer employees of the Department of State, but work on a contract through AT&T. "This is a bad precedent to allow," said Representative Gary Ackerman (D-NY). "You could wind up with every federal agency taxing the citizenry

a second time for basic information." In contrast, Nyda Budig, spokeswoman for the State Department's Bureau of Consular Affairs, said privatizing the function improved service and saved most taxpayers money by making users pay for it.

But critics of the contract arrangement think it should be the department and not customers who pay for the service. The House passed a State Department authorization bill that would earmark $5 million to pay for 800 number lines to be run by the contractors. Although similar language is not in a comparable Senate bill, Representative Ackerman said it may be approved by budget negotiators. (Daniel, Lisa, "Passport Office Charging Callers," *Federal Times*, August 4, 1997: 7)

CIA Criticized for Withholding Information

The New York Times criticized the CIA's withholding of information about its own files on crimes in Latin America, as truth commissions in several countries began to investigate the human rights abuses of the past. At the same time, *The New York Times* acknowledged that the CIA had released some records on the 1954 military coup it organized in Guatemala, and had promised more coup records in the months ahead.

Nevertheless, the CIA has declassified practically nothing on the security forces that have killed more than 110,000 Guatemalans since the coup. "Washington trained and supported some of these forces. It also backed abusive internal security organizations in Nicaragua, Haiti, Honduras and El Salvador. It owes the victims of these groups whatever information it has." The editorial concluded that the agency's continued secrecy serves to protect it from embarrassment. ("History That Remains Hidden," *The New York Times*, August 5, 1997, http://www.newyorktimes.com/ yr/ mo/day/editorial/05tue3.html)

Cold War Deception Fueled UFO Controversy

According to CIA historian Gerald Haines, during the 1950s and 1960s, the Air Force and CIA "willfully misled" the public by claiming that thousands of sightings of unidentified flying objects were caused by ice crystals, temperature inversions, and other natural causes, when actually they were produced by the flight of super-secret spy planes. Writing in the declassified version of *Studies of Intelligence*, Haines concluded that more than half of all UFO sightings in the United States for decades "were accounted for by manned Reconnaissance flights."

During this time, believers in UFOs thrived on the belief that the U.S. government covered up crucial information about mysterious flying objects. Haines said that in thousands of cases, they were right. His study found that the government concocted the explanations both to calm fears about UFOs and to maintain secrecy about its most advanced espionage aircrafts at the time, the U-2 and the SR-71 Blackbird.

National security officials justified their deception "to allay public fears and protect an extraordinarily sensitive national security project," wrote Haines. "While perhaps justified, this deception added fuel to the...conspiracy theories and the cover-up controversy" of later years. Questioned in early August 1997, Air Force Brigadier General Ronald said, "I cannot confirm or deny that we lied. The Air Force is committed to providing accurate and timely information within the confines of national security." The spokesman said, "Corporately and institutionally, there is no Air Force or Defense Department game plan" currently in place to intentionally mislead the public in order to conceal secrets. UFO experts and government secrecy watchdogs said the CIA study is a refreshingly revealing document but unlikely to repair the government's credibility problem among those who believe that the government has tried to conceal evidence of extraterrestrial visitors to Earth. (Priest, Dana, "Cold War UFO Cover-up Shielded Spy Planes," *Washington Post*, August 5, 1997: A4)

Intelligence Community Delays Release of Historic Records

The annual report of the Historical Advisory Committee (HAC) is highly critical of the intelligence community, primarily the Central Intelligence Agency, for maintaining barriers to opening the historical record of United States foreign policy and diplomacy. The government-appointed panel was created following the embarrassment that resulted from the publication in the late 1980s of a volume of the *Foreign Relations of the United States* (FRUS) that ignored the U.S. government's use of covert activities to influence U.S.-Iranian relations in the mid-1950s. For four years the CIA has acknowledged conducting at least eleven covert activities during the Cold War, but has declassified enough information to delineate U.S. foreign policy only in British Guyana. As a result, a number of volumes of the FRUS are delayed, awaiting the outcome of repeated declassification appeals.

The report states that "a number of FRUS compilations now stand in Never-never Land, and the HAC is forced to contemplate recommending against publication because the thirty-year-old historical record is or will fall grossly short of a complete record including the relevant intelligence involvement." The committee said it is "increasingly disinclined" to resort to stating in Prefaces to the FRUS that the volume in question constitutes an inaccurate and incomplete record when the committee "knows that the documentary record is, or is likely to be, available in government archives." The committee said many covert activities have been revealed in various official (e.g., Congressional hearings) and semi-official (memoirs by CIA agents) sources. "Such a compromise is especially ludicrous with regard to the specific covert activities now acknowledged by the CIA."

The Report of the Advisory Committee on Historical Diplomatic Documentation to the United States Department of State came in the form of a June 26, 1997, letter to Secretary of State Madeleine Albright from Chairman War-ren F. Kimball. The report came weeks after the CIA acknowledged it had destroyed some records of covert activities undertaken in the 1950s and 1960s, but the agency said destruction was to clear out shelf space, not to conceal its activities. CIA spokesman Mark Mansfield said, "The reason why information would be withheld concerns protection of sources and methods." But Dr. Kimball said the committee was not trying to publish such sensitive information. (Haworth, Karla, "Committee of Historians Says CIA Balks at Releasing 30-Year-Old Documents," *The Chronicle of Higher Education*, August 11, 1997, Academe Today electronic news service)

[Ed. Note: The report is available on-line at http://www.fas.org/sgp/advisory/hac96.html]

Privatizing the Public's Business Deplored

In an opinion piece, Robert Kuttner said, "A hallmark danger of this era is that the public's business is becoming privatized. Industry wants to replace public agencies and public processes with private contractors and private deals. And there is far too little public protest." He observed that the Food and Drug Administration appears to be "public enemy number one." As an example of efforts to weaken the FDA, he pointed to the proposed tobacco accord reached through secret negotiations. Kuttner said "a group of self-appointed spokesmen for the public's health and some state attorneys general, lured by the prospect of a large payment from the tobacco industry, have cut a proposed deal that limits the industry's total liability for damages and reins in the FDA."

Kuttner then pointed to efforts by the medical-device industry to limit the FDA's ability to ensure the safety and efficacy of everything from artificial heart valves to super-tampons. The $50-billion-a-year medical device business is one of America's most profitable. He said this industry hopes to get Congress to pass legislation that would partly privatize the FDA's function of certifying safe products. "Instead of having to pass muster with the FDA, a manufacturer could submit a new product to a private review firm selected by the very company seeking approval." And these same private consultants could do other contract work for the device manufacturers, setting up a conflict of interest.

Kuttner asked, "What entrepreneur would put other business at risk by vetoing a client's new product application?" The author maintained that instead of trying to cripple the FDA, industry should be thankful for it, since the FDA offers their products a worldwide seal of approval that consumers can trust—contributing to the industry's global preeminence. (Kuttner, Robert, "Privatizing the Public's Business," *Washington Post*, August 29, 1997: A23)

SEPTEMBER

Gag Ordered on Air Force Readiness Reports

Louis Finch, Defense Department Deputy Undersecretary for Readiness, issued a gag order to members of his staff who go on field trips to assess military readiness. In the August 7 memorandum, he also reserved the right to declare secret what they learn. According to his ground rules, trip information:

➤ "...will not contain editorializing, opinions, or speculations of team members or others."
➤ "...will not be transferred electronically among participants or shared with others without my consent."
➤ "...will not be printed on letterhead, contain reference to intended recipient, or indicate coordinating officials until it is in final form."
➤ "...will not contain the names of anyone visited in the field."

Finch's memo was issued after a draft "trip report" concluded "limited wartime sortie generation capability exists today" in the Air Force, because so many planes can't fly for lack of engines and spare parts. The report also said morale was low among active-duty personnel and that they distrust senior leaders. (Wilson, George C., "Gag Order Issued on Readiness Reports," *Federal Times*, September 1, 1997: 11)

Film Makers Warned about Bomb Blasts, but not the General Public

During the 1950s, the government assured the public that there was no health threat from atmospheric nuclear tests. Yet at the same time, the Atomic Energy Commission (AEC) regularly warned film manufacturers about fallout that could damage their products according to a review of documents made public as part of an "openness initiative" by former Secretary of Energy Hazel O'Leary. The non-profit Institute for Energy and Environmental Research said Eastman Kodak had threatened to sue the Atomic Energy Commission when some of its film was fogged before use and the problem was traced to fallout from U.S. and Russian nuclear tests. The AEC then promised to warn Kodak about future tests.

The National Cancer Institute said in August that radioactive iodine-131 fallout from the blasts had probably caused 10,000 to 75,000 extra thyroid cancers. Senator Tom Harkin (D-IA) said, "It really is odd that the government would warn Kodak about its film but it wouldn't warn the general public about the milk it was drinking." Iodine-131 is absorbed by cows and incorporated into milk. In humans, it concentrates in the thyroid gland, where it can cause cancer. Senator Harkin said that part of his thyroid was removed 17 years ago and that his brother died of thyroid cancer last year. (Wald, Matthew L., "U.S. Alerted Photo Film Makers, Not Public, About Bomb Fallout," *The New York Times*, September 30, 1997: A18)

[Ed. Note: The final fallout report of the National Cancer Institute is available online at http://rex.nci.nih.gov/massmedia/Fallout/index.html.]

CIA Reveals U.S. Intelligence Budget at $26.6 billion

After 50 years of secrecy, under pressure from a Freedom of Information lawsuit, the CIA disclosed that the United States spends $26.6 billion a year on intelligence matters. The agency, which itself spends about $3 billion a year, oversees a covertly appropriated sum from which billions are drawn by other government intelligence agencies, including the National Security Agency and the National Imagery and Mapping Agency. CIA director George Tenet said the disclosure "does not jeopardize" national security and "serves to inform the American people." Kate Martin, the attorney who filed the lawsuit, said, "Now we can begin to have some real democratic debate on the size of the intelligence budget. The CIA's refusal to disclose the figure didn't protect national security. It shut citizens out of the debate about the usefulness and future of the CIA." Martin, director of the Center for National Security Studies, filed the suit on behalf of the Federation of American Scientists' government secrecy project. (Weiner, Tim, "For First Time, U.S. Discloses Spying Budget," *The New York Times*, October 16, 1997: 27)

Government Contractor Threatens to Sue to Prevent Release of Transplant Data

The United Network for Organ Sharing, a private group that operates the national organ donor network, is threatening to sue the federal government to prevent the release of data on individual heart and kidney transplant centers. The Richmond, Virginia-based contractor oversees the organ allocation system and compiles information about organ transplants that is submitted to the U.S. Department of Health and Human Services. The records include median waiting times and the numbers of organ offers that are turned down both for medical and non-medical reasons. The requests for the records were filed by *The Plain Dealer* under the Freedom of Information Act (FOIA) in June 1996. Since then, *The Detroit Free Press*, ABC News, and two grass-roots transplant groups have made similar requests. On October 16, federal officials informed UNOS that they will release the data unless a federal judge orders otherwise.

Charles E. Fiske of the National Transplant Action Committee asked, "But what is UNOS there for? Is it there to protect patients or to protect the institutions?" (Wendling, Ted, Dave Davis, and Joan Mazzolini, "Organ Donor Group Threatens Suit to Keep Files Private," *The Plain Dealer* [Cleveland, OH], October 31, 1997: 10-A)

[Ed. Note: In mid-November, under threats that the government was preparing to release turndown data for organ transplants, UNOS's board voted unanimously to release the information. (Wendling, Ted, Dave Davis, and Joan Mazzolini. "Florida, California Lead in Organ Turndowns," *The Plain Dealer* [Cleveland, OH], November 21, 1997: 1A)

NOVEMBER

Compromise Reached on Sampling for the 2000 Census

Following months of controversy about the potential use of sampling in the 2000 Census, the White House and Republican Congressional leaders reached a compromise on the use of the politically sensitive statistical technique. They agreed to allow the administration to experiment with statistical sampling to achieve a more accurate count but gave Republicans time and resources to challenge the technique in court. The issue has been controversial because it could affect the future political composition of the House of Representatives.

House Republican leaders have opposed the administration's planned use of statistical sampling to supplement traditional person-by-person head counts, fearing the technique could be used to produce more House districts dominated by racial minorities, who tend to vote for Democrats. They also argue that sampling is unconstitutional. The administration and Congressional Democrats argued that minorities traditionally have been undercounted in the decennial census and that by using statistical sampling, undercounting will be reduced. The compromise helped clear the way for final passage of the fiscal year 1998 appropriations bill for the Departments of Commerce, Justice, and State. (Pianin, Eric, and Helen Dewar, "Congress Also Clears FDA Changes, Works Late on Spending Bills," *Washington Post*, November 10, 1997: A04)

National Academy of Sciences Exempted from Open Access Law

Congress passed legislation to exempt the National Academy of Sciences from a law mandating open access to its deliberations and federal oversight of its committees, but the Academy "will have to provide extensive public information about many aspects of its work." Activist groups argued in lawsuits that the NAS committees, which traditionally are appointed without public consultation and conduct key meetings in private, violated the 1972 Federal Advisory Committee Act. That law requires open meetings, "balanced" committee membership, and federal oversight for organizations that advise the federal government.

The NAS countered that Congress never intended the FACA to apply to the Academy, which must apply its own professional standards for committee membership and maintain confidentiality in meetings to ensure that its advice is "independent from government...as well as from potential outside political and special-interest pressures." (Suplee, Curt, "Congress Addresses Access to Academy of Sciences," *Washington Post*, November 17, 1997: A21)

Plan Revealed to Blame Castro if Glenn Mission Failed

Previously classified records revealed that had John Glenn's space flight in February 1952 failed, American military planners were thinking of blaming Fidel Castro. The operation was called "Operation Dirty Trick," and according to long-secret documents recently made public, the idea was "to provide irrevocable proof that, should the MERCURY manned orbit flight fail, the fault lies with the Communists et al. Cuba." The planners suggested in a February 2, 1962 memo that this could be accomplished "by manufacturing various pieces of evidence which would prove electronic interference on the part of the Cubans." (Lardner, George, Jr., and Walter Pincus, "Military Had Plan to Blame Cuba If Glenn's Space Mission Failed," *Washington Post*, November 19, 1997: A2)

National Archives Destroys Naval Research Laboratory Historical Records

Archivist of the United States John Carlin has ordered an investigation into the destruction by the National Archives of records that the Naval Research Laboratory considered of permanent historical value. Carlin said, "If the process is flawed, or the evaluation criteria are inadequate, then obviously the situation must be fixed." Paul Gaffney, the Chief of Naval Research, wrote to Carlin on November 13, stating that "the historical record of our nation's scientific and technical heritage has suffered a serious and irreparable loss." The destroyed records included material that documented the work of the pioneers of American radar, path-breaking acoustic and oceanographic research, early sonar research, the first U.S. satellite program, and the early rocket-based astronomical research.

Gaffney contends that Naval Research Laboratory personnel received no notification of the National Archives' plan to destroy records they considered permanently valuable and which constituted the core of the agency's corporate memory. Carlin contends the records were destroyed following procedures established years ago for evaluating naval laboratory records, and that National Archives staff did not consider the destroyed material to meet the tests for permanent value. Carlin pointed out that the Navy had been notified about the pending destruction and had "raised no objection." (Miller, Page Putnam, "Archivist Orders an Investigation of Recent Destruction of Naval Laboratory Records," *NCC Washington Update*, vol. 3, #46, November 19, 1997)

DECEMBER

Tape Transcripts Reveal Nixon White House Media Strategy

Transcripts of Nixon White House tapes released in October further reveal a president obsessed with efforts to improve his image and eagerly plotting to discredit his detractors. The National Archives released 200 hours of conversations after a long court battle. In a July 2, 1971, tape-recorded discussion with aide Charles Colson, Nixon said the best way to intimidate the nation's three major television networks was to keep the constant threat of an antitrust suit hanging over them. Colson played a major role in pressuring the news media to change their critical coverage of the Nixon Administration. Colson told Nixon "keeping this case in a pending status gives one hell of a club on an economic issue that means a great deal to those three networks...something of a sword of Damocles."

Nixon responded, "Our gain is more important than the economic gain. We don't give a goddamn about the economic gain. Our game here is solely political....As far as screwing them is concerned, I'm very glad to do it." The White House kept the Justice Department from filing suit until April 1972 when the government accused the networks of monopolizing prime-time entertainment with their own programs. The suits were dismissed in 1974 after the Nixon White House refused to turn over subpoenaed records. (Pincus, Walter, and George Lardner, Jr., "Nixon Hoped Antitrust Threat Would Sway Network Coverage," *Washington Post*, December 1, 1997: A1)

U.S. Role in Melting Nazi Gold Revealed in Long-secret Documents

According to long-secret documents that the Federal Reserve Bank of New York plans to release to a conference of historians tracking Nazi gold, in 1952, the United States melted down gold plates, buttons, coins, and smoking-pipe ornaments that were apparently looted from Hitler's victims. The gold bars were then turned over to European central banks. Jewish groups and the United States government plan to use the documents to press their case that $54 million in gold remained in the possession of the Tripartite Commission for the Restitution of Monetary Gold (the panel assembled to return looted assets to central banks), and should be given to Holocaust survivors and their heirs.

Other recently declassified documents from American archives reveal details from recent investigations of the trail of wartime assets that have now spanned the globe. For example, a declassified coded message released by the National Security Agency shows what happened to millions of dollars paid by the United States and Switzerland for the care of prisoners of war held by the Japanese. The newly released transcript of a coded message written by Swiss officials—the neutral country that handled the funds—shows that a secret deal was reached in August 1944 by Swiss and Japanese officials to divert 40 percent of those funds to pay off Japan's debts to Swiss businesses. (Sanger, David E., "U.S. Melted Down Gold Items from Nazis," *The New York Times*, December 1, 1997: A8)

U.S. Argues that Cutting Would Jeopardize Nixon Tapes

A federal court ordered the National Archives to return all "personal or private conversations" on the Nixon White House tapes to the late president's estate. In an appeal brief Justice Department lawyers said this would jeopardize "virtually all" of the 950 reels of tape from the Nixon presidency that Congress confiscated by law in 1974 to keep Nixon from destroying them. The Justice Department said that it has no obligation to cut out portions of the tapes to satisfy the demands of Nixon's estate. Nixon's privacy interests, the Justice brief said, will be preserved because the original tapes will be kept intact in a special vault, without any provision for public access. A hearing is scheduled for late February. (Lardner, George, Jr., "U.S. Argues Against Return of Excerpts of Nixon Tapes," *Washington Post*, December 2, 1997: A17)

U.S. Sued for Violating Freedom of Information Act

Public Citizen filed a federal lawsuit in U.S. District Court for the District of Columbia to enforce recent federal statutes designed to make it easier for the public to obtain access to government information. The suit charged that seven major federal agencies have not complied with statutes requiring that they make available guides and indices to help the public obtain agency records. "The Clinton Administration has failed to live up to its commitment to make government information more open to the public," said Michael Tankersley, the Public Citizen Litigation Group attorney who filed the suit.

In 1995, Congress directed all federal agencies to compile a current and complete inventory of their information resources, including directories that could be used to establish an electronic service for locating major government information systems. The following year, in the Electronic Freedom of Information

Act Amendments, Congress directed agencies to make available a guide containing an index, with a description of all major information and record locator systems, and a handbook describing how to obtain information from these systems under the Freedom of Information Act (FOIA) and other statutes.

According to Public Citizen, the Office of Management and Budget (OMB) was supposed to take a leadership role in implementing these requirements. But many agencies, including the OMB, have ignored these mandates. The seven agencies named as defendants are the OMB, the Office of Administration in the Executive Office of the President, the Office of the U.S. Trade Representative, the Department of Education, the Department of Energy, the Department of Justice, and the Department of State. "This lawsuit will force these agencies to give the public the tools needed to navigate through the bureaucratic corridors of cyberspace," said Lucinda Sikes, another Public Citizen representative working on the case. (Public Citizen press release, "Federal Agencies Violating Freedom of Information Act, Lawsuit Alleges," December 4, 1997)

[Ed. Note: The press release is available on-line at http://www.citizen.org/foia-suit.htm]

Tobacco Industry Turns Over Documents to Congress

A dramatic confrontation between Representative Thomas Bliley (R-VA) and the tobacco industry has resulted in a cache of sensitive internal company documents being turned over to a Congressional committee—a departure from years of legal maneuvering to keep industry secrets hidden. Over 800 documents were delivered to Congress, less than 24 hours after Bliley, a long-time industry supporter, issued a subpoena for them. "Today's development will give Congress the information it needs to make more informed and responsible decisions" on the proposed settlement, Bliley said.

The documents were not released publicly, however, and Bliley gave no indication of when that might happen, saying only that the committee will establish "a bipartisan process for reviewing and disclosing" them. "These documents are only the tip of the iceberg," said Senator Patrick Leahy (D-VT). And Minnesota Attorney General Hubert H. Humphrey said, "The smoking guns are trickling out, but the smoking howitzers remain under lock and key." Matthew Myers, of the National Center for Tobacco-Free Kids, said he hoped that Bliley's comments were not an indication that the documents would be kept private. "It's as important for the American public to see these documents as for Congress—so that the citizens of the country can make an informed decision about what Congress should do," Myers said. (Torry, Saundra, and John Schwartz, "Tobacco Industry Delivers Documents to Congress," *Washington Post*, December 6, 1997: A9)

White House Continues Pattern of Belated Release of Subpoenaed Material

Throughout the summer and fall of 1997, many articles have appeared in the press about the belated released of subpoenaed material to Congress, including video tapes, concerning President Clinton's fundraising activities for the 1996 presidential campaign. This article is about notes taken in the White House during discussions of the growing campaign finance controversy. Although the notes appear to add little to the ongoing campaign finance investigations, they could become a new source of controversy for the Clinton Administration. White House spokesman Lanny J. Davis said he could not explain the delay in finding the notes, which he acknowledged fall within the scope of subpoenas for materials relating to fundraising in the White House that were issued as long ago as March 24. (Schmidt, Susan, "White House Gives Aide's Notes to Congress," *Washington Post*, December 9, 1997: A6)

Attorney General Declines to Hand Over FBI Memo to Congress

Attorney General Janet Reno refused to comply with a Congressional subpoena for a confidential memorandum in which FBI Director Louis Freeh urged her to seek an independent counsel in the campaign finance scandal. The House Government Reform and Oversight Committee, having called Reno and Freeh to testify at a hearing on December 9, sought the memorandum as part of its investigation of Reno's handling of the independent counsel issue. Reno declined to provide the document, pointing to the need to protect an ongoing investigation and to preserve the confidentiality of the decision-making process within the Department of Justice. (Suro, Roberto, "Reno Declines to Hand Over Freeh Memo," *Washington Post*, December 9, 1997: A6)

Judge Orders Government to Pay Sanctions for Withholding Information

In a follow-up to a *Less Access* item from four years ago, a federal judge ordered the U.S. government to pay sanctions of $285,864 for the "dishonest" and "reprehensible" conduct of the White House and Justice Department in failing to reveal to the court key information about the membership of the health care reform task force chaired by Hillary Rodham Clinton. "[It] is clear that the decisions here were made at the highest levels of government, and the government itself is—and should be—accountable when its officials run amok," U.S. District Court Judge Royce C. Lamberth wrote in his opinion. "It seems that some government officials never learn that the cover-up can be worse than the underlying conduct." (Locy, Toni, "Government Ordered to Pay Sanctions for Dishonest About Health Care Task Force," *Washington Post*, December 19, 1997: A21)

EPA Plans Expansion of "Right-to-know"

The Environmental Protection Agency (EPA) announced plans for an ambitious project to expand its "right-to-know" initiatives so that people who live near hundreds of factories in five major industries can have easy on-line access to additional data about the pollution from those plants. This is the first time profiles of the environmental performance of the producers of oil products, steel and other metals, autos, and paper have been made available, indicating which factories may present the biggest environmental problems.

Industries argued that the evaluation is misleading. The project expands on the *Toxics Release Inventory*, an annual survey published on-line and in printed reports that has been credited with encouraging companies to voluntarily control their pollution.

The new project is called the Sector Facility Indexing Project, but the affected industries consider it the Scarlet Letter Initiative, because they fear that it will unfairly identify some of them as polluters. The industries are trying to block the project, arguing that the release of the information will confuse and alarm the public. (Cushman, John H., Jr., "EPA Is Pressing Plan to Publicize Pollution Data," *The New York Times*, August 12, 1997, http://newyorktimes.com/library/cyber/week/081297pollute.html)

Americans Can Provide More Information About Themselves

The Clinton Administration announced that for the first time, Americans will be able to choose more than one racial category to describe themselves on census and other federal forms. The decision ends a long-standing practice of requiring people to identify themselves as a member of only one racial group despite growing complaints that the nation's racial composition is increasingly diverse. "This gives far more flexibility for people to express their multiracial heritage," said OMB Director Franklin Raines. How the census collects data is important because the numbers are used to redraw political boundaries, enforce civil rights protections, and administer many programs that depend on racial data.

In the last census, Americans could mark just one box and were given these choices: white, black, American Indian, Eskimo, Aleut, or several Asian or Pacific Islander groups. The result was a set of population figures that could be neatly tabulated, but left many dissatisfied at being forced to choose one heritage over another. Nearly 10 million Americans marked "other" rather than choose one of the basic categories. In the 2000 Census, people can check off as many categories as they like, yielding a much more complex view of the American population. (Vobejda, Barbara,

"Census Expands Options for Multiracial Families," *Washington Post*, October 30, 1997: A11)

Best Federal Government Web Sites Chosen

Joyce Kasman Valenza, a high school librarian, wrote an article for a Philadelphia newspaper featuring a number of local, state, and federal government Web sites that she believed best that exemplified Thomas Jefferson's axiom, "Whenever the people are well-informed, they can be trusted with their own government." Valenza said, "To Jefferson, an informed citizenry was essential to the proper functioning of a democracy. Self-government would not be possible unless citizens were well-educated and had free access to information. Jefferson would have really liked the World Wide Web." She observes that young citizens can read the actual texts of laws, speeches, judicial decisions, and, of course, political propaganda. Among the best of the federal executive and legislative branch Web sites she chose are:

➤ http://www.whitehouse.gov/WH/Welcome.html
➤ http://www.whitehouse.gov/WH/kids/html/kidshome.html
➤ http://www.odci.gov/cia/publications/pubs.html
➤ http://www.state.gov/www/background-notes/index.html
➤ http://www.state.gov/www/regionsdigital.html
➤ http://www.census.gov
➤ http://thomas.loc.gov/

➤ http://lcweb2.loc.gov/frd/cs/cshome.html

The judicial branch is represented by a Web site hosted by Northwestern University, instead of the federal government. It is a multimedia database of U.S. Supreme Court information: http://oyez.at.nwu.edu/oyez.html. (Valenza, Joyce Kasman, "Sites That Provide Government Information to the People: Laws, Speeches and Court Decisions Are Among a Wealth of Documents at Local, State and Federal Levels," *Philadelphia Inquirer*, November 13, 1997: F04)

Government Printing Office Thrives in Electronic Age

The Government Printing Office (GPO), the federal government's publisher, has used new technology to make information available to the public so effectively that Congress has considered changing the agency's name to reflect the cyberspace age. Eric Peterson, staff director of the Joint Committee on Printing, said GPO has "been on the forefront of helping the government emerge from the classic printing environment to electronic information access." For example, before GPO made the *Federal Register* available on the Internet in 1994, government presses printed 33,000 copies a night at an average of 225 pages per issue. Currently, GPO prints 23,000 paper copies, while 1 million copies are downloaded every month from the Internet. Federal laws, in the *United States Code*, fill 35 bound volumes that cost about $2,000. The same information fits on one compact disc that sells for $37. At the same time, sales of the disc have fallen since GPO made the *United States Code* available on the Internet for free.

Senator John Warner (R-VA), who chairs the Joint Committee on Printing, wants GPO to ensure that all government documents are made accessible to the public, especially through electronic formats at libraries. Warner wants to channel all federal government publications printed by a private business or other another agency through GPO's Superintendent of Documents. "Free and open access to information created at taxpayer expense is the principle which has enabled the United States to endure and prosper for over 200 years," Warner said. (Johnson, Mark, "Venerable GPO thrives in Cyberspace," *Richmond Times Dispatch*, November 30, 1997: A2)

[Ed. Note: The GPO Access system is found on-line at http://www.access.gpo. gov.]

THIS MODERN WORLD

by TOM TOMORROW

IN THE ONLINE MAGAZINE *SALON*,* SIXTIES RADICAL TURNED RABID CONSERVATIVE *DAVID HOROWITZ* RECENTLY WROTE ONE OF THOSE TEACHER BASHING PIECES SO IN VOGUE AMONG RIGHTWINGERS THESE DAYS... STATING IN PART:

> Teachers -- despite the widespread myth -- are overpaid and underworked ... (they) are not required to be at their job more than six hours and 20 minutes a day. When you add to that the fact that teachers only work nine months out of the year, and then calculate teachers' pay on the basis of the eight-hour-day and 11-and-a-half-month year that the rest of us work, the pay for a seventh-grade science teacher in New York City is between $60 and $70 an hour. That amounts to an annual salary of well over $100,000 ...

*WHICH ALSO FEATURES THIS CARTOON.

NOW, FOR STARTERS, MR. HOROWITZ'S SPECIOUS CALCULATION OF WHAT TEACHERS "REALLY" MAKE COMPLETELY IGNORES THE FACT THAT THEIR SALARIES--WHICH ARE IN REALITY QUITE MODEST--MUST LAST THE *ENTIRE YEAR*... TEACHERS DON'T GO INTO *SUSPENDED ANIMATION* DURING THE SUMMER MONTHS, FOLKS...

SEE YOU NEXT SEPTEMBER, MRS. WILSON!

GLUB!

AND FURTHER...TEACHERS MAY ONLY SPEND "SIX HOURS AND 20 MINUTES A DAY" MANAGING CROWDED CLASSROOMS FULL OF HYPERACTIVE CHILDREN--A HEROIC FEAT UNTO ITSELF--

--BUT IF THEY HOPE TO HAVE LESSON PLANS PREPARED OR HOMEWORK GRADED, THEY MUST ALSO WORK SEVERAL HOURS AT HOME MOST NIGHTS--NOT TO MENTION WEEKENDS...

...NONE OF WHICH EXACTLY ADDS UP TO THE LIFE OF *DECADENT LEISURE* PORTRAYED BY--WELL, BY OVERPAID AND UNDERWORKED *RIGHTWING COMMENTATORS*...

FRANKLY, THIS WHOLE TREND OF SCAPEGOATING SCHOOLTEACHERS-- *SCHOOLTEACHERS*, FOR GOD'S SAKE--LEAVES *US* FLABBERGASTED... *AND* MAKES US WONDER HOW LOW THESE PEOPLE CAN POSSIBLY *SINK*...

PERHAPS WE COULD GAIN A SHORT-TERM POLITICAL ADVANTAGE WITH A WELL-ORCHESTRATED CAMPAIGN AGAINST *LITTLE LEAGUE COACHES!*

I KNOW-- LET'S TAKE A FIRM STAND AGAINST *CUTE PUPPIES*-- AND *BUTTERFLIES!*

SIGH... I MISS THE *SOVIET UNION*...

TOM TOMORROW © 3-12-97

APPENDIX B

The Project Censored Media Activists and Alternative/ Independent Writers Resource Guide

Compiled by Nicola Mazumdar with the assistance of Yvonne Jolley-Crawford, Brian Foust, Kimberly Starbuck, and Todd Hillstrom

In modern complex societies people are dependent on the media to provide reliable, complete, and relevant information about the world in which they live. Sound decision making in our shared public life as well as in our private lives depends upon access to such high quality information. Without it, democracy functions poorly, public life degenerates, and private lives are endangered. Sadly, the mainstream media—too often and on too many subjects—has failed dismally in providing this quality information. Competition in the "marketplace of ideas" has failed to assure that the truth emerge. Lower quality "products" (untruths) have emerged victorious, in part because the marketplace is skewed, and the truth falls victim.

This *Censored* Resource Guide is presented as a contribution to the opening of that marketplace of ideas. In it you will find magazines and periodicals that produce high-quality original investigative journalism, news and perspectives absent from the mainstream media, and rigorous information-rich reports and analyses. You will also find pieces presented with style and an absence of the pseudo-objectivity which has too often drained the life and the truth out of mainstream news reports. Wherever possible, we have included e-mail addresses and Web sites. A scan of the Web sites will reveal the richness of the sources and introduce you to the print versions of the listed publications. (See, for instance, the Web sites of the two sources of our number one *Censored* story—*The Bulletin of Atomic Scientists* and *In These Times*—and the Web site of CAQ, source of three of the top ten *Censored* stories.) More detailed information on selected on-line media resources is provided in Appendix C.

We provide a list of organizations that are media warriors. They work to increase resources for independent journalists, to advance media literacy, to work for First Amendment freedoms, to monitor the media, and to make media distortions public. (Check out, for instance, the Web sites of Adbusters, FAIR, or the Television Project.)

There is a list of wire services and other electronic news providers that expand the news and stories available to print journalists, radio and television broadcasters, and to you personally. (See the Web site of PEACENET, LABORNET, for instance). There is also a list of alternative/independent broadcast, film, and video producers whose work is unparalleled. The Web site of WINGS, for instance, gives instructions on how to produce your own reporting and have it broadcast. We also provide a list of major national broadcast and cable media that you may contact with complaints or comments, as well as contact information for the Federal Communications Commission.

We have indicated with a ✎ some publications that have stated they accept freelance work. A "$" indicates that we are aware they pay freelancers. Many periodicals listed herein may also accept freelance submissions, but if they did not answer that particular question on our questionnaire, they will not have these symbols by their names. You are encouraged to contact any of these publications directly concerning freelance submissions and payment rates.

You are also encouraged to make your opinions known to the resources listed in this guide. Contrary to popular belief, letters to the editor, phone calls, faxes, and e-mail can make a difference. A small group of well-organized campaigners can get the attention of a local, regional, or national media outlet, and can force changes in unjust situations. Many of the organizations listed here can help with those campaigns.

This information was current as of late 1997. If you become aware of any changes, corrections, or additions to the list, please send them to: Project Cen-

sored Resource Guide, Project Censored, Sonoma State University, Rohnert
Park, CA 94928 (E-mail: project.censored@sonoma.edu).

TABLE OF CONTENTS-CENSORED RESOURCE GUIDE

ALTERNATIVE/INDEPENDENT PUBLICATIONS AND PERIODICALS

14850 MAGAZINE
Public Communications, Inc.
95 Brown Road, Suite 210
Ithaca, NY 14850
Ph: 607/257-1831
Fax: 607/257-1873
http://www.14850.com

A little of everything, from humor to
local interest

ABYA YALA NEWS: JOURNAL OF
THE SOUTH AND MESOAMERICAN
INDIAN RIGHTS CENTER
P.O. Box 28703
Oakland, CA 94604
Ph: 510/834-4263
Fax: 510/834-4264
http://www.nativeweb.org/abyayala
E-mail: saiic@igc.apc.org

Environmental and human rights issues
with focus on indigenous people in
Latin America and elsewhere

ADBUSTERS: A MAGAZINE OF
MEDIA AND ENVIRONMENTAL
STRATEGIES
The Media Foundation
1243 West Seventh Avenue
Vancouver, British Columbia V6H 1B7
Canada
Ph: 604/736-9401
Fax: 604/737-6021
http://www.adbusters.org/adbusters/

Strategies for fighting mind pollution
from advertising

THE ADVOCATE
6922 Hollywood Boulevard, Suite 1000
Los Angeles, CA 90028
Ph: 213/871-1225
Fax: 213/467-6805
http://www.advocate.com
E-mail: newsroom@advocate.com

Leading national gay and lesbian news
magazine

AFRICA NEWS ✎
P.O. Box 3851
Durham, NC 27702
Ph: 919/286-0747
Fax: 919/286-2614
http://www.africanews.org
E-mail: newsdesk@afnews.org

Disseminates stories from African news organizations

AGAINST THE CURRENT
Center for Changes
7012 Michigan Avenue
Detroit, MI 48210
Ph: 313/841-0161
Fax: 313/841-8884
http://www.igc.apc.org/solidarity
E-mail: efc@igc.apc.org

Promoting dialogue among activists, organizers, and serious scholars of the left

AKWESASNE NOTES
Mohawk Nation
P.O. Box 196
Rooseveltown, NY 13683-0196
Ph: 518/358-9531
Fax: 613/575-2935
E-mail: notes@glen-net.ca

News of Mohawk and other indigenous peoples

ALBION MONITOR
P.O. Box 1025
Occidental, CA 95465
http://www.monitor.net/monitor
E-mail: editor@monitor.net

Critical news and commentary on "the news you're missing"

ALTERNATIVE PRESS REVIEW ✎$
C.A.L. Press
P.O. Box 1446
Columbia, MO 65205-1446
Ph: 573/442-4352
E-mail:
jmcquinn@mail.coin.missouri.edu

Promoting and supporting alternative, liberating media

ALTERNATIVE THERAPIES IN
HEALTH AND MEDICINE
101 Columbia
Aliso Viejo, CA 92656
Ph: 714/722-6167
Fax: 714/650-5653

ALTERNATIVES
Lynne Rienner Publishers
1800 30th Street, Suite 314
Boulder, CO 80301-1032
Ph: 303/444-6684
Fax: 303/444-0824
http://www.rienner.com
E-mail: peacock@rienner.com

Alternative views in international relations, politics, and Third World study

ALTERNATIVES
1718 M Street, NW, #245
Washington, DC 20036
Ph: 202/588-9888
Fax: 202/588-1818
E-mail: NLGJA@aol.com

News and reports from the National Gay and Lesbian Journalists Association

ALTERNATIVES JOURNAL
Faculty of Environmental Studies
University of Waterloo
Waterloo, Ontario N2L 3G1
Canada
Ph: 519/885-4567 Ext. 6783
Fax: 519/746-0292
E-mail: alternat@fes.uwaterloo.ca

Critical and informed analysis of environmental issues

THE AMERICAN EDITOR ✎$
ASNE
11690 B Sunrise Valley Drive
Reston, VA 20191-1409
Ph: 703/453-1122
Fax: 703/453-1133
http://www.asne.org
E-mail: asne@asne.com

AMERICAN JOURNALISM REVIEW
8701 Adelphi Road
Adelphi, MD 20783
Ph: 301/431-4771
Fax: 301/431-0097
http://www.ajr.org
E-mail: editor@ajr.umd.edu

THE AMERICAN PROSPECT
P.O. BOX 383080
Cambridge, MA 02238
http://epn.org/prospect.html
E-mail: prospect@epn.org

"A journal for the liberal imagination"

AMICUS JOURNAL
40 West 20th Street
New York, NY 10011
Ph: 212/727-2700
Fax: 212/727-1773
http://www.nrdc.org/eamicus/back/mag a.html
E-mail: amicus@nrdc.org

Thought and opinion on environmental affairs and policies of international significance

ANARCHY
A Journal of Desire Armed
P.O. Box 2647
Peter Stuyvesant Station
New York, NY 10009
Ph: 212/332-9660

Radical, anti-authoritarian, critical views on religion, moralism, politics, and ideology

THE ANIMAL'S AGENDA ✎
P.O. Box 25881
Baltimore, MD 21224
Ph: 410/675-4566
Fax: 410/675-0066
http://www.animalsagenda.org
E-mail: office@animalsagenda.org

News magazine dedicated to animal rights

ANNALS OF IMPROBABLE
RESEARCH ✎
P.O. Box 380853
Cambridge, MA 02238
Ph: 617/491-4437
http://www.improb.com
E-mail: air@improb.com

Science humor, politics, and culture

ANTIPODE
238 Main Street
Cambridge, MA 02142
Ph: 800/835-6770
Fax: 617/547-0789
http://www.staff.uiuc.edu/~dwilson2/antipode.html

Marxist, socialist, anarchist, anti-racist, and feminist analysis of environmental and geographical issues

ARENA MAGAZINE: THE AUSTRALIAN MAGAZINE OF LEFT POLITICAL, SOCIAL, AND CULTURAL COMMUNITY ✎
P.O. Box 18
North Carlton, Victoria 3054
Australia
Ph: 011-61-03-9416-5166
Fax: 011-61-03-9415-1301
E-mail: arena@vicnet

Forum for reflection, critique, and analysis on local and global social and political issues

ARMS SALES MONITOR
Federation of American Scientists
307 Massachusetts Avenue, NE
Washington, DC 20002
Ph: 202/675-1018
Fax: 202/675-1010
http://www.fas.org/asmp/
E-mail: llumpe@fas.org

Highlight U.S. government policies on arms exports and conventional weapons proliferation

ASIAN LABOUR UPDATE
Asia Monitor Resource Center
444 Nathan Road, 3-B
Kowloon, Hong Kong
Ph: 011-852-2332-1346
Fax: 011-852-2385-5319
E-mail: amrc@hk.super.net

Reports on labor issues in the Asia-Pacific Region

THE BAFFLER ✎$
P.O. Box 378293
Chicago, IL 60637
Ph: 773/493-0413
Fax: 773/493-0515
http://www.voyagerco.com/misc/killerapp/baffler.html

An independent journal of cultural criticism and literature

THE BEAT WITHIN
Pacific News Service/YO!
450 Mission Street, #204
San Francisco, CA 94105
Ph: 415/243-4364
http://www.pacificnews.org/yo/beat/

A weekly newsletter of writing and art by incarcerated youth

THE BEST OF PNS
Pacific News Service
450 Mission Street, Room 204
San Francisco, CA 94105
Ph: 415/243-4364
http://www.pacific.news.org/inn/index.html

BEYOND TV ✎
The Television Project
2311 Kimball Street
Silver Springs, MD 20910
Ph: 301/588-4001
Fax: 301/588-4001
http://www.tvp.org
E-mail: apluhar@tvp.org

Quarterly newsletter aimed at empowering parents to use television wisely

THE BIG ISSUE: COMING UP FROM
THE STREETS
Fleet House
57-61 Clerkenwell Road
London, EC1M 5NP
England
Ph: 011-44-171-490-4127
Fax: 011-44-171-490-1791
E-mail: london@bigissue.co.uk

Magazine of the campaign on behalf of
homeless people, giving voice to their
concerns, and highlighting the major
social issues of the day

BILL OF RIGHTS JOURNAL
Center for Constitutional Rights
666 Broadway, 7th Floor
New York, NY 10012
Ph: 212/614-6464
Fax: 212/614-6499
http://gopher.wm.edu/MWSL/LJ/BORJ

Covers issues involving freedoms guaranteed by the Constitution and Bill of
Rights

BLACK SCHOLAR
P.O. Box 2869
Oakland, CA 94618-0069
Ph: 510/547-6633
Fax: 510/547-6679
E-mail: blkschlr@aol.com

An independent intellectual journal of
the African-American experience

BLK
P.O. Box 83912
Los Angeles, CA 90083-0912
Ph: 310/410-0808
Fax: 310/410-9250
http://www.blk.com
E-mail: newsroom@blk.com

News magazine for black, lesbian, and
gay community

THE BODY POLITIC
P.O. Box 2363
Binghamton, NY 13902
Ph: 607/648-2760
Fax: 607/648-2511
E-mail: annebower@delphi.com

BOGONG: JOURNAL OF THE
CANBERRA AND THE SOUTHEAST
REGION ENVIRONMENTAL
CENTER ✎
Kingsley Street, Acton, GPO 1875
Canberra, ACT 2601
Australia
Ph: 011-61-02-6248-0885
Fax: 011-61-02-6247-3064
http://www.spirit.net.au/envoz/eccser/
core.html
E-mail: caserec@peg.apc.org

Reports on environmental issues and current affairs in southeast Australia, and issues of national and international significance

BORDER/LINES
400 Dover Court Road
Toronto, Ontario M67 3E7
Canada
Ph: 416/534-3224
Fax: 416/534-2301
http://www.interlog.com/~kavik/border.htm
E-mail: borderin@idirect.com

Designed to fill the space between academic journals and specialist cultural magazines

THE BOSTON PHOENIX ✎$
126 Brookline Avenue
Boston, MA 02215
Ph: 617/536-5390
Fax: 617/859-8201
http://www.bostonphoenix.com

BOSTON REVIEW
E53-407, MIT
30 Wadsworth Street
Cambridge, MA 02139
Ph: 617/253-3642
Fax: 617/252-1549
http://www.bookwire.com/bbrhome.html
E-mail: bostonreview@mit.edu

Combines commitments to public reason with literary imagination

BOYCOTT QUARTERLY
Center for Economic Democracy
P.O. Box 30727
Seattle, WA 98103-0727
E-mail: boycottguy@aol.com

Comprehensive coverage of boycotts across the political spectrum and around the world

BREAKTHROUGH
P.O. Box 1442
San Francisco, CA 94114

A magazine of international and domestic politics and activism

BRIARPATCH: SASKATCHEWAN'S INDEPENDENT NEWS MAGAZINE
2138 McIntyre Street
Regina, Saskatchewan S4P 2R7
Canada
Ph: 306/525-2949

Covers labor, environment, women's rights, and politics from a socialist perspective

BROADCASTING & CABLE MAGAZINE
1705 DeSales Street, NW, Suite 600
Washington, DC 20036
Ph: 202/659-2340

BROWARD-PALM BEACH
16 NE 4th Street, Suite 200
Ft. Lauderdale, FL 33301
Ph: 954/233-1600
Fax: 954/233-1571
http://www.newtimes.com

News, entertainment, investigative journalism

BULLETIN IN DEFENSE
OF MARXISM
P.O. Box 1317
New York, NY 10009

Issues of the global and domestic class
struggle from the perspective of the
American Trotskyist tradition

BULLETIN OF CONCERNED
ASIAN SCHOLARS
3239 9th Street
Boulder, CO 80304
Ph: 303/449-7439
http://csf.colorado.edu/bcas/bcashome.
html
E-mail: doub@csf.colorado.edu

Challenging accepted formulas for
understanding Asia, the world, and
ourselves

THE BULLETIN OF THE
ATOMIC SCIENTISTS
Education Foundation for
Nuclear Science
6042 South Kimbark Avenue
Chicago, IL 60637
Ph: 773/702-2555
Fax: 773/702-0725
http://www.bullatomsci.org
E-mail: bullatomsci@igc.apc.org

International security, military affairs,
nuclear issues

BUSINESS ETHICS
P.O. Box 8349
Minneapolis, MN 55408
Ph: 800/601-9010
Fax: 612/879-0699
http://condor.depaul.edu/ethics/
bizethics.html
E-mail: BizEthics@aol.com

Promoting ethical business practices,
encouraging responsible and successful
companies

THE CALIFORNIA PRISONER
P.O. Box 1019
Sacramento, CA 95812-1019
Ph: 916/441-4214
Fax: 916/441-4297

Newspaper of the Prisoner's Rights
Union, committed to restoring fundamental civil rights to prisoners and
their families

CALIFORNIA PRISON FOCUS
2489 Mission Street, #28
San Francisco, CA 94110
http://www.igc.org/justice.cpf

CALYPSO LOG ✎$
The Cousteau Society
870 Greenbrier Circle, Suite 402
Chesapeake, VA 23320
Ph: 757/523-9335Fax: 757/523-2747
http://www.cousteau.org
E-mail: cousteau@infi.net

Focused on protection and improvement of the quality of life for future
generations

CANADIAN DIMENSION
707-228 Notre Dame Avenue,
Room 401
Winnipeg, Manitoba R3B 1N7
Canada
Ph: 204/957-1519
Fax: 204/943-4617
http://www.canadiandimension.mb.ca/
cd/index/htm
E-mail: nfo@canadiandimension.mb.ca

Covers Canadian politics, culture, and
issues of environment and labor

CAPITAL EYE ✎$
Center for Responsive Politics
1320 19th Street, NW, #700
Washington, DC 20036
Ph: 202/857-0044
Fax: 202/857-7809
http://www.crp.org
E-mail: info@crp.org

Covers money-in-politics at the federal,
state, and local levels

CAQ ✎$
CovertAction Quarterly
1500 Massachusetts Avenue, NW,
#732
Washington, DC 20005
Ph: 202/331-9763
Fax: 202/331-9751
http://www.caq.com
E-mail: caq@igc.org

Investigative journalism exposing
malfeasance and covert activities in
government, corporations, and other
areas affecting the public

CASCADIA TIMES
25-6 NW 23rd Place, #406
Portland, OR 97210
Ph: 503/223-9036
Fax: 503/736-0097
http://cascadia.times.org
E-mail: cascadia@spiritone.com

Investigative journalism covering politics, environment, and other issues in
the Pacific Northwest

CHAIN REACTION
P.O. Box 45, O'Conner
Acton, 2601
Australia
Ph: 011-61-06-248-0289
Fax: 011-61-06 248-0289
E-mail: chain@peg.pegasus.oz.au

Environmental issues from a global
perspective

CHALLENGE
P.O. Box 4119
Jaffa, 61411
Israel
Ph: 011-972-3-792270
Fax: 011-972-3-792270
E-mail: chall@baraka.org

News and opinion on Israel, the occupied territories, and Palestine

CHARTIST
18 Southcote Road
London, N19 5BJ
England
Ph: 011-44-171-254-8601
E-mail: chalkp@sbu.ac.uk

Focused on the contemporary rele-
vance of democratic socialism

CHICAGO INK
5706 South University Avenue
Chicago, IL 60637
Ph: 773/955-2047
Fax: 773/702-7718
http://student-www.uchicago.edu/orgs/
ink/uchicago
E-mail: jkw3@midway.uchicago.edu

A progressive paper critiquing Chicago
politics and the media

CHICAGO LIFE MAGAZINE
P.O. Box 11311
Chicago, IL 60611-0311
Ph: 773/528-2737
E-mail: achicagolife@mcs.com

Politics, health, and environmental
issues emphasizing improving quality
of life

THE CHRONICLE OF
HIGHER EDUCATION
1255 23rd Street, NW
Washington, DC 20037
Ph: 202/466-1000
Fax: 202/296-2691
http://www.chronicle.com
E-mail: editor@chronicle.com

THE CHRONICLE OF
PHILANTHROPY
1255 23rd Street, NW, 7th Floor
Washington, DC 20037
Ph: 202/466-1200
Fax: 202/466-2078
http://www.philanthropy.com
E-mail: editor@philanthropy.com

CINEASTE
200 Park Avenue
New York, NY 10009
Ph: 212/982-1241
Fax: 212/982-1241

Art and politics of the cinema

CINECISM: A QUARTERLY
FILM REPORT
P.O. Box 40254
Washington, DC 20016-0254

Critical news and commentary on films
and the media

THE CIRCLE
1530 East Franklin Avenue
Minneapolis, MN 55404
Ph: 612/879-1760
Fax: 612/879-1712
http://nic.com/circle/homepage/html
E-mail: circlemplsa@aol.com

CITY PAPER
Baltimore's Free Weekly
812 Park Avenue
Baltimore, MD 21201
Ph: 410/523-2300
Fax: 410/523-2222

CIVIL LIBERTIES
American Civil Liberties Union
125 Broad Street
New York, NY 10004
Ph: 212/549-2500
Fax: 212/549-2646
http://www.aclu.org

Issues of civil liberties including
on-line information on Internet free
speech issues

CO-OP AMERICA QUARTERLY
1612 K Street, #600
Washington, DC 20006
Ph: 202/872-5307
Fax: 202/331-8166
http://www.coopamerica.org/default.htm
E-mail: info@coopamerica.org

A magazine for building economic
alternatives

COLUMBIA JOURNALISM REVIEW
Columbia University
700 Journalism Building
New York, NY 10027
Ph: 212/854-1881
Fax: 212/854-8580
http://ublib.buffalo.edu/libraries/
e-resources/ejournals/records/cjr.html

Assesses the performance of journalism
and stimulating continuing improvements in the profession

COMMUNITIES MAGAZINE
P.O. BOX 169
Masonville, CO 80541
Ph: 970/593-5615
Fax: 970/593-5615
http://www.ic.org

Focus on "intentional communities,"
including ecovillages, co-housing,
urban housing cooperatives, and other
projects

COMMUNITY MEDIA REVIEW
The Journal of the Alliance for Com-
munity Media
666 11th Street, NW, Suite 806
Washington, DC 20001
Ph: 202/393-2650
Fax: 202/393-2653
http://www.thesphere.com/ACTV/acm.
html
E-mail: AllianceCM@aol.com

Newsletter reporting on political and
regulatory issues in the media; reports
on emerging information systems

COMPARATIVE STUDIES:
SOUTH AFRICA, ASIA &
THE MIDDLE EAST
Duke University Press,
Journal Division
P.O. Box 90660
Durham, NC 27708
Ph: 919/687-3614
http://www.duke.edu/web/dupress
E-mail: Ki.acupub.duke.edu.

Comparative studies of South Asia,
Africa, and the Middle East

CONGRESSIONAL QUARTERLY
WEEKLY REPORT
1414 22nd Street, NW
Washington, DC 20037
Ph: 202/887-8500
Fax: 202/728-1863
http://voter96.cqalert.com/moll/wrabout
.htm

CONSCIOUS CHOICE
Journal of Ecology & Natural Living
920 North Franklin Street, Suite 301
Chicago, IL 60610-3119
Ph: 312/440-4373
Fax: 312/751-3973
http://www.consciouschoice.com
E-mail: editor@consciouschoice.com

Sustainable patterns of living, environmental issues, and natural alternatives

CONSUMER REPORTS
101 Truman Avenue
Yonkers, NY 10703
Ph: 914/378-2000
http://www.consumerreports.org

CORPORATE CRIME REPORTER
1209 National Press Building
Washington, DC 20045
Ph: 202/737-1680

Legal weekly covering issues of corporate and white-collar crime

COUNTER MEDIA
1573 North Milwaukee Avenue, #517
Chicago, IL 60622
Ph: 312/243-8342
http:/www.cs.uchicago.edu/cpsr/
countermedia/
E-mail: lquilter@igc.apa.org

Covers protests, actions, and issues ignored by conventional media sources

COUNTERPOISE
1716 Williston Road
Gainesville, FL 32608
Ph: 352/335-2200
Fax: call first
http://www.lib.lsu.edu/hum/
counterpoise.html
E-mail: willett@afn.org

Alternative review journal of the Alternative Task Force on Social Responsibility of the American Library Association

COUNTERPUNCH ✎$
P.O. Box 18675
Washington, DC 20036
Ph: 202/986-3665
Fax: 202/986-0974
http://www.newsun.com/counter.html

D.C.-based newsletter on power and evil in Washington

CRONE CHRONICLES: A JOURNAL
OF CONSCIOUS AGING
Box 81
Kelly, WY 83011
Fax: 307/733-8639
http://www.feminist.com/crone.htm

CUBA UPDATE
Center for Cuban Studies
124 West 23rd Street
New York, NY 10011
Ph: 212/242-0559
Fax: 212/242-1937
http://www.eden.com/fineprint/40289.
html

THE CULTURAL ENVIRONMENT
MONITOR
3508 Market Street
Philadelphia, PA 19104
Ph: 215/387-8034
Fax: 215/387-1560

CULTURAL SURVIVAL
QUARTERLY ✎
96 Mt. Auburn Street
Cambridge, MA 02138
Ph: 617/441-5400
Fax: 617/441-5417
http://www.cs.org/csq/csqguid.html
E-mail: csinc@cs.org

Focus on survival of indigenous
peoples through preservation of their
rights in a changing world

CULTURE WATCH
Data Center
464 19th Street
Oakland, CA 94612
Ph: 510/835-4692
Fax: 510/835-3017
http://www.igc.org/culturewatch/
E-mail: masildatactr@tmn.com

Monthly newsletter which tracks and
monitors the political and social
agenda of the religious right

THE DAILY CITIZEN
P.O. Box 57365
Washington, DC 20037
Ph: 202/429-6929
Fax: 202/659-1145

DALLAS OBSERVER
2130 Commerce Avenue
Dallas, TX 75201
Ph: 214/757-9000
Fax: 214/757-8593
http://www.newtimes.com

News, entertainment, investigative
reporting

THE DAYTON VOICE ✎$
1927 North Main Street
Dayton, OH 45405
Ph: 513/275-8855
Fax: 513/275-6056
E-mail: thevoice@commkey.net

Locally oriented news and entertainment weekly

DE TODO UN POCO ✎
2830 5th Street
Boulder, CO 80304
Ph: 303/444-8565
Fax: 303/545-2074
E-mail: tmoore@igc.apc.org

Issues in Central America, Mexico,
the Caribbean, and U.S. influence in
the region

DEFENSE MONITOR
1500 Massachusetts Avenue, NW
Washington, DC 20005
Ph: 202/862-0700
Fax: 202/862-0708
http://www.cdi.org
E-mail: info@cdi.org

Opposes policies that increase the
danger of war

DEMOCRATIC LEFT
Democratic Socialists of America
180 Varick Street, 12th Floor
New York, NY 10014
Ph: 212/727-8610
Fax: 212/727-8616
http://www.dsausa.org/index.html
E-mail: dsa@dsausa.org

DENVER WESTWORD
1621 18th Street, #150
Denver, CO 80202
Ph: 303/296-7744
Fax: 303/296-3566
http://newtimes.com

News, entertainment, investigative
reporting

DETROIT METRO TIMES
743 Beaubien, Suite 301
Detroit, MI 48226
Ph: 313/961-4060
Fax: 313/961-6598

News, investigative reports

THE DETROIT SUNDAY JOURNAL
450 West Fort
Detroit, Michigan 48226
Ph: 313/964-5655
Fax: 313/964-5554
http://www.rust.net/~workers/strike.html
E-mail: detjourn@aol.com

A publication by the striking journalists of *The Detroit News* and *The Detroit
Free Press*

DIOXIN DIGEST
P.O. Box 6806
Falls Church, VA 22040
Ph: 703/237-2249
Fax: 703/237-8389
http://essential.org/cchw
E-mail: cchw@essential.org

DISSENT
521 Fifth Avenue, Suite 1700
New York, NY 10017
Ph: 212/595-3084
Fax: 212/595-3084
http://www.igc.apc.org/dissent
E-mail: dissent@igc.apc.org

Leading periodical of social democracy
in the United States

DOLLARS AND SENSE: WHAT'S
LEFT IN ECONOMICS ✎$
1 Summer Street
Somerville, MA 02143
Ph: 617/628-8411
Fax: 617/628-2025
http://www.igc.apc.org/dollars/
E-mail: dollars@igc.apc.org

Reporting on issues of social justice
and economic policy

DOUBLE TAKE ✎
1317 West Pettigrew Street
Durham, NC 27705
Ph: 919/660-3669
Fax: 919/660-3688
http://www.duke.edu/doubletake/
E-mail: dtmag@acpub.duke.edu

Compelling writing and photography in
the best tradition of documentary work

E: THE ENVIRONMENTAL
MAGAZINE ✎$
P.O. Box 5098
Westport, CT 06881
Ph: 203/854-5559
Fax: 203/866-0602
http://www.emagazine.com
E-mail: emagazine@prodigy.net

Independent, national environmental
magazine

THE EARTH FIRST! JOURNAL
P.O. Box 1415
Eugene, OR 97440
Ph: 541/344-8004
Fax: 541/344-7688
http://www.envirolink.org
E-mail: earthfirst@igc.apc.org

The voice of the radical environmental
movement

EARTH ISLAND JOURNAL ✎$
300 Broadway, Suite 28
San Francisco, CA 94133-3312
Ph: 415/788-3666
Fax: 415/788-7324
http://www.earthisland.org/ei/
E-mail: journal@earthisland.org

Focused on conserving, preserving, and
restoring the earth

THE ECOLOGIST
c/o MIT Press Journals
55 Hayward Street
Cambridge, MA 02142
Ph: 617/253-2889
Fax: 617/258-6779
http://www.gold.net/ecosystem/ecolog.htm
E-mail: ecologist@gn.apc.org

Covers ecological issues and supports
small-scale agriculture and democra-
tized political power

ECONEWS ✎
879 Ninth Street
Arcata, CA 95521
Ph: 707/822-6918
Fax: 707/822-0827
http://www.nfcandeconews.to
E-mail: nec@igc.apc.org

Forestry, wildlife, toxics, recycling, off-
shore oil, energy, air and water quality

THE EL SALVADOR WATCH
c/o CISPES
19 West 21st Street, Room 502
New York, NY 10010
Ph: 212/229-1290
Fax: 212/645-645-7280
http://www.cispes.org
E-mail: cispesnatl@igc.apc.org

EMERGE: BLACK AMERICA'S
NEWS MAGAZINE ✎$
One B.E.T. Plaza, 1900 W Place, NE
Washington, DC 20018-1211
Ph: 202/608-2093
Fax: 202/608-2598
http://www.emergemag.com
E-mail: emergemag@compuserve.com
or emergeed@aol.com

News analysis and commentary from
the African-American perspective

ENVIRONMENTAL HEALTH
MONTHLY
P.O. Box 6806
Falls Church, VA 22040
Ph: 703/237-2249
Fax: 703/237-8389
http://essential.org/cchw
E-mail: cchw@essential.org

ENVIRONMENTAL IMPACT
REPORTER ✎$
P.O. Box 1834
Sebastopol, CA 95473
Ph: 707/823-8744
Fax: 707/823-7481
E-mail: juliana@monitor.net

ESSENCE MAGAZINE
1500 Broadway
New York, NY 10036
Ph: 212/642-0600
http://www.essence.com

News and commentary for African-
American women

EVERYONE'S BACKYARD ✎
Center for Health, Environment
and Justice
P.O. Box 6806
Falls Church, VA 22040-6806
Ph: 703/237-2249
Fax: 703/237-8389
http://essential.org/cchw
E-mail: cchw@essential.org

EXTRA!
Fairness and Accuracy in Reporting
130 West 25th Street
New York, NY 10001
Ph: 212/633-6700
Fax: 212/727-7668
http://www.fair.org
E-mail: info@fair.org

Media criticism featuring articles on
biased reporting, censored news, media
mergers, and more

EYE MAGAZINE
301 South Elm Street, Suite 405
Greensboro, NC 27401
Ph: 910/370-1702
Fax: 910/370-1603
http://www.infi.net/~eye/
E-mail: eye@nr.infi.net

Vintage film, trippy technologies, scientific obscurities, B movies, conspira-
cies, retro TV, and more

FACTSHEET 5 ✎$
c/o Seth Friedman
P.O. Box 170099
San Francisco, CA 94117-0099
Ph: 415/668-1781
http://www.factsheet5.com
E-mail: seth@factsheet5.com

Guide to the 'zine revolution; resources
and reviews of thousands of underground publications

FAT!SO?
P.O. Box 423464
San Francisco, CA 94142-3464
Ph: 1-800/OHFATSO
http://www.fatso.com
E-mail: marilyn@fatso.com

For people who don't apologize for their
size

FELLOWSHIP MAGAZINE
Fellowship of Reconciliation
Box 271, 521 North Broadway
Nyack, NY 10960
Ph: 914/358-4601
Fax: 914/358-4924
http://www.nonviolence.org/~nvweb/for
E-mail: fellowship@igc.org

Seeks to replace violence, war,
racism, and economic injustice with
nonviolence, peace, and justice

FEMINIST LIBRARY NEWSLETTER
5 Westminster Bridge Road
London, SE17XW
England
Ph: 011-44-171-928-7789

FEMINIST MAJORITY REPORT
1600 Wilson Boulevard, #801
Arlington, VA 22209
Ph: 703/522-2214
http://www.feminist.org

News and reports on politics, culture,
women's health, reproductive rights,
events, career opportunities, and the
multi-dimensional nature of feminism

FIFTH ESTATE ✎
4632 Second Avenue
Detroit, MI 48201
Ph: 313/831-6800

Longest-running English language
anarchist publication in U.S.

FIRST THINGS: A JOURNAL OF
RELIGION AND PUBLIC LIFE
156 5th Avenue, Suite 400
New York, NY 10010

To advance a religiously-informed
public philosophy for the ordering of
society

FOOD & WATER JOURNAL
Food & Water, Inc.
RR1, Box 68D
Walden, VT 05873
Ph: 802/563-3300
Fax: 802/563-3310

FOOD FIRST NEWS ✎$
Institute for Food &
Development Policy
398 60th Street
Oakland, CA 94618
Ph: 510/654-4400
Fax: 510/654-4400
E-mail: foodfirst@igc.apc.org

Information and reader action guide for
ending world hunger and poverty

FOOD NOT BOMBS MENU
3145 Geary Boulevard, #12
San Francisco, CA 94118
Ph: 800/884-1136
http://www.eci.com/dave/fnb.html

FORWARD MOTION
P.O. Box 150311
Brooklyn, NY 11215-0311
Ph: 718/789-6483
Fax: 718/789-2551
E-mail: fmlink@igc.org

FREE INQUIRY: THE
INTERNATIONAL SECULAR
HUMANIST MAGAZINE
P.O. Box 664
Amherst, NY 14226

FRONT LINES RESEARCH
Planned Parenthood Federation
of America
810 Seventh Avenue
New York, NY 10019
Ph: 212/261-4721
Fax: 212/261-4352

FUSE MAGAZINE
401 Richmond Street West, Suite 454
Toronto, M5V 3A8
Canada
Ph: 416/340-8026
Fax: 416/340-0484
http://www.eden.com/fineprint/81331.
html
E-mail: fuse@interlog.com

Art and the art world, culture and
politics

GENDER & MASS MEDIA
Stockholm University-JMK
P.O. Box 27861
Stockholm, 11593
Sweden

GENEWATCH
The Council for Responsible Genetics
5 Upland Road, Suite 3
Cambridge, MA 02140
Ph: 617/868-0870
Fax: 617/491-5344
http://essential.org/crg/

National bulletin dedicated to the
social implications of technology

GLAADlines and GLAAD-Alert ✎
1360 Mission Street, Suite 200
San Francisco, CA 94103
Ph: 415/861-2244
Fax: 415/861-4893
http://www.glaad.org
E-mail: glaad@glaad.org

On-line resource for promoting fair,
accurate, inclusive media representation of lesbian, gay, bisexual, and
transgender people

GLOBAL EXCHANGE
2017 Mission Street, Suite 303
San Francisco, CA 94110
Ph: 415/255-7296
Fax: 415/255-7498
http://globalexchange.org
E-mail: gx-info@globalexchange.org

Promoting people-to-people ties and
building international partnership
around the world

GLOBAL PESTICIDE CAMPAIGNER
Pesticide Action Network
116 New Montgomery, #810
San Francisco, CA 94105
Ph: 415/541-9140
Fax: 415/541-9253
http://www.panna.org/panna
E-mail: panna@panna.org

Environmental, health, and other information about pesticides, ecological pest control, and sustainable agriculture

GNOSIS MAGAZINE
A Journal of Western Inner Tradition
P.O. Box 1427
San Francisco, CA 94114
Ph: 415/974-0600
http://www.lumen.org

Devoted to the exploration of the spiritual and esoteric paths of the Western hemisphere

GRASSROOTS FUNDRAISING
JOURNAL
P.O. Box 11607
Berkeley, CA 94712
Ph: 510/704-8714
Fax: 510/649-7913
http://www.chardonpress.com
E-mail: chardn@aol.com

Fundraising and community-organizing resources for social change

THE GREEN CITY CALENDAR
P.O. Box 31251
San Francisco, CA 94131
Ph: 415/285-6556
Fax: 415/285/6563
E-mail: planetdrum@igc.apc.org

Urban environmental events in the Bay Area

GREEN MAGAZINE
P.O. Box 381, Mill Harbour
London, E14 9TW
England

THE GUARDIAN (MANCHESTER)
Guardian Newspapers, Ltd.
164 Deansgate
Manchester, M60 2RR
England
Ph: 011-44-161-832-7200
Fax: 011-44-161-876-5362

GUARDIAN WEEKLY
164 Deansgate
Manchester, M60 2RR
England
Ph: 011-44-161-832-7200
Fax: 011-44-161-876-5362

GUILD NOTES
National Lawyers Guild
126 University Place, 5th Floor
New York, NY 10003
Ph: 212/627-2656
Fax: 212/627-2404
http://www.nlg.org
E-mail: coordinator@nlg.org

Newsletter of the national lawyer's guild

HA!
P.O. Box 1282
Carrboro, NC
http://www.unc.edu/~cherylt
E-mail: gmonster@email.unc.edu

'zine which is a venue for women's
voices and self-expression

HEALTH LETTER ✎
1600 20th Street, NW
Washington, DC 20009
Ph: 202/588-1000
Fax: 202/588-7796

Critical information on health care
issues

HIGH COUNTRY NEWS ✎$
P.O. Box 1090
Paonia, CO 81428
Ph: 303/527-4898
http://www.hcn.org
E-mail: betsym@hcn.org

Covers public land and rural communities in ten Western states

HIP MAMA ✎
The Parenting Zine
Box 9097
Oakland, CA 94613
Ph: 800/585-4508
http://www.hipmama.com
E-mail: hipmama@sirius.com

'zine for progressive families—covering
the culture and politics of parenting

HUMAN EVENTS MAGAZINE
1 Massachusetts, NW
Washington, DC 20001
Ph: 202/216-0600

The national conservative weekly,
founded in 1944

THE HUMAN QUEST ✎
1074 23rd Avenue North
St. Petersburg, FL 33704-3228
Ph: 813/894-0097
Fax: 813/894-0539

Journal of religious humanism; encouraging spiritual evolution and the free
exchange of ideas and opinions

THE HUMANIST
American Humanist Association
7 Harwood Drive, Box 1188
Amherst, NY 14226-7188
Ph: 716/839-5080
Fax: 716/839-5079
http://humanist.net/
E-mail: humanism@juno.com

HUMAN RIGHTS TRIBUNE
Human Rights Internet
8 York Street, Suite 302
Ottawa, Ontario K1N 5S6
Canada
Ph: 613/789-7407
Fax: 613/789-7414
http://www.hri.ca
E-mail: hri@hri.ca

Web site has links to human rights
Web sites worldwide; job postings from
human rights organizations, databases

HUMAN RIGHTS WATCH
485 Fifth Avenue
New York, NY 10017
Ph: 212/972-8400
Fax: 212/972-0905
http://www.hrw.org
E-mail: hrwnyc@hrw.org

HUNGRY MIND REVIEW
1648 Grand Avenue
St. Paul, MN 55105
Ph: 612/699-2610
Fax: 612/699-0970
http://www.bookwire.com/hmr
E-mail: hmreview@winternet.com

Quarterly book review magazine
geared toward iconoclastic reader who
frequents independent bookstores

THE IDLER
15 Street Stephens Gardens
London, W2 5NA
England
Ph: 011-44-171-792-3501

I.F. MAGAZINE
The Media Consortium
2200 Wilson Boulevard,
Suite 102-231
Arlington, VA 22201
Ph: 800/738-1812
Fax: 703/920-1802

IMAGES
Gay & Lesbian Alliance
Against Defamation
1360 Mission Street, Suite 200
San Francisco, CA 94103
Ph: 415/861-2244
Fax: 415/861-4893
http://www.glaad.org
E-mail: glaad@glaad.org

IN THESE TIMES
2040 North Milwaukee Avenue,
2nd Floor
Chicago, IL 60647-4002
Ph: 773/772-0100
Fax: 773/772-4180
http://www.inthesetimes.com
E-mail: itt@inthesetimes.com

Provides independent news and views
you won't find anywhere else

THE INDEPENDENT FILM
& VIDEO MONTHLY
625 Broadway, 9th Floor
New York, NY 10012
Ph: 212/807-1400
Fax: 212/677-8732
http://www.virtualfilm.com/AIVF/
independent.html

INDEX ON CENSORSHIP ✎$
Writers & Scholars Educational Trust
33 Islington High Street
London, N1 9LH
England
Ph: 011-44-171-278-2313
Fax: 011-44-171-278-1878
http://www.oneworld.org/index_oc/
E-mail: indexoncenso@gn.apc.org

INFUSION: TOOLS FOR ACTION
AND EDUCATION
Center for Campus Organizing
P.O. Box 748
Cambridge, MA 02142
Ph: 617/357-9363
Fax: 617/547-5067
http://envirolink/envirolink.org/orgs/
eco/infusion/index.html
E-mail: cco@igc.apc.org

INSIGHT ✎$
3600 New York Avenue, NE
Washington, DC 20002
Ph: 202/636-8810
Fax: 202/529-2484
http://www.insightmag.com
E-mail: 76353.2113@compuserve.com

News and investigative reports

INTELLIGENCE REPORT ✎
Southern Poverty Law Center
400 Washington Avenue
Montgomery, AL 36104
Ph: 334/264-0286
Fax: 334/264-8891
http://www.splcenter.org/klanwatch.
kw-4.html

Reports on white supremacist
organizations and extreme anti-
government groups

INTERNATIONAL JOURNAL
OF HEALTH SERVICES
Baywood Publishing
P.O. Box 337
26 Austin Avenue
Amityville, NY 11701
Ph: 516/691-1270
Fax: 516/691-1770
http://www.baywood.com
E-mail: baywood@baywood.com

Health and social policy, political
economy, sociology, history, philosophy, ethics and law in health and
health care

INTERNATIONAL VIEWPOINT
BP 85, 75522
Paris, CEDEX 11F
France
Ph: 011-33-1-43792960
Fax: 011-33-1-43792961
E-mail: inprecor@igc.apc.org

News analysis magazine published
under auspices of the Fourth International

IRE: INVESTIGATIVE REPORTERS
AND EDITORS
138 Neff Annex Missouri School
of Journalism
Columbia, MO 65211
Ph: 573/882-2042
http://www.ire.org

ISSUES IN SCIENCE AND
TECHNOLOGY
1636 Hobart Street, NW
Washington, DC 20009
Ph: 202/965-5648

JOURNAL OF COMMUNITY
PRACTICE
School of Social Work, CB #3550
University of North Carolina
Chapel Hill, NC 27599
Ph: 800/342-0678
Fax: 800/895-0582

Journal of organizing, planning,
development, and change

JOURNAL OF PESTICIDE
REFORM ✎
Northwest Coalition for Alternatives
to Pesticides
P.O. Box 1393
Eugene, OR 97440
Ph: 541/334-5044
Fax: 541/344-6923
http://www.efn.org/~ncap
E-mail: info@pesticide.org

JOURNAL OF PRISONERS
ON PRISONS
University of Manitoba
Box 54 University Centre
Winnipeg, Manitoba R3T 2N2
Canada
http://www.synapse.net/~arrakis/jpp/
jpp.html

Contributions by prisoners and former
prisoners

JOURNALISM QUARTERLY
George Washington University
Journalism Program
Washington, DC 20052
Ph: 202/994-6226

JUMP CUT
P.O. Box 865
Berkeley, CA 94701
http://www.sa.ua.edu/TCF/res/
journals/jc/jumpcut.htm

Review of contemporary media from a
political activist orientation

KICK IT OVER
P.O. Box 5811, Station A
Toronto, Ontario M5W 1P2
Canada
http://www.eden.com/fineprint/42840.
html
E-mail: KIO@web.apc.org

Anarchism, feminism, and the politics
of everyday life

KINESIS: NEWS ABOUT WOMEN
THAT'S NOT IN THE DAILIES
1720 Grant Street, #301
Vancouver, British Columbia
V5L 2Y6 Canada

News, features, art reviews, commentary of and for women to work actively
for social change

LA GACETA
P.O. Box 5536
Tampa, FL 33675
Ph: 813/248-3921
Fax: 813/247-5357
E-mail: lagaceta@aol.com

Politically-oriented trilingual weekly
newspaper, published since 1922

L.A. WEEKLY
P.O. Box 4315
Los Angeles, CA 90078
Ph: 213/465-9909
Fax: 213/465-3220
http://www.laweekly.com~laweekly
E-mail: editorial@laweekly.com

News, entertainment, investigative reporting

LABOR NEWS FOR WORKING
FAMILIES ✎
I.I.R., 2521 Channing Way, #5555
Berkeley, CA 94720
Ph: 510/643-6814
Fax: 510/642-6432
http://socrates.berkeley.edu/~iir/
workfam/home.html

Highlights union policies and benefits including family leave, child care, elder care, flexible work

LABOR NOTES
7435 Michigan Avenue
Detroit, MI 48210
Ph: 313/842-6262
Fax: 313/842-0227
E-mail: labornotes@igc.apc.org

Issues and events of labor reform at grass-roots level

LABORATORY MEDICINE
American Society of Clinical
Pathologists
2100 West Harrison Street
Chicago, IL 60612
Ph: 800/638-4931 or 312/738-1336
Fax: 312/738-0101
http://www.ascp.org

LAMBDA BOOK REPORT:
A REVIEW OF CONTEMPORARY
GAY AND LESBIAN LITERATURE
P.O. Box 73910
Washington, DC 20056
Ph: 202/462-7924
Fax: 202/462-5264
E-mail: LBREditor@aol.com

LAPIS MAGAZINE ✎
New York Open Center
83 Spring Street
New York, NY 10012
Ph: 212/334-0210
Fax: 212/219-1347
http://www.opencenter.org
E-mail: nyoc@aol.com

Addresses both the inner world of soul and spirit and the outer world of politics, society, and ecology

LATIN AMERICAN PERSPECTIVES
2455 Teller Road
Newbury Park, CA 91320
Ph: 805/499-0721
Fax: 805/499-0871
http://www.sagepub.com
E-mail: order@sagepub.com

LEFT BUSINESS OBSERVER ✎$
250 West 85th Street
New York, NY 10024-3217
Ph: 212/874-4020
Fax: 212/874-3137
http://www.panix.com/~dhenwood/
LBO-home.html
E-mail: dhenwood@panix.com

News and analysis of economics, finance, business, and politics

LEFT CURVE
P.O. Box 472
Oakland, CA 94604
Ph: 510/763-7193
http://www.wco.com/~leftcurv
E-mail: leftcurve@wco.com

Artist-produced magazine addressing problems of cultural forms emerging from problems of modernity

LEGAL TIMES
1730 M Street, NW, Suite 802
Washington, DC 20036
Ph: 202/457-0686
Fax: 202/457-0718
http://www.counsel.com

Weekly legal newspaper

LIBRARIANS AT LIBERTY
CRISES Press, Inc.
1716 SW Williston Road
Gainesville, FL 32608
Ph: 352/335-2200
Fax: call first
E-mail: willett@afn.org

Aims to give people working in libraries and related fields an unconstrained opportunity to express their professional concerns

LINGUAFRANCA
A Review of Academic Life
22 West 38th Street
New York, NY 10018
http://www.linguafranca.com
E-mail: edit@linguafranca.com

A magazine for anyone with an intellectual, and a morbid, curiosity about academic goings-on

LM MAGAZINE
P.O. Box 769 Murray Hill Station
New York, NY 10156
http://www.informinc.co.uk
E-mail: im@infominc.co.uk

A loud-mouthed free speech magazine that dares to publish what others are frightened to whisper

LONDON INDEPENDENT
40 City Road
London, EC1Y 2DB
England

LOS ANGELES NEW TIMES
1950 Sawtelle Boulevard, Suite 200
Los Angeles, CA 90025
Ph: 310/477-0403
Fax: 310/478-9873
http://www.newtimes.com

News, entertainment, investigative reporting

LOWDOWN ✎
London Terrace Station
P.O. Box 20065
New York, NY 10011
E-mail: spectator@newslet.com

A twice-monthly populist newsletter featuring Jim Hightower

LRA'S ECONOMIC NOTES
145 West 28th Street, 6th Floor
New York, NY 10001
Ph: 800/875-8775

Labor, economics, and politics for labor policy makers

MEDIA BYPASS ✎$
P.O. Box 5326
Evansville, IN 47716
Ph: 812/477-8670
Fax: 812/477-8677
http://www.4bypass.com
E-mail: newsroom@4bypass.com

Unsuppressed national news for concerned Americans

MEDIA, CULTURE AND SOCIETY ✎
Sage Publications
CCIS, Block J, Harrow Campus,
Waford Road
Middlesex
England
Ph: 011-44-181-911-5941
Fax: 011-44-181-911-5942
E-mail: c.s.sparks@westminster.ac.uk

MEDIA CULTURE REVIEW
77 Federal Street
San Francisco, CA 94107
Ph: 415/284-1420
Fax: 415/284-1414
http://www.mediademocracy.org
E-mail: congress@igc.org

Commentary and criticism from the
alternative press and elsewhere on
media, technology and culture

MEDIA MATTERS
Media Alliance
814 Mission Street, Suite 205
San Francisco, CA 94103
Ph: 415/546-6334
Fax: 415/546-6218
http://www.media-alliance.org/
E-mail: ma@igc.org

MEDIA REPORT TO WOMEN ✎
10606 Mantz Road
Silver Spring, MD 20903-1247
Ph: 301/445-3231
E-mail: sheilagib@aol.com

Reports on news, research, and
commentary about the media's
depiction of women and girls

MEDIAFILE
814 Mission Street, Suite 205
San Francisco, CA 94103
Ph: 415/546-6334
Fax: 415/546-6218
http://www.media-alliance.org
E-mail: ma@igc.org

MIAMI NEW TIMES
2800 Biscayne Boulevard
Miami, FL 33137
Ph: 305/576-8000
Fax: 305/571-7677
http://www.newtimes.com

News, entertainment, and investigative
reporting

MIDDLE EAST REPORT
1500 Massachusetts Avenue, NW,
Suite 119
Washington, DC 20005
Ph: 202/223-3677
Fax: 202/223-3604
http://www.merip.org
E-mail: merip@igc.org

Offering an independent critical voice
on the Middle East

MONTHLY REVIEW
An Independent Socialist Magazine
122 West 27th Street
New York, NY 10001
Ph: 212/691-2555
Fax: 212/727-3676
http://www.peacenet.org/
MonthlyReview
E-mail: mreview@igc.apc.org

An independent socialist magazine

MOTHER JONES
731 Market Street, Suite 600
San Francisco, CA 94103
Ph: 415/665-6637
Fax: 415/665-6696
http://www.motherjones.com
E-mail: query@motherjones.com

Investigative journalism; home of
"mojowire"

MOTHERING
The Magazine of Natural Family Living
P.O. Box 1690
Santa Fe, New Mexico 87504
Ph: 800/984-8116

MOUTH: THE VOICE OF
DISABILITY RIGHTS
61 Brighton Street
Rochester, New York 14607
Ph: 716/244-6599

Social, political, legislative issues,
activism, and resources

MS. MAGAZINE
230 Park Avenue
New York, NY 10169
Ph: 212/445-6100
http://www.womweb.com
E-mail: ms@echonyc.com

Founding magazine of the feminist
movement, ad-free, national and international focus on issues affecting
women

MSRRT NEWSLETTER
("Library Alternatives") ✎
Chris Dodge/Jan DeSirey
4645 Columbus Avenue South
Minneapolis, MN 55407
Ph: 612/541-8572
http://www.cs.unca.edu/~davidson/msrrt
E-mail: dodge@sun.hennepin.lib.mn.us

Networking information and commentary for activist library workers, and
reviews of materials from independent
presses/media

MULTINATIONAL MONITOR
P.O. Box 19405
Washington, DC 20036
Ph: 202/387-8034
Fax: 202/234-5176
http://essential.org
E-mail: monitor@essential.org

Tracks corporate activity, especially in
the Third World

NACLA REPORT ON THE
AMERICAS
475 Riverside Drive, Suite 454
New York, NY 10115
Ph: 212/870-3146
http://www.igc.apc.org/nacla/nacla.html

Politics, economics, and culture of
Latin America and the Caribbean; foreign policy issues

THE NATION
72 Fifth Avenue
New York, NY 10011
Ph: 212/242-8400
Fax: 212/463-9712
http://www.thenation.com
E-mail: nation@igc.org

Investigative journalism, a leading
forum for leftist debate; home of Radio
Nation and the Nation Institute

NATIONAL CATHOLIC REPORTER
P.O. Box 419281
Kansas City, MO 64141
Ph: 816/531-0538
Fax: 816/968-2280
http://www.naccath.com

NATIONAL REVIEW
150 East 35th Street
New York, NY 10016
Ph: 212/679-7330
Fax: 212/696-0309
http://www.nationalreview.com/

Opinion and commentary from a conservative perspective

NATIVE AMERICAS
Akwe:kon's Journal of Indigenous Issues
Cornell University, 300 Caldwell Hall
Ithaca, New York 14853
Ph: 800/9NATIVE

Combines academic research and
Native knowledge, tradition and culture

THE NEIGHBORHOOD WORKS
Center for Neighborhood Technology
2125 West North Avenue
Chicago, IL 60647
Ph: 773/278-4800
Fax: 773-278-3840
http://www.cnt.org/tnw/
E-mail: tnwedit@cnt.org

Practical approaches for activists and
organizers

THE NEW CITIZEN
Citizens for Media Literacy
34 Wall Street, #407
Asheville, NC 28801
Ph: 704/255-0182
Fax: 704/254-2286
E-mail: cml@main.nc.us
http://www.main.nc.us/cml/

THE NEW INTERNATIONALIST ✎$
55 Rectory Road
Oxford, OX4 1BW
England
Ph: 011-44-186-572-8181
Fax: 011-44-186-579-3152
http://www.newint.org/
E-mail: ni@newint.org

Report on people, ideas, and action
in the fight for sustainable world
development

NEW MARITIMES
P.O. Box 31269
Halifax, Nova Scotia B3K 5Y5
Canada
Ph: 902/425-6622

Culture and politics in the Maritime
provinces of Canada

NEW PERSPECTIVES QUARTERLY
10951 West Pico Boulevard, 3rd Floor
Los Angeles, CA 90064
Ph: 310/474-0011
E-mail: npq@pacificnet.ne/

THE NEW REPUBLIC
1220 19th Street, NW
Washington, DC 20036
Ph: 202/331-7494
Fax: 202/331-0275
http://magazines.enews.com/magazines/
tnr
E-mail: tnr@aol.com

NEW SCIENTIST
1150 18th Street, NW, #725
Washington, DC 20036
Ph: 888/800-8077
Fax:202/331-2082
http://www.newscientist.com

Devoted to science and technology and
their impact on the world and the way
we live

NEW STATESMAN & SOCIETY
7th Floor, Victoria Station House
191 Victoria Street
London, SWIE SNE
England

NEW TIMES, INC.
P.O. Box 5970
Denver, CO 80217

News, entertainment, and investigative
reporting

NEWS FROM INDIAN COUNTRY
Rt. 2, Box 2900A
Hayward, WI 54843
Ph: 715/634-5226
http://www.journalism.wisc.edu-nfic
E-mail: newsfic@aol.com

NEWS ON EARTH ✎
London Terrace Station
P.O. Box 20065
New York, NY 10011
E-mail: spectator@newslet.com

Monthly newsletter on environment for
time-challenged readers

NEWSLETTER ON INTELLECTUAL
FREEDOM ✎
American Library Association
50 East Huron Street
Chicago, IL 60611
Ph: 312/280-4223
Fax: 312/280-4227
http://www.ala.org/oif.html
E-mail: jkrug@ala.org

NEWSPAPER RESEARCH JOURNAL
Scripps Hall School of Journalism
Ohio University
Athens, OH 45701
Ph: 614/593-2590
Fax: 614/593-2592

Bridges the gap between newspaper
industry and academe

NEWSPRINTS
Essential Information
P.O. Box 19405
Washington, DC 20036
Ph: 202/387-8030
Fax: 202/234-5176
http://essential.org/newsprints
E-mail: newsprints@essential.org

THE NONVIOLENT ACTIVIST
Magazine of the War Resisters League
339 Lafayette Street
New York, NY 10012
Ph: 212/228-0450
Fax: 212/228-6193
http://www.nonviolence.org/~nvweb/wrl/
E-mail: wri@igc.apc.org

Political analysis from a pacifist perspective

NORTH COAST XPRESS ✎$
P.O. Box 1226
Occidental, CA 95465
Ph: 707/874-3104
Fax: 707/874-1453
http://www.north-coast-xpress.com/~doretk/
E-mail: doretk@sonic.net

Environmental, social, political, economic, academic activism; voices of underrepresented minorities

NUTRITION ACTION HEALTH LETTER
Center for Science in the Public Interest
1875 Connecticut Avenue, NW, Suite 300
Washington, DC 20009-5728
Ph: 202/322-9110
Fax: 202/265-4954
http://www.cspinet.org/

THE OBJECTOR: A MAGAZINE OF CONSCIENCE AND RESISTANCE
655 Sutter, #514
San Francisco, CA 94102
Ph: 415/474-3002
Fax: 415/474-2311
http://www.libertynet.org/ccco/
E-mail: cccowr@peacenet.org

Magazine of the Central Committee for Conscientious Objectors

OFF OUR BACKS: A WOMEN'S NEWSJOURNAL
2337-B 18th Street, NW
Washington, DC 20009
Ph: 202/234-8072
Fax: 202/234-8092
E-mail: compuserve: 73613.1256

National and international news on feminist issues

THE OJIBWE NEWS
1106 Paul Bunyan Drive, NE
Bemidji, MN 56601
Ph: 218/751-1655
Fax: 218/251-0650
Weekly native news with focus on reservations within Minnesota

OMB WATCH
1742 Connecticut Avenue, NW
Washington, DC 20009-1171
Ph: 202/234-8494
Fax: 202/234-8584
http://ombwatch.org/ombwatch.html
E-mail: ombwatch@rtk.net

ON THE ISSUES
Choices Women's Medical Center, Inc.
97-77 Queens Boulevard, Suite 1120
Forest Hills, NY 11374
Ph: 718/459-1888 Ext. 209
Fax: 718/997-1206
E-mail: 74013.352@compuserve.com

Quarterly women's feminist magazine

OPEN EYE
BM Open Eye
London, WC1N 3XX
England

ORGANIZING
Overbrook Hall
5600 City Avenue
Philadelphia, PA 19131
Ph: 215/878-4253
Fax: 215/879-3148

Helping community groups develop
local leadership, covers issues of community organizing

OUR SCHOOLS/OUR SELVES
A Magazine for Canadian Education
Activists
107 Earl Grey Road
Toronto, Ontario M4J 3L6 Canada
Ph: 416/463-6978
Fax: 416/463-6978

Analysis of educational issues and
information for education activists

OUR TIMES
Canada's Independent Labour
Magazine
390 Dufferin Street
Toronto, Ontario M6K 9Z9 Canada
Ph: 416/531-5762
Fax: 416/533-2397

Social change through unionism and
democratic socialism

OUT MAGAZINE
110 Green Street, Suite 600
New York, NY 10012
Ph: 212/334-9119
Fax: 212/334-9227
E-mail: outmag@aol.com

General interest gay and lesbian
magazine

PACIFIC SUN ✎$
P.O. Box 5553
Mill Valley, CA 94942
Ph: 415/383-4500
Fax: 415/383-4159
E-mail: psun@aol.com

Events and issues in Marin and
Sonoma

PBI/USA REPORT ✎
Peace Brigades International/USA
2642 College Avenue
Berkeley, CA 94704
Ph: 510/540-0749
Fax: 510/849-1247
http://www.igc.apc.org/pbi/index.html
E-mail: pbiusa@igc.apc.org

Reports on the work of PBI and on the political situations where members work

PEACE MAGAZINE
736 Bathurst Street
Toronto, Ontario M5S 2R4
Canada
Ph: 416/533-7581
Fax: 416/531-6214
http://www.peacemagazine.org
E-mail: mspencer@web.net

PEACE NEWS FOR NONVIOLENT REVOLUTION
5 Caledonian Road
London, N1 9DX
England
E-mail: peacenews@gn.apc.org

News of peace movements and non-violent action

PEACE REVIEW: A TRANS-NATIONAL QUARTERLY
Peace & Justice Studies
University of San Francisco
2130 Fulton Street
San Francisco, CA 94117
Ph: 415/422-6349 or 415/422-6496
Fax: 415/388-2631 or 415/422-2772
E-mail: eliasr@usfca.edu

Focuses on issues and controversies the underlie the promotion of a peaceful world

PEACEWORK ✎
American Friends Service Committee
2161 Massachusetts Avenue
Cambridge, MA 02140
Ph: 617/661-6130
Fax: 617/354-2832
http://www.afsc.org/nero/nepw.htm
E-mail: pwork@igc.apc.org

Serves movements for nonviolent social change and promotes grassroots action from national and international perspective

THE PERMACULTURE ACTIVIST
P.O. Box 1209
Black Mountain, NC 28711
Ph: 704/683-4946
http://cst.colorado.edu.perma/faq.1.3.html

Stories and resources for ecological landscape design, organic agriculture, and natural building

PHOENIX NEW TIMES
1201 East Jefferson
Phoenix, AZ 85034
Ph: 602/271-0040
Fax: 602/3409-8806
http://www.newtimes.com

News, entertainment, investigative journalism

PITTSBURGH POST-GAZETTE
P.O. Box 957
Pittsburgh, PA 15222
Ph: 412/263-1100

POZ MAGAZINE
1279 Old Chelsea Station
New York, NY 10113-1279
Ph: 212/242-2163
http://www.poz.com
E-mail: edit@poz.com

Quality of life issues for anyone
impacted by AIDS and HIV

PR WATCH
Center for Media and Democracy, Inc.
3318 Gregory Street
Madison, WI 53711
Ph: 608/233-3346
Fax: 608/238-2236
http://www.prwatch.org/
E-mail: 74250.735@compuserve.com

PREVAILING WINDS MAGAZINE
Center for the Preservation
of Modern History
P.O. Box 23511
Santa Barbara, CA 93121
Ph: 805/899-3433
Fax: 805/899-4773
http://www.prevailingwinds.org
E-mail: patrick@silcom.com

Produces research and exposes of U.S.
government corruption and malfeasance (large research collection at
CPMH)

PRINCETON PROGRESSIVE
REVIEW
315 West College
Princeton University
Princeton, NJ 08544
http://www.princeton.edu/~progrev
E-mail: progrev@princeton.edu

A journal of news analysis, occasional
cultural critique, voicing social justice

PRISON LEGAL NEWS ✎
2400 NW 80th Street, Suite 148
Seattle, WA 98117
Ph: 561/547-9716
http://www.prisonlegalnews.org
E-mail: pln@prisonlegalnews.org

Challenging the current prison industrial complex by providing timely news
and law reporting

PRISON NEWS SERVICE
P.O. Box 5052, Station A
Toronto, Ontario M5W 1W4
Canada
E-mail: sage!pns@noc.tor.hookup.net

News and analysis from the prisons of
U.S. and Canada written mainly by
prisoners

PROBE
Box 1321
Cathedral Station
New York, NY 10025

Critical, independent newsletter on science, media and health

THE PROGRESSIVE ✎
409 East Main Street
Madison, WI 53703
Ph: 608/257-4626
Fax: 608/257-3373
http://www.progressive.org/

Progressive reporting and political
analysis; political cartoons and feature

PROGRESSIVE LIBRARIAN
Library Studies and Information
P.O. Box 2203
Times Square Station
New York, NY 10108
Ph: 212/647-7833
http://home.earthlink.net/~rlitwin/
proglib.html

Political ramifications of profession of
librarian; forum of open exchange on
library issues

PROGRESSIVE POPULIST
P.O. Box 150517
Austin, TX 78715-0517
Ph: 512/447-0455
http://www.eden.com/~reporter/
E-mail: reporter@eden.com

A newspaper that believes people are
more important than corporations

PROGRESSIVE REVIEW
1739 Connecticut Avenue, NW
Washington, DC 20009
Ph: 202/232-5544
Fax: 202/234-6222
http://emporium.turnpike.net/P/ProRev/
E-mail: ssmith@igc.org

Washington's most unofficial voice

PROPAGANDA REVIEW
Media Alliance
814 Mission Street, Suite 205
San Francisco, CA 94103
Ph: 415/546-6334
http://www.media-alliance.org
E-mail: ma@igc.org

THE PROUT JOURNAL ✎
People's News Agency
7627 16th Street, NW
P.O. Box 56466
Washington, DC 20040
Ph: 202/829-2278
Fax: 202/829-0462
E-mail: prout@prout.org

The holistic socio-economic ideas of
the Progressive Utilization Theory

PUBLIC CITIZEN MAGAZINE
1600 20th Street, NW
Washington, DC 20009
Ph: 202/588-1000
Fax: 202/588-7799
http://www.citizen.org/ or
gopher://gopher.essential.org/hh/ftp/
pub/public citizen
E-mail: pnye@citizen.org

Consumer rights, safety issues, corporate and business accountability, environmental issues, and citizen
empowerment

THE PUBLIC EYE
Political Research Associates
120 Beacon Street, Suite 202
Somerville, MA 02143
Ph: 617/661-9313
Fax: 617/661-0059
http://www.publiceye.org/pra
E-mail: publiceye@igc.opc.org

Focuses on issues pertaining to the
U.S. right and stories underrepresented
in the mainstream media

THE PUBLIC i
Center for Public Integrity
1634 I Street, NW, Suite 902
Washington, DC 20006
Ph: 202/783-3900
Fax: 202/783-3906
http://www.publicintegrity.org/
E-mail: contact@publicintegrity.org

QUILL ✎
Society of Professional Journalists
16 South Jackson Street, P.O. Box 77
Greencastle, IN 46135-0077
Ph: 765/653-3333
Fax: 765/653-4631
http://www.spj.org
E-mail: maiospj@link2000.net

RACHEL'S ENVIRONMENT &
HEALTH WEEKLY ✎
c/o Environmental Research
Foundation
P.O. Box 5036
Annapolis, MD 21403-7036
Ph: 410/263-1584
Fax: 410/263-8944
E-mail: erf@rachel.clark.net

Reports on medical and scientific studies linking environment and health

RADICAL AMERICA
237A Holland
Somerville, MA 02144
Ph: 617/628-6585
Fax: 617/628-6585

RADICAL TEACHER
P.O. Box 102
Kendall Square Post Office
Cambridge, MA 01242
http://www.eden.com/fineprint/41225.
html

RAISE THE STAKES:
THE PLANET DRUM REVIEW
P.O. Box 31251
San Francisco, CA 94131
Ph: 415/285-6556
Fax: 415/285-6563
E-mail: planetdrum@igc.apa.org

International publication about bi-
regionalism

RANDOM LENGTHS ✎$
Harbor Independent News
P.O. Box 731
1117 South Pacific Avenue
San Pedro, CA 90733
Ph: 310/519-1016
Fax: 310/832-1000
E-mail: 71632.210@compuserve.com

RAW MATERIALS REPORT:
JOURNAL OF MINERAL POLICY,
BUSINESS AND ENVIRONMENT ✎
P.O. Box 44 062
Stockholm, S-100 73
Sweden
Ph: 011-46-8-744-0065
Fax: 011-46-8-744-0066
http://www.rmg.se
E-mail: raw.materials.group@rmg.se

Issues of contemporary interest to the
world raw materials supply

REASON ✎$
3415 South Sepulveda Boulevard,
Suite 400
Los Angeles, CA 90034
Ph: 310/391-2245
Fax: 310/390-8986
http://www.reason.com

Reports on public policy and culture
from a dynamic libertarian perspective

THE RECORDER
625 Polk Street
San Francisco, CA 94102
Ph: 415/749-5400

RED PEPPER
Socialist Newspaper Publications, Ltd.
3 Gunthorpe Street
London, E1 7RP
England
Ph: 011-44-171-247-1702
http://www.rednet.co.uk/redpepper
E-mail: redpepper@online.rednet.co.uk

Uniting socialist forces with British
Labour Party

RETHINKING SCHOOLS ✎
1001 East Keefe Avenue
Milwaukee, WI 53212
Ph: 414/964-9646 or 800/669-4192
Fax: 414/964-7220
http://www.rethinkingschools.org
E-mail: RS Business@aol.com

Provides an alternative to mainstream
educational materials, committed to
issues of equity and social justice

REVOLUTIONARY WORKER
P.O. Box 3486
Chicago, IL 60654

RFD: A JOURNAL FOR GAY MEN
EVERYWHERE
P.O. Box 68
Liberty, TN 37095
Ph: 615/536-5176

A reader-written journal for gay men
focusing on country living, and encouraging alternative lifestyles

ROLLING STONE
1290 Avenue of the Americas,
2nd Floor
New York, NY 10104
Ph: 212/484-1616
Fax: 212/767-8203
http://www.rollingstone.com

Rock and politics at the cutting edge

RYERSON REVIEW OF
JOURNALISM
350 Victoria Street
Toronto, Ontario M5B 2K3 Canada
Ph: 416/979-5000
http://www.ryerson/RRJ

S.O.A. WATCH
P.O. Box 3330
Columbus, GA 31903
Ph: 706/682-5369
Fax: same as above
http://www.derechos.org/soaw/

Reporting on School of America Watch

THE SAN FRANCISCO BAY
GUARDIAN ✎$
520 Hampshire
San Francisco, CA 94110
Ph: 415/255-3100
Fax: 415/255-8762
http://www.sfbg.com
E-mail: sfguardian@aol.com

To print the news and raise hell!

SANTA BARBARA NEWS PRESS
715 Anacapa Street
Santa Barbara, CA 93101
Ph: 805/564-5200
http://www.sbcoast.com

SANTA CRUZ SENTINEL
P.O. Box 638
Santa Cruz, CA 95061
Ph: 408/423-4242
Fax: 408/429-9620

SECRECY & GOVERNMENT
BULLETIN ✎
Federation of American Scientists
307 Massachusetts Avenue, NE
Washington, DC 20002
Ph: 202/675-1012
Fax: 202/675-1010
http://www.fas.org/sgp/
E-mail: saftergood@igc.apc.org

Reports on new developments in government secrecy policy

SF FRONTLINES
3311 Mission Street, Suite 25
San Francisco, CA 94110
Ph: 415/642-3704
Fax: 415/643-8581
E-mail: progress@ix.netcom.com

Newspaper for a new progressive
majority

SF WEEKLY
185 Berry Street, Suite 3800
San Francisco, CA 94107
Ph: 415/541-0700
Fax: 415/777-1839
http://www.sfweekly.com

SHELTERFORCE
The Journal of Affordable Housing
Strategies
439 Main Street
Orange, NJ 07050
http://www.nhi.org/online/issues.html

SHUNPIKING DISCOVERY
MAGAZINE
P.O. Box 31377
Halifax, Nova Scotia B3K 5Z1
Canada
Ph: 902/455-4922
Fax: 902/455-7599

General interest discovery magazine

SOCIAL JUSTICE ACTION
QUARTERLY ✎
600 West 113th Street, #215
New York, NY 10025
Ph: 212/222-9081
E-mail: jlp24@columbia.edu

To organize and educate social service
workers and students around radical
left actors and issues

SOCIAL POLICY
25 West 43rd Street, Room 620
New York, NY 10036-7406
Ph: 212/354-8525
Fax: 212/642-1956
http://www.socialpolicy.org
E-mail: socpol@igc.apc.org

Reporting on culture, politics, political
and social movements

SOJOURNERS
2401 15th Street, NW
Washington, DC 20009
Ph: 202/328-8842
Fax: 202/328-8757
http://www.sojourners.com/sojourners
E-mail: sojourn@ari.net

Grassroots network for personal,
community, and political
transformation rooted in prophetic
biblical tradition

THE SONOMA COUNTY
INDEPENDENT ✎$
540 Medocino Avenue
Santa Rosa, CA 95401
Ph: 707/527-1200
Fax: 707/527-1288
http://www.metroactive.com/sonoma
E-mail: indy@livewire.com

News, dining, and arts

SOUTHERN EXPOSURE
P.O. Box 531
Durham, NC 27702
Ph: 919/419-8311 Ext. 26
Fax: 919/419-8315
http://sunsite.unc.edu/Southern_
Exposure/
E-mail: Southern@igc.apc.org

Award-winning magazine focused on
fighting for a better South

SPIN
6 West 18th Street
New York, NY 10011
Ph: 212/633-8200
Fax: 212/633-9041
E-mail: spinonline@aol.com

News, issues, and profiles in
alternative music

SPIRIT OF CRAZY HORSE
Leonard Peltier Defense Committee
International Office
P.O. Box 583
Lawrence, KS 66044
Ph: 785/842-5774
Fax: 785/842-5796
http://www.unicom.net/peltier/index.html
E-mail: lpdc@idir.net

ST. LOUIS JOURNALISM REVIEW
8380 Olive Boulevard
St. Louis, MO 63132
Ph: 314/991-1699
Fax: 314/997-1898

STAY FREE! ✎
Prince Street Station
P.O. Box 306
New York, NY 10012
Ph: 212/995-5882
Fax: 212/477-5074
http://sunsite.unc.edu/stayfree
E-mail: stayfree@sunsite.unc.edu

A 'zine that casts a critical eye on
commercialism and pop culture

THE STRANGER
1122 East Pike Street, Suite 1225
Seattle, WA 98122
Ph: 206/323-7002
Fax: 206/323-7203
http://www.thestranger.com
E-mail: postmaster@thestranger.com

News, entertainment, investigative
reporting

STUDENT PRESS LAW CENTER
REPORT ✎
1101 Wilson Boulevard, Suite 1910
Arlington, VA 22901
Ph: 703/807-1904
Fax: 703/807-2109
http://www.splc.org
E-mail: splc@splc.org

Reports on cases, controversies, and
legislation relating to free press rights
of student journalists

THE SUN
107 North Roberson Street
Chapel Hill, NC 27516
Ph: 919/942-5282

SYNTHESIS/REGENERATION:
A MAGAZINE OF GREEN SOCIAL
THOUGHT
WD Press, P.O. Box 24115
St. Louis, MO 63130
Ph: 314/727-8554
Fax: Call first
E-mail: jsutter@igc.apc.org

TASK FORCE CONNECTIONS
National Task Force on AIDS
Preservation
973 Market Street, Suite 600
San Francisco, CA 94103
Ph: 415/356-8110
Fax: 415/356-8138

TEACHING TOLERANCE
Southern Poverty Law Center
400 Washington Avenue
Montgomery, AL 36104
Ph: 334/264-0286
Fax: 334/264-3121
http://www.splcenter.org/
teachingtolerance/h-1.html

Magazine promoting tolerance in a
diverse society

TEAMSTER
International Brotherhood of Teamsters
25 Louisiana Avenue, NW
Washington, DC 20001
Ph: 202/624-6911
Fax: 202/624-6918
http://www.teamster.org
E-mail: ibtcomm@aol.com

Newsletter of the organization of 1.4
million members, focused on fighting
for the future of working families

TEEN VOICES MAGAZINE ✎
Women Express, Inc.
P.O. Box 120-027
Boston, MA 02112-0027
Ph: 617/426-5505
Fax: 617/426-5577
http://www.teenvoices.com
E-mail: womenexp@teenvoices.com

An interactive, educational forum that
challenges media images of young
women

TERRAIN ✎
Northern California's Environmental
Magazine
2530 San Pablo Avenue
Berkeley, CA 94702
Ph: 510/548-2220
E-mail: terrain@igc.org

TEXAS OBSERVER ✎$
307 West 7th Street
Austin, TX 78701-2917
Ph: 512/477-0746
Fax: 512/474-1175
http://texasobserver.org
E-mail: observer@eden.com

Focuses on progressive politics
and the arts in Texas

THIRD FORCE
Center for Third World Organizing
1218 East 21st Street
Oakland, CA 94606-9950
Ph: 510/533-7583
Fax: 510/533-0923
http://www.igc.org/ctwo/
E-mail: ctwo@igc.org

Reports on labor, low income issues,
communities of color, and community
activism and organizing

THIS MAGAZINE
35 Rivera Drive, #17
Markham, Ontario M5V 3A8
Canada
Ph: 416/979-8400
E-mail: this magazine@intacc.web.net

Culture, politics, labor, and feminism
in Canada and internationally

THRESHOLD
Student Environmental Action
Coalition (SEAC)
P.O. Box 1168
Chapel Hill, NC 27514-1168
Ph: 919/967-4600
Fax: 919/967-4648
E-mail: seac@igc.apc.org

TIBET PRESS WATCH
International Campaign for Tibet
1825 K Street, NW, Suite 520
Washington, DC 20006
Ph: 202/785-1515
Fax: 202/785-4343
http://www.savetibet.org

TIKKUN
P.O. Box 1778
Cathedral Station
New York, NY 10025
Ph: 212/864-4110
Fax: 212/864-4137
http://www.tikkun.com/

Culture, politics, philosophy; topics of particular concern to the Jewish community

TOWARD FREEDOM
209 College Street
Burlington, VT 05401
Ph: 802/658-2523
Fax: 802/658-3738
E-mail: TFmag@aol.com
http://homepages.together.net/~tfmag/

International news, analysis, and advocacy for human justice and liberties

TRADEWOMEN: A MAGAZINE FOR WOMEN IN BLUE COLLAR WORK
P.O. Box 2622
Berkeley, CA 94702
Ph: 510/433-1378
http://www.emf.net/~cheetham/gtrmc-l.html

Labor issues, legislation; issues of women in the trades; Bay Area resources

TRANSITION
Van Serg Hall, 25 Francis Avenue, B11
Cambridge, MA 02138
Ph: 617/496-2847
Fax: 617/496-2877
E-mail: transit@fas.harvard.edu

TRANSPORTATION ALTERNATIVES
115 West 30th Street, #1207
New York, NY 10001
Ph: 212/629-3311
Fax: 212/629-8334
http://www.transalt.org
E-mail: info@transalt.org

News and advocacy for greater use of human-powered transportation in New York City

TRICYCLE: THE BUDDHIST REVIEW
92 Vandam Street
New York, NY 10013
Ph: 212/645-1143
http://www.tricycle.com

A magazine to help you spin the dharma

TURNING THE TIDE: JOURNAL OF ANTI-RACIST ACTIVISM, RESEARCH & EDUCATION ✎
People Against Racist Terror
P.O. Box 1055
Culver City, CA 90232-1055
Ph: 310/288-5003
E-mail: mnovickttt@igc.org

Constructive solutions to racism

TYNDALL WEEKLY REPORT
135 Rivington Street
New York, NY 10002
Ph: 212/674-8913
Fax: 212/979-7304

U: THE NATIONAL COLLEGE
MAGAZINE
1800 Century Park East, #820
Los Angeles, CA 90067-1503
Ph: 310/551-1381
Fax: 310/551-1659
http://www.umagazine.com
E-mail: editor@umagazine.com

Economy and politics from a global
perspective

UNCLASSIFIED
Association of National Security
Alumni
2001 S Street, NW, Suite 740
Washington, DC 20009
Ph: 202/483-9325

UNDERGROUND PRESS
CONFERENCE
Mary Kuntz Press
P.O. Box 476617
Chicago, IL 60647
Ph: 312/486-0685
Fax: 312/226-1168

THE URBAN ECOLOGIST
Urban Ecology
405 14th Street, Suite 900
Oakland, CA 94612
Ph: 510/251-6330
Fax: 510/251-2117
http://www.best.com/~schmitty/ueindex
.shtml
E-mail: urbanecology@igc.apc.org

Issues and action in sustainable urban
development

URGENT ACTION BULLETIN ✎
Survival International
11-15 Emerald Street
London, WC1N 3QL
England
Ph: 011-44-171-242-1441
Fax: 011-44-171-242-1771
http://www.survival.org.uk
E-mail: survival@gn.apc.org

URGENT ACTION NEWSLETTER
Urgent Action Program Office
Amnesty International USA
P.O. Box 1270
Nederland, CO 80466-1270
Ph: 303/440-0913
Fax: 303/258-7881
http://www.amnesty-usa.org
E-mail: sharris@igc.apc.org

UTNE READER
1624 Harmon Place, Suite 330
Minneapolis, MN 55403
Ph: 612/338-5040
Fax: 612/338-6043
http://www.utne.com
E-mail: editor@utne.com

Digest of materials reprinted from
alternative and independent media

THE VETERAN ✎
Vietnam Veterans of America
1224 M Street, NW
Washington, DC 20005
Ph: 202/628-2700
Fax: 202/628-5880
http://www.vva.org

The official voice of Vietnam Veterans
of America

VIBE
205 Lexington Avenue, 3rd Floor
New York, NY 10016
Ph: 212/522-7092
Fax: 212/522-4578
http://www.vibe.com

News and features about goings-on in
urban culture

VILLAGE VOICE
36 Cooper Square
New York, NY 10003
Ph: 212/475-3300
Fax: 212/475-8944
http://www.villagevoice.com

VOCES DE LA FRONTERA ✎
P.O. Box 340195
Austin, TX 78734-0195
Ph: 512/264-0834
Fax: 512/264-0834
E-mail: beecreek@aol.com

Providing space for *maquiladora* workers to express themselves, coverage of
independent democratic union strug-
gles, a bilingual publication

WAR AND PEACE DIGEST ✎
War and Peace Foundation
32 Union Square East
New York, NY 10003-3295
Ph: 212/777-6626
Fax: 212/777-2552

Anti-nuclear publication, promoting
peace, social justice and media reform

WASHINGTON FREE PRESS
1463 East Republican, #178
Seattle, WA 98112
Ph: 206/860-5290
http://www.speakeasy.org/wfp
E-mail: freepres@scn.org

THE WASHINGTON MONTHLY
Washington Monthly Co.
1611 Connecticut Avenue, NW
Washington, DC 20009
Ph: 202/462-0128
Fax: 202/332-8413
http://enews.com/magazines/wash_
month/magazines.enews

THE WASHINGTON SPECTATOR ✎
London Terrace Station
P.O. Box 20065
New York, NY 10011
E-mail: spectator@newslet.com

Twice-monthly commentary on national
politics

WE INTERNATIONAL
Centre for Urban and Community
Studies
736 Bathurst Street
Toronto, Ontario M5S 2R4
Canada
Ph: 416/516-2600
Fax: 416/531-6214
http://www.web.net/~weed/
E-mail: weed@web.net

Examines women's multiple relationships with their environment

WHO CARES: A JOURNAL
OF SERVICE AND ACTION
511 K Street, NW, Suite 1042
Washington, DC 20005
Ph: 202/628-1691
Fax: 202/628-2063
http://www.whocares.org
E-mail: info@whocares.mag

WHOLE EARTH MAGAZINE
1408 Mission Avenue
San Rafael, CA 94901
Ph: 415/256-2800
Fax: 415/256-2808
E-mail: wer@well.com

Access to tools, ideas, and practices;
reviews of books and products to help
people help themselves

WHY MAGAZINE
Challenging Hunger and Poverty
505 Eighth Avenue, 21st Floor
New York, NY 10018
Ph: 212/629-8850
Fax: 212/465-9274

WILLAMETTE WEEK ✎$
Portland's Newsweekly
822 SW 10th Avenue
Portland, OR 97205
Ph: 503/243-2122
Fax: 503/243-1115

News, entertainment, investigative
reporting

WOMEN IN ACTION
P.O. Box 1837
Quezon City Main
Quezon City 1100
Philippines
Ph: 011-63-2-967297

International feminism and women's
issues on sharing

WOMEN'S EDUCATION
DES FEMMES
Canadian Congress for Learning
Opportunities for Women
47 Main Street
Toronto, Ontario M4E 2V6
Canada
Ph: 416/699-1909
Fax: 416/699-2145
E-mail: cclow@web.apc.org

WOMEN'S HEALTH LETTER
2245 East Colorado Boulevard,
Suite 104
Pasadena, CA 91107-3651
Ph: 626/798-0638
Fax: 626/798-0639

Addresses key health concerns of
females; strong emphasis on prevention
and alternative health care solutions

WOMEN'S REVIEW OF BOOKS
Center for Research on Women
Wellesley College
Wellesley, MA 02181
Ph: 617/283-2087
Fax: 617/283-3845

WOMEN'S WORLD
Women's International
Cross Cultural Exchange
Box 4934
Kampala
Uganda
Ph: 256 41 266007/8
Fax: 256 41 268676
E-mail: Isis-WICCE@mulka.gn.apc.org

THE WORKBOOK ✎
Southwest Research and
Information Center
P.O. Box 4524, 105 Stanford, SE
Albuquerque, NM 87106
Ph: 505/262-1862
Fax: 505/262-1864

Helping people gain access to vital
information that can help them assert
control over their lives

WORKPLACE DEMOCRACY:
THE MAGAZINE OF EMPLOYEE
OWNERSHIP AND PARTICIPATION
University of Amherst
111 Draper Hall
Amherst, MA 01003-0001

WORLD POLICY JOURNAL
65 Fifth Avenue, Suite 413
New York, NY 10003
Ph: 212/229-5808
Fax: 212/229-5579
http://worldpolicy.org/
E-mail: pera@newschool.edu

WORLD PRESS REVIEW
200 Madison Avenue, Suite 2104
New York, NY 10016
Ph: 212/889-5155
Fax: 212/889-5634
E-mail: worldpress@worldpress.org

WORLD RIVERS REVIEW
1847 Berkeley Way
Berkeley, CA 94703
Ph: 510/848-1155
Fax: 510/848-1008
http://www.irn.org
E-mail: irn@igc.apc.org

WORLD WATCH
Worldwatch Institute
1776 Massachusetts Avenue, NW
Washington, DC 20036
Ph: 202/452-1999
Fax: 202/296-7365
http://www.worldwatch.org

YES: POSITIVE FUTURES
NETWORK ✎$
P.O. Box 10818
Bainbridge Island, WA 98110
Ph: 206/842-0216
Fax: 206/842-5208
http://www.futurenet.org
E-mail: yes@futurenet.org

To help shape and support the evolution of sustainable cultures and communities

YO-YOUTH OUTLOOK ✎$
Pacific News Service
450 Mission Street, Room 204
San Francisco, CA 94105
Ph: 415/243-4364
http://www.pacificnews.org/yo/
E-mail: yo@pacificnews.org

Newspaper by and about young people

YOGA JOURNAL
2054 University Avenue, Suite 600
Berkeley, CA 94704
Ph: 510/841-9200
Fax: 510/644-3101
http://www.yogajournal.com

Z MAGAZINE
18 Millfield Street
Woods Hole, MA 02543
Ph: 617/251-0755
Fax: 617/251-0756
http://www.lbbs.org
E-mail: Lydia.Sargent@lbbs.org

Independent political magazine of critical thinking on political, cultural, social, and economic life in the U.S.

MEDIA-RELATED ORGANIZATIONS: FREEDOM OF INFORMATION, MEDIA ANALYSIS, MEDIA LITERACY, JOURNALISTIC RESOURCES

ADBUSTERS
The Media Foundation
1243 West Seventh Avenue
Vancouver, British Columbia
V6H 1B7 Canada
Ph: 604/736-9401
Fax: 604/737-6021
http://adbusters.org/adbusters/

ADVOCATES FOR YOUTH'S
MEDIA PROJECT
10999 Riverside Drive, Suite 300
North Hollywood, CA 91602
Fax: 818/762-9769
http://www.advocatesforyouth.org

(AIM) ACCURACY IN MEDIA
4455 Connecticut Avenue, NW, Suite 330
Washington, DC 20005
Ph: 202/364-4401
Fax: 202/364-4098
http://www.aim.org
E-mail: ar@aim.org

ALLIANCE FOR COMMUNITY
MEDIA
666 11th Street, NW, Suite 806
Washington, DC 20001-4542
Ph: 202/393-2650
Fax: 202/393-2653
http://www.alliancecm.org
E-mail: acm@alliancecm.org

ALLIANCE FOR CULTURAL
DEMOCRACY
P.O. Box 192244
San Francisco, CA 94119
Ph: 415/437-2721 or 212/533-3032
Fax: 718/488-8296
http://www.f8.com/ACD
E-mail: cdemocracy@aol.com

ALLIANCE FOR DEMOCRACY/
UW GREENS INFOSHOP
731 State Street
Madison, WI 53703
Ph: 608/262-9036
Fax: 608/251-3267
http://www.sit.wisc.edu/democrac/
E-mail: wisc-eco@igc.apc.org

ALTERNATIVE MEDIA, INC.
P.O. Box 21308
Washington, DC 20009
Ph: 202/588-9807
Fax: 202/588-9809
http://www.alternativemedia.com/
E-mail: mpaulsen@aminc.com

ALTERNATIVE PRESS CENTER
P.O. Box 33109
Baltimore, MD 21218-0401
Ph: 410/243-2471
Fax: 410/235-5325
http://www.igc.apc.org/altpress/
E-mail: altpress@igc.apc.org

AMERICAN HELLENIC
MEDIA PROJECT
P.O. Box 1150
New York, NY 10028
http://hri.org/ahmp/alert.html
E-mail: ahmp@hri.org

AMERICAN LIBRARY
ASSOCIATION OFFICE FOR
INTELLECTUAL FREEDOM
50 East Huron Street
Chicago, IL 60611
Ph: 312/280-4223 or 800/545-2433
Fax: 312/280-4227
http//: www.ala.org/oif.html
E-mail: oif@ala.org

AMERICAN SOCIETY OF
JOURNALISTS AND AUTHORS
1501 Broadway, Suite 302
New York, NY 10036
Ph: 212/398-1934
Fax: 212/768-7414
http://www.asja.org
E-mail:
102535.2427@compuserve.com

ARTICLE 19: INTERNATIONAL
CENTRE AGAINST CENSORSHIP
33 Islington High Street
London, N1 9LH
England
Ph: 011-44-171-278-9292
Fax: 011-44-171-713-1356
http://www.gn.apc.org/article19/
E-mail: article19@gn.apc.org

ASIAN AMERICAN JOURNALISTS
ASSOCIATION
1765 Sutter Street, Suite 1000
San Francisco, CA 94115
Ph: 415/346-2051
Fax: 415/931-4671
http://www.aaja.org/
E-mail: aaja1@aol.com

ASSOCIATION FOR EDUCATION
JOURNALISM AND MASS
COMMUNICATION
University of South Carolina
1621 College Street
Columbia, SC 29208
Ph: 803/777-2005

ASSOCIATION OF ALTERNATIVE
NEWSWEEKLIES
1660 L Street, NW, Suite 316
Washington, DC 20036
Ph: 202/822-1955
Fax: 202/822-0929
http://aan.org
E-mail: rkarpel@intr.net

ASSOCIATION OF AMERICAN
PUBLISHERS
71 Fifth Avenue
New York, NY 10003
Ph: 212/255-0200
Fax: 212/255-7007
http://www.publishers.org/

BERKELEY MEDIA STUDIES
GROUP
2140 Shattuck Avenue, Suite 804
Berkeley, CA 94704
Ph: 510/204-9700
Fax: 510/204-9710
E-mail: bmsg@bmsg.org

BEYOND MEDIA
1629 Asbury Avenue
Evanston, IL 60201
Ph: 847/869-6888

BLACK PRESS INSTITUTE
2711 East 75th Place
Chicago, IL 60649
Ph: 312/375-8200
Fax: 312/375-8262

BLACK WOMEN IN PUBLISHING
P.O. Box 6275
FDR Station
New York, NY 10150
Ph: 212/772-5951

CALIFORNIA FIRST AMENDMENT
COALITION
926 J Street, Suite 1406
Sacramento, CA 95814-2708
Ph: 916/447-2322
Fax: 916/447-2328
http://cfac.org

CAMPAIGN FOR PRESS &
BROADCASTING FREEDOM
8 Cynthia Street
London, N1 9LF
England
Ph: 011-44-171-278-4430
Fax: 011-44-171-837-8868

CAMPUS ALTERNATIVE
JOURNALISM PROJECT
Center for Campus Organizing
P.O. Box 748
Cambridge, MA 02142
Ph: 617/357-9363
Fax: 617/547-5067
http://www.envirolink.org/orgs/cco/
journalism/index.html
E-mail: cco@igc.apc.org

THE CENTER FOR COMMERCIAL-
FREE PUBLIC EDUCATION
Home of the Unplug campaign
360 Grand Avenue
P.O. Box 385
Oakland, CA 94610
Ph: 510/268-1100
Fax: 510/268-1277
E-mail: unplug@igc.apc.org

CENTER FOR DEMOCRATIC
VALUES
5700 Cass Avenue, Room 2426
Detroit, MI 48202
Ph: 313/577-0828
Fax: 313/577-8585
http://www.igc.apc.org/cdv
E-mail: RAronso@cll.wayne.edu

THE CENTER FOR DEMOCRACY
AND TECHNOLOGY
1634 I Street, Suite 1100
Washington, DC 20001
Ph: 202/637-9800
Fax: 202/637-0968
http:www.cdt.org
E-mail: info@cdt.org

CENTER FOR INTEGRATION AND
IMPROVEMENT OF JOURNALISM
San Francisco State University
San Francisco, CA
Ph: 415/243-4364
http://www.journalism.sfsu.edu/www/
ciij/ciij.htm

CENTER FOR INVESTIGATIVE
REPORTING
500 Howard Street, Suite 206
San Francisco, CA 94105-3000
Ph: 415/543-1200
Fax: 415/543-8311
http://www.muckraker.org/pubs/
paper-trails/index.html
E-mail: CIR@igc.org

CENTER FOR MEDIA
AND DEMOCRACY
3318 Gregory Street
Madison, WI 53711
Ph: 608/233-3346
Fax: 608/238-2236
http://www.prwatch.org/
E-mail: 74250.735@compuserve.com

CENTER FOR MEDIA AND
PUBLIC AFFAIRS
2100 L Street, NW, Suite 300
Washington, DC 20037-1526
Ph: 202/223-2942
Fax: 202/872-4014
http://www.cmpa.com/html/2100.html

CENTER FOR MEDIA
EDUCATION
1511 K Street, NW, Suite 518
Washington, DC 20005
Ph: 202/628-2620
Fax: 202/628-2554
http://www.cme.org/cme
E-mail: cme@cme.org

CENTER FOR MEDIA LITERACY
4727 Wilshire Boulevard, Suite #403
Los Angeles, CA 90010
Ph: 213/931-4177
Fax: 213/931-4474
E-mail: cml@medialit.org
http://www.medialit.org

CENTER FOR PUBLIC INTEGRITY
1634 I Street, NW, Suite 902
Washington, DC 20006
Ph: 202/783-3900
Fax: 202/783-3906
http://www.publicintegrity.org
E-mail: contact@publicintegrity.org

CENTER FOR THIRD WORLD
ORGANIZING
1218 East 21st Street
Oakland, CA 94606-9950
Ph: 510/533-7583
Fax: 510/533-0923
E-mail: ctwo@igc.org
http://ctwo.org/

CENTER FOR WAR, PEACE
AND THE NEWS MEDIA
New York University
10 Washington Place, 4th Floor
New York, NY 10003
Ph: 212/998-7960
Fax: 212/995-4143
http://www.nyu.edu/globalbeat

CITIZENS FOR MEDIA LITERACY
34 Wall Street, Suite 407
Asheville, NC 28801
Ph: 704/255-0182
Fax: 704/254-2286
http://www.main.nc.us/cml/
E-mail: cml@main.nc.us

COMMITTEE TO PROTECT
JOURNALISTS
330 Seventh Avenue, 12th Floor
New York, NY 10001
Ph: 212/465-1004
Fax: 212/465-9568
http://www.cpj.org
E-mail: info@cpj.org

COMMON CAUSE
1250 Connecticut Avenue, NW,
6th Floor
Washington, DC 20036
Ph: 202/833-1200
Fax: 202/659-3716
http://www.commoncause.org

COMMUNICATIONS CONSORTIUM
AND MEDIA CENTER
1333 H Street, NW, Suite 700
Washington, DC 20005
Ph: 202/682-1270
Fax: 202/682-2154
http://www.womenofcolor.org/about.htm

COMMUNITY MEDIA WORKSHOP
c/o Columbia College
600 South Michigan Avenue
Chicago, IL 60605-1996
Ph: 312/663-1600 Ext. 5498
Fax: 312/663-3227
http://www.mcs.net/~commnews
E-mail: commnews@mcs.net

CONSEIL DE PRESSE DE QUEBEC
1000, rue Fullum, 2 étage, bureau
C239
Montreal, Quebec H2K 3L7 Canada
Ph: 514/529-2818
Fax: 514/873-4434

CONSUMER PROJECT
ON TECHNOLOGY
P.O. Box 19367
Washington, DC 20036
Ph: 202/387-8030
Fax: 202/234-5176
http://essential.org/cpt
E-mail: love@tap.org

ELECTRONIC FRONTIER
FOUNDATION
1550 Bryant Street, Suite 725
San Francisco, CA 94103
Ph: 415/436-9333
Fax: 415/436-9993
http://www.eff.org
E-mail: eff@eff.org

EMPOWERMENT PROJECT
3403 Highway 54 West
Chapel Hill, NC 27516
Ph: 919/967-1963
Fax: 919/967-1863
http://www.webcom.com/empowerment

ESSENTIAL INFORMATION
P.O. Box 19405
Washington, DC 20036
Ph: 202/387-8030
Fax: 202/234-5176
http://essential.org

FAIRNESS AND ACCURACY
IN REPORTING
(FAIR)
130 West 25th Street
New York, NY 10001
Ph: 212/633-6700
Fax: 212/727-7668
http://www.fair.org
E-mail: info@fair.org

FEMINISTS FOR FREE
EXPRESSION
2525 Times Square Station
New York, NY 10108
Ph: 212/702-6292
Fax: 212/702-6277
http://www.well.com/user/freedom
E-mail: FFE@aol.com

FREEDOM FORUM
First Amendment Center
1207 18th Avenue South
Nashville, TN 37212
Ph: 615/321-9588
Fax: 615/321-9599
http://www.fac.org
E-mail: info@fac.org

FREEDOM FORUM WORLD
CENTER
1101 Wilson Boulevard
Arlington, VA 22209
Ph: 703/528-0800
Fax: 703/522-4831
http://www.freedomforum.org
E-mail: news@freedomformu.org

FREEDOM OF EXPRESSION
FOUNDATION
171-B Claremont Aveue
Long Beach, CA 90803
Ph: 562/434-2284
http://www.csulb.edu/~research/Cent/
lamend.html
E-mail: crsmith@csulb.edu

FREEDOM OF INFORMATION
CENTER
University of Missouri at Columbia
127 Neff Annex
Columbia, MO 65211
Ph: 573/882-4856
Fax: 573/884-4856
http://www.missouri.edu/~foiwww
E-mail: athleen_edwards@jmail.
jour.missouri.edu

FREEDOM OF INFORMATION
CLEARINGHOUSE
P.O. Box 19367
Washington, DC 20036
Ph: 202/588-7790
http://www.citizen.org/public_citizen/
litigation/foic/foic.html

FUND FOR INVESTIGATIVE
JOURNALISM
5120 Kenwood Drive
Annandale, VA 22003
Ph: 703/750-3849
http://www.fij.org

GOVERNMENT ACCOUNTABILITY
PROJECT
810 First Street, NE, Suite 630
Washington, DC 20002-3633
Ph: 202/408-0034
Fax: 202/408-9855
http://www.halcyon.com/tomgap

THE GUSTAVUS MYERS CENTER
FOR THE STUDY OF HUMAN
RIGHTS IN NORTH AMERICA
2582 Jimmie
Fayetteville, AR 72703-3420
Ph: 501/442-4600 or 501/575-4301
E-mail: jbennet@comp.uark.edu

HEAL
Hanford Education Action League
1408 West Broadway
Spokane, WA 99201
Ph: 509/326-3370
Fax: 509/326-2932
http://www.iea.com/~heal
E-mail: heallfi@aol.com

HISPANIC EDUCATION
AND MEDIA GROUP, INC.
P.O. Box 221
Sausalito, CA 94966
Ph: 415/331-8560
Fax: 415/331-2636

THE HUCK BOYD NATIONAL
CENTER FOR COMMUNITY MEDIA
School of Journalism
105 Kedzie Hall
Kansas State University
Manhattan, KS 66506
Ph: 913/532-6890
Fax: 913/532-5484
http://www.jnc.ksu.edu/~hbnc/hbnc.html

IN CONTEXT
Context Institute
P.O. Box 946
Langley, WA 98260
Ph: 360/221-6044
Fax: 360/221-6045
http://www.context.org

INDEPENDENT PRESS
ASSOCIATION
P.O. Box 191785
San Francisco, CA 94119-1785
E-mail: indypress@igc.org

INDEPENDENT PROGRESSIVE
POLITICS NETWORK
P.O. Box 170610
Brooklyn, NY 11217
http://www.ippn.org
E-mail: indpol@igc.apc.org

INDUSTRIAL WORKER
103 West Michigan Avenue
Ypsilanti, MI 48197-5438
Ph: 313/483-3548
Fax: 313/483-4050
http://parsons.iww.org/~iw/index_text.
html
E-mail: iww@igc.apc.org

INFACT
Campaign for Corporate Accountability
256 Hanover Street
Boston, MA 02113
Ph: 617/742-4583
Fax: 617/367-0191
http://www.infact.org
E-mail: infact@igc.apc.org

INSTITUTE FOR ALTERNATIVE
JOURNALISM
77 Federal Street
San Francisco, CA 94107
Ph: 415/284-1420
Fax: 415/284-1414
http://www.mediademocracy.org
E-mail: alternet@alternet.org

INSTITUTE FOR PUBLIC
ACCURACY
65 Ninth Street, Suite 3
San Francisco, CA 94103
Ph: 415/552-5378
Fax: 415/552-6787
E-mail: institute@igc.org

INTERNATIONAL ACTION CENTER
39 West 14th Street, Room 206
New York, NY 10011
Ph: 212/633-6646
Fax: 212/633-2889
http://www.iac.org
E-mail: iacinter@org

INTERNATIONAL CONSORTIUM
OF INVESTIGATIVE JOURNALISTS
Center for Public Integrity
1634 I Street, NW, Suite 902
Washington, DC 20006
Ph: 202/783-3900
Fax: 202/783-3906
http://www.publicintegrity.org/

INVESTIGATIVE JOURNALISM
PROJECT
Fund for Constitutional Government
122 Maryland Avenue, NE, Suite 300
Washington, DC 20002
Ph: 202/546-3732
Fax: 202/543-3156

THE INVESTIGATIVE REPORTING
FUND (FIRE)
2 Wall Street, Suite 203
Asheville, NC 28801-2710
Ph: 704/259-9179
Fax: 704/251-1311
http://www.main.nc.us/fire
E-mail: calvina@main.nc.us

Dedicated to research and reporting on
critical issues affecting North Carolina

JUST THINK FOUNDATION
80 Liberty Ship Way, Suite 1
Sausalito, CA 94965
Ph: 415/289-0122
Fax: 415/289-0123
http://www.justthink.org
E-mail: think@justthink.org

KLANWATCH AND MILITIA
TASK FORCE
Southern Poverty Law Center
400 Washington Avenue
Montgomery, AL 36104
Ph: 334/264-0286
Fax: 334/264-8891
http://www.splcenter.org/splc.html

LEONARD PELTIER DEFENSE
COMMITTEE
P.O. Box 583
Lawrence, KS 66044
Ph: 785/842-5774
Fax: 785/842-5796
http://www.unicom.net/Peltier/index.
html
E-mail: lpdc@idir.net

LEONARD PELTIER
FREEDOM CAMPAIGN
Box 522
Charlottesville, VA 22902
Ph: 804/823-2845

MEDIA ACCESS PROJECT
1707 L Street, NW
Washington, DC 20036
Ph: 202/232-4300
Fax: 202/223-5302
http://www.mediaaccess.org/

MEDIA ACTION RESEARCH
CENTER (MARC)
475 Riverside Drive, #1948
New York, NY 10115
Ph: 212/870-3802
Fax: 212/870-2171

MEDIA ALLIANCE
814 Mission Street, Suite 205
San Francisco, CA 94103
Ph: 415/546-6334
Fax: 415/546-6218
http://www.media-alliance.org
E-mail: ma@igc.org

MEDIA COALITION/AMERICANS
FOR CONSTITUTIONAL FREEDOM
139 Fulton Street, Suite 302
New York, NY 10038
Ph: 212/587-4026
Fax: 212/587-2436
E-mail: mediacoalition@sprintmail.com

THE MEDIA CONSORTIUM
2200 Wilson Boulevard, Suite 102-231
Arlington, VA 22201
Ph: 800/737-1812
Fax: 703/920-1802

THE MEDIA & DEMOCRACY
INSTITUTE
77 Federal Street
San Francisco, CA 94107
Ph: 415/284-1420
Fax: 415/284-1414
http://www.alternet.org/an/Congress.
html
E-mail: congress@igc.org

THE MEDIA EDUCATION
FOUNDATION
26 Center Street
Northampton, MA 01060
Ph: 800/897-0089 or 413/584-8500
Fax: 800/659-6882 or 413/586-8398
http://www.igc.apc.org/mef/
E-mail: mediaed@igc.apc.org

THE MEDIA INSTITUTE
1000 Potomac Street, NW, Suite 301
Washington, DC 20007
Ph: 202/298-7512
Fax: 202/337-7092
http://www.mediainst.org
E-mail: tmi@clark.net

MEDIA NETWORK/ALTERNATIVE
MEDIA INFORMATION CENTER
39 West 14th Street, #403
New York, NY 10011
Ph: 212/929-2663
Fax: 212/929-2732

MEDIA WATCH
P.O. Box 618
Santa Cruz, CA 95061-0618
Ph: 408/423-6355
Fax: 408/423-6355
http://www.mediawatch.com
E-mail: mwatch@cruzio.com

MEDIAWORKS COMMUNITY
GRAPHIC COMMUNICATION
17 Buitenkant Street
6th Floor Norlen House
Cape Town 8001
South Africa
Ph: 011-27-21-461-0368/9
Fax: 011-27-21-461-0385
E-mail: mediawks@iafrica.com

MEIKLEJOHN CIVIL LIBERTIES
INSTITUTE
P.O. Box 673
Berkeley, CA 94701
Ph: 888/848-0599
Fax: 510/848-6008
E-mail: mcli@igc.org

NATIONAL ASIAN AMERICAN
TELECOMMUNICATION
ASSOCIATION
346 9th Street, 2nd Floor
San Francisco, CA 94103
Ph: 415/863-0814
Fax: 415/863-7428
http://www.naatanet.org

NATIONAL ASSOCIATION OF
BLACK JOURNALISTS
University of Maryland
3100 Taliaferro Hall
College Park, MD 20742
Ph: 301/405-8500
Fax: 301/405-8555
http://www.nabj.org
E-mail: nabj@nabj.org

NATIONAL ASSOCIATION
OF HISPANIC JOURNALISTS
National Press Building, Suite 1193
Washington, DC 20045
Ph: 202/662-7145
Fax: 202/662-7144
http://www.nahj.org
E-mail: liz@nahj.org

NATIONAL ASSOCIATION OF
MINORITY MEDIA EXECUTIVES
5746 Union Mill Road, Box 310
Clifton, VA 20124
Ph: 703/830-4743

NATIONAL ASSOCIATION OF
RADIO TALK SHOW HOSTS
566 Commonwealth Avenue, Suite 601
Boston, MA 02115
Ph: 617/437-9757
Fax: 617/437-0797
http://www.talkshowhosts.com

NATIONAL CAMPAIGN FOR FREE-
DOM OF EXPRESSION
918 F Street, NW, #609
Washington, DC 20004
Ph: 202/393-2787
Fax: 202/347-7376
http://www.artswire.org/~ncfe/
E-mail: ncfe@artswire.org

NATIONAL COALITION AGAINST
CENSORSHIP
275 7th Avenue, 20th Floor
New York, NY 10001
Ph: 212/807-6222
Fax: 212/807-6245
http://www.ncac.org
E-mail: ncac@netcom.com

NATIONAL COMMITTEE AGAINST
REPRESSIVE LEGISLATION
3321 12th Street, NE
Washington, DC 20017
Ph: 202/529-4225
Fax: 202/526-4611
E-mail: ncarl@aol.com

NATIONAL CONFERENCE
OF EDITORIAL WRITERS
6223 Executive Boulevard
Rockville, MD 20852
Ph: 301/984-3015

NATIONAL EDUCATIONAL
MEDIA NETWORK
655 13th Street, Suite 1
Oakland, CA 94612
Ph: 510/465-6885
Fax: 510/465-2835
http://www.nemn.org
E-mail: nemn@nemn.org

NATIONAL FORUM ON
INFORMATION LITERACY
American Library Association
50 East Huron Street
Chicago, IL 60611

NATIONAL LESBIAN & GAY
JOURNALISTS ASSOCIATION
1718 M Street, NW, #245
Washington, DC 20036
Ph: 202/588-9888
Fax: 202/588-1818
E-mail: nlgja@aol.com

NATIONAL TELEMEDIA COUNCIL
120 East Wilson Street
Madison, WI 53703
Ph: 608/257-7712
Fax: 608/257-7714
http://danenet.wicip.org./ntc
E-mail: ntc@danenet.wicip.org

NATIONAL WOMEN'S HEALTH
NETWORK
1325 G Street, NW
Washington, DC 20005
Ph: 202/347-1140

NATIONAL WRITERS UNION
113 University Place
New York, NY 10003
Ph: 212/254-0279
Fax: 212/254-0673
http://www.nwu.org/nwu/
E-mail: nwu@nwu.org

NEW MEXICO MEDIA LITERACY
PROJECT
6400 Wyoming Boulevard, NE
Albuquerque, NM 87109
Ph: 505/828-3129
Fax: 505/828-3320
http://www.nmmlp.org

THE NEWSPAPER GUILD
8611 Second Avenue
Silver Spring, MD 20910
Ph: 301/585-2990
Fax: 301/585-0668
http://www.newsguild.org/

NEWSWATCH CANADA
School of Communication
Simon Fraser University
8888 University Drive
Burnaby, BC V5A 1S6
Canada
Ph: 604/291-4905
Fax: 604/291-4024
http://newswatch.cprost.sfu.ca/
newswatch
E-mail: censored@sfu.ca

NICAR: NATIONAL INSTITUTE
FOR COMPUTER-ASSISTED
REPORTING
138 Neff Annex
University of Missouri
Columbia, MO 65211
Ph: 573/882-2042
Fax: 573/882-5431
http://www.nicar.org
E-mail: ourire@muccmail.missouri.edu

ORGANIZATION OF
NEWS OMBUDSMEN
c/o Art Nauman, *Sacramento Bee*
P.O. Box 15779
Sacramento, CA 95852
Ph: 916/442-8050
http://www.infi.net/ono/

THE PAUL ROBESON FUND
FOR INDEPENDENT MEDIA
Paul Robeson Foundation
666 Broadway, #500
New York, NY 10012
Ph: 212/302-8477

PEACE AND FREEDOM
Women's International League for
Peace and Freedom
1213 Race Street
Philadelphia, PA 19107
Ph: 215/563-7110

POLITICAL RESEARCH
ASSOCIATES
120 Beacon Street, Suite 202
Somerville, MA 02143-4304
Ph: 617/661-9313
Fax: 617/661-0059
http://www.publiceye.org/pra/
E-mail: publiceye@igc.apc.org

PROGRESSIVE MEDIA PROJECT
409 East Main Street
Madison, WI 53703
Ph: 608/257-4626
Fax: 608/257-3373
http://www.progressive.org/media
project.htm
E-mail: pmproj@itis.com

PROJECT CENSORED
Sociology Department
Sonoma State University
1801 East Cotati Avenue
Rohnert Park, CA 94928-3609
Ph: 707/664-2500
Fax: 707/664-2108
http://www.sonoma.edu/ProjectCensored
E-mail: project.censored@sonoma.edu

PROJECT ON GOVERNMENT
OVERSIGHT
1900 L Street NW, Suite 314
Washington, DC 20036
Ph: 202/466-5539
Fax: 202/466-5596
http://www.mnsinc.com/pogo/
E-mail: mpogo@pogo.org or
defense@pogo.org

PUBLIC MEDIA CENTER
446 Green Street
San Francisco, CA 94133
Ph: 415/434-1403
Fax: 415/986-6779

REPORTER'S COMMITTEE FOR
FREEDOM OF THE PRESS
1101 Wilson Boulevard, Suite 1910
Arlington, VA 22209
Ph: 703/807-2100
Fax: 703/807-2109

ROCKY MOUNTAIN MEDIA WATCH
P.O. Box 18858
Denver, CO 80218
Ph: 303/832-7558
Fax: 303/832-7558
http://www.imagepage.com/rmmw/index
.html

SOCIETY OF ENVIRONMENTAL
JOURNALISTS
P.O. Box 27280
Philadelphia, PA 19118-0280
Ph: 215/836-9970
Fax: 215/836-9972
http://www.sej.org
E-mail: SEJoffice@aol.com

SOUTHWEST ALTERNATIVE
MEDIA PROJECT
1519 West Main Street
Houston, TX 77006
Ph: 713/522-8592
Fax: 713/522-0953
http://www.swamp.org
E-mail: cyberia@swamp.org

THE TELEVISION PROJECT
2311 Kimball Place
Silver Springs, MD 20910
Ph: 301/588-4001
Fax: 301/588-4001
http://www.tvp.org
E-mail: mapluhar@tvp.org

THE THOMAS JEFFERSON CENTER
FOR THE PROTECTION OF FREE
EXPRESSION
400 Peter Jefferson Place
Charlottesville, VA 22901-8691
Ph: 804/295-4784
Fax: 804/296-3621

TREATMENT REVIEW
AIDS Treatment Data Network
611 Broadway, Suite. 613
New York, NY 10012-2809
Ph: 800/734-7104
Fax: 212/260-8869
http://www.aidsnyc.org/network
E-mail: atdn@aidnyc.org

WE INTERRUPT THIS MESSAGE
965 Mission Street, Suite 220
San Francisco, CA 94103
Ph: 415/537-9437
Fax: 415/537-9439

WOMEN FOR MUTUAL SECURITY
Women's Peace Movement and MEDIA
5110 West Penfield Road
Columbia, MD 21045
Ph: 410/730-7483
Fax: 410/964-9248
http://www.iacenter.org/wms/
E-mail: foerstel@aol.com

WOMEN IN COMMUNICATIONS
10605 Judicial Drive, Suite A-4
Fairfax, VA 22030
Ph: 703/359-9000
Fax: 703/359-0603

WOMEN'S INSTITUTE FOR
FREEDOM OF THE PRESS
3306 Ross Place, NW
Washington, DC 20008-3332
Ph: 202/966-7783
Fax: 202/966-7783
http://www.igc.org/wifp/
E-mail: wifponline@igc.apc.org

WORLD PRESS FREEDOM
COMMITTEE
c/o The Newspaper Center
11600 Sunrise Valley Drive
Reston, VA 22091
Ph: 703/648-1000
Fax: 703/620-4557

YOUTH ACTION FORUM
Youth Action Network
67 Richmond Street, West, Suite 410
Toronto, Ontario MS4 125
Canada
Ph: 800/718-LINK or 416/368-2277
Fax: 416/368-8354
E-mail: ak027@torfres.net

WIRE SERVICES/ELECTRONIC NEWS SERVICES

ALTERNET
Alternative News Network
77 Federal Street
San Francisco, CA 94107
Ph: 415/284-1420
Fax: 415/284-1414
http://www.alternet.org

AMERICAN NEWS SERVICE
289 Fox Farm Road
Brattleboro, VT 05301
Ph: 800/654-6397
Fax: 802/254-1227
http://www.americannews.com

ASSOCIATED PRESS
50 Rockerfeller Plaza
New York, NY 10020

ASSOCIATED PRESS RADIO NET-
WORK
1825 K Street, NW, Suite 710
Washington, DC 20006

COX ENTERPRISES, INC.
P.O. Box 105357
Atlanta, GA 30348
Ph: 404/843-5123

GANNETT NEWS SERVICE
1000 Wilson Boulevard
Arlington, VA 22229
Ph: 703/276-5898
Fax: 703/558-3902

INTER PRESS SERVICE
Global Information Network
1293 National Press Building
Washington, DC 20045
Fax: 202/662-7164
E-mail: ipsgin@igc.apc.org

KNIGHT-RIDDER NEWS SERVICE
790 National Press Building
Washington, DC 20045
Ph: 202/383-6080

LATIN AMERICA DATA BASE
Latin America Institute
University of New Mexico
801 Yale Boulevard, NE
Albuquerque, NM 87131-1016
Ph: 800/472-0888 or 505/277-6839
Fax: 505/277-5989
http://ladb.unm.edu/
E-mail: info@ladb.unm.edu

PACIFIC NEWS SERVICE
450 Mission Street, Room 506
San Francisco, CA 94105
Ph: 415/243-4364
http://www.pacific.news
E-mail: pacificnews@pacificnews.org

PEACENET, LABORNET, ECONET,
CONFLICTNET, WOMEN NET
Institute for Global Communications
Presidio Building 1012
P.O. Box 29904
San Francisco, CA 94129
Ph: 415/561-6100
Fax: 415/561-6101
http://www.igc.org
E-mail: mlockwood@igc.org

PEOPLE'S NEWS AGENCY
7627 16th Street, NW
P.O. Box 56466
Washington, DC 20040
Ph: 202/829-2278
Fax: 202/829-0462
E-mail: proutwdc@prout.org

REUTERS INFORMATION
SERVICES
1700 Broadway
New York, NY 10019
Ph: 212/603-3300

UNITED PRESS INTERNATIONAL
1510 H Street
Washington, DC 20005
Ph: 202/898-8000

**ALTERNATIVE/
INDEPENDENT
BROADCAST/FILM,
VIDEO PRODUCERS,
AND ORGANIZATIONS**

ALTERNATIVE RADIO
2129 Mapleton
Boulder, CO 80304
Ph: 303/444-8788
Fax: 303/546-0592

ALTERNATIVE VIEWS
P.O. Box 7295
Austin, TX 78713
Ph: 512/918-3386

BLACK PLANET PRODUCTIONS/
NOT CHANNEL ZERO
P.O. Box 435
Cooper Station
New York, NY 10003-0435
Ph: 212/886-3701
Fax: 212/420-8223

CALIFORNIA NEWSREEL
149 9th Street, Suite 420
San Francisco, CA 94103
Ph: 415/612-6196
Fax: 415/621-6522
http://www.newsreel.org
E-mail: Newsreel@ix.netcom.com

COMMON GROUND
Stanley Foundation
216 Sycamore Street, Suite 500
Muscatine, IA 52761
Ph: 319/264-1500
http://www.commonground.org

CUBA VA VIDEO/FILM PROJECT
12 Liberty Street
San Francisco, CA 94110
Ph: 415/282-1812
Fax: 415/282-1798

DEEP DISH TV
339 Lafayette Street
New York, NY 10012
Ph: 212/473-8933
http://www.igc.org/deepdish
E-mail: deepdish@igc.org

DIVA-TV
(Damned Interfering Video Activists)
12 Wooster Street
New York, NY 10013
http://www.actupny.org/diva/
DIVA-TV.html
E-mail: divatv@aidsnyc.org

EARTH COMMUNICATIONS
(Radio for Peace International)
SJO 577, P.O. Box 025216
Miami, FL 33102-5216
Ph: 011-506-249-1821 (Costa Rica)
Fax: 011-506-249-1095 (Costa Rica)
E-mail: rfpicr@sol.racsa.co.cr

FIRE: FEMINIST INTERNATIONAL
RADIO ENDEAVOR
c/o Radio for Peace International
P.O. Box 88
Santa Ana, Costa Rica
Ph: 011-506-249-1821
Fax: 011-506-249-1929
http://www.wings.org

FREE RADIO BERKELEY/FREE
COMMUNICATIONS COALITION
1442A Walnut Street, #406
Berkeley, CA 94709
Ph: 510/464-3041
http://www.freeradio.org
E-mail: frbspd@crl.com

FREE SPEECH TV (FSTV)
P.O. Box 6060
Boulder, CO 80306
Ph: 303/442-8445 or 303/442-5693
Fax: 303/442-6472
http://www.freespeech.org
E-mail: fstv@fstv.org

GLOBALVISION
1600 Broadway, Suite 700
New York, NY 10019
Ph: 212/246-0202
Fax: 212/246-2677
http://www.globalvision.org/globalvision
E-mail: roc@igc.apc.org

HIGHTOWER RADIO
P.O. Box 13516
Austin, TX 78711
Ph: 512/477-5588
Fax: 512/478-8536
http://essential.org/hightower/
E-mail: hightower@essential.org

THE INDEPENDENT
Association of Independent Video
and Film (AIVF)
625 Broadway, 9th Floor
New York, NY 10012
Ph: 212/473-3400
Fax: 212/677-8732

INDEPENDENT TELEVISION
SERVICE
51 Federal Street, Suite 401
San Francisco, CA 94107
Ph: 415/356-8383
Fax: 415/356-8391
http://www.itvs.org
E-mail: itvs@itvs.org

INTERNATIONAL MEDIA
PROJECT/NATIONAL RADIO
PROJECT/"MAKING CONTACT"
830 Los Trancos Road
Portola Valley, CA 94028
Ph: 650/851-7256
Fax: 650/851-0731
http://www.igc.org/makingcontact
E-mail: contact@igc.org

JUDITH HELFAND PRODUCTIONS
125 Riverside Drive, 10B
New York, NY 10024
Ph: 212/875-0456
Fax: 212/501-0889
http://www.itvs.org/programs/babyg
E-mail: jhp@igc.org

L.A. ALTERNATIVE MEDIA
NETWORK
8124 West 3rd Street, #208
Los Angeles, CA 90048
Ph: 213/655-5720
Fax: 310/458-6566
http://home.labridge.com/~laamn/
E-mail: sekler@labridge.com

LABOR BEAT
37 South Ashland Avenue
Chicago, IL 60607
Ph: 312/226-3330
http://shogan.wwa.com/~bgfolder.lb
E-mail: lduncan@igc.apc.org

MIX: NEW YORK LESBIAN &
GAY EXPERIMENTAL FILM/
VIDEO FESTIVAL
341 Lafayette Street, #169
New York, NY 10012
Ph: 212/501-2309
Fax: 212/571-5155
http://www.echonyc.com/~mix/home.
html
E-mail: mix@echonyc.com

P.O.V. (Point Of View)
220 West 19th Street, 11th Floor
New York, NY 10011-4035
Ph: 212/989-8121
Fax: 212/989-8230

PACIFICA RADIO ARCHIVES
3729 Cahuenga Boulevard West
North Hollywood, CA 91604
Ph: 818/506-1077
Fax: 818/506-1085
http://www.ppspacifica.org
E-mail: ppspacific@igc.apc.org

PAPER TIGER TV
339 Lafayette Street
New York, NY 10012
Ph: 212/420-9045
Fax: 212/420-8223
http://www.papertiger.org
E-mail: tigertv@bway.net

PEOPLE'S VIDEO NETWORK
2489 Mission Street, #28
San Francisco, CA 94110
Ph: 415/821-6545 or 415/821-7575
Fax: 415/821-5782
E-mail: npcsf@igc.apc.org

PEOPLE'S VIDEO NETWORK
39 West 14th Street
New York, NY 10071
Ph: 212/633-6646
Fax: 212/633-2889
http://www.peoplesvideo.org

RADIO FOR PEACE
INTERNATIONAL
P.O. Box 88
Santa Ana, Costa Rica
Ph: 011-506-249-1821
Fax: 011-506-249-1095
http://www.clark.net/pub/cwilkins/rfpi
E-mail: rfpicr@sol.racsa.co.cr

RADIO NATION
72 Fifth Avenue
New York, NY 10011
Ph: 212/242-8400
Fax: 212/675-3499
E-mail: radio@thenation.com

THE RADIO PROJECT
818 Elmwood Avenue, #4
Rochester, NY 14620-2918
Ph: 716/256-2370
Fax: 716/256-2370
E-mail: tom.lane@lol.shareworld.com

RISE & SHINE PRODUCTIONS
Rheedlen Center for Children
300 West 43rd Street
New York, NY 10036
Ph: 212/265-5909

THE SQUEALER
c/o Squeaky Wheel
175 Elmwood Avenue
Buffalo, NY 14201-1419
Ph: 716/884-7172

TAOS TALKING PICTURES
TTP Festival/Media Literacy Project
216 M North Pueblo Road, #216
Taos, NM 87571
Ph: 505/751-0637
Fax: 505/751-7385
http://www.taosnet.com/ttpix/
E-mail: ttpix@taosnet.com

TELEMUNDO NETWORK
2470 West 8th Avenue
Hialea, FL 33010
Ph: 305/889-6907
Fax: 305/882-8700

THIRD WORLD NEWSREEL
Camera News Inc.
335 West 38th Street, 5th Floor
New York, NY 10018
Ph: 212/947-9277
Fax: 212/594-6417

TV-FREE AMERICA
1611 Connecticut Avenue, NW
Washington, DC 20009
Ph: 202/887-0436
Fax: 202/518-5560
http://essential.org/orgs/tvfa
E-mail: tvfa@essential.org

VIDEO DATABANK
112 South Michigan Avenue, 3rd Floor
Chicago, IL 60603
Ph: 312/345-3550
Fax: 312/541-8073

THE VIDEO PROJECT: FILMS
AND VIDEOS FOR A SAFE AND
SUSTAINABLE WORLD
200 Estates Drive
Ben Lomond, CA 95005
Ph: 408/336-0160 or 800/PLANET
Fax: 408/336-2168
http://www.videoproject.org
E-mail: videoproject@igc.org

THE WITNESS
333 Seventh Avenue, 13th Floor
New York, NY 10001
http://www.witness.org
E-mail: witness@lchr.org

WINGS: WOMEN'S
INTERNATIONAL NEWS
GATHERING SERVICE
"Raising Voices Through Radio
Worldwide"
P.O. Box 332200
Austin, TX 78764
Ph: 800/798-9703
http://www.wings.org
E-mail: wings@igc.apc.org

ZEITGEIST FILMS, LTD.
247 Centre Street, 2nd Floor
New York, NY 10013
Ph: 212/274-1989
Fax: 212/274-1644
http://www.zeitgeistfilm.com

NATIONAL BROADCAST AND CABLE MEDIA AND FCC

ABC
47 West 66th Street
New York, NY 10023
Ph: 212/456-7777

C-SPAN (1 or 2)
400 North Capitol Street, NW,
Suite 650
Washington, DC 20001
Ph: 202/737-3220
Fax: 202/737-3323

CBS
524 West 57th Street
New York, NY 10019
Ph: 212/975-4321

CHICAGO TRIBUNE
435 North Michigan Avenue
Chicago, IL 60611
Ph: 312/222-3232

CNN
One CNN Center
Box 105366
Atlanta, GA 30348
Ph: 404/827-1500

COPLEY NEWS SERVICE
1100 National Press Building
Washington, DC 20045
Ph: 202/737-6960

ESPN
ESPN Plaza
935 Middle Street
Bristol, CT 06010
Ph: 860/585-2000

FEDERAL COMMUNICATIONS
COMMISSION
1919 M Street, NW
Washington, DC 20554
Ph: 202/418-0200

FOX BROADCASTING
P.O. Box 900
Beverly Hills, CA 90213
Ph: 310/277-2211

THE LOS ANGELES TIMES
Times-Mirror Square
Los Angeles, CA 90053
Ph: 800/528-4637

MTV
1515 Broadway, 24th Floor
New York, NY 10036
Ph: 212/258-8712

NATIONAL PUBLIC RADIO
635 Massachusetts Avenue, NW
Washington, DC 20001
Ph: 202/414-2000
Fax: 202/414-3329

NBC
30 Rockerfeller Plaza
New York, NY 10112
Ph: 212/664-4444

THE NEW YORK TIMES
229 West 43rd Street
New York, NY 10036
Ph: 212/556-1234

PACIFICA NETWORK NEWS/
PACIFICA NATIONAL
PROGRAMMING
"DEMOCRACY NOW"
2390 Champlain Street, NW
Washington, DC 20009
Ph: 202/588-0988
Fax: 202/588-0561
http://www.pacifica.org

PBS
1320 Braddock Place
Alexandra, VA 22314
Ph: 703/739-5000
Fax: 703/739-5295

UNITED BROADCASTING
P.O. Box 13516
Austin, TX 78711
Ph: 512/477-5588
Fax: 512/478-8536

THE WALL STREET JOURNAL
200 Liberty Street
New York, NY 10281

WASHINGTON POST
1150 15th Street, NW
Washington, DC 20071
Ph: 202/334-6000

APPENDIX C

The Project Censored Guide to On-line Resources

Compiled by Jeffrey A. Fillmore, Project Censored net.geek

The 1998 Guide to On-line Resources highlights Web sites associated with mass media research and criticism, alternative press associations, and organizations dedicated to maintaining a free exchange of information on the Internet. Additionally, we have included several Web sites regarding the proliferation of weapons as related to the top *Censored* news story of 1997.

All of the following sites are conveniently linked at:

THE PROJECT CENSORED WEB SITE

http://www.sonoma.edu/ProjectCensored/
E-mail: project.censored@sonoma.edu
Project Censored net.geek: fillmore@sonoma.edu

For inclusion in next year's Guide to On-line Resources or to be linked from the Project Censored Web site send e-mail to Project Censored at: project.censored@sonoma.edu

MEDIA WATCH AND THE ALTERNATIVE PRESS

ALTERNATIVE PRESS CENTER
http://www.igc.apc.org/altpress/
E-mail: altpress@igc.apc.org

"The Alternative Press Center (APC) is a non-profit collective dedicated to providing access to and increasing public awareness of the alternative press. Founded in 1969, it remains one of the oldest self-sustaining alternative media institutions in the United States... For more than a quarter of a century, the Alternative Press Index has been recognized as a leading guide to the alternative press in the United States and around the world."

AMERICAN CIVIL LIBERTIES UNION
http://www.aclu.org/
E-mail: aclu@aclu.org

"The American Civil Liberties Union is the nation's foremost advocate of individual rights—litigating, legislating, and educating the public on a broad array of issues affecting individual freedom in the United States."

THE CENTER FOR INVESTIGATIVE REPORTING (CIR)
http://www.muckraker.org/
E-mail: cir@igc.org

"CIR is the only non-profit, tax-exempt news organization in the United States established specifically to do investigative journalism and is supported by reporting fees, foundation grants, and individual donations... The Center was founded on the premise that if democracy is to succeed, the people must be informed and power made accountable."

THE CENTER FOR MEDIA EDUCATION
http://tap.epn.org/cme/
E-mail: cme@cme.org

"The Center for Media Education (CME) is a national non-profit organization dedicated to improving the quality of the electronic media. CME fosters telecommunications policy making in the public interest through its research, advocacy, public education, and press activities."

FAIR (Fairness and Accuracy In Reporting)
http://www.igc.org/fair/
E-mail: fair@fair.org

"FAIR (Fairness & Accuracy In Reporting) is the national media watch group offering well-documented criticism in an effort to correct media bias and imbalance. FAIR focuses public awareness on the narrow corporate ownership of the press, the media's allegiance to official agendas, and their insensitivity to women, labor, minorities, and other public interest constituencies. FAIR seeks to invigorate the First Amendment by advocating for greater media pluralism and the inclusion of public interest voices in national debates."

THE INSTITUTE FOR ALTERNATIVE JOURNALISM (IAJ)
http://www.igc.apc.org/an/
E-mail: alternet@mediademocracy.org

"IAJ is a non-profit organization dedicated to strengthening and supporting independent and alternative journalism, and to improving the public's access to independent information sources."

THE LOS ANGELES ALTERNATIVE MEDIA NETWORK
http://home.labridge.com/~laamn/index.html
E-mail: sekler@labridge.com

"The Los Angeles Alternative Media Network (LAAMN) is a network of journalists in print, radio, video, TV, film, as well as Internet publishers, photographers, musicians, artists, and media watch activists who have come together to develop a strong presence for the independent, alternative media in Los Angeles. Through cross-collaboration, we intend to reach a wide audience with a progressive message and report on the developing social, political, and cultural movements of the time, providing a 'voice for the voiceless' throughout the Southland. We are culturally inclusive, opposed to racism, sexism, and homophobia, and function democratically as a network of working groups around various projects. We stand for tolerance, justice, equality, and human rights as opposed to corporate-controlled media which stand for profit and keeping the majority of people ignorant of political, economic and social issues which impact them."

MEDIA ALLIANCE
http://www.media-alliance.org/
E-mail: mainfo@igc.org

"Media Alliance is a non-profit organization which serves media professionals, other non-profit organizations and the general public in the San Francisco Bay Area. For twenty years, Media Alliance has worked to promote fairness and accuracy in the media in the Bay Area and nationwide. Our 3,500 members include professional journalists, freelance writers, activists, students, and other interested individuals."

MEDIA AWARENESS NETWORK
http://www.schoolnet.ca/medianet/
E-mail: info@media-awareness.ca

"The Media Awareness Network is a Canadian non-profit organization dedicated to media education and media issues affecting children and youth. The Network hosts a World Wide Web site in English and French—with 'one stop shopping' for educators, students, community leaders, and others interested in knowing more about the media and its influences."

THE MEDIA AND DEMOCRACY CONGRESS
http://www.igc.apc.org/an/Congress.html
E-mail: congress@mediademocracy.org

"On October 16-19, 1997, in the media capital of the world, New York City, over 1,100 people convened for the second Media and Democracy Congress. In order to support public interest journalism and the independent media, we continue to call on all concerned journalists, producers, activists, critics, and teachers to insist that the media system be held accountable in its democratic role."

NEWSWATCH CANADA
http://edwina.cprost.sfu.ca/newswatch/
E-mail: censored@sfu.ca

"NewsWatch Canada (formerly Project Censored Canada) undertakes independent research on the diversity and thoroughness of news coverage in Canada's media, with a focus on identifying blind spots and double standards. It began as a collaborative project of the communication departments at Simon Fraser University and the University of Windsor and the Canadian Association of Journalists."

THE PROGRESSIVE MEDIA PROJECT
http://www.progressive.org/mediaproj.htm
E-mail: project@progressive.org

"The Progressive Media Project was launched in January 1993 to give voice to those in diverse communities who have been shut out of the mainstream media. We solicit and edit op-ed articles from a wide cross-section of journalists, academics, and grass-roots activists. We distribute to papers throughout the nation, and our work has been published in a host of papers including the *Los Angeles Times*, *Newsday*, the *Chicago Tribune*, *The Miami Herald*, *The Christian Science Monitor*, the *Houston Chronicle*, the *Fort Worth Star-Telegram*, Cleveland's *Plain Dealer*, *The Pittsburgh Post-Gazette*, *The Kansas City Star*, the *Omaha World Herald*, *The Buffalo News*, *The Des Moines Register*, the *Milwaukee Sentinel*, the *Las Vegas Review Journal*, *The Sacramento Bee*, and many more."

INTERNET-RELATED RESOURCES

CENTER FOR DEMOCRACY AND TECHNOLOGY
http://www.cdt.org/
E-mail: info@cdt.org

"The Center For Democracy and Technology is a non-profit public interest organization based in Washington, DC. CDT works to develop and advocate public policies that advance Constitutional civil liberties and democratic values in new computer and communications technologies."

ELECTRONIC FRONTIER FOUNDATION
http://www.eff.org/
E-mail: ask@eff.org

"The Electronic Frontier Foundation works to ensure that the civil liberties guaranteed in the Constitution and the Bill of Rights are applied to new communications technologies. EFF is a respected voice for the rights of users of online technologies."

FREE SPEECH TV
http://www.freespeech.org/
E-mail: joey@freespeech.org

"Free Speech TV is a World Wide Web video broadcast hub, housing over 300 on-demand RealMedia files, with new programs posted daily."

INSTITUTE FOR GLOBAL
COMMUNICATIONS
http://www.igc.org/igc/
E-mail: support@igc.org

"Our Mission: To expand and inspire movements for peace, economic and social justice, human rights, and environmental sustainability around the world by providing and developing accessible computer networking tools."

VOTERS TELECOMMUNICATIONS
WATCH
http://www.vtw.org/
E-mail: vtw@vtw.org

"The Voters Telecommunications Watch (VTW) is a New York-based citizen-based Internet civil liberties group. We organize citizens in individual Congressional districts, lobby on state and Federal legislation, and occasionally raise money for a worthy cause."

THE INTERNATIONAL ARMS TRADE

THE ARMS SALES MONITORING
PROJECT
http://www.fas.org/asmp/
E-mail: llumpe@fas.org

"The Arms Sales Monitoring Project works for restraint in the global production and trade of weapons. Project staff produce a newsletter, the *Arms Sales Monitor*, which reports and analyzes U.S. government policies on conventional arms exports and weapons proliferation. The ASM Project works in alliance with other Washington, D.C. based groups concerned about U.S. and global arms trading through the Arms Transfers Working Group. The Project also works with the media to highlight the impact and true costs of U.S. and global arms sales."

CENTER FOR DEFENSE
INFORMATION
http://www.cdi.org/
E-mail: Info@cdi.org/

"Founded in 1972 as an independent monitor of the military, the Center for Defense Information is a private, non-governmental, research organization. Its directors and staff believe that strong social, economic, political, and military components and a healthy environment contribute equally to the nation's security... CDI's Conventional Arms Trade Project exists to inform the public, media, scholars, and government officials about the conventional arms trade. While much attention is paid to the proliferation of the so-called weapons of mass destruction, i.e., nuclear, biological, and chemical weapons, it is the ordinary conventional weapons, from AK-47s and M16s to landmines, tanks, fighter aircraft which are responsible for the vast majority of deaths and casualties in the world's conflicts."

THE BULLETIN OF THE ATOMIC SCIENTISTS ONLINE
http://www.bullatomsci.org/
E-mail: brendan@interaccess.com

The Bulletin of the Atomic Scientists is not a technical publication—it's the world's premier magazine on nuclear weapons and international affairs. Their Web site features a 'Nuclear FAQ,' five years' worth of articles on topics like weapons, the former Soviet republics, military spending, and the global arms trade; a history of our famous 'Doomsday Clock'; and much more."

FEDERATION OF AMERICAN SCIENTISTS-PROJECT ON GOVERNMENT SECRECY
http://www.fas.org/sgp/
E-mail: saftergood@igc.apc.org

"Through research, advocacy, and public education, the Project on Government Secrecy works to challenge excessive government secrecy and to promote public oversight. The Project supports journalists and fosters enhanced public awareness of secrecy issues through publication of the *Secrecy & Government Bulletin*. In the current year, the Project is working in particular towards a favorable resolution of the various secrecy reform initiatives and their successful implementation."

PROGRAM FOR ARMS CONTROL, DISARMAMENT, AND CONVERSION (PACDC)
http://cns.miis.edu/pacdc/
E-mail: pacdc@miis.edu

"PACDC's major activities and products include a World Wide Web site containing updated information on the acquisition and disposal of conventional armaments, published studies, and policy analysis, workshops and conferences, consultation to non-governmental organizations (NGOs), national governments and the United Nations, and advocating those policy solutions most likely to promote the reduction of violence through arms control and disarmament."

APPENDIX D

TOP 5 CENSORED REPRINTS

Compiled by Nicola Mazumdar, Catherine Hickinbotham, and Tricia Boreta

1 CENSORED

Clinton Administration Aggressively Promotes U.S. Arms Sales Worldwide

"COSTLY GIVEAWAYS"

By Lora Lumpe; *The Bulletin of Atomic Scientists*; October 1996

After World War II, the United States shipped a mountain of unwanted military equipment—armored vehicles, aircraft, naval vessels, and infantry weapons—to Europe and Asia. Some of this equipment, like the C-47 transport planes and M-2 "half-tracks" sent 40 years ago to contain Soviet influence, is still used by militaries in Latin America, Asia, and Africa.

Now the end of the Cold War has left the United States with another heap of excess equipment. Some unneeded weapons are being destroyed or transferred to civilian agencies, but most will end up in the hands of foreign militaries. Since 1990, the United States has transferred approximately $7 billion worth of military equipment, including 3,900 heavy tanks and 500 ground-attack jets, primarily to developing countries. Large quantities of small arms and light weapons have also been exported.

Giving away excess weapons is believed to be cheaper than destroying or storing them, and weapon transfers are seen as an easy way to gain favor. In 1990-94, 80 percent of all excess transfers were giveaways; in 1995, half were.

In 1990, 10 countries purchased surplus weapons or received weapons grants from the Defense Department. Five years later, that number had expanded to 60. Over the same period, the Pentagon offered to export $8.5 billion worth of military equipment at little or no charge. Although actual deliveries were only made public beginning in 1993, according to the Defense Department, from 1993 through 1995 it shipped items valued at $1.9 billion.

Some excess equipment is transferred to further specific policy goals, such as narcotics control, military cooperation, or encouraging participation in peacekeeping operations. However, surplus arms giveaways may exacerbate human rights problems and frustrate arms control. An individual transfer may appear benign, but in the aggregate these transfers raise concerns about fiscal responsibility, congressional oversight, weapons proliferation, and human rights.

Even older equipment, like M-60 tanks and F-4 aircraft purchased in the 1960s or 1970s, can be formidable if upgraded and modified. These weapons may seem dated to the U.S. armed services, but they often become the centerpiece of foreign militaries: A ship discarded by the U.S. Navy will become the flagship for Bahrain. Similarly, the hundreds of free tanks sent to Greece, Turkey, Egypt, and Morocco have given them large, modern tank armies they could not otherwise afford.

In addition, many other countries have large surplus arms holdings, and if they use U.S. export policies to justify similar behavior, the result could be an even greater flood of weapons transfers.

BUILDING DOWN

The United States has reduced force levels by nearly one-third since 1990. But even without these post-Cold War reductions, the massive buildup of the 1980s made it inevitable that excess arms would pile up.

Vast quantities of weapons have been retired during the past five years. The military has shed older equipment first, particularly that bought in the 1960s or earlier. But the services are now retiring large numbers of newer, more advanced weapons. Built in the 1970s and 1980s, these weapons were used by U.S. forces only a few years ago. Some combat equipment now being retired has served only half—or less—of its expected lifetime.

Each of the military services has wide discretion in deciding what is excess and how to dispose of it. With the approval of the Defense Department and Congress, they export unwanted arms through a variety of sales, grants, and leases.

THE ARMY. In the 1980s, the army's entire inventory of armored vehicles, helicopters, artillery, and logistics and communications gear was modernized. Now the army has declared more than 3,000 transport and attack helicopters and 6,000 battle tanks and armored personnel carriers as excess. Many have been exported, often at little or no cost to their recipients.

As a result of the Conventional Forces in Europe (CFE) Treaty, the number of U.S.-held tanks in Europe has decreased from 6,000 to 1,200. In 1990, the United States gave Egypt 700 M-60s (original cost: $1.3 million each); Egypt paid only transportation costs. Others were distributed to Bahrain, Brazil, Greece, Morocco, Oman, Portugal, Spain, Taiwan, Thailand, and Turkey.

By 1992 the army had 6,000 ongoing or proposed excess-equipment deals in the works. In September 1993, it held a tent sale, inviting potential customers from NATO, Egypt, Israel, Japan, Saudi Arabia, Singapore, South Korea, and Taiwan to spend five days browsing through weapons on offer. Ted Gandy, the deputy director of weapons development for Army Missile Command, hoped the bazaar would help the army unload $300 million worth of surplus missiles.

The army has also announced plans to offer foreign militaries 600 surplus AH-1 Cobra attack helicopters and UH-1 Huey utility helicopters.

THE NAVY. Ship strength peaked in 1987, just 31 vessels short of the Reagan Administration's goal of a 600-ship navy. By 1995, the fleet had been reduced to 373 ships; it is expected to stand at 330-346 vessels by 2001. The nearly 200 decommissioned ships include modern frigates, guided-missile destroyers, and amphibious assault ships.

Some of these ships will be "mothballed." Others will be cannibalized for spare parts or cut up for scrap. Yet others will be used in weapons tests—either as targets or as a platform on which to mount test weapons. A few, like the four Iowa-class battleships reactivated in the 1980s, will become museums.

But most will be sold, given away, or leased to foreign navies. Between 1990 and 1995, the navy transferred 39 frigates, five guided-missile destroyers, and 13 tank-landing ships. Several more guided-missile frigates have been leased or given away in 1996.

The navy also wants to unload some of its 300 carrier-based F-18A/B Hornet fighter jets so that it can procure newer F/A-18C/D and E/F planes. Spain bought 30 of these earlier planes last year.

THE AIR FORCE. The air force is shedding large numbers of planes in order to maintain and acquire more sophisticated strike and transport aircraft. It is retiring all FB-111 fighter-bombers and EF-111 Raven electronic warfare/jammer aircraft, most F-4 Phantom fighters, more than 100 A-10 attack aircraft, and hundreds of early model F-15 Eagles and F-16 Falcons.

These aircraft, designed to fight the Soviet Union in the 1980s, remain potent: The F-4 is one of the most widely used Western aircraft designs; 1,300 F-4s currently serve in nine air forces around the world. The F-111 Aardvark, which first flew during the Vietnam War, was used in the 1986 bombing raid on Tripoli, Libya. The F-15 and F-16 are still the backbone of the U.S. Air Force, performing both anti-air and ground-attack missions.

Over the past five years, the air force has sold or given away more than 900 planes, including 82 used F-16s. Now it wants to sell 300-400 early model Falcons to fund the procurement of 80-100 new F-16s. Possible buyers include the Czech Republic, Poland, Chile, and Argentina. In addition, Jordan will get 16 F-16s under a nearly no-cost lease, as a reward for making peace with Israel.

TRANSFER MECHANISMS

Most of the rules covering foreign sales of new weapons also apply to transfers of excess arms. Recipients are expected to use surplus arms only for internal security, "legitimate self-defense," or to participate in regional or collective military arrangements consistent with the U.N. Charter. The president must certify that arms shipped to a recipient "will strengthen the security of the United States and promote world peace." Similarly, eligibility is subject to certain provisions regarding human rights, terrorism, counter-narcotics, and third-party transfers. Some surplus arms transfers require notification of Congress, and a few require congressional approval.

There are four primary mechanisms under which surplus weapons are transferred to foreign nations:

CONVENTIONAL FORCES IN EUROPE TREATY. The CFE, which was signed in 1990 and took force in November 1992, limits the number of tanks, armored combat vehicles, artillery, attack helicopters, and fixed-wing combat aircraft based in the center of Europe.

By the end of 1994, parties to the treaty had destroyed more than 37,000 conventional weapons. But CFE also gave the United States and other NATO members—in particular, Germany, Italy, and the Netherlands—an opportunity to transfer military equipment from central Europe to other regions, and NATO members in southern and northern Europe have been the principal beneficiaries. Between 1991 and 1993, the United States shipped nearly 2,000 tanks, more than 600 armored personnel carriers, and 180 artillery pieces to Greece, Turkey, Spain, Portugal, and Norway, at no cost to the recipients.

EXCESS DEFENSE ARTICLES PROGRAM. The Pentagon disposes of most surplus weapons through the Excess Defense Articles (EDA) program, which was initiated in 1976. The quantity and value of EDA transfers have grown in recent years, and the number of countries authorized to receive EDA has expanded dramatically.

EDA may be defined as any weapons that—for whatever reason—the military services no longer want. When they are transferred, the services must estimate their value, using Defense Department guidelines that suggest "fair" prices ranging from 5 to 50 percent of original cost, depending on the equipment's age and condition. But surplus items are frequently underpriced.

A 1994 General Accounting Office (GAO) review of EDA pricing found that the air force undervalued most excess items by more than 30 percent. The study also found that the army priced excess trucks at 5 to 10 percent of their original acquisition value, regardless of condition. The GAO concluded that the values the services assigned to excess equipment were "generally unreliable."

In one sense, of course, these deeply discounted prices are irrelevant, because the weapons are usually offered for free on an "as is, where is" basis.

But the tendency to undervalue surplus equipment complicates any effort to determine the true value of these exports. Calculations based on acquisition costs tend to overstate the case, but the services' low-ball prices tend to understate it. Well over $500 million worth of military equipment (in original value) has actually been transferred in each of the past few years.

Militaries seeking excess defense articles must go through a process similar to that required to purchase new weapons under the U.S. foreign military sales program. The process begins when a government or eligible organization submits a request to the Defense Department. Depending on the type of weapons desired, the request is sent to one of the services or to the Defense Logistics Agency.

Section 502A of the Foreign Assistance Act directs that excess defense articles "be provided whenever possible rather than providing such articles by the procurement of new items." However, complaints from the weapons industry led Congress to amend the law in 1993 to require the president to "consider the effects of the transfer of the excess defense articles on the national technological and industrial base, particularly the extent, if any, to which the transfer reduces the opportunities of entities in the national technology and industrial base to sell new equipment to the country or countries to which the excess defense articles are transferred." The Defense Department now tries to avoid competing with U.S. companies that manufacture similar goods or services.

Next, the EDA coordinating committee evaluates the recipient's military requirements and its ability to effectively use the equipment, as well as the regional military balance and foreign policy considerations. Most committee members are Defense and State Department officials, but Commerce Department representatives were recently added to protect the U.S. arms industry's interests.

If the coordinating committee agrees to the transfer, the Pentagon's Defense Security Assistance Agency must formally notify Congress of the proposed export. Barring congressional opposition, the Defense Department can deliver most types of equipment 15 to 30 days after notification.

Transfers of naval vessels are handled differently. Congress must authorize any grant, lease, or sale of a ship that is less than 20 years old—but it usually approves these transfers without controversy.

The Foreign Assistance Act specifies which countries are eligible for aid and for what purposes. In 1986, Section 516 authorized gifts of both lethal and non-lethal equipment to fellow NATO members Greece, Italy, Portugal, Spain, and Turkey. But eligibility has steadily expanded. In 1988, "major non-NATO allies on the southern and southeastern flank of NATO" (Egypt and Israel) became eligible for free military equipment. In 1991, certain allies in the Persian Gulf War were added. Eligible states now include Bahrain, Egypt, Greece, Israel, Jordan, Morocco, Oman, Portugal, Senegal, and Turkey.

Because of their improved economies, Italy and Spain are no longer eligible for grants, although they can still purchase weapons at bargain-basement prices. Pakistan would be eligible if nuclear-weapons-related sanctions cutting off U.S. military aid were lifted.

The vast majority of grants are transferred under Section 516, but Congress and the executive branch have added several other categories of eligibility.

In 1989, Congress added Section 517, which allows weapons transfers for counter-narcotics purposes. These transfers are made to democracies with major drug-producing or drug-transit problems, whose armed forces "do not engage in a consistent pattern of gross violations of internationally recognized human rights." Colombia has been the prime beneficiary of this provision.

In 1990, Congress approved Section 518, authorizing the grant of small arms and non-lethal items to "friendly countries and to international organizations and private and voluntary organizations" trying to protect endangered species and conserve natural resources. This section has been used only once, when 12 Cessna Skymaster observation/light-attack aircraft were given to Botswana in 1993.

Also added in 1990, Section 519 is a catch-all that authorizes grants of non-lethal items to any country for which the administration has requested and justified foreign military financing in the same fiscal year. After Section 516, this is the most widely used grant mechanism. Argentina has been the big winner under this provision, but Bahrain, Bangladesh, Botswana, Ethiopia, Hungary, Oman, the Philippines, Romania, Tunisia, Uruguay, and Zimbabwe have also benefited from aircraft giveaways.

Section 520, added in 1994, permits transfers to regional and international organizations. Transfers to U.N. operations are supposed to be credited against unpaid U.N. dues, but no transfers have yet taken place under this authority.

EMERGENCY "DRAWDOWNS." The executive branch can also draw on Defense Department equipment, services, or training to help out in an emergency.

Under Section 506 of the Foreign Assistance Act, the president may transfer up to $150 million of defense articles for this purpose each year. The executive branch has used this provision on several occasions, often in conjunction with disaster relief. Only limited combat equipment has been transferred under this section.

Section 552 of the Foreign Assistance Act permits the transfer of equipment for peacekeeping operations. President Clinton used this provision to send pickup trucks to the Palestinian and Haitian police forces in March 1995.

Israel has received the most emergency military aid. In 1991, Congress created a special draw-down account to compensate Israel for the heightened threat to its security posed by Iraq's invasion of Kuwait. The legislation authorized the president to provide Israel with up to $775 million of U.S. military equipment from stocks based in Europe. Israel received 15 F-15s and 50 F-16s, 24 Apache attack helicopters, and 10 Blackhawk helicopters.

LEASES AND LOANS. The United States leases weapons if it might want them back, or if the recipient cannot afford to purchase them. In these deals, the lessee pays only the equivalent of depreciation, although it must pay the cost of restoration or replacement if the articles are damaged, lost, or destroyed. In cases of cooperative military research and development projects or joint training exercises, the lease is cost-free.

Leases and loans are carried out under the Arms Export Control Act, which requires the executive branch to notify Congress 30 days before entering into any agreement valued at $14 million or more. Leases cannot run longer than five years, but they may be renewed.

Although the government maintains the title on leased weapons, leasing has become a mechanism for transferring a good deal of equipment. According to the State Department, in 1995 the United States signed new lease agreements with 15 foreign militaries, the United Nations, and NATO, distributing military equipment valued at $366 million.

POLICY ISSUES

Large quantities of now-surplus military equipment—much of it modern and lethal—is cascading from the United States to countries in the developing world, without much debate about the giveaway policy or its long-term effects.

FISCAL RESPONSIBILITY. The end of the Cold War and concerns about the budget deficit have led to a reduction in more visible foreign military assistance. Surplus transfers have come to supplement, or in some cases even supplant, traditional forms of aid. Congressional "deficit hawks" have taken the scalpel to more visible forms of foreign aid, but giving away approximately $7 billion of surplus weapons has aroused scant opposition, in part because giveaways are viewed as cheaper than storing or destroying surplus arms.

Aside from the question of whether the United States gets a fair price for its older equipment, there is a more fundamental issue: The services and their allies in Congress appear to be giving away still-useful equipment just to justify their requests for new items. Much of the equipment now called "excess" is still serviceable; in fact, a lot of it was purchased or reconditioned in the 1980s.

For example, to make room for new ships that the Senate Armed Services Seapower Subcommittee wants, the navy is unloading active-duty vessels—destroyers, frigates, amphibious, and support ships. The navy also wants to sell five of its billion-dollar Ticonderoga-class cruisers to make room for new billion-dollar destroyers.

In a similar case, the air force, aircraft manufacturers, and some members of Congress argue for the production of the F-22 and Joint Strike fighters by citing the dangerous proliferation of advanced aircraft—including the F-15s, F-16s, and F/A-18s the air force and navy are unloading.

Any immediate savings gained by giving arms away (as opposed to destroying them) should be weighed against potential downstream costs. If these weapons contribute to the outbreak of warfare, or if they encourage surplus arms exports by other nations, they may end up costing American taxpayers a great deal. The Pentagon could end up spending far more than it has saved if it has to defend against contingencies enabled by surplus arms shipments. In the worst case, U.S. forces might actually be called on to intervene in a conflict fueled by U.S. weapons transfers.

A particularly dangerous initiative is the air force plan to sell old weapons to directly fund the procurement of new ones. In early 1994, the air force announced that it would buy 90 new F-16C/D aircraft with the proceeds of sales of some 360 older model F-16A/B fighter jets. U.S. Air Force Vice Chief of Staff Michael Carns said the scheme would give him "brand new war-fighting planes at no cost to the taxpayer." Lockheed Martin, which manufactures the F-16, is lobbying hard for the plan, which would give the company hundreds of millions of dollars in upgrade work on the older planes as well as orders for new ones.

The air force plan involves $5 billion worth of aircraft. There are precedents for such "off-budget" procurement, but none of this magnitude. In 1993 Congress allowed the army to use the $197 million it received for excess M-48 and M-60 tanks to upgrade M-1s, and it permitted $15.2 million from M-113 sales to be used to purchase Bradley Fighting Vehicles. In 1994, the House Armed Services Committee suggested that the navy sell excess Mk-46 torpedoes to offset the cost of the Mk-50 Advanced Light Weight Torpedo.

The potential downstream costs of this practice are considerable, something the government recognizes when another country is the seller: The U.S. government protests vociferously when other governments pursue similar policies. In 1991, the Western press expressed outrage at China's practice of buying new weapons with the proceeds of foreign sales. And U.S. government officials denounced a Russian plan in the early 1990s to finance arms industry conversion through arms sales. In both cases, U.S. officials criticized the creation of a dangerous and short-sighted bureaucratic interest in selling weapons abroad.

CONGRESSIONAL OVERSIGHT. Although it appears as if Congress oversees surplus weapons transfers, the reality is somewhat different. Because they are not required to vote on gifts, drawdowns, and leases—except in the case of ships—busy members pay little attention.

Only about 20 percent of the members of the House and Senate—those serving on the foreign affairs committees—may even be aware of surplus arms transfers. Further, the executive branch notifies Congress of proposed transfers, not actual deliveries. The GAO reported in 1994 that the "relevant Congressional committees do not know how many transfers were actually executed and what the total acquisition and current values of EDAs transferred to various recipients were."

REGIONAL ARMS RACES. The executive branch claims it considers the implications of surplus transfers carefully. For example, the transfer of M-60 tanks to Egypt in 1990 was conditioned on the promise that Egypt retire one older tank for each M-60 it received. The transfer thus resulted in only a qualitative, not quantitative, improvement.

In other cases, however, U.S. weapons are sometimes sent to both sides of regional rivalries. Consider the arms that the United States has given to Turkey and Greece. Significant quantities of surplus arms are also going to Argentina and Chile, which have embarked on a nascent arms race. And American surplus arms continue to flow to both Israel and Egypt, which are in a cold peace.

In 1994, Admiral Edward Shaefer, director of naval intelligence, said Turk-ish-Greek animosity was one of "the most worrisome situations developing in Europe, and the one most dangerous to NATO as an institution." Shaefer pointed out that "Greece has acquired virtually a completely modernized surface force from the United States, Germany, and the Netherlands." In turn, Turkey has been given eight Knox-class frigates. The United States has transferred hundreds of tanks, aircraft, and artillery as well as 16 warships to this antagonistic pair.

And it is not just the United States at work here. Germany has been selling off the East German arsenal, which it inherited when the two countries reunited. An enormous supply of used equipment came on the market as Russia demobilized. And the Netherlands is selling older ships, aircraft, and army vehicles.

East European countries have tried to export tanks and other combat equipment that exceed CFE limits, much as the United States did. When Poland and Czechoslovakia marketed their surplus weapons in Syria and Iran, however, it caused great alarm in Washington.

HUMAN RIGHTS. Several countries that receive large quantities of U.S. arms through surplus programs are engaged in conflict or have poor human rights records. Where government repression or other abuses are prevalent, the transfer of small arms, light weapons, ammunition, bombs, and missiles can take an immediate toll. Even "non-lethal" equipment—observation and transport planes and helicopters—is used to locate targets.

In a June 1995 report, the State Department cited the Turkish government for "mystery killings," disappearances, and political repression. Most of these abuses involved the Kurdish population and Turkey's 12-year-long war against Kurdish militants, during which it has destroyed 2,000 villages, killed thousands—primarily civilians—and displaced millions.

The State Department acknowledges that Turkey has employed American-supplied weapons in attacks on non-combatant populations, and admits that Turkey has used M-113 armored personnel carriers and Cobra and Blackhawk helicopters in indiscriminate attacks on Kurdish villages. Turkey was given 250 M-113s as part of the CFE reductions, and it got 28 free Cobra helicopters under Section 516 of the Foreign Assistance Act. In addition, the United States has given Turkey hundreds of howitzers.

In Bahrain, government forces have fired into crowds demonstrating for a restoration of the parliament, which the ruling al-Khalifa family dissolved in 1975. When members of Congress asked the administration to state its position on the demands of the Bahraini opposition, the State Department responded for the record that "the United States supports expansion of political participation for all Bahrainis." Nonetheless, from 1993 to 1995 the United States gave Bahrain's rulers two C-130 military transport planes, six observation/light-attack jets, 22 Cobra attack helicopters, 2,000 .38 caliber pistols, and 120 grenade launchers. In addition, the Pentagon transferred 60 M-60 tanks under a lease arrangement.

According to the State Department's latest human rights report, the Colombian police and armed forces committed "widespread human rights abuses" in 1995, including political and extrajudicial killings, kidnappings, and torture. In addition to fighting narcotics traffickers, the Colombian armed forces and police are waging war against several left-wing political groups. Washington has expressed concern that U.S. military aid was being diverted to fight insurgents and sympathetic civilians. Yet Colombia remains the largest recipient of weapons giveaways under the counter-narcotics provision.

Israel, the leading beneficiary of U.S. military and economic aid, used U.S.-supplied arms in a deadly assault in Lebanon earlier this year, in which an ambulance and a U.N. refugee camp were apparently targeted when they were thought to be shielding Hezbollah guerrillas. Israel has been given nearly 65,000 M-16A1 rifles, 2,500 M-204 grenade launchers, 24 Apache attack helicopters, and 65 F-15 and F-16 fighter-bomber jets.

Morocco, a major U.S. weapons recipient, is governed by a highly repressive monarchy that has illegally occupied the Western Sahara for 20 years. In 1991, the United Nations brokered a fragile peace agreement between Morocco and the Polisario Front guerrillas, who are seeking independence. However, Morocco has obstructed the peace process, and a resumption of fighting appears likely. In the past five years Morocco has received a substantial number of small arms, tanks, and attack aircraft.

THE "INDUSTRIAL BASE." The arms industry has divided views on the surplus weapons program. Small companies tend to support the program, because they often receive contracts to upgrade and repair transferred equipment. In addition, free or reduced-price transfers undercut foreign competitors and strengthen the link between U.S. and foreign militaries, which increases future business opportunities for the U.S. weapons industry.

On the other hand, the major contractors have argued that giveaways pose unfair competition and undermine the health of the "defense industrial base." Some segments of industry have been hard hit, particularly helicopter and ammunition makers.

As a result, those most likely to express opposition to sales or giveaways of surplus arms are the major arms manufacturers. Alliant Tech Systems, for example, criticized a gift to Greece of 58,000 rounds of tank ammunition, which caused Greece to cancel a $30 million order. Alliant argued in December 1993 that the government should "adopt demilitarization as the preferred strategy for disposing of unusable ammunition. This will lessen the pressure to give excess stocks away to potential foreign customers, while providing a source of income to help sustain the ammunition industrial base."

REDUCING THE RISK

Surplus weapons transfers will continue to be a prominent part of U.S. security assistance for the next several years, as the remainder of the weapons retired at the end of the Cold War are disbursed. When the armed services can save money by transferring appropriate equipment to responsible end users, the practice would appear to benefit all involved—the services, U.S. taxpayers, and recipients.

But it is foolish to transfer weapons simply because the military services want newer, fancier equipment—especially when the process of unloading older weapons exacerbates regional arms races.

Some additional guidelines might reduce the risk that U.S. arms transfers will imperil innocent lives abroad or endanger American soldiers. These policy recommendations would also minimize the burden on U.S. taxpayers.

The U.S. government should:

PROVIDE A FULL ACCOUNTING OF ALL SURPLUS ARMS TRANSFERS, USING REALISTIC VALUES FOR THE EQUIPMENT. In 1994, the GAO called for fuller reporting by the executive branch on EDA transfers and lease arrangements. In particular, the oversight agency saw a need for Congress to be informed about the actual quantity of items delivered. The administration subsequently began to provide this information in the "Congressional Presentation Document." However, many of the official statistics on arms exports routinely omit surplus arms transfers. When equipment is leased, only the rental fees are included in total export figures. Omitting the full value of these transfers dramatically undercounts the total level of U.S. arms exports. Mispricing by the services also understates the total value of these exports.

In 1994, the Defense Department agreed with the GAO that the armed services had often failed to adhere to proper guidelines for pricing excess equipment, and said it would reinforce its guidance and procedures for pricing. But there is no evidence that this problem has been corrected. In 1995, Defense Security Assistance Agency figures still misstated acquisition prices. The services told GAO investigators that they have no incentives for adhering to the pricing guidelines, because they gain no economic advantage from these transfers. Rather, it is in their interest to get rid of excess equipment as quickly as possible to minimize storage and maintenance costs. Some sort of carrot or stick needs to be devised to improve adherence to pricing procedures.

PROHIBIT THE DIRECT FUNDING OF NEW WEAPONS WITH PROCEEDS FROM SALES OF OLD OR SURPLUS ARMS. Using arms sales proceeds to fund new weapons procurement might seem like a good idea, but the effect of such a policy could be disastrous, with taxpayers forced to fund higher levels of Pentagon spending to counter threats posed by increasingly sophisticated weapons that have been distributed by their own government. Moreover, such a policy sets a dangerous precedent for other exporters to follow.

SET AND ENFORCE ANNUAL CAPS ON THE AMOUNT OF SURPLUS ARMS TRANSFERS EACH COUNTRY IS ELIGIBLE TO RECEIVE. Congress does not vote on the level of surplus arms to be sent to individual countries. In fact, members of Congress and their staffs are generally unaware of the level of surplus arms transfers each country is receiving until well after the exports have taken place. Because the services' valuations are unreliable, these caps should be based on acquisition costs.

If policy makers are unwilling to set annual country-specific caps, they should, at a minimum, set a firm cap on the total value of surplus weapons that may be transferred in a given year. The Pentagon is currently permitted to export EDA worth $250 million in original acquisition value annually, in addition to warships and their munitions. Despite this cap, weapons worth more than $500 million per year are actually being transferred.

A bill pending in the Senate would raise the limit on giveaways to $350 million per year in current value, and set no cap at all on EDA sales, although it would eliminate the current exemption for naval vessels and their munitions. This bill could vastly increase arms exports. Given the services' pricing practices, allowing transfers that the services value at $350 million could easily translate into the export of several billions of dollars of equipment in terms of original cost.

PROHIBIT SURPLUS WEAPONS TRANSFERS TO REPRESSIVE REGIMES. Despite laws that would seem to bar military aid to governments that are "gross and consistent" abusers of human rights, the United States has given billions of dollars of surplus arms to repressive regimes. Sections 516 and 519 contain a clause exempting weapons transfers from all legal restrictions, including those relating to human rights.

Congress should repeal this clause. Transfers of surplus military equipment should be subject to all laws enacted to minimize the potential negative consequences of arms exports. In addition, Congress and the executive branch should block surplus arms transfers to repressive regimes, even if the government in question is an ally.

Such regimes are by nature unstable, and giving them free weapons is not sound policy. In addition to abetting in the repression of the citizens of those countries, these transfers imperil U.S. security when new and unfriendly regimes inherit their U.S. supplied arsenals.

Lora Lumpe is director of the Arms Sales Monitoring Project at the Federation of American Scientists (FAS) in Washington, DC.

Reprinted by permission of *The Bulletin of the Atomic Scientists*, copyright ©1996 by the Educational Foundation for Nuclear Science, 6042 South Kimbark Avenue, Chicago, IL 60637, USA. A one-year subscription is $36. This article was adapted from a 1996 FAS report, "Recycled Weapons: American Exports of Surplus Weapons, 1990-1995." The full report including footnotes is available for $5 from FAS, 307 Massachusetts Avenue, NE, Washington, DC 20002.

"GUNS 'R' US"

By Martha Honey;
In These Times; August 11, 1997

On June 7, the House unanimously approved, by voice vote, the Arms Transfer Code of Conduct. If enacted, the code would significantly change the rules of the game for arms exports.

U.S. arms dealers currently sell $10 billion in weapons to non-democratic governments each year, according to Caleb Rossiter, director of the Demilitarization for Democracy project. Dubbed the "No Arms to Dictators" bill, the code would prohibit U.S. commercial arms sales or military aid and training to foreign governments that are undemocratic, abuse human rights, or engage in aggression against neighboring states. The president, who will have the authority to make these determinations, can exempt undemocratic countries on the grounds of national security, but Congress has eight months to overturn any waivers.

The bill faces a number of legislative hurdles before becoming law. Nevertheless, the House vote was an important victory for a coalition of some 300 grass-roots, religious and Washington-based advocacy groups that have taken on the powerful weapons industry and its government allies. Over the past five years, the doves have put together a broad congressional coalition, exemplified by the code's co-sponsors, liberal Cynthia McKinney (D-GA) and conservative Dana Rohrabacher (R-CA).

A White House speech writer under Reagan, Rohrabacher has softened his views since the end of the Cold War. "We have a higher standard of morality now," he told the Orange County Weekly. "With the [Cold] War over, there's no excuse for selling weapons to regimes that will use them to repress their own people."

Yet ironically, the Clinton Administration is moving in the opposite direction. Arguing that arms exports are a boon to the U.S. economy, the president, along with the Defense, Commerce and State Departments, is aggressively promoting the arms industry at every opportunity. During 1993, Clinton's first year in office and the peak of the post-Gulf War arms-buying frenzy, U.S. foreign military contracts soared to $36 billion, a level unprecedented during the Cold War and more than double what Bush approved in 1992. By 1995, U.S. government-negotiated sales had leveled off at between $9 billion and $13 billion a year.

The United States, Britain, Russia, France, and China dominate today's $32 billion global arms trade. But the United States has pulled out in front. According to the U.S. government's own estimates, Washington's share of the business jumped from 16 percent in 1988 to 50 percent between 1992 and 1994. The sky seems to be the limit. According to a 1995 Pentagon forecast, the United States accounts for 63 percent of worldwide arms deals already signed for the period between 1994 and 2000.

The Clinton Administration has accelerated arms exports despite the global downturn in military production and defense budgets since the end of the Cold War. After peaking in 1987, world military spending dropped 40 percent to $811 billion in 1996, the lowest since 1966, according to the International Institute for Strategic Studies.

The overall U.S. military budget is one-third smaller than at its peak in the mid-'80s. In real terms, however, U.S. defense spending is still higher than during the Carter Administration. Rather than embark on a serious program of defense cuts and economic conversion—the illusory "peace dividend" promised with the end of the Cold War—the Clinton Administration is phasing out its conversion programs, opting instead to help boost the profits of military manufacturers through overseas sales.

The foreign policy risks of escalating arms exports are enormous. Most U.S. weaponry is sold to the Middle East and other strife-torn regions, helping to fan the flames of war instead of promoting stability. More than 40 percent of the international sales of major conventional weapons between 1984 and 1994 went to nations at war such as Iraq, Somalia, and Sudan, according to the United Nations Development Program's 1994 Human Development Report. Civilians are increasingly the major victims of war. They accounted for half of all war deaths during the first half of this century, 64 percent in the '60s and 74 percent in the '80s. The share of civilian casualties appears to be higher still in the '90s.

The United States has been a major arms supplier to nations at war. Since 1985, participants in 45 ongoing conflicts received over $42 billion worth of U.S. weapons, according to a 1995 World Policy Institute report. Among the major conflicts in 1993 and 1994, 90 percent involved one or more parties that had received U.S. weapons or military technology prior to the outbreak of fighting. International arms sales also put U.S. troops based around the world at growing risk. In discussing this so-called "boomerang effect," the CIA's Nonproliferation Center noted in 1995 that "the acquisition of advanced conventional weapons and technologies by hostile countries could result in significant casualties being inflicted on U.S. forces or regional allies." In fact, the last five times that the United States has sent troops into conflict—in Panama, Iraq-Kuwait, Somalia, Haiti, and Bosnia—American forces faced adversaries that had previously received U.S. weapons, military technology, or training.

The Pentagon and defense contractors then turn around and use the presence of advanced U.S. weapons in foreign arsenals to justify increased spending on new leading-edge weapons back home so that the United States can maintain its military superiority. For instance, the export of F-15 and F-16 tactical fighters to U.S. allies in Europe, Asia and the Middle East is being used to justify the development of the F-22, the "next generation" fighter that has already cost taxpayers $16 billion. Air Force officials are already proposing F-22 production costs be offset through overseas sales of the plane, which will undoubtedly provoke calls for yet another new fighter.

But it's NATO expansion, the foreign policy centerpiece of Clinton's second term, that offers the biggest potential bonanza for U.S. weapons exporters. U.S. arms dealers are salivating at the prospect of the new states upgrading and retrofitting their militaries with Western weapons and equipment.

"The stakes are high," Joel Johnson of the Aerospace Industries Association told *The New York Times*. "Whoever gets in first will have a lock for the next quarter-century." It's no coincidence that the globe-trotting president of the U.S. Committee to Expand NATO is Bruce Jackson, whose other hat is director of strategic planning at Lockheed Martin, which wants its F-16 fighters to replace Central Europe's Soviet MIG-21s.

A bipartisan group of 20 senators, including Jesse Helms (R-NC) and Patrick Leahy (D-VT), took issue with President Clinton's contention that "NATO expansion is in our national interests." In a joint letter, the senators expressed doubts about forcing these relatively poor, fledgling democracies "to spend money on arms, when expenditures for the infrastructure critical to economic growth are more pressing." The letter promises "intense" debate about NATO expansion in the Senate, which must ratify new NATO members by a two-thirds vote.

Arms merchants and their Pentagon flacks are leaving no stone unturned in their export drive. The United States is contemplating the removal of a 20-year U.S. ban on sales of advanced fighter aircraft to Latin America. Imposed during the Carter Administration when military dictators ruled most of the region, proponents of lifting the ban argue that with the end of the Cold War and the revival of democracy in most of Latin America, countries like Chile or Brazil should be allowed to buy F-16s if they want them.

In a declaration issued at a Carter Center meeting in April, former Costa Rican president Oscar Arias warned that lifting the ban would suck up money better spent on human development programs and derail international efforts to ratchet down military spending in volatile regions. Arguing that the removal of the ban "could undermine regional military balances or stimulate an arms race," Senators Joseph Biden (D-DE) and Christopher Dodd (D-CT) introduced a bill in July to extend the export moratorium for another two years. Clinton is expected to make a decision after he visits Latin America in October.

Given that international arms sales exacerbate conflicts and drain scarce resources from developing countries, why does the Clinton Administration push them so vigorously? The official answer is, most often, jobs. But the government's own studies reveal that this rationale doesn't hold much water. The Office of Management and Budget estimates that for every 100 jobs created by weapons exports, 41 are lost in non-military U.S. firms that must compete with foreign companies that were granted access to the U.S. market in indirect payment for weapons purchases. U.S. arms exporters are also increasingly negotiating "offset" agreements, which sweeten the pot for foreign buyers by sending production (technologies and jobs) overseas along with American weapons. Even as U.S. arms exports soar, some 2.2 million defense industry workers lost their jobs between 1988 and 1996.

Political contributions by arms manufacturers reinforce this cozy relationship. During last year's election campaign, the top 25 weapons exporters contributed $10.8 million, according to a study by the World Policy Institute. This marks a 56 percent increase in political action committee (PAC) and soft money contributions over the previous peak of $6.9 million during the 1991-92 election cycle. The "leader of the PACs"—contributing more than $2.3 million to last year's campaign—was Lockheed Martin, the world's largest arms manufacturer.

Unlike in any other industry, U.S. taxpayers fully underwrite the research and development costs for weapons systems. In 1995, the arms industry successfully lobbied for the abolition of "recoupment fees," a small government tax on foreign weapons sales that brought in about $500 million each year to help offset R&D costs. Arguing that recoupment fees made U.S. weapons uncompetitive, the industry convinced Congress to allow the president to waive them.

U.S. dominance of the global arms market has been accomplished as much through subsidies as sales: In 1995, more than half of the $15 billion in U.S. arms exports was paid with government grants, subsidized loans, tax breaks, and promotional activities. The result is a net transfer of dollars from the U.S. Treasury to weapons manufacturers. Arms export subsidies are the second largest category of corporate welfare, surpassed only by agricultural subsidies.

Currently, 6,500 full-time government employees in the Defense, Commerce, and State Departments are engaged in promoting and financing weapons exports through a maze of programs. The Pentagon's Foreign Military Financing program provided $3.2 billion in grants in 1995 to foreign countries—chiefly Israel and Egypt—to buy American military equipment. U.S.AID Economic Support Fund grants totaling $2.1 billion in 1995 went to help offset the costs of arms purchases. The Commerce Department subsidized outstanding military-related loans given by the Export-Import Bank to the tune of $2.1 billion in 1995. The Defense Department writes off another $1 billion each year for bad or forgiven weapons-purchase loans to foreign countries. Thirty-four countries, including Zaire, Turkey, Liberia, and Sudan, owe the United States $14 billion in military loans, according to a 1996 Pentagon report; most of these loans will likely be written off.

In 1995, Lockheed Martin and other defense industry giants won congressional approval for the newest and potentially largest subsidy package. The $15 billion Defense Export Loan Guarantee Fund covers military contractor losses when foreign customers cannot afford to honor weapons sales agreements. East European NATO aspirants are now tapping this fund. In May, Romania became

the first country to use the fund to underwrite the purchase of $23 million in unmanned reconnaissance planes.

The Defense Department also gives away, leases, sells at a deep discount, or lends surplus weapons stocks. "While other, more visible forms of military aid have been cut since the end of the Cold War, shipments of surplus arms through a variety of programs have increased dramatically," says Lora Lumpe, director of the Federation of American Scientists' Arms Sales Monitoring Project. These giveaways—which include tanks, attack helicopters, bombers, and pistols—have been used to fan regional arms rivalries (between Greece and Turkey, for instance) and to commit human rights violations in countries such as Bahrain, Colombia, and Morocco.

"Recycled Weapons," a 1996 study co-authored by Lumpe, found that the U.S. military is giving away still useful equipment in order to justify the procurement of new weapons. The Air Force "Boneyard," a four square-mile stretch of Arizona desert outside Tucson, provides rust-free storage for 5,200 planes, 75 percent of which are still in operating condition. "We could have air superiority with what we have in the Boneyard," Rossiter of Demilitarization for Democracy told The New York Times.

Rather than trekking out to the Boneyard, potential buyers more often show up at overseas air shows and expos, which are also financed by taxpayers at an annual cost of about $125 million. Once offering stripped-down export models, U.S. arms dealers at today's arms marts display top-of-the-line diesel submarines, portable surface-to-air missiles, jet fighters, missile systems, and other high-tech weaponry. If the price is right, any type of weapon (except for nuclear, biological, chemical, or long-range missiles) is available.

In this era of balanced budgets and belt tightening at home, the multibillion dollar bevy of subsidies for arms exporters needs to be weighed against cuts in other government programs. The 1996 welfare reform law will cut federal support for poor families by about $7 billion annually over the next five years, an amount almost equal to the yearly subsidies given to U.S. weapons manufacturers. There are parallels as well between some of the specific welfare and warfare programs. The welfare law cuts child nutrition programs by $500 million and food stamps by $2.1 billion a year. On the other side of the ledger, arms export subsidies include recoupment fee waivers of $500 million and $2.1 billion in U.S.AID Economic Support Fund grants each year.

It is, in essence, the poor at home and abroad who pay the price for escalating arms exports. In a joint statement issued recently in New York, eight Nobel Peace Prize recipients—including Oscar Arias, Elie Wiesel, José Ramos Horta of East Timor and the Dalai Lama—who support an international Arms Transfer Code of Conduct declared, "Millions of civilians have been killed in conflict this century, and many more have lost their loved ones, their homes, their spirit. In a world where 1.3 billion people earn less than $1 a day, the sale of weapons simply perpetuates poverty. Our children urgently need schools and health care centers, not machine guns and fighter planes. Our children also need to be protected from violence. The dictators of this world, not the poor, clamor for arms."

But flanked against such eloquent, straightforward logic is the mighty U.S. arms industry and its government allies. "The brakes are off the system," says Lawrence Kolb, a Brookings Institute fellow and former assistant secretary of defense under Ronald Reagan. "It has become a money game: an absurd spiral in which we export arms only to have to develop more sophisticated ones to counter those spread out all over the world.... It is very hard for us to tell other people—the Russians, the Chinese, the French—not to sell arms, when we are out there peddling and fighting to control the market."

Martha Honey is director of the Institute for Policy Studies' Peace and Security Program.

Reprinted by permission of *In These Times*, 2040 North Milwaukee Avenue, 2nd Floor, Chicago, IL 60647-4002, Tel: 773/772-0100.

2 CENSORED

Personal Care and Cosmetic Products May Be Carcinogenic

"TO DIE FOR"
By Joel Bleifuss;
In These Times; February 17, 1997

In the course of one day, an American woman might color her hair with Clairol Nice 'n' Easy Permanent Shampoo-in Haircolor (natural medium brown); wash it with Vidal Sassoon shampoo, Stylist Choice; cover her face with Cover Girl Replenishing Ultra-Finish Cream Makeup; rub her body with Lubriderm lotion; brush her teeth with Crest Tartar Control toothpaste; douche her vagina with Massengill Country Flowers; and then dust her crotch with Johnson & Johnson talcum powder.

By the time she concludes her beauty regimen, this woman will have absorbed into her body five chemical compounds that are known carcinogens. She also will have exposed herself four times to a group of chemicals that are often contaminated with a carcinogenic by-product or that regularly react to form a potent carcinogen during storage and use.

The Food and Drug Administration (FDA) oversees the cosmetics industry, sort of. The agency divides cosmetics into 13 categories: skin care, fragrances, eye makeup, other makeup, manicure products, hair dyes, shampoos and other hair products, deodorants, shaving products, bath oils, mouthwashes, tanning products, and baby products.

But while the FDA classifies, it does not regulate. An FDA document posted on the agency's World Wide Web home page explains that "a cosmetic manufacturer may use any ingredient or raw material and market the final product without government approval."

There are a few exceptions. Cosmetic manufacturers are prohibited from using seven known toxins, including hexachlorophene, mercury compounds, and chloroform. As for the remaining 8,000 raw materials used in the formulation of cosmetics, the industry regulates itself.

Let's look at the products used in the beauty regimen mentioned above.

➤ The Clairol hair dye contains Quaternium-15, which releases carcinogenic formaldehyde, and Cocamide DEA, which can be contaminated with carcinogenic nitrosamines or react to produce a nitrosamine during storage or use.
➤ The Vidal Sassoon shampoo, like the hair dye, contains Cocamide DEA.
➤ The Cover Girl makeup contains titanium dioxide, which is carcinogenic; talc, which is a carcinogen similar to asbestos; and TEA, which, like Cocamide DEA, is associated with carcinogenic nitrosamines.
➤ The Lubriderm lotion contains TEA.
➤ The Crest toothpaste contains titanium dioxide; saccharin, which is a carcinogen; and FD&C Blue #1, which is a carcinogen.

➤ The Massengill douche contains FD&C Blue #1.

➤ The Johnson & Johnson talcum powder contains the asbestos-like mineral talc.

If the FDA deems a cosmetic product a danger to public health, it can yank it from the shelves, as it did in 1972 with acne soaps that contained hexachlorophene. But the FDA has failed to act, even as evidence mounts, on some of the most common cosmetic ingredients that double as deadly carcinogens. This raises the question: Is the FDA more concerned with protecting public health or with the bottom line of the "personal-care" industry, which rakes in $20 billion a year, mostly from women?

Among the cosmetic toxins that consumer advocates are most concerned about are nitrosamines, a group of potent carcinogens that contaminate a wide range of cosmetic products, from shampoos to hand lotions and sunscreens. One of these nitrosamines, N-nitrosodiethanolamine (NDELA), is formed when a common contaminant of such cosmetic ingredients as TEA and Cocamide DEA interacts with the nitrites that many cosmetic-makers use as preservatives.

The Cancer Prevention Coalition, a Chicago-based health-advocacy group founded by University of Illinois-Chicago pathologist Samuel Epstein, wants nitrosamine-contaminated cosmetics banned. Coalition program director Melissa Troester puts it this way: "Nitrosamines have been identified as one of the most potent classes of carcinogens, having caused cancer in more than 40 different animal species as well as in humans. The FDA should take regulatory action against companies manufacturing cosmetic products; responsible corporations should remove these avoidable contaminants from their products; and the public should boycott all products containing nitrosamines."

In the mid-'70s, the nitrosamine contamination of cooked bacon and other nitrite-treated meats became a public health issue. Since then, the food industry, which is more strictly regulated than the cosmetic industry, has drastically lowered the amount of nitrosamines found in nitrite-processed meats. (A risk, however, may still exist. A study of children up to age 10 in Los Angeles County between 1980 and 1987 found that children who ate more than 12 hot dogs a month had nine times the normal risk of developing childhood leukemia.)

Today, nitrosamines contaminate cosmetics at significantly higher levels than those cooked bacon once contained. While people don't eat cosmetics, their skin absorbs the nitrosamines in products such as lotion and sunscreen. Writing in the journal *Carcinogenesis* in 1985, National Cancer Institute scientists William Lijinsky and Robert Kovatch reported that NDELA is the specific nitrosamine "to which human exposure is the greatest," since it occurs "in cosmetics" and is "absorbed readily through the skin."

In 1978, the International Agency for Research on Cancer surveyed the available research and concluded: "In view of the widespread exposure to appreciable concentrations of NDELA, efforts should be made to obtain epidemiological information. Although no epidemiological data [are] available, NDELA should be regarded for practical purposes as if it were carcinogenic to humans."

The FDA has long known that the nitrosamines in cosmetics pose a risk to public health. On April 10, 1979, FDA Commissioner Donald Kennedy called on the cosmetic industry to "take immediate measures to eliminate, to the extent possible, NDELA and any other N-nitrosamines from cosmetic products." He went on to warn that "cosmetic products may be analyzed by the FDA for nitrosamine contamination and that individual products could be subject to enforcement action."

In the 18 years since the FDA issued that warning, cosmetics manufacturers have done little to remove nitrosamines from their products, and the FDA has done even less to ensure that the industry does so. All the while, evidence mounts that nitrosamines are a danger to public health.

In 1985, Lijinsky and Kovatch discovered that NDELA was more carcinogenic than originally thought. In a research paper titled "Induction of Liver Tumors in Rats by NDELA at Low Doses," the two scientists conclude: "NDELA was at one time thought to be a 'weak' carcinogen, but recent studies have shown that it is reasonably potent.... Not only does NDELA induce tumors over a wide range of doses, but it is a multipotent carcinogen, inducing [cancers in rats] in a number of different organs."

The FDA intermittently tests personal-care products for NDELA. In 1992, the agency found one product that contained NDELA at a concentration of 2,960 parts per billion. (The FDA keeps brand names confidential.) The European Union strictly regulates nitrosamine-producing chemicals and bans cosmetic products containing NDELA at a level of more than 50 parts per billion.

The following year, in the course of investigating sunscreens for nitrosamines, FDA chemists discovered the carcinogen NMPABAO. This nitrosamine is created when the sunscreen known as "padimate O" interacts with the nitrites in cosmetic preservatives such as BNPD.

As the FDA's Donald Havery and Hardy Chou observed in a 1992 paper presented to an American Chemical Society symposium on nitrosamines, "The FDA has conducted surveys of sunscreens and other personal-care products for NMPABAO since 1986. Analysis showed that many of the products containing padimate O also contained NMPABAO, some at elevated levels, especially when the product contained the [preservative] BNPD."

Indeed, between 1986 and 1992, the FDA tested 88 cosmetic products containing padimate O and found that 57 of those products were contaminated with the nitrosamine NMPABAO. In 1991, one product was found to contain the nitrosamine in the incredible concentration of 20,520 parts per billion. And in

1992, all 14 products tested contained the carcinogens.

Though the FDA has refused to officially address this danger, individual agency scientists are not reticent about speaking out. In their 1992 presentation to the American Chemical Society, Havery and Chou pointed out that cosmetic corporations continue to introduce new products that contain the chemical precursors of nitrosamines.

The Cancer Prevention Coalition, for example, is concerned about No-Rinse Shampoo and No-Rinse Body Bath, which were recently introduced by N/R Laboratories of Centerville, Ohio. The target market is outdoor enthusiasts who want to keep clean while camping. But such cleanliness may come at a price. The top two ingredients of these no-rinse products are TEA and Cocamide DEA, which, since they don't get rinsed off with water, are largely absorbed into the body.

The continued use of such ingredients, say Havery and Chou, contradicts what should be a social goal: keeping "human exposure to N-nitrosamines to the lowest level technologically feasible by reducing levels in all personal-care products." They add: "With the information and technology currently available to cosmetic manufacturers, N-nitrosamine levels can and should be further reduced in consumer products."

Women—and men—should demand that the FDA regulate cosmetics as it does food. And while waiting for the FDA to act, they should carefully check the ingredients on the label before they buy cosmetic chemical concoctions.

Research assistance was provided by Jennifer Patterson.

Reprinted by permission of *In These Times*, 2040 North Milwaukee Avenue, 2nd Floor, Chicago, IL 60647-4002, Tel: 773/772-0100.

"TAKE A POWDER"

By Joel Bleifuss;
In These Times; March 3, 1997

Women who frequently use talcum powder on their genital area significantly increase their risk of getting cancer. Yet despite clear evidence of an association between the mineral talc and ovarian cancer, both the U.S. Food and Drug Administration and the cosmetic industry's main trade group refuse to acknowledge these findings and to regulate the use of talc.

A 1992 study published in the medical journal *Obstetrics & Gynecology* examined the history of talc use in 235 white women with ovarian cancer and 239 white women without the disease in the Boston metropolitan area. The research team, led by Bernard Harlow of Harvard Medical School's Obstetrics and Gynecology Epidemiology Center, found that women who regularly applied talc to their genital area increased their risk of contracting ovarian cancer three-fold.

In the study, 49 percent of the women with ovarian cancer and 39 percent of those without the disease reported some level of genital exposure to talc. The researchers found that the "most frequent method of talc exposure was use as a dusting powder directly to the perineum." Further, they noted that "brand or generic 'baby powder' was used most frequently and was the category associated with a statistically significant risk of ovarian cancer." Fourteen percent of the women with ovarian cancer in the study had applied talc to their perineum an estimated 10,000 or more times during the years when they were ovulating with an intact genital tract-compared to 7 percent of women without the disease.

The researchers warned that "given the poor prognosis for ovarian cancer, any potentially harmful exposures [to talc] should be avoided, particularly those with limited benefits. For this reason, we discourage the use of talc in genital hygiene, particularly as a daily habit."

The study concluded that about 10 percent of all ovarian cancer cases may be attributed to the frequent use of talc. Ovarian cancer, the incidence of which is on the rise, is the fourth deadliest cancer among women, killing about 14,000 American women each year.

Talc, a mineral related to asbestos, has been an object of scientific scrutiny for decades. As early as 1968, scientists examining cosmetic talcum products discovered that 22 of those they analyzed had, on average, a mineral fiber content of 19 percent. In 1971, researchers discovered talc particles deeply embedded in 75 percent of ovarian tumors studied.

Such evidence led the FDA in 1973 to draft a resolution that would have limited the amount of asbestos-like fibers in cosmetic-grade talc to less than 0.1 percent. But no ruling was ever made, and the cosmetics industry was left to police itself and rid baby powder and other talc products of asbestos-like fibers.

To their credit, cosmetic manufacturers appear to have reduced the volume of asbestos-like fibers found in the 77,000 metric tons of cosmetic-grade talc that the U.S. cosmetics industry uses each year—at least that's what the industry and FDA claim. But even without asbestos-like fibers, talc is a matter of concern.

In 1993, the National Toxicology Program conducted an animal study of "non-asbestiform talc" (talc which does not contain asbestos-like fibers) and concluded that when inhaled, it was carcinogenic to rats. The study was requested by the National Institute of Occupational Safety and Health, which has been a more rigorous protector of public health than the FDA.

So is talc harmful?

It's important to remember that the Food, Drug, and Cosmetics Act regulates cosmetics differently from food, says Arthur Whitmore, the FDA's Cosmetic Technology Branch spokesman. In the case of cosmetics, he adds, "The burden of proof is on the FDA to prove that a product is harmful under condition of use." Don Havery, an FDA cosmetics researcher, puts it this way: "You don't see a lot of regulatory action because it is very difficult to prove harm."

But what is considered proof? According to the Cosmetic Toiletry and Fragrance Association (CTFA), the trade group of the $20-billion-a-year cosmetics industry, "no scientific study

CARCINOGENS IN SHAMPOOS AND LOTIONS

The FDA is not doing enough to ensure that many foods and cosmetics are free of carcinogenic nitrosamines, according to William Lijinsky, the former director of the Chemical Carcinogenesis Program at the National Cancer Institute's Frederick Cancer Research and Development Center. The fewer tests that are done, the fewer problems there will be to find. "It is very logical," he explains. "If you don't look, you don't find."

FDA cosmetics researcher Donald Havery describes Lijinsky, who is now retired, as the scientist who has "done more work than anybody for testing nitrosamines for carcinogenicity." Nitrosamines are potent carcinogens that have been frequently found to contaminate shampoos and lotions.

Lijinsky says he was particularly concerned to hear FDA Commissioner David Kessler, in a November 1995 radio interview, dismiss "as myth from long ago" the role of nitrites—precursors to nitrosamines—in promoting human cancer. Lijinsky says Kessler failed to realize "that the nitrosamines are the most potent carcinogens we know and active at extremely low concentrations in animals." In a letter he wrote to Kessler in response to the radio interview, Lijinsky pointed out that nitrosamines are so carcinogenic that they "give rise to tumors within the short lifespan of a rat." And, he added, "There is no doubt that such reactions occur in humans."

Lijinsky says the level of nitrites allowed in food should be further limited, and that the FDA should closely monitor and control the level of nitrosamines—or other nitrosamine precursors, such as DEA—in cosmetic ingredients. By itself, DEA is harmless, but when combined with nitrites, it forms the potent carcinogen NDELA, which is the nitrosamine most commonly found in cosmetics.

In 1979, then FDA Commissioner Donald Kennedy threatened regulatory action if the cosmetics industry did not "take immediate measures to eliminate, to the extent possible, NDELA and any other N-nitrosamines from cosmetic products." Since then, the FDA has monitored the level of nitrosamines found in cosmetic products. But from 1985 to 1996, the FDA analyzed only 47 cosmetic products for NDELA, 23 of which were found to be contaminated with the nitrosamine. Havery says that his office has only one chemist and "he does work other than nitrosamines."

Lijinsky has some sympathy for the FDA's surveillance program. "NDELA, the principal nitrosamine in cosmetics, is absorbed through the skin particularly in an oily solution [like lotion], and it is quite a potent carcinogen," he says. "But one of the problems is that it is difficult and expensive to measure, and there are thousands of products that have to be monitored, so I can understand why they don't do it."

One way to avoid the problem of monitoring all these cosmetic products would be to regulate the amount of DEA allowed in cosmetics. The European Union restricts DEA contamination to 1 percent of any cosmetic ingredient. DEA is currently found in much higher levels in products in the United States. According to Havery, an unpublished FDA study of 20 cosmetic raw ingredients found DEA in concentrations of up to 13 percent. However, only two of the FDA's samples exceeded the manufacturer's specifications-based on limits provided by the Cosmetic, Toiletry, and Fragrance Association, an industry group. The CTFA advises its members that DEA levels should not exceed 5 percent of a final cosmetic product—significantly higher than the European level.

has ever demonstrated that talc causes ovarian cancer." The CTFA official position paper on talc maintains that "the latest toxicologic and epidemiologic studies conducted on talc" were reviewed at a 1994 workshop entitled "Talc: Consumer Uses and Health Perspectives," co-sponsored by the FDA and the International Society of Regulatory Toxicology and Pharmacology. According to the CTFA, workshop participants concluded that "when taken together, the results of these studies [linking talc use and ovarian cancer] are insufficient to demonstrate any real association."

That conclusion, however, contradicts the assessment of Bernard Harlow, whom workshop organizers had asked to review the latest epidemiological studies examining potential links between talc use and ovarian cancer. Harlow presented his review at the workshop and later published it in the journal, *Regulatory Toxicology and Pharmacology*. The review's data show that four of eight studies since 1982 "implicated use of body powders" with increased ovarian cancer risks of 50 percent or more. He concludes that from an epidemiological point of view, it is "plausible" that any genital application of talc increases a woman's risk of ovarian cancer by as much as 80 percent.

"The studies that are out there suggest there is a risk," says Harlow. Asked whether his family uses talc products, he replies that they never used talc-based baby powder on their daughter. "My wife certainly doesn't use any talcum powder in her genital area," he says. "I certainly wouldn't recommend it."

So why does the CTFA cite the workshop to refute the link between talc and ovarian cancer? And why has the FDA not taken action, since ample evidence points to such a link? Despite repeated queries, the FDA failed to respond to this question by press time.

It's hard not to conclude that the FDA has no interest in finding proof. For their part, researchers know what other avenues need to be explored. Harlow ends his review of the talc-ovarian cancer connection by saying "the greatest need is to confirm or deny the reports of talc embedded in human ovarian tissue and the report of easy transportation of particles through the female reproductive tract."

The Chicago-based Cancer Prevention Coalition has petitioned the FDA to require that all cosmetic talcum-powder products carry a warning such as: "Talcum powder causes cancer in laboratory animals. Frequent talc application in the female genital area increases the risk of ovarian cancer." The FDA could also follow the example of the European Union, which stipulates that talcum powder, like Johnson & Johnson baby powder, is not to be used in products for children under three years old.

3 CENSORED

Big Business Seeks to Control and Influence U.S. Universities

"PHI BETA CAPITALISM: UNIVERSITIES IN SERVICE TO BUSINESS"

By Lawrence Soley; *CovertAction Quarterly* (CAQ); Spring 1997

There has been a "virtual explosion over the past several years in the number and variety of university-industry alliances," concluded the National Academy of Sciences. The "relationship between academe and business is more cordial than it has been for decades," agreed the *Chronicle of Higher Education*, "...the sectors are increasingly resembling each other." Thus quietly, while the right wing blows smoke, denouncing universities for harboring radicals, and the media hold up mirrors reflecting fanciful images of left-wing domination, a major change in the role of higher education is taking place: Large corporations, conservative foundations, and well-heeled executives are buying the ivory tower and transforming it into an annex for industry. Across the country, well-funded defense contractors are seducing physics and electrical engineering departments; pharmaceutical and biotech firms are wooing molecular biology, biochemistry, and medicine

departments; and IBM and a few high-tech chip makers are bedding down with university computer science departments. Increasingly, industry is creating endowed professorships, funding think tanks and research centers, sponsoring grants, contracting for research, and influencing who is hired as faculty and consultants. Under this cozy arrangement, students, faculty, and universities serve the interests of corporations, not the public, as they sell off academic freedom and intellectual independence.

The auctioning of academe to the highest bidder extends from the Midwestern college that adopts a corporate logo for its sports team to the selling off of major research programs at top universities. At the Massachusetts Institute of Technology (MIT), for example, a number of elaborate programs serve corporate interests. One of these is MIT's Industrial Liaison Program (ILP), which charges 300 corporations from $10,000 to $50,000 per year in membership fees. Like campaign contributions, the fees buy corporations "access"—in this case to research reports by MIT faculty, to 70 symposia and faculty seminars, and to personal attention from MIT academics. As the ILP catalog describes it, MIT places "at the disposal of industry the expertise and resources of all the schools, departments, and laboratories of MIT."

Professors are encouraged to participate in the ILP by an inducement program patterned after the coupons on the top of Betty Crocker cake mixes. They can redeem "points" they accumulate by involvement with member corporations for travel to professional conferences, computer equipment, office furniture, or other prizes. MIT awards each faculty member one point for each unpublished article that is made available to an ILP member, two points for a phone conversation or a brief campus meeting with a corporate member, 12 points for a visit to a company's headquarters or lab, and so forth. Each point is worth about $35 in prize money.

Another program that ties MIT to industry is the New Products Program (NPP), a joint project of the mechanical engineering, electrical engineering, and management departments. Under it, corporations pay the university $500,000 to develop a new product within two years. Three faculty members and four graduate students are assigned to work on the product, and the students wind up devoting more than half of their time to it. In effect, students pay big bucks to participate in an internship.

Program Director Woodie Flowers said he is "90 percent sure" that MIT will shut down NPP by September and open a new program under the School of Engineering. The National Science Foundation, Ford, ITT, Xerox, GM, and Polaroid have already committed $30 million to be spread out over an 11-year period.

Similarly, Rensselaer Polytechnic Institute operated the Center for Product Innovation which conducted research for corporate clients. Its supporters—including Timex, General Dynamics, and Norelco—underwrote the center and funded specific projects. One of the center's most widely heralded projects was redesigning a coffeepot for Norelco. The University of Texas's Center for Technology Venturing also works on projects for corporate clients such as 3M, Ford, and Dell Computer Corp.

POURING RIGHTS & WRONGS

The University of Minnesota (U. of M)—described by former National Endowment for the Humanities head Lynne Cheney as a bastion of political correctness—typifies the extent of the alliance between industry and academia. In 1996, for example, U. of M signed an exclusive agreement with Coca-Cola, giving the soft drink exclusive "pouring rights" on campus and making it the official sponsor of on-campus promotional events, such as the "Diet Coke Volleyball Classic." Its College of Liberal Arts houses the Personnel Decisions, Inc. Professorship of Organizational and Counseling Psychology, funded by a firm that develops psychological tests given to prospective employees; the Mithun Land Grant Chair of Advertising, named for an owner of the Twin Cities' largest advertising agency; and the Elmer Andersen Chair in Corporate Responsibility, named for a former Minnesota governor and CEO of the H.B. Fuller Co., a paint and adhesives manufacturer that exports products banned in the United States, including the toxic glue sniffed by street children in Third World countries. U. of M's business school is named for the owner of the Carlson Travel Network, the university's preferred travel agency; and professors in the medical school have used their laboratories to conduct research for firms such as Curative Technologies and Endotronics, in which they had financial interests. Within the School of Journalism is a research center called the *China Times* Center for Media and Social Studies, funded by a Taiwanese newspaper magnate and political leader that "seeks humbly to promote" democracy in China, Taiwan's bête noire. The university "needs to make no apology for affiliating with private industry. This is part of our mission; always has been," says retiring U. of M President Nils Hasselmo.

CEOS AND THEIR BOARDS

Hasselmo's attitude is similar to that of other university presidents, who increasingly come from corporate board rooms, foundation suites, and smoke-filled back rooms. Michigan State University's president is Peter McPherson, a former Bank of America executive who worked in the Ford and Reagan Administrations. The new chief of the University of Massachusetts is former state senate leader William F. Bolger, and the new head of Wesleyan College is former Agency for International Development and National Public Radio chief Douglas J. Bennet, Jr.

One reason why university boards of trustees prefer presidents like McPherson and Bolger is that these individuals promote university-industry ties. As the head of Michigan State University's industrial relations office observed, the institution is now "trying to make an atmosphere where faculty members feel they can be more entrepreneurial.... I think that with Peter McPherson [as] our

president [this will happen], he's had a business background and he's encouraging this kind of thing."

Adding to the happy atmosphere of collegiality, university presidents and chancellors often serve on the boards of directors of corporations that have close ties to the universities. University of Texas (UT) Chancellor William Cunningham sits on the boards of Jefferson-Pilot Corp., John Hancock Fund Management Co., and La Quinta Motor Inns, Inc., which established UT's La Quinta Motor Inns, Inc. Centennial Professor of Business. And until several conflicts of interest concerning Cunningham were exposed, he was also paid $40,000 annually as a board member of Freeport-McMoRan Corp., a New Orleans-based mining company accused of environmental pollution. After the chancellor's ties came under public fire, he resigned his board seat and cashed in his stock options, netting a $650,422 profit.

Some of the fruits of the Cunningham/Freeport relationship remain: For a contribution of less than one-twelfth the cost of the building's construction, UT named its molecular biology building after Freeport's CEO James Robert ("Jim Bob") Moffett and his wife. Freeport had also endowed a professorship in UT's geology department, held by a professor doing geological research for Freeport in Indonesia, where the company collaborates with Suharto's dictatorship. Freeport's contract for this research allowed it to review any academic articles the professor wrote before they were submitted for publication.

Cunningham is one of many university administrators serving on corporate boards. City University of New York Chancellor Ann Reynolds sits on the boards of Abbott Laboratories, Owens-Corning, American Electric Power, Humana, Inc., and the Maytag Corp. Her $150,000 annual salary as chancellor is approximately doubled by what she gets as a board member.

President Stephen Trachtenberg of George Washington University is on the boards of Loctite Corp., MNC Financial, and the Security Trust Co.

Universities return the favor. The domination of university boards of trustees by captains of industry further explains why these boards appoint presidents and chancellors with pro-industry biases. New York University's board includes former CBS owner Laurence Tisch, Hartz Mountain chief Leonard Stern, Salomon Brothers brokerage firm founder William B. Salomon, and real estate magnate-turned-publisher Mortimer Zuckerman. The composition of boards at smaller colleges is similar. The board of trustees of the University of St. Thomas in St. Paul, Minnesota, includes executives from Montgomery Ward & Co., Graco, Inc., 3M, Waldorf Corp., Opus Corp., and Honeywell.

PAYING FOR SECRETS

Although universities often claim that corporate monies come without strings attached, this is often not the case. Contracts for research, such as the one between Freeport-McMoRan and the University of Texas, frequently include provisions giving corporations some control over the dissemination of research results. A study published in the *New England Journal of Medicine* reported that the majority of companies entering into biomedical research agreements with universities require that the findings be "kept confidential to protect [their] proprietary value beyond the time required to file a patent."

According to the National Cancer Institute's Steven Rosenberg, this secrecy is impeding scientific research. He contends that "open discussion among scientists, even about the preliminary results of ongoing experiments... can play an important part in advancing research." Instead of an early and fruitful exchange of ideas, the secrecy agreements have imposed "the ethical and operational rules of business" on scientific researchers.

Not all contracts contain language that merely restricts when research findings can be made public. Some contain paragraphs giving the corporate contractor the right to determine whether the results can ever be released. A British pharmaceutical corporation, the Boots Company, gave $250,000 to the University of California San Francisco for research comparing its hypothyroid drug, Synthroid, with lower-cost alternatives. Instead of demonstrating Synthroid's superiority as Boots had hoped, the study found that the drugs were bioequivalents. Professor Betty Dong, who conducted the study, submitted her findings to the *Journal of the American Medical Association*, which subjected it to rigorous blind-review. The information could have saved consumers $356 million if they had switched to a cheaper alternative, but would have undermined Synthroid's domination of the $600 million synthetic hormone market.

When Boots found out about the scheduled article, it stopped publication, citing provisions in the research contract that results "were not to be published or otherwise released without [Boots's] written consent." After Boots announced that the research was badly flawed, Dong was unable to counter the claim because she could not release the study.

IF THE SHOE FITS

Even contracts that appear benign can have strings that choke academic freedom. In 1996, the University of Wisconsin signed a multimillion-dollar contract with Reebok, granting the running shoe manufacturer exclusive rights to make and market athletic apparel bearing the Wisconsin logo. In addition to paying coaches for promotional appearances for Reebok, giving financial support for the university's athletic program, and providing student internships at Reebok's headquarters, the contract included an Orwellian clause: "The university will not issue any official statement that disparages Reebok... [and] will promptly take all reasonable steps to address any remark by any university employee, including a coach, that disparages Reebok."

Although university administrators publicly disclosed many other provisions of the Reebok contract, they kept the speech-restriction clause secret until the last moment. When it was finally disclosed—as the contract was going before the board of trustees for approval— dozens of UW professors signed a letter of opposition. Embarrassed by the flak and the exposure of their willingness to sell out the First Amendment and academic freedom, university administrators retreated, asking Reebok to cancel the speech-prohibition paragraph. Facing a public relations disaster, Reebok quickly agreed.

Not content with buying specific research projects and athletic programs, corporations have put their stamp on academic departments by endowing chairs. The Carlson Travel, Tour, and Hospitality Professorship at U. of M, endowed by the owner of the Carlson Travel Network, provides money for the Carlson Chair for research on issues of interest to the travel industry. The executive vice president of the Minnesota Restaurant, Hotel, and Resort Associations praised this research funding, saying, "We'll have data on who comes to Minnesota and why, why people fail to return, and other statistics that we need to make decisions about advertising, marketing, and promotion." Even when there are no visible strings, says University of New Mexico professor Gilbert Merkx, "there is always a natural inclination to be grateful to the donor." Cal Bradford, a former fellow at the U. of M's Humphrey Institute for Public Policy, says that outside funds "determine what universities will teach and research, what direction the university will take.... If universities would decide that they need an endowed chair in English, and then try to raise the money for it, it would be one thing. But that's not what happens. Corporate donors decide to fund chairs in areas where they want research done. Their decisions decide which topics universities explore and which aren't." After he criticized university ties to corporations, Bradford's contract at the Humphrey Institute wasn't renewed.

TIES THAT BLIND

Two changes in federal laws have helped cultivate the current relationship between universities and business: the 1980 Bayh-Dole Act (University and Small Business Patent Procedures Act PL 96-517), which was supplemented by a 1983 executive order extending the legislation to large corporations; and the 1981 Recovery Tax Act (PL 97-34). The 1980 law and the executive order allowed universities to sell corporations patent rights derived from taxpayer-funded research. The result is a covert transfer of resources from the public to the private sector. The 1981 law made the arrangement even more lucrative for corporations by increasing the tax deductions they could claim for "donations" made to universities.

Corporations jumped at the opportunity. While federal tax dollars fund about $7 billion worth of research, corporations—for a relatively small investment—can buy access to the results, at just a fraction of the actual cost. Given this direct subsidy in taxpayers' dollars, plus the tax benefits, it is little wonder that corporate dollars going to universi-

ties almost tripled from $235 million in 1980 to $600 million in 1986. By 1991, the annual corporate investment had increased to $1.2 billion, and by 1996 to around $2 billion.

The benefits to corporations from these investments is demonstrated by an agreement between Sandoz Pharmaceuticals and the Dana-Farber Institute, a Harvard University teaching hospital. Sandoz gave Dana-Farber a ten-year, $100 million grant for research on cancer drugs. In return, Sandoz got the rights to any discoveries made by professors who had accepted Sandoz dollars, even if the actual discoveries weren't funded by the Swiss pharmaceutical giant. Under this agreement, Sandoz was given the commercial rights for a method of identifying a mutant gene linked to colon cancer, even though the mutant gene research was primarily funded by the U.S. government—that is, U.S. taxpayers.

This windfall of corporate welfare does not come without some work by the corporations. In May 1996, after several Republican budget cutters suggested that funding for scientific research be scaled back, university representatives and corporate CEOs met privately with House Speaker Newt Gingrich to lobby against cuts in biomedical research. After the meeting—which included representatives from universities and executives from Biogen Corp., Bristol-Myers Squibb, Chiron Corp., and Pioneer Hi-Bred International—Gingrich endorsed a $655 million *increase* in federal funding for the National Institutes of Health, $175 million more than the agency had requested. The success of the lobbying effort indicates the power and influence of the new university-industrial complex.

The biotech and pharmaceutical executives lobbied Gingrich because federal research funding represents a significant government subsidy for their industries, which receive the benefits of the work without paying for it. However, government grants are just one method involving universities for transferring resources from the public to the private, for-profit sector. Another transfer occurs when universities use federal and state tax dollars and tuition monies to build state-of-the-art research facilities. Corporations then use them and save the cost of building their own. When the low pay of graduate students—who comprise the majority of research assistants—is added to the equation, universities can perform bargain-basement research tailored to corporate needs.

The high costs associated with conducting cutting edge research provides a plausible explanation for the soaring tuition fees of the last decade. Although universities have long claimed that grants and contracts for scientific research subsidize programs in the liberal arts and humanities, this is not the case, according to a financial analysis conducted by the *Chicago Tribune*. Using financial records obtained from the University of Rhode Island, the *Tribune* found that tuition dollars—including those from students in the liberal arts and humanities—subsidize scientific research.

Although the university's president disputed the study's methods, he nevertheless conceded that around $400 of each student's tuition may subsidize research. While the subsidy is small, what corporations get from taxpayers through research grants and laboratory construction at universities points to a larger problem. What he didn't say is that this type of research has changed the purpose of universities, making them centers for corporate R&D rather than centers of instruction—servants of Mammon rather than of Minerva.

Lawrence Soley teaches at Marquette University in Milwaukee and is author of Leasing the Ivory Tower *(Boston: South End Press, 1995).*

Reprinted by permission of *CovertAction Quarterly* (CAQ), 1500 Massachusetts Avenue, NW, #732, Washington, DC 20005, Tel: 202/331-9763. The full text of the article with footnotes is available from CAQ for $8 in the U.S. and $10 elsewhere.

4 CENSORED

Exposing the Global Surveillance System

"SECRET POWER: EXPOSING THE GLOBAL SURVEILLANCE SYSTEM"
By Nicky Hager;
CovertAction Quarterly (CAQ);
Winter 1996/1997

For 40 years, New Zealand's largest intelligence agency, the Government Communications Security Bureau (GCSB)—the nation's equivalent of the U.S. National Security Agency (NSA)—had been helping its Western allies to spy on countries throughout the Pacific region, without the knowledge of the New Zealand public or many of its highest elected officials. What the NSA did not know is that by the late 1980s, various intelligence staff had decided these activities had been too secret for too long, and were providing me with interviews and documents exposing New Zealand's intelligence activities. Eventually, more than 50 people who work or have worked in intelligence and related fields agreed to be interviewed.

The activities they described made it possible to document, from the South Pacific, some alliance-wide systems and projects which have been kept secret elsewhere. Of these, by far the most important is ECHELON.

Designed and coordinated by NSA, the ECHELON system is used to intercept ordinary e-mail, fax, telex, and telephone communications carried over the world's telecommunications networks. Unlike many of the electronic spy systems developed during the Cold War, ECHELON is designed primarily for non-military targets: governments, organizations, businesses, and individuals in virtually every country. It potentially affects every person communicating between (and sometimes within) countries anywhere in the world.

It is, of course, not a new idea that intelligence organizations tap into e-mail and other public telecommunications networks. What was new in the material leaked by the New Zealand intelligence staff was precise information on where the spying is done, how the system works, its capabilities and shortcomings, and many details such as the code names.

The ECHELON system is not designed to eavesdrop on a particular individual's e-mail or fax link. Rather, the system works by indiscriminately intercepting very large quantities of communications and using computers to identify and extract messages of interest from the mass of unwanted ones. A chain of secret interception facilities has been established around the world to tap into all the major components of the international telecommunications networks. Some monitor communications satellites, others land-based communications networks, and others radio communications. ECHELON links together all these facilities, providing the U.S. and its allies with the ability to intercept a large proportion of the communications on the planet.

The computers at each station in the ECHELON network automatically search through the millions of messages intercepted for ones containing pre-programmed key words. Key words include all the names, localities, subjects, and so on that might be mentioned. Every word of every message intercepted at each station gets automatically searched—whether or not a specific telephone number or e-mail address is on the list.

The thousands of simultaneous messages are read in "real time" as they pour into the station, hour after hour, day after day, as the computer finds intelligence needles in telecommunications haystacks.

SOMEONE IS LISTENING

The computers in stations around the globe are known, within the network, as the ECHELON Dictionaries. Computers that can automatically search through traffic for key words have existed since at least the 1970s, but the ECHELON system was designed by NSA to interconnect all these computers and allow the stations to function as components of an integrated whole. The NSA and GCSB are bound together under the five-nation UKUSA signals intelligence agreement. The other three partners—all with equally obscure names—are the Government Communications Headquarters (GCHQ) in Britain, the Communications Security Establishment (CSE) in Canada, and the Defense Signals Directorate (DSD) in Australia.

The alliance, which grew from cooperative efforts during World War II to intercept radio transmissions, was formalized into the UKUSA agreement in 1948 and aimed primarily against the USSR. The five UKUSA agencies are today the largest intelligence organizations in their respective countries. With much of the world's business occurring by fax, e-mail, and phone, spying on these communications receives the bulk of intelligence resources. For decades before the introduction of the ECHELON

system, the UKUSA allies did intelligence collection operations for each other, but each agency usually processed and analyzed the intercept from its own stations.

Under ECHELON, a particular station's Dictionary computer contains not only its parent agency's chosen key words, but also has lists entered in for other agencies. In New Zealand's satellite interception station at Waihopai (in the South Island), for example, the computer has separate search lists for the NSA, GCHQ, DSD, and CSE in addition to its own. Whenever the Dictionary encounters a message containing one of the agencies' key words, it automatically picks it and sends it *directly* to the headquarters of the agency concerned. No one in New Zealand screens, or even sees, the intelligence collected by the New Zealand station for the foreign agencies. Thus, the stations of the junior UKUSA allies function for the NSA no differently than if they were overtly NSA-run bases located on their soil.

The first component of the ECHELON network are stations specifically targeted on the international telecommunications satellites (Intelsats) used by the telephone companies of most countries. A ring of Intelsats is positioned around the world, stationary above the equator, each serving as a relay station for tens of thousands of simultaneous phone calls, fax, and e-mail. Five UKUSA stations have been established to intercept the communications carried by the Intelsats.

The British GCHQ station is located at the top of high cliffs above the sea at

Morwenstow in Cornwall. Satellite dishes beside sprawling operations buildings point toward Intelsats above the Atlantic, Europe, and, inclined almost to the horizon, the Indian Ocean. An NSA station at Sugar Grove, located 250 kilometers southwest of Washington, DC, in the mountains of West Virginia, covers Atlantic Intelsats transmitting down toward North and South America. Another NSA station is in Washington State, 200 kilometers southwest of Seattle, inside the Army's Yakima Firing Center. Its satellite dishes point out toward the Pacific Intelsats and to the east.

The job of intercepting Pacific Intelsat communications that cannot be intercepted at Yakima went to New Zealand and Australia. Their South Pacific location helps to ensure global interception. New Zealand provides the station at Waihopai and Australia supplies the Geraldton station in West Australia (which targets both Pacific and Indian Ocean Intelsats).

Each of the five stations' Dictionary computers has a code name to distinguish it from others in the network. The Yakima station, for instance, located in desert country between the Saddle Mountains and Rattlesnake Hills, has the COWBOY Dictionary, while the Waihopai station has the FLINTLOCK Dictionary. These code names are recorded at the beginning of every intercepted message, before it is transmitted around the ECHELON network, allowing analysts to recognize at which station the interception occurred.

New Zealand intelligence staff has been closely involved with the NSA's Yakima station since 1981, when NSA pushed the GCSB to contribute to a project targeting Japanese embassy communications. Since then, all five UKUSA agencies have been responsible for monitoring diplomatic cables from all Japanese posts within the same segments of the globe they are assigned for general UKUSA monitoring. Until New Zealand's integration into ECHELON with the opening of the Waihopai station in 1989, its share of the Japanese communications was intercepted at Yakima and sent unprocessed to the GCSB headquarters in Wellington for decryption, translation, and writing into UKUSA-format intelligence reports (the NSA provides the code-breaking programs).

"COMMUNICATION" THROUGH SATELLITES

The next component of the ECHELON system intercepts a range of satellite communications not carried by Intelsat. In addition to the UKUSA stations targeting Intelsat satellites, there are another five or more stations homing in on Russian and other regional communications satellites. These stations are Menwith Hill in northern England; Shoal Bay, outside Darwin in northern Australia (which targets Indonesian satellites); Leitrim, just south of Ottawa in Canada (which appears to intercept Latin American satellites); Bad Aibling in Germany; and Misawa in northern Japan.

A group of facilities that tap directly into land-based telecommunications systems is the final element of the ECHE-LON system. Besides satellite and radio, the other main method of transmitting large quantities of public, business, and government communications is a combination of water cables under the oceans and microwave networks over land. Heavy cables, laid across seabeds between countries, account for much of the world's international communications. After they come out of the water and join land-based microwave networks they are very vulnerable to interception. The microwave networks are made up of chains of microwave towers relaying messages from hilltop to hilltop (always in line of sight) across the countryside. These networks shunt large quantities of communications across a country. Interception of them gives access to international undersea communications (once they surface) and to international communication trunk lines across continents. They are also an obvious target for large-scale interception of domestic communications.

Because the facilities required to intercept radio and satellite communications use large aerials and dishes that are difficult to hide for too long, that network is reasonably well documented. But all that is required to intercept land-based communication networks is a building situated along the microwave route or a hidden cable running underground from the legitimate network into some anonymous building, possibly far removed. Although it sounds technically very difficult, microwave interception from space by United States spy satellites also occurs. The worldwide network of facilities to intercept these communications is largely undocumented, and because New Zealand's GCSB does not participate in this type of interception, my inside sources could not help either.

NO ONE IS SAFE FROM A MICROWAVE

A 1994 exposé of the Canadian UKUSA agency, *Spyworld*, co-authored by one of its former staff, Mike Frost, gave the first insights into how a lot of foreign microwave interception is done. It described UKUSA "embassy collection" operations, where sophisticated receivers and processors are secretly transported to their countries' overseas embassies in diplomatic bags and used to monitor various communications in foreign capitals.

Since most countries' microwave networks converge on the capital city, embassy buildings can be an ideal site. Protected by diplomatic privilege, they allow interception in the heart of the target country. The Canadian embassy collection was requested by the NSA to fill gaps in the American and British embassy collection operations, which were still occurring in many capitals around the world when Frost left the CSE in 1990. Separate sources in Australia have revealed that the DSD also engages in embassy collection. On the territory of UKUSA nations, the interception of land-based telecommunications appears to be done at special secret intelligence facilities. The U.S., U.K., and Canada are geographically well placed to intercept the large amounts of the world's communications that cross their territories.

The only public reference to the Dictionary system anywhere in the world was in relation to one of these facilities, run by the GCHQ in central London. In 1991, a former British GCHQ official spoke anonymously to Granada Television's *World in Action* about the agency's abuses of power. He told the program about an anonymous red brick building at 8 Palmer Street where GCHQ secretly intercepts every telex which passes into, out of, or through London, feeding them into powerful computers with a program known as "Dictionary." The operation, he explained, is staffed by carefully vetted British Telecom people: "It's nothing to do with national security. It's because it's not legal to take every single telex. And they take everything: the embassies, all the business deals, even the birthday greetings, they take everything. They feed it into the Dictionary." What the documentary did not reveal is that Dictionary is not just a British system; it is UKUSA-wide.

Similarly, British researcher Duncan Campbell has described how the U.S. Menwith Hill station in Britain taps directly into the British Telecom microwave network, which has actually been designed with several major microwave links converging on an isolated tower connected underground into the station.

The NSA Menwith Hill station, with 22 satellite terminals and more than 4.9 acres of buildings, is undoubtedly the largest and most powerful in the UKUSA network. Located in northern England, several thousand kilometers from the Persian Gulf, it was awarded the NSA's "Station of the Year" prize for 1991 after its role in the Gulf War. Menwith Hill assists in the interception of microwave communications in another way as well, by serving as a ground station for U.S. electronic spy satellites. These intercept microwave trunk lines and short range communications such as military radios and walkie talkies. Other ground stations where the satellites' information is fed into the global network are Pine Gap, run by the CIA near Alice Springs in central Australia and the Bad Aibling station in Germany. Among them, the various stations and operations making up the ECHELON network tap into all the main components of the world's telecommunications networks. All of them, including a separate network of stations that intercepts long distance radio communications, have their own Dictionary computers connected into ECHELON.

In the early 1990s, opponents of the Menwith Hill station obtained large quantities of internal documents from the facility. Among the papers was a reference to an NSA computer system called Platform. The integration of all the UKUSA station computers into ECHELON probably occurred with the introduction of this system in the early 1980s. James Bamford wrote at that time about a new worldwide NSA computer network code named Platform "which will tie together 52 separate computer systems used throughout the world. Focal point, or 'host environment,' for the massive network will be the NSA headquarters at Fort Meade. Among those included in Platform will be the British SIGINT organization, GCHQ."

LOOKING IN
THE DICTIONARY

The Dictionary computers are connected via highly encrypted UKUSA communications that link back to computer databases in the five agency headquarters. This is where all the intercepted messages selected by the Dictionaries end up. Each morning the specially "indoctrinated" signals intelligence analysts in Washington, Ottawa, Cheltenham, Canberra, and Wellington log on at their computer terminals and enter the Dictionary system. After keying in their security passwords, they reach a directory that lists the different categories of intercept available in the databases, each with a four-digit code. For instance, 1911 might be Japanese diplomatic cables from Latin America (handled by the Canadian CSE), 3848 might be political communications from and about Nigeria, and 8182 might be any messages about distribution of encryption technology.

They select their subject category, get a "search result" showing how many messages have been caught in the ECHELON net on that subject, and then the day's work begins. Analysts scroll through screen after screen of intercepted faxes, e-mail messages, etc., and, whenever a message appears worth reporting on, they select it from the rest to work on. If it is not in English, it is translated and then written into the standard format of intelligence reports produced anywhere within the UKUSA network—either in entirety as a "report," or as a summary or "gist."

INFORMATION CONTROL

A highly organized system has been developed to control what is being searched for by each station and who can have access to it. This is at the heart of ECHELON operations and works as follows.

The individual station's Dictionary computers do not simply have a long list of key words to search for. And they do not send all the information into some huge database that participating agencies can dip into as they wish. It is much more controlled.

The search lists are organized into the same categories, referred to by the four digit numbers. Each agency decides its own categories according to its responsibilities for producing intelligence for the network. For GCSB, this means South Pacific governments, Japanese diplomatic, Russian Antarctic activities, and so on.

The agency then works out about 10 to 50 key words for selection in each category. The key words include such things as names of people, ships, organizations, country names, and subject names. They also include the known telex and fax numbers and Internet addresses of any individuals, businesses, organizations, and government offices that are targets. These are generally written as part of the message text and so are easily recognized by the Dictionary computers.

The agencies also specify combinations of key words to help sift out communications of interest. For example, they might search for diplomatic cables containing both the words "Santiago" and "aid," or cables containing the word "Santiago" but not "consul" (to avoid the masses of routine consular communications). It is these sets of words and numbers (and combinations), under a particular category, that get placed in the Dictionary computers. (Staff in the five agencies called Dictionary Managers enter and update the key word search lists for each agency.)

The whole system, devised by the NSA, has been adopted completely by the other agencies. The Dictionary computers search through all the incoming messages and, whenever they encounter one with any of the agencies' key words, they select it. At the same time, the computer automatically notes technical details such as the time and place of interception on the piece of intercept so that analysts reading it, in whichever agency it is going to, know where it came from, and what it is. Finally, the computer writes the four-digit code (for the category with the key words in that message) at the bottom of the message's text. This is important. It means that when all the intercepted messages end up together in the database at one of the agency headquarters, the messages on a particular subject can be located again. Later, when the analyst using the Dictionary system selects the four-digit code for the category he or she wants, the computer simply searches through all the messages in the database for the ones which have been tagged with that number.

This system is very effective for controlling which agencies can get what from the global network because each agency only gets the intelligence out of the ECHELON system from its own numbers. It does not have any access to the raw intelligence coming out of the system to the other agencies. For example, although most of the GCSB's intelligence production is primarily to serve the UKUSA alliance, New Zealand does not have access to the whole ECHELON network. The access it does have is strictly controlled. A New Zealand intelligence officer explained: "The agencies can all apply for numbers on each other's Dictionaries. The hardest to deal with are the Americans.... [There are] more hoops to jump through, unless it is in their interest, in which case they'll do it for you."

There is only one agency which, by virtue of its size and role within the alliance, will have access to the full potential of the ECHELON system—the agency that set it up. What is the system used for? Anyone listening to official "discussion" of intelligence could be forgiven for thinking that, since the end of the Cold War, the key targets of the massive UKUSA intelligence machine are terrorism, weapons proliferation, and economic intelligence. The idea that economic intelligence has become very important, in particular, has been carefully cultivated by intelligence agencies intent on preserving their post-Cold War budgets. It has become an article of faith in much discussion of intelligence. However, I have found no evidence that these are now the primary concerns of organizations such as NSA.

QUICKER INTELLIGENCE, SAME MISSION

A different story emerges after examining very detailed information I have been given about the intelligence New Zealand collects for the UKUSA allies and detailed descriptions of what is in the yards-deep intelligence reports New Zealand receives from its four allies each week. There is quite a lot of intelligence collected about potential terrorists, and there is quite a lot of economic intelligence, notably intensive monitoring of all the countries participating in GATT negotiations. But by far, the main priorities of the intelligence alliance continue to be political and military intelligence to assist the larger allies to pursue their interests around the world. Anyone and anything the particular governments are concerned about can become a target.

With capabilities so secret and so powerful, almost anything goes. For example, in June 1992, a group of current "highly placed intelligence operatives" from the British GCHQ spoke to the London *Observer*: "We feel we can no longer remain silent regarding that which we regard to be gross malpractice and negligence within the establishment in which we operate." They gave as examples GCHQ interception of three charitable organizations, including Amnesty International and Christian Aid. As the *Observer* reported: "At any time GCHQ is able to home in on their communica-

tions for a routine target request," the GCHQ source said. In the case of phone taps the procedure is known as Mantis. With telexes it is called Mayfly. By keying in a code relating to Third World aid, the source was able to demonstrate telex "fixes" on the three organizations. "It is then possible to key in a trigger word which enables us to home in on the telex communications whenever that word appears," he said. "And we can read a pre-determined number of characters [on] either side of the key word." Without actually naming it, this was a fairly precise description of how the ECHELON Dictionary system works. Again, what was not revealed in the publicity was that this is a UKUSA-wide system. The design of ECHELON means that the interception of these organizations could have occurred anywhere in the network, at any station where the GCHQ had requested that the four-digit code covering Third World aid be placed.

Note that these GCHQ officers mentioned that the system was being used for telephone calls. In New Zealand, ECHELON is used only to intercept written communications: fax, e-mail, and telex. The reason, according to intelligence staff, is that the agency does not have the staff to analyze large quantities of telephone conversations.

Mike Frost's exposé of Canadian "embassy collection" operations described the NSA computers they used, called Oratory, that can "listen" to telephone calls and recognize when key words are spoken. Just as we can recognize words spoken in all the different tones and accents we encounter, so too, according to Frost, can these computers. Telephone calls containing key words are automatically extracted from the masses of other calls and recorded digitally on magnetic tapes for analysts back at agency headquarters. However, high volume voice recognition computers will be technically difficult to perfect, and my New Zealand-based sources could not confirm that this capability exists. But, if or when it is perfected, the implications would be immense. It would mean that the UKUSA agencies could use machines to search through all the international telephone calls in the world, in the same way that they do written messages. If this equipment exists for use in embassy collection, it will presumably be used in all the stations throughout the ECHELON network. It is yet to be confirmed how extensively telephone communications are being targeted by the ECHELON stations for the other agencies.

The easiest pickings for the ECHELON system are the individuals, organizations, and governments that do not use encryption. In New Zealand's area, for example, it has proved especially useful against already vulnerable South Pacific nations which do not use any coding, even for government communications (all these communications of New Zealand's neighbors are supplied, unscreened, to its UKUSA allies). As a result of the revelations in my book, there is currently a project under way in the Pacific to promote and supply publicly available encryption software to vulnerable organizations such as democracy movements in countries with repressive governments. This is one practical way of curbing illegitimate uses of the ECHELON capabilities.

One final comment. All the newspapers, commentators, and "well placed sources" told the public that New Zealand was cut off from US intelligence in the mid-1980s. That was entirely untrue. The intelligence supply to New Zealand did not stop, and instead, the decade since has been a period of increased integration of New Zealand into the U.S. system. Virtually everything—the equipment, manuals, ways of operating, jargon, codes, and so on, used in the GCSB—continues to be imported entirely from the larger allies (in practice, usually the NSA). As with the Australian and Canadian agencies, most of the priorities continue to come from the U.S., too.

The main thing that protects these agencies from change is their secrecy. On the day my book arrived in the book shops, without prior publicity, there was an all-day meeting of the intelligence bureaucrats in the prime minister's department trying to decide if they could prevent it from being distributed. They eventually concluded, sensibly, that the political costs were too high. It is understandable that they were so agitated.

Throughout my research, I have faced official denials or governments refusing to comment on publicity about intelligence activities. Given the pervasive atmosphere of secrecy and stonewalling, it is always hard for the public to judge what is fact, what is speculation, and what is paranoia. Thus, in uncovering New Zealand's role in the NSA-led alliance, my aim was to provide so much detail about the operations—the technical systems, the daily work of individual staff members, and even the rooms in which they work inside intelligence facilities—that readers could feel confident that they were getting close to the truth. I hope the information leaked by intelligence staff in New Zealand about UKUSA and its systems such as ECHELON will help lead to change.

Nicky Hager is author of Secret Power: New Zealand's Role in the International Spy Network *(Nelson, New Zealand: Craig Potton, 1996). This article was adapted from the book, which is available through CAQ.*

Reprinted by permission of *CovertAction Quarterly* (CAQ), 1500 Massachusetts Avenue, NW, #732, Washington, DC 20005, Tel: 202/331-9763. The full text of the article with footnotes is available from CAQ for $8 in the U.S. and $10 elsewhere.

5 CENSORED

United States Companies are World Leaders in the Manufacture of Torture Devices for Internal Use and Support

"SHOCK VALUE: U.S. STUN DEVICES POSE HUMAN-RIGHTS RISK"

By Anne-Marie Cusac; *The Progressive*; September 1997

Amnesty International lists the United States in the same class as Algeria and China in a March 1997 report. All three countries appear under a section titled, "Recent Cases of the Use of Electroshock Weapons for Torture or Ill-Treatment."

A decade ago, the United States did not often show up as a culprit in Amnesty reports. But lately, the United States has become a leading manufacturer and exporter of push-button electric-shock devices, which Amnesty claims are unsafe and are ending up in the hands of torturers. Of the 100 companies listed in the report, forty-two are U.S.-based. According to Amnesty, countries that have received stun weapons exported from the United States in the last decade include Yemen, Panama, Saudi Arabia, Mexico, Argentina, the Philippines, the United Arab Emirates, Ecuador, Cyprus, and Thailand.

One company the report cites is Arianne International of Palm Beach Gardens, Florida, which makes the "Myotron"—a compact version of the stun gun "available in pearl, black, or white," a salesperson tells me over the telephone. The company advertises the device as "small enough to carry on a big key ring and flat enough to carry in a shirt pocket. It's five times more powerful than the best police stun gun." A related device, the "Myotron-TM Venu," is marketed especially to women.

Other prominent U.S.-based manufacturers of stun weaponry include Stun Tech of Cleveland, Ohio, known for its stun guns, stun shields, and especially its stun belts; Nova Products, Inc., of Cookeville, Tennessee, maker of tasers, along with other electronic devices; and Safe Defense Co., of Greenville, North Carolina, which, according to the company's president, markets its stun guns to the general public through variety stores, "gun shops, pawn shops, uniform stores, and flea markets."

Another company that makes an appearance in the Amnesty report is B-West Imports, Inc., of Tucson, Arizona, which in 1995 joined a South African company called Paralyzer Protection. B-West brings in Paralyzer shock batons and shields that deliver a charge of between 80,000 and 120,000 volts.

A B-West advertising brochure claims, "The Paralyzer stun baton is the result of a unique process developed by German scientists and doctors. The extensive testing done by the Department of Medicine at the University of Dusseldorf resulted in the correlation of volts, amps, and frequency to render a would-be assailant helpless without any damage to skin, eyes, or internal organs."

Amnesty takes issue with that account. "The professor has since told Amnesty International that he was not specifically involved in developing the 'Paralyzer' range of stun guns and batons, but simply tested a particular stun device for another company in March 1985, the results of which cannot be applied directly to other stun devices," the report states.

The report also devotes considerable attention to Tasertron, of Corona, California, the first company to manufacture the taser—a weapon that shoots two wires attached to darts with metal hooks from as far away as thirty feet. When the hooks catch in a victim's skin or clothing, the device delivers a debilitating shock. Los Angeles police officers used the device against Rodney King in 1991.

A version of the weapon, the Air Taser, launches "two small probes attached to fifteen feet of TASER wire" through the air, according to the manufacturer, Air Taser, Inc., of Scottsdale, Arizona. Because the device uses air instead of gunpowder to power the shot, it is not regulated by the gun-control laws that apply to other tasers, which are banned for sale to consumers. The company has multiple Internet sites, complete with visuals. One image shows a small woman in high heels and a short skirt shocking a much larger man in a black knit cap. A jagged charge travels from her hand to his chest, where it creates a small explosion. "The AIR TASER sends powerful T-Waves™ through the wires (and up to two cumulative inches of clothing) into the body of the assailant, jamming his nervous system and incapacitating him," proclaims the ad.

Air Taser also markets a new product it calls the Auto Taser. "Imagine an automotive defense system that fights back," the company says. "Any attempt to touch the AUTO TASER zaps the thief with an unforgettable, yet non-lethal 5,900 milliwatt electron pulse. A thief can't steal what he can't touch." The accompanying photograph shows a dark parking lot. A man reaches through a car window and lightning runs up his arm to his shoulder. He is grimacing and is falling backwards.

Air Taser claims its corporate mission is "to raise mankind above violent behavior by developing products which enable people to protect themselves without causing injury or death to another human being."

But these devices also prove quite handy for people who want to commit crimes. In Britain, a country that prohibits handguns, stun weapons became a favorite tool of muggers until the government banned them.

Amnesty International and the American Civil Liberties Union (ACLU) both claim the devices are unsafe and may actually encourage sadistic acts by police officers and prison guards. "Stun belts offer enormous possibilities for abuse and the infliction of gratuitous pain," says Jenni Gainsborough of the ACLU's National Prison Project. She adds that because use of the belt leaves little physical evidence, this increases "the likelihood of sadistic, but hard-to-prove, misuse of weapons."

"It's possible to use anything for torture, but it's a little easier to use our devices," admits John McDermit, head of Nova Products.

In 1991, Terence Allen, a specialist in forensic pathology who served as deputy medical examiner for both the Los Angeles and San Francisco coroner's offices, linked the taser to fatalities. "The taser contributed to at least these nine deaths," Allen wrote in the *Journal of Forensic Sciences.* "It seems only logical that a device capable of depolarizing skeletal muscle can also depolarize heart muscle and cause fibrillation under certain circumstances."

With electrical current, Allen tells me, "the chance of death increases with each use. This may have been a factor in Los Angeles. Some of the people who died there had been shocked as many as seven times."

Warns Allen: "I think what you're going to see is more deaths" from stun weapons.

As a result of his own work in forensic pathology, Allen is convinced that stun devices are already being abused in U.S. police stations and prisons. Some authorities, he says, can't resist exploiting the power they have over people in their custody to "force them to lose control of their muscles."

Allen describes a seventeen-year-old boy in Los Angeles who was accused of stealing. "They used a stun gun to extract a confession from him," he says. "He had burns that exactly fit the probes." Allen is referring to the case of Jaime Ramirez. Before dawn on November 30, 1986, officers William Lustig and Robert Rodriguez stopped Ramirez, who was carrying a sack full of stereo parts, according to the *Los Angeles Times*. The two officers shocked the boy repeatedly with a stun gun in an attempt to force him to confess to stealing the equipment.

Ramirez sued the city. He testified that Lustig "told me that if I didn't tell the truth, he was going to burn me," reported the *Los Angeles Times*. Both officers then used the stun gun on Ramirez. "I felt like I was being burned," the *Los Angeles Times* quoted Ramirez as saying. "I could not keep my legs still.... I was feeling the pressure in my heart. I could not breathe freely." The two officers lost their jobs. Both were convicted and served time behind bars. The city of Los Angeles settled with Ramirez for $300,000.

Los Angeles is not the only American city where police officers abuse people with electroshock weapons. Phoenix, Arizona, is home to Sheriff Joe Arpaio, author of *America's Toughest Sheriff: How We Can Win the War Against Crime*. But, under Arpaio's charge, the Maricopa County Jails have come under some harsh criticism. In March 1996, the Department of Justice's civil-rights division filed a report on the jails that strongly condemns

"the fact that all jail guards carry stun guns. The easy availability of these weapons," the Department of Justice examiner concluded, "has contributed to the excessive use of force."

Guards at the Maricopa County Jails have been known to use the stun gun against an inmate "simply to see its effect," the report states. It also cites "use of a stun device on a prisoner's testicles while in a restraint chair."

The Maricopa County Jail disputes nearly every charge in the Department of Justice report. They are "allegations by prisoners, unsubstantiated remarks," says Lisa Allen, coordinator of communications for the sheriff's office. The county complains that the Department of Justice report does not provide inmate names, dates, or times of the alleged incidents. But in fact, the report draws on videotapes and jail documents in addition to prisoner testimony.

"I've seen the photos. I've talked with inmates. I've seen the letters. I have dates. I have times," says Nick Hentoff, a criminal and civil-rights attorney in Phoenix who says he has represented clients in "about a dozen suits " against the Maricopa County Jails involving stun weapons. He says the county jails "have countless videos that show it." Hentoff's client, Bart David, currently has a lawsuit pending against the county. He claims that guards at one of the jails shocked him in the testicles.

In 1996, the *Phoenix New Times*, a newsweekly, reported the death of jail inmate Scott Norberg at the Maricopa County Jails. Norberg died while fighting with officers who were attempting to confine him in a restraining chair while strapping a towel around his mouth "to keep him from spitting."

During the struggle, jailers shocked Norberg multiple times with stun guns. Inmates who witnessed Norberg's death estimated that he had been shocked between eight and twenty times. Guards estimated the number of shocks at between two and six. "An examination of Norberg's corpse commissioned by Norberg's family puts the number at twenty-one," wrote *New Times* reporter Tony Ortega.

Although the medical examiner ruled the death an accident, "at least one detention officer...contradicts the scenario that Norberg suddenly went limp," wrote Ortega. "In fact, she claims she tried to tell the guards that they were suffocating Norberg, who had literally turned purple. She says an officer snapped back at her, 'Who gives a fuck?'"

"Their policy is stun first, ask questions later," says Hentoff. He claims to have seen "dozens of pictures" of jail inmates with stun burns. "You'll see two little marks close together like vampire bites on their bodies," says Hentoff. "Those are the stun-gun marks."

In a letter released on August 3, 1997, Amnesty International detailed several more recent incidents of mistreatment at the Maricopa County Jails, including an inmate who "allegedly sustained broken teeth and spine and knee injuries after being kicked and beaten and stunned repeatedly with a stun gun." After the beating, the prisoner alleges, he was confined for five hours in a restraining chair.

A second inmate fell asleep during processing in a central-intake room. "A stun gun was allegedly used to wake him up," says Amnesty. The prisoner claims he was then thrown against a wall.

Ortega talked to a nurse in July who spilled the beans on her co-workers at the Maricopa County Jails. She told him many guards "seem to delight in treating inmates badly." One time, "she saw a detention officer bring a man suffering from abdominal pain into a clinic," Ortega reported. "The man refused to say what was wrong with him, so the detention officer zapped the patient with a stun gun to make him talk. 'None of us could believe it,' she says."

Amnesty International claims the Commerce Department is not limiting sales of electronic devices overseas. "The United States will say it opposes torture, and it's a party to the convention against torture," says Brian Wood of Amnesty International. "However, as each month goes by, more and more of these electric-shock weapons are exported, and information is withheld about where, exactly, they're sent to. This is unacceptable, especially since Amnesty first raised this issue with the U.S. government over a decade ago."

Although Amnesty has asked the United States to guarantee that it will not knowingly export electroshock devices to torturing states, the Clinton Administration has yet to agree to slow the brisk U.S. trade in stun devices. In response to Amnesty's campaign, over the past few months governments in Germany, Belgium, and the United Kingdom have announced that they will tighten prohibitions on the trade in stun weapons. Though electric torture is on the rise worldwide, the U.S. Commerce Department does not group electroshock weapons with torture items, whose export it restricts. Instead, it classifies such devices as police equipment, which makes them easily exportable. The stun belt is considered offensive (as opposed to defensive) police equipment, so it still must receive a license before export to most countries. But, as Michael Lelyveld reported last year in *The Journal of Commerce*, manufacturers in NATO countries import stun devices as general merchandise and the U.S. Commerce Department does not track them.

"The lack of official data raises the possibility that this country may be the world's biggest source of such products," wrote Lelyveld. "But without tighter regulation, it is impossible to know."

One NATO country that uses electronic weapons for torture is Turkey. Amnesty's report cites the case of Mediha Curabaz, a twenty-five-year-old nurse. Police detained her on the street in 1991 and took her to the political branch of the Adana police headquarters. "They were making baseless accusations about people I work with and about people from the Adana Nurse's Association, on whose committee I serve," the Amnesty report quotes Curabaz as saying. "They asked me to support their allegations.... When I refused, they beat me furiously all over, took me in the room used for hanging people up by their arms or legs, and gave me electric shocks through my fingers, sexual organs, and nipples, saying degrading things about my body. They said, 'You will certainly do what we say if we give you the electric truncheon.' They thrust the electric truncheon violently into my sexual organs, and I felt a pain as if I was being drilled there with an electric drill."

NATO countries can also provide an easy route for manufacturers intent on shipping their devices to other torturing states. "It begs the question, should the United States export them at all?" says Lelyveld.

Would the United States, under any circumstances, ever allow the export of the stun belt, for instance, to a torturing state? "I would not feel comfortable saying 'never under any circumstances,'" says a Commerce Department spokesperson.

The U.S. government itself is a big user of stun devices, especially stun guns, electroshock batons, and electric shields. In June 1996, Amnesty International asked the U.S. Bureau of Prisons to suspend use of the electroshock belt—citing the possibility of physical danger to inmates and the potential for misuse. The agency has not complied.

Amnesty International has come down particularly hard on the state of Wisconsin—which has a place of prominence in the March report for its plan to use the stun belt on chain gangs. That plan has now gone into effect. Wisconsin's new chain gang started work at Fox

Lake prison on June 2. The state has conducted no studies on the use of the belt on chain-gang members, even though physical work and summer heat could contribute to a dangerous level of stress on an inmate's heart if he were shocked.

The first inmate to wear the belt on the Wisconsin chain gang was seventeen-year-old Clark Krueger. Though Krueger is a minor, he is doing time as an adult. But he is still subject to anti-smoking laws that apply to minors. And Krueger likes to smoke. He has been caught with cigarettes five times, enough to earn him 180 days in the segregation unit or a stint on the chain gang, according to Mary Neuman, the administrative captain at Fox Lake in charge of supervising the new work crews. Clark opted for the chain gang.

The state's use of the belt on a minor is of special concern to Amnesty. Brian Wood calls it a "violation of the international convention on the rights of the child."

When Fox Lake guards objected to the state's plan to dress all members of the crew in stun belts, the Department of Corrections asked the prison to place the belt on at least one inmate at a time. Now the guards in charge of the gang are "moving it from one inmate to another from one day to the next," says Gerald Berge, the warden at Fox Lake.

When I visit the prison, Berge tells me the prisoners are at work off prison grounds, at a cemetery in the city of Fox Lake. I follow Berge's car down several miles of rural roads. It is a bright, windy July day—the first cool afternoon in a week. The graveyard lies next to a marsh and a curving river. Some of the headstones in the graveyard are more than 100 years old.

We watch as an inmate shifts a gravestone forward. A second worker dumps gravel behind the marker to prop it up. The inmates wear standard-issue green clothing and bright yellow vests. Each has twenty-five-inch leg restraints with padded cuffs around the ankles. They are chained to themselves, not each other. It is impossible to tell which inmate wears the stun belt under his clothes. Mary Neuman says that, for security reasons, she can't let me know who has it on.

Two guards advise the work crew. A third stands back and watches, a rifle slung over his shoulder.

I am surprised. Wasn't the stun belt supposed to make supervision with guns unnecessary?

Even if the entire work crew were to wear the stun belt, a guard with a gun would watch over them, says Berge. "The statute says one of the guards will be armed."

When it comes to the stun belt, Berge is no cheerleader. "I would not feel comfortable having inmates out here all in stun belts without restraints," he says.

"I think, frankly, the stun belt is more appropriate for transport," Berge goes on. "We don't have experience with inmates in stun belts working. It's hard to endorse that."

I ask Berge if he would feel comfortable if the crew were wearing only individual leg chains, and no belt. "Yes," he says.

Is he concerned about possible injury? "Not really," he says. Then he qualifies the point. "If we had an inmate who had a cardiac condition that we were not aware of, that's where the danger would be."

After a few minutes of conversation, Neuman brings over inmate Earl Simington, who has agreed to talk with me about his experience on the chain gang. Simington is typical of the inmates assigned to the crew—someone let out on parole, who, as Neuman puts it, "didn't get the message" and has landed back in prison. He is currently serving a thirty-month sentence.

"I have three misdemeanors and one felony on my record, and I'll be twenty-seven at the end of July," says Simington. He tells me his felony conviction was for possession of fifteen grams of marijuana.

Simington volunteered for the new chain gang because he was bored. "It's not for the pay," he tells me (inmates on the chain gang make between twenty and thirty cents per hour, according to Berge). "It makes my time go faster."

Before he started work on the chain gang, the prison required Simington to sign a form giving officers permission to make him wear the belt and to shock him with it if he misbehaves.

He then practiced working outside cutting grass while wearing the belt. Simington is most concerned about the belt's weight, and the discomfort from wearing it in the heat. The belt has a good heft, he tells me. He says if it were mandatory daily wear, he wouldn't volunteer for the chain gang. "No one will want to be out there" if they have to wear it, he says.

Simington can't remember seeing any medical information on the form he signed. "I was never told, except, 'you may lose your bodily functions,'" he says. "I don't know if there are any long-term effects or damage or anything like that. I would want to find out if there are bad side effects. I don't know how long it's been studied on people."

Simington believes he has signed away his rights when it comes to the device. "When I signed that waiver form, that was saying, hey, you volunteered," he says. "If you get hurt you can't bring repercussions if it's because of your behavior."

Simington says the stun belt is too much. "We're already doing time. We're already chained. What more?"

Manufacturers of electroshock weapons continue to wave aside allegations that use of their devices is dangerous and may constitute a gross violation of human rights. And they are making innovations on some old favorites. A new stun weapon that may soon arrive at a police department near you: electroshock razor wire, specially designed for surrounding demonstrators who get out of hand.

Anne-Marie Cusac is Managing Editor of The Progressive. *Her story, "Stunning Technology," which appeared in the July 1996 issue, won the George Polk award for magazine reporting.*

Reprinted by permission from *The Progressive*, 409 East Main Street, Madison, WI 53703, Tel: 608/257-3373.

About the Author

Peter Phillips came to Sonoma State University in 1994 as an Assistant Professor of Sociology. He teaches classes in Media Censorship, Power, Class Stratification, and Social Welfare. He assumed the directorship of Project Censored in the Spring of 1996. His first book was *Censored 1997: The News that Didn't Make the News* (Seven Stories Press, 1997).

Phillips had a long career in human service administration. His experiences include two and half decades of community service and social activism, including serving both as a CETA administrator and a Head Start director.

Phillips earned a B.A. degree in Social Science in 1970 from Santa Clara University, and an M.A. degree in Social Science from California State University at Sacramento in 1974. Several years of adjunct college teaching led him to the University of California, Davis, where he earned an M.A. in Sociology in 1991 and a Ph.D. in Sociology in 1994. His doctoral dissertation was entitled *A Relative Advantage: Sociology of the San Francisco Bohemian Club.*

Phillips is a fifth generation Californian, who grew up on a family-owned farm west of the Central Valley town of Lodi. He has a 26-year-old son named Jeff, also a University of California, Davis, graduate. Phillips lives today in rural Sonoma County with his cat, Spaghetti, and two pet chickens, Millie and Booster.

PROJECT CENSORED MISSION STATEMENT Project Censored, founded in 1976, is a non-profit project within the Sonoma State University Foundation, a 501(c)3 organization. Its principle objective is the advocacy for and protection of First Amendment rights and freedom of information in the United States. Through a faculty, student, community partnership, Project Censored serves as a national press/media ombudsman by identifying and researching important national news stories that are under-reported, ignored, misrepresented, or censored by media corporations in the United States. It also encourages and supports journalists, faculty, and student investigations into First Amendment and freedom of information issues through its Project Censored Yearbook, Censored Alert Newsletter, and nationwide advocacy.

Index

How to Nominate a Censored Story

Some of the most interesting stories Project Censored evaluates are sent to us as nominations from people all over the world. These stories are clipped from small-circulation magazines or the back pages of local newspapers. If you see a story and wonder why it hasn't been covered in the mainstream media, we encourage you to send it to us as a Project Censored nomination. To nominate a *Censored* story send us a copy of the article and include the name of the source publication, the date that the article appeared, and page number(s).

CRITERIA FOR PROJECT CENSORED NEWS STORIES NOMINATIONS

1. A censored news story is one which contains information that the general United States population has a right and need to know, but to which it has had limited access.

2. The news story is timely, on-going, and has implications for a significant number of residents in the United States.

3. The story has clearly defined concepts and is backed up with solid, verifiable documentation.

4. The news story has been publicly published, either electronically or in print, in a circulated newspaper, journal, magazine, newsletter, or similar publication from either a foreign or domestic source.

5. The news story has direct connections to and implications for people in the United States, which can include activities that U.S. citizens are engaged in abroad.

We evaluate stories year-round and post important under-published stories on our World Wide Web site every month. However, the final deadline for nominating a *Censored* of the year is October 15th. Please send regular mail nominations to the address below or e-mail nominations to: project.censored@sonoma.edu. Our phone number for more information on Project Censored is 707-664-2500.

> Project Censored Nominations
> Sociology Department
> Sonoma State University
> 1801 East Cotati Avenue
> Rohnert Park, CA 94928

Thank you for your support.

> Peter Phillips
> Director, Project Censored